W9-CCN-465

Medicine on Trial

Other books in ABC-CLIO's On Trial Series

Charles L. Zelden, Series Editor

Gay Rights on Trial, Lee Walzer

The Human Body on Trial, Lynne Curry

Native American Sovereignty on Trial, Bryan H. Wildenthal

Pornography on Trial, Thomas C. Mackey

Racial Violence on Trial, Christopher Waldrep

Religion on Trial, James John Jurinski

Voting Rights on Trial, Charles L. Zelden

Medicine ON TRIAL

A Handbook with Cases, Laws, and Documents

Elisabeth A. Cawthon

A B C CLIO

Santa Barbara, California • Denver, Colorado • Oxford, England

For E. A. C., J. S. S., E. C. S., and A. C. S.

Library of Congress Cataloging-in-Publication Data
Cawthon, Elisabeth A., 1957–
Medicine on trial : a handbook with cases, laws, and documents / Elisabeth A. Cawthon.
p. cm. — (ABC-CLIO's on trial series)
Includes bibliographical references and index.
ISBN 1-85109-564-0 (hardcover : alk. paper); 1-85109-569-1 (eBook)
1. Medical laws and legislation—United States—History. 2. Medical jurisprudence—United States—History. I. Title. II. Series: On trial.
KF3821.C39 2004
344.7304'1—dc22

2003025780

08070605041 0987654321

ABC-CLIO, Inc.
130 Cremona Drive, P.O. Box 1911
Santa Barbara, California 93116–1911

This book is printed on acid-free paper.
Manufactured in the United States of America

Contents

Series Foreword

The volumes in the On Trial series explore the many ways in which the U.S. legal and political system has approached a wide range of complex and divisive legal issues over time—and in the process defined the current state of the law and politics on these issues. The intent is to give students and other general readers a framework for understanding how the law in all its various forms—constitutional, statutory, judicial, political, and customary—has shaped and reshaped the world in which we live today.

At the core of each volume in the series is a common proposition: that in certain key areas of American public life, we as a people and a nation are "on trial" as we struggle to cope with the contradictions, conflicts, and disparities within our society, politics, and culture. Who should decide if and when a woman can have an abortion? What rights, if any, should those with a different sexual orientation be able to claim under the Constitution? Is voting a basic right of citizenship, and if so, under what rules should we organize this right—especially when the application of any organizing rules inevitably results in excluding some citizens from the polls? And what about the many inconsistencies and conflicts associated with racial tensions in the country? These are just some of the complex and controversial issues that we as a people and a nation are struggling to answer—and must answer if we are to achieve an orderly and stable society. For the answers we find to these disputes shape the essence of who we are—as a people, community, and political system.

The concept of being "on trial" also has a second meaning fundamental to this series: the process of litigating important issues in a court of law. Litigation is an essential part of how we settle our differences and make choices as we struggle with the problems that confront us as a people and a nation. In the 1830s, Alexis de Tocqueville noted in his book *Democracy in America*, "There is hardly a political question in the United States which does not sooner or later turn into a judicial one" (Tocqueville 1835, 270). This insight is as true today as it was in the 1830s. In *The Litigious Society*, Jethro K. Lieberman notes: "To express amazement at American litigiousness is akin to professing astonishment at learning that the roots of most Americans lie in other lands. We have been a litigious nation as we have been an immigrant one. Indeed, the two are related" (Lieberman 1983, 13). Arriving in the United States with different backgrounds, customs, and lifestyle preferences, we inevitably clashed as our contrasting visions of life in the United States—its culture, society, and politics—collided. And it was to the courts and the law that we turned as a neutral forum for peaceably working out these differences. For, in the United States at least, it is the courthouse that provides the anvil on which our personal, societal, and political problems are hammered out.

The volumes in this series therefore take as their central purpose the important task of exploring the various ways—good and bad, effective and ineffective, complex and simple—in which litigation in the courts has shaped the evolution of particular legal controversies for which we as a people are "on trial." And, more important, the volumes do all this in a manner accessible to the general reader seeking to comprehend the topic as a whole.

These twin goals—analytical and educational—shape the structure and layout of the volumes in the series. Each book consists of two parts. The first provides an explanatory essay in four chapters. Chapter 1 introduces the issues, controversies, events, and participants associated with the legal controversy at hand. Chapter 2 explores the social, economic, political, and/or historical background to this topic. Chapter 3 describes in detail the various court decisions and actions that have shaped the current status of the legal controversy under examination. In some cases that will be done through a close examination of a few representative cases, in others by a broader but less detailed narrative of the course of judicial action. Chapter 4 discusses the impact of these cases on U.S. law—their doctrinal legacy—as well as on U.S. society—their historical, sociological, and political legacy.

Part 2, in turn, provides selective supplementary materials designed to help readers more fully comprehend the topics covered in the chapters of Part 1. First are documents aimed at helping the reader better appreciate both the issues and the process by which adjudication shaped these matters. Selected documents might include court opinions (excerpted or whole), interviews, newspaper accounts, or selected secondary essays. Next comes an alphabetically formatted glossary providing entries on the people, laws, cases, and concepts important to an understanding of the topic. A chronology next provides the reader an easily referenced listing of the major developments covered in the book, and a table of cases lists the major court decisions cited. And last, an annotated bibliography describes the key works in the field, directing a reader seeking a more detailed examination of the topic to the appropriate sources.

In closing, as you read the books in this series, keep in mind the purposefully controversial nature of the topics covered within. The authors in the series have not chosen easy or agreeable topics to explore. Much of what you read may trouble you, and should. Yet it is precisely these sorts of contentious topics that need the most historical analysis and scrutiny. For it is here that we are still "on trial"—and all too often, as regards these matters, the jury is still out.

Charles L. Zelden
Ft. Lauderdale, Florida

Preface and Acknowledgments

How and why law and medicine became intertwined in American courtrooms are the subject of this exploration of past and current medicolegal controversies. This study considers the role of the courts in relation to medicine within the past 150 years in the United States. The volume also considers how medicine has affected American judicial decisions. Both relationships—law's impact upon medicine and medicine's effect upon law—have been vital and have undergone great change in that time period. Medicine now seems an inextricable aspect of American trials of all sorts, and the law has had such an effect upon medicine as a field that the term *medicolegal* currently is recognized as a legitimate adjective. But it was by no means a given that the two areas should mix. Even throughout the nineteenth century, the academic disciplines of law and medicine seemed to have little in common.

By the twenty-first century, however, Americans have become accustomed to medical experts serving as witnesses in courtrooms in a wide variety of cases. In judicial discussions of murder, child custody, the rights of the mentally ill, end-of-life issues, abortion, contraception, compulsory vaccination, product liability, and many other topics, medical personnel currently have a leading role to play. On the other hand, courts increasingly intrude into medical situations, including the physician-patient relationship. Of particular interest in this study are the germinations of several medicolegal controversies that trouble law and medicine in the twenty-first century and indeed have spread beyond those two fields to nettle

American society as a whole. Discussions of controversies concerning law and medicine are no longer confined to courtrooms; in trying to resolve medicolegal disputes, courts actually have created additional turmoil within the larger society.

For example, policymakers, lawyers, and doctors are extremely concerned about the problem of malpractice suits against physicians and other healthcare professionals; work stoppages by clamorous physicians have highlighted what these doctors believe to be a malpractice crisis that threatens patients' quality of care as well as physicians' right to remain in practice. State legislatures as well as Congress have considered proposals to limit the sums awarded by juries in malpractice actions. Such a step is a radical response to a situation that is perceived as an emergency by many, including physicians such as neurosurgeons and obstetricians, other health workers (notably midwives), trial lawyers, as well as the public as a whole. One of the topics under consideration here is how the malpractice controversy arose from the various types of medical-product liability claims heard with particular intensity by U.S. courts in the past half-century.

Another highly contentious area of medicolegal discussion has been the question of the "right to die." From reading U.S. court decisions in cases from the 1970s onward, one can conclude that courts often have been involved in discussions about physician-assisted suicide (PAS), euthanasia, and questions surrounding the termination of life support. But what have those decisions meant for law, medicine, and American society in general? From the U.S. Supreme Court to courts at a much lower level, U.S. judicial forums have considered cases on the right to die and have come to decisions that themselves engender controversies. Much the same can be said of medicolegal questions related to the beginning of life. Abortion, contraception, assisted reproduction (AR), and injury-at-birth cases have bloodied the courts and have often bruised courts' standing with the public at large.

The implications of such controversies on the medical profession are profound, going right to the question of how healers should comport themselves. Ironically, even in ancient Greece physicians had to forswear being engaged in certain practices that still bring doctors into court today. The Hippocratic oath required (and still mandates) that physicians swear they will neither administer fatal poisons nor perform abortions. The oath further cautions that physicians must use their judgment and ability to help the sick and to refrain from doing damage to any person—the famous admonition to "do no harm." Physicians currently face the challenge of reconciling that ancient charge with their modern duties, duties that bring them into direct contact with not only patients but a host of other parties (such as government agencies, drug companies, hospital managements, insurance providers, and, of course, the courts) that seek to regulate their conduct. The changing ethical and professional position of physicians within American society is not the main focus of this book. Still, the volume does include considerations of several instances in which courts have held doctors to certain ethical standards in connection with explosive issues such as abortion and the administration of what Hippocrates would have called fatal draughts by the hands of persons such as Dr. Jack Kevorkian.

Interestingly, several important historical developments connecting law and medicine are not particularly well known or widely discussed among scholars. Legal historians have not written much, for example, about the field of forensic medicine and the increasing authority of some of its most active practitioners—forensic pathologists. The inclusion of forensic pathology within courtrooms, particularly in helping to solve murder cases, has been a notable change when medicine or any other subject was "on trial" in the past 150 years, and therefore it is a key theme in this study. This volume also explores a related historical development: the rise to hero status of forensic pathologists. Some among that grim specialty have become heroes to the American public; in current popular culture, forensic pathologists are pivotal figures who see that justice is done in difficult murder cases. This volume aims to demonstrate how, and especially through which important exemplars of its practice, forensic pathology as a field yielded those unlikely celebrities.

A project this broad in scope merely can give the flavor of the debates that are spotlighted rather than convey all of their nuances. Written for neither medical lawyers nor forensic medicine specialists, this volume is aimed, instead, at the general reader. Besides spotlighting the judicial handling of medicolegal dramas, this study explains the historical developments underlying and accompanying courtroom controversies.

Bringing an introductory-level treatment of this complex subject into focus for the lay reader has required the skill and generosity of several persons.Without the enthusiasm and keen historical ability of series editor Charles Zelden, this particular project never would have come to pass. Dr. Zelden brims with good cheer, but he also wields an incisive editor's pen. His ability to zero in on lapses in logic and explanation while remaining diplomatic is rare indeed. ABC-CLIO's editors Alicia Merritt, Carla Roberts, and Jessica Bothwell, as well as several other members of the staff of the press, have been unfailingly efficient as the manuscript was under consideration and in production.

Several colleagues in the History Department at the University of Texas at Arlington offered moral support and specific suggestions about the manuscript. Department chair Donald Kyle provided tangible assistance in managing the overflow enrollment in one of my classes during the semester that I was completing the writing. James Cotton untangled in record time, some technical difficulties in my word processing.

Several reference librarians were of tremendous help in guiding me through databases and documents collections: Ann Kelley of the University of Texas at Arlington and the staff at the University of Texas Southwestern Medical Center Library were especially knowledgeable and enthusiastic about problem solving on my behalf. I also appreciate the assistance of the staff at the National Institutes of Health, History of Medicine Division, in Bethesda, Maryland; the Wellcome Institute in London; and the Boston Athenaeum, which provided access to rare materials.

Students in undergraduate and graduate legal history classes forced me to refresh my knowledge of the cases on which this study is predicated. I am grateful to them for their energy and talent in discussing "great trials" over the past few years. Professor Marjorie Levine-Clark of the University of Colorado at Denver adeptly critiqued an early draft of part of this research.

I remain grateful to Professor Charles McCurdy of the University of Virginia for helping me understand the importance of the *Guiteau* case and encouraging my interest in medicolegal history. My generation of legal historians is indebted to Professor McCurdy not only for his scholarship but also for his kindness.

My cheerful husband engineered trips to the zoo for the rest of our household on some sunny Saturdays so that I might stay inside at the computer. My toddler daughters offered many charming distractions from the troubling stories in which I was immersed.

Writing about these controversial and often tragic cases makes me doubly thankful for the supportive presence and continuing good health of my family.

Elisabeth A. Cawthon

Part One

1
Introduction

Vision and Reality: Public Perceptions about Medicine in the Courtroom

The phrase *medicine on trial* conjures up a wide range of images for modern Americans. Largely as a result of memorable dramatic portrayals and mass media coverage of physicians in the courtroom, most Americans readily imagine scenes of a surgeon defending himself from a malpractice suit, a forensic expert testifying about a victim's cause of death, or a doctor explaining his decision to hasten the demise of a terminally ill patient. Although medicolegal subjects such as medical malpractice, forensic pathology, and assisted suicide would not seem the stuff of Hollywood or the tabloids, they have become topics that affect not only American courtrooms, but also popular culture.

The film *The Verdict,* for instance, tells a heartbreaking story. An arrogant physician is accused of negligence in the case of a young woman who has lapsed into a coma. The doctor is defended by the religious organization that runs the hospital at which the alleged negligence occurred. The physician and the church officials are of the same elite social class as the judge hearing the suit. The patient is from a working-class background. The victim and her family are represented by a lawyer (played by Paul Newman) who is initially an ambulance chaser, but who finds redemption as he investigates and tries the case. In the end, the lawyer's personal empathy for the victim and her family finally win out. Much to the surprise of even the Paul Newman character, the jury asks if it may return an award greater than that requested. And so, played out on the movie screen, justice is served by the workings of our legal system.

The reality of medical malpractice is a much more complex matter. The term *malpractice crisis* has become commonplace among the American public in the early twenty-first century. In front of state capitols throughout the United States, physicians have staged demonstrations (coupled with work stoppages) to highlight the spiraling cost of malpractice insurance premiums. Many insurance companies contend that jury awards in malpractice cases have become too high and that increased insurance premiums are the only method of financing coverage for physicians. Particularly in specialties such as obstetrics—where practitioners often are the subject of malpractice claims due to injuries allegedly incurred at birth—medical personnel are limiting their care for new patients, moving to jurisdictions where jury awards are limited, and/or leaving their practices altogether. Many states, as well as the federal government, are considering legislation that would establish caps on the portions of medical malpractice awards that compensate victims for pain and suffering rather than for tangible economic loss, such as medical bills. The advocacy groups for trial lawyers, however, argue that to limit jury awards is a fundamental infringement on U.S. constitutional rights. After all, it is the patient who has been injured, not the doctor. They contend that physicians must be brought to task for carelessness, and they cite examples of medical horror stories to show that a few incompetent physicians have made malpractice suits a necessary part of American justice.

The disparity between fact and fiction is less apparent when one looks at the doctor as an expert witness. Medical personnel in the courtroom emerge as much more positive figures in television programs and novels devoted to a branch of medical expertise unlikely to create heroes: forensic pathology. Writers such as Erle Stanley Garner, P. D. James, and Patricia Cornwell place forensic pathology at the center of a number of their fictional presentations. Gardner's Perry Mason novels, for instance, drew a great deal of inspiration from one of the most well-respected medical examinerships in the nation, that of Maryland under Dr. Russell Fisher. Hollywood has offered dramatizations of several celebrity coroners and medical examiners (MEs), for example the actor Jack Klugman's character, Dr.

Quincy, who anchored a long-running television series in the 1970s. More recently, television series such as *Diagnosis Murder, Crossing Jordan,* and *CSI: Miami* have all painted pathologists as young, energetic, and talented.

Once regarded even by other physicians as the beastly science, this specialized area of medicine has emerged as an area of expertise where celebrities are made. The first celebrity coroner appeared in England in the early twentieth century as a result of his successful testimony in several well-publicized murder cases. Although he never left England, Dr. Bernard Spilsbury became known, via newspaper accounts, throughout the world in the first three decades of the twentieth century as an expert whose word practically ensured convictions when he appeared for the prosecution. His successor, Dr. Keith Simpson, utilized television as effectively as Spilsbury employed the print media. Simpson traveled the world as a forensic consultant and had many contacts with American colleagues who modeled their own techniques on his. The best example of a celebrity pathologist in modern America has been Dr. Thomas Noguchi, the Los Angeles County coroner between 1967 and 1982. Noguchi, a well-respected pathologist among his peers, was thrown into a wider limelight as a result of his supervision of celebrity-death inquiries in his jurisdiction. Like Simpson, Noguchi was an articulate commentator on the field of forensic pathology and his place within the field; both men published autobiographies that were international bestsellers.

Another image to which Americans have become accustomed—one based not on fiction but on facts reported in the evening news—involves the public polarization caused by doctors' actions in controversial areas. One of the most contentious of these issues is physician-assisted suicide (PAS). Jack Kevorkian, a pathologist who lost his license to practice medicine in 1991, has participated in several suicides by persons with terminal or incurable illnesses. Kevorkian is an extremely controversial figure within medical and legal circles and among the American public. Kevorkian and others who believe in PAS are willing to go to jail in defense of that belief. Their actions have forced U.S. citizens to consider extraordinarily difficult questions that transcend both medicine and law—questions that will be answered in light of the actions of the courts. Kevorkian and his brethren thus represent the dilemmas that medicine has faced in confronting questions of ethics and morality within a legal setting.

With their perspectives shaped by both reality and fiction, modern Americans therefore view physicians within courtrooms as functioning in several different roles, all of which are at odds with one another. To the general public, physicians are key players (often, but not always, unsympathetic ones) within a nationwide malpractice crisis. They are popular investigators of violent crimes who always catch the criminal. And they are the precipitants of volatile debates about the "right to die" and other divisive questions concerning biomedical ethics. How did such conflicting images of medical personnel in the courtroom arise?

A key reason for public confusion about how medicine fits into the courtroom is that medicine's role in American society has changed in fundamental ways in the past 150 years. Whereas prior to the mid–nineteenth century most medical practitioners were not sufficiently well organized to govern their own professional affairs, much less have an impact on public policy or law, the later part of the nineteenth century saw a rapid improvement in professional development and organization in the medical community. In at least one key area of medical practice—that connected to the new field of psychiatry—the recently organized medical experts in their field immediately made a splash on a national level. Psychiatrists became particularly active in the public view as expert witnesses in trials when the mental states of accused persons were at issue. The impact of psychiatrists as expert witnesses in court cases involving psychiatric matters was dramatic. As discussed in Chapters 2 and 3, almost as soon as psychiatry had developed its own internal standards, it was asked by courts to give advice in high-profile cases concerning the insanity defense.

In most areas of medicine, however, the recently formed and self-conscious groups of medical professionals began to have an impact on local and state policies before they made a difference at the national level. For instance, as state medical societies demonstrated a preference for medical examinerships as opposed to coronerships, state legislatures responded positively to their recommendations in the early twentieth century. State medical organizations at the end of the nineteenth century also lobbied their legislatures to write laws giving those medical organizations control over professional medical licensure, qualification, and discipline. Physicians' groups, in addition, tried to limit competition from other medical practitioners such as midwives and pharmacists. Many state laws concerning medicine in the mid-1800s evidenced a clear bias toward physicians rather than other types of medical personnel. In time, courts (including the U.S. Supreme Court) recognized organizations of medical professionals and gave them the power to regulate entry into the profession and to license practitioners. That legal recognition of physicians' collective authority is discussed in Chapter 3.

But courts also held that with the authority to define, regulate, and limit competition in one's profession came certain responsibilities. Particularly as medical professionals began to associate themselves more and more with hospitals, courts took a heavier hand in protecting the rights of patients. With the dawn of the twentieth century, it became clear that physicians viewed hospital practice as prestigious and desirable. In turn, when medical care was based in hospitals, there were far more numerous opportunities for surgery and the use of more advanced technology in patient care. The greater the invasion of the human body and the pocketbook, the greater was the potential for misuse of physicians' authority. As discussed in Chapter 3, courts in the early twentieth century began to set expectations for the professional conduct of healthcare personnel; courts required that medical care be given according to established professional standards. Far from conferring too much authority on doctors, courts' reliance on well-known standards of care seemed to contribute to a much greater willingness by patients to sue their physicians for malpractice, as was apparent by the soaring number of malpractice actions in the mid–twentieth century.

Early twentieth-century medical innovations such as X rays and routine surgeries on body cavities (made possible through advances in antiseptic techniques as well as anesthetics) inspired courts to ensure that physicians and hospitals were not infringing on the basic human rights of patients. More complex technological and medicinal advancements later in the twentieth century inspired still further oversight by the courts of physicians' treatment of patients. Issues related to the beginning and end of life have been particularly affected by the intervention of the courts. Because technology has greatly affected the ability of medicine to keep ill patients alive or to save the lives of babies newly born, the debate concerning how to manage the care of fragile patients has inspired judicial action.

In cases such as the *Quinlan* decision of 1976 (discussed in Chapter 3), U.S. courts told the medical profession that it could not be the sole—or even the key—authority on end-of-life questions. Thus the

Quinlan case was a watershed in regard to right-to-die issues. It also indicated American society's discomfort with medicine's ability to manage its new technologies. *Quinlan* was the first major court ruling involving the fate of a patient who was kept alive through artificial means. The case addressed the fact that the law had not yet provided a definition of the end of life. Medical authorities had attempted to set criteria as to when life ceased, and yet healthcare providers had no cohesive stance about how they were to act when confronted with individual crises at the end of life. Some doctors admitted openly during the *Quinlan* case that the use of "Do Not Resuscitate" codes (to indicate that resuscitation was not to be performed on a terminally ill patient) was routine in hospital settings. Still, many physicians remained unwilling to disconnect artificial means of life support, such as respirators, even at the request of family members of patients who were in prolonged vegetative states. To keep a patient alive almost indefinitely, in other words, now was possible. But should medical personnel have the authority to allow or prohibit the continuation of heroic measures? What role should family members play in such decisions when patients are incapacitated? In *Quinlan,* the courts gave notice that they would be arbiters in these types of end-of-life controversies. Though courts refused to stake out a claim to being the *sole* decision makers, in *Quinlan* and subsequent right-to-die cases, such as the *Cruzan* case (1990) and the *Glucksberg* and *Vacco* decisions (1997), the courts argued that physicians and other healthcare providers required some judicial oversight. The chance of patients' fundamental rights (such as the right to live) being abused simply was too great.

In *Roe v. Wade* (1973), courts announced a similar policy with respect to the subject of the beginning of life. While recognizing the impulse and authority of states to make laws on controversial subjects such as PAS and abortion, U.S. courts have enunciated standards that transcend state regulations. In certain instances, such as the Supreme Court's enunciation of a privacy right covering matters of contraception and abortion, courts have grounded patient rights in the U.S. Constitution—a clear limitation on states' authority. And yet courts' underlining of patient rights has not been absolute, as the abortion controversy itself has shown; courts continue to hold that there is a realm of proper state action in regard to the regulation of citizens' health.

Although some recent authors have contended that courts' increasing management of medicine and medical practitioners has been at best ineffective and at worst a disaster, this study presents a less gloomy view. In spite of the inability of courts to solve deeply divisive controversies such as the abortion debate, I contend that especially with respect to beginning- and end-of-life issues the U.S. judicial system has been responsive to changes in medicine and medical technology while still allowing scope for action by states and localities.

A Wider Context: The Medicalization of Courtrooms

In one sense, this study tells of twin historical developments: Medicine has become a major factor in judicial settings in the past 150 years, and courts increasingly have begun to exert authority over medicine and its practitioners. The evolution of medicine as a force within and concerning U.S. courtrooms has not happened in a vacuum. Both the history and current status of these medicolegal controversies in the United States—and our public conceptions about them—are closely connected with developments in other nations. Some medicolegal practices came straight from England to America in the 1600s and 1700s. The coroner, for example, was the public officer in England who was responsible for investigating all cases of sudden or violent death, or death that occurred in certain institutional settings, such as jails and almshouses. A medieval office, the coronership survived into the early modern era with its reputation sullied. Among other weaknesses, the sixteenth- and seventeenth-century English coroner was perceived by the public as highly politicized, reluctant to engage in controversy, and overly concerned with the collection of fees. With the English migration to the New World, this concept of the coronership was transplanted from England to North America with all of its shortcomings. Consequently, Chapter 2 includes a discussion of the origins and historical development of the coronership and the medical examinership. Within the small and specialized group of persons who have become experts in forensic pathology, there has been considerable transatlantic sharing of knowledge and personnel. England's Bernard Spilsbury and Keith Simpson were widely admired and emulated among their professional colleagues in the United States, for example, and New York

City's Milton Helpern was regarded as a world-class representative of his field. In fact, the first instances of the ME as hero arose in England.

American physicians and legal experts concerned with other fields in medicine often have looked to England for inspiration, and vice versa, as they practiced their craft. Particularly when fields of medicine have a bearing on criminal or civil court cases, the connection between medicolegal matters in the United States and the English legal tradition is readily apparent. In regard to expert medical testimony on the mental state of accused persons, for instance, U.S. authorities until the present day often have cited the British M'Naghten Rules from the 1840s as important tests for insanity. On the other hand, one of the most convincing medical experts on the nineteenth-century English law of insanity was the American physician Isaac Ray. In the twentieth century, eminent American judges such as Benjamin Cardozo testified before the British parliament about the operation (or lack thereof) of legal standards for insanity. The close relationship between English and U.S. law concerning the insanity defense is highlighted in Chapter 3.

The experiences of English lawmakers also have informed American legislators and judges. When Louis Brandeis searched for data to support his contention, in the case of *Muller v. Oregon,* that manual labor could be harmful to female laundry workers, he utilized example after example drawn from the British parliamentary papers. Chapter 3 considers the development of the Brandeis brief and other methods of introducing scientific and medical evidence into courtrooms.

A study concerned with medicine in the courtroom must take into account the fact that other nations have addressed some of the same controversies in medicolegal matters that the United States currently faces. To craft policies relating to assisted suicide, for example, U.S. state legislatures and courts recently have examined the experiences of Switzerland and the Netherlands—nations that allow much more legal freedom for physicians to assist in the deaths of their patients. Chapter 4 describes several foreign alternatives to the state-by-state approach to regulating PAS currently in force and which the U.S. Supreme Court seems to have endorsed in the *Vacco* and *Glucksberg* decisions. Some legal controversies that affect foreign nations originated with American products or policies that were marketed abroad. To what extent should U.S. courts take cognizance of lawsuits under such circumstances? In deciding whether to allow foreign nationals access to U.S. courts in breast-implant cases, for instance, U.S. state courts have considered whether compensation is available in the plaintiffs' home jurisdictions. In many instances of product liability lawsuits connected with medicine, nations such as Great Britain and Germany have more efficient compensation schemes than the United States—largely as a result of their being caught off guard by the thalidomide births of the 1950s and 1960s (described in Chapter 2).

Foundations: Methods and Goals of the Study

This book concentrates on a selection of current medicolegal controversies, with an explanation of some of their historical roots and likely future trends. My emphasis has been on leading cases, particularly U.S. Supreme Court decisions, although it should be noted that several pivotal decisions (with *Quinlan* a major example) were at the state supreme court or appeals court level. With regard to some controversies, such as medical-product liability, I have discussed less well-known decisions in order to convey the sense of how courts decided ordinary cases on a certain subject. With respect to one important type of case, class action lawsuits, I have not attempted to survey all of the hundreds of decisions that the courts have made, but only to represent certain trends within the judicial response.

Certain elements of the arguments in this study are original. In particular, the changing role of forensic pathologists in the twentieth-century United States and the United Kingdom and the connections between those nations' forensic scientists form a subject that has not been considered thoroughly among legal historians. Yet most of the rest of this study builds on existing works. Paul Starr's *The Social Transformation of American Medicine* in particular has provided much of the framework for the history of medicine that appears in this study.

Starr, for example, describes in much greater detail than can be shown here the process by which hospitals were founded and eventually became businesses in the nineteenth century. Whereas hospitals in America once had been mostly charitable or religious institutions that cared for persons either too poor or too far from their homes to rely on family assistance, they have now become institutions that compete for paying patients with curable afflictions. The association between affiliated physicians and hospitals grew much closer as hospitals turned into enterprises with a greater concern for revenue. Revenue concerns, in turn, raised issues that inevitably drew doctors and hospitals into the legal realm. For example, could patients without insurance be shunted off by private hospitals to public facilities? Only in the later twentieth century did Congress mandate that emergency patients had the right to be stabilized and treated at the first medical facility that saw them. As discussed in Chapter 3, court cases arise regularly under the legislation guaranteeing emergency medical care regardless of the ability to pay (the 1986 federal law known as EMTALA).

Another important development in healthcare with implications for the law, Starr notes, was the management of hospitals by large corporations in the middle of the twentieth century. Increasingly, neither individual physicians nor even groups of doctors within a particular facility made hospital policies. Those policies were set (usually for reasons of cost and with an eye toward potential liability) more often than not by the management of groups of hospitals. In a variety of areas of medicine and on an everyday basis, patient treatment is affected by those policies. For example, in Texas hospitals that were a part of the Healthcare Corporation of America (HCA) system in the early 1990s, healthcare workers were expected to follow guidelines set by the hospital's management company about when premature newborns must be resuscitated. Those criteria were not developed in individual circumstances (for example when a premature baby was suffering from severe abnormalities), and they were not to be impacted by parents' wishes. Such management from afar could and did give rise to "wrongful life" cases, like that of *Miller v. Columbia/HCA* (see Chapter 3), in which courts had to decide whether hospitals or their parent companies were liable for the astronomical continuing costs of having resuscitated a desperately ill baby.

Starr argues that by the 1970s, American medical providers were increasingly under scrutiny from other institutions. Healthcare had come under the purview of the federal government as the result of programs such as Medicare and Medicaid in the 1960s. This federal oversight was the result of a new social vision, but it was tied nonetheless to the escalating costs of medicine. Increasing federal oversight also was related to a public lack of confidence in medicine. Greater technological advances had once brought the hope that medicine could solve ever-greater numbers of problems. Yet by the

1970s, complex medical technology—at a much higher cost—appeared to create additional dilemmas. That crisis of confidence spilled over into a judicial oversight of areas of medicine that previously had not been the subject of court cases, most especially in right-to-die cases such as *Quinlan* (1976), *Cruzan* (1990), and *Glucksberg* and *Vacco* (1997).

Still, in his justifiably celebrated book, Starr does not emphasize the interactions between law and medicine or the development of medicolegal studies as a field. In fact, few works exploring the totality of medicolegal issues are available for the layperson. Books on legal medicine written for physicians usually emphasize avoiding liability in the first place. They also quite rightly recommend that the physician who expects that he or she will be the object of a lawsuit should consult an experienced malpractice attorney.

Yet in spite of the rarity of historical studies that are medicolegal in subject matter, several excellent historians of medicine and law do provide contexts in which current medicolegal controversies can be considered. Roy Porter's far-reaching and detailed *The Greatest Benefit to Mankind*, for example, considers the paradox that an increasingly "powerful, science-based biomedical tradition" (p. 12) cannot serve all of the medically needy persons in the world. David Rothman, in *Strangers at the Bedside,* chronicles the increasing oversight by nonmedical authorities (such as legislators and philosophers interested in ethics) of healthcare in mid- to late twentieth-century America. Roger Dworkin provides thoughtful and broad coverage of many topics in biomedical ethics that have been the subject of legal discussion. In his book *Limits—The Role of the Law in Bioethical Decision Making,* Dworkin concludes that the legal responses to medical and ethical quandaries have ranged between ill advised, ineffective, and positively harmful. In many respects, Ben Rich takes an opposite view to Dworkin's, in Rich's book *Strange Bedfellows: How Medical Jurisprudence Has Influenced Medical Ethics and Medical Practice.* Rich contends that the modern influence of the law upon medicine has contributed to the solving of thorny problems in medical ethics.

Although not primarily historical in methodology, recent works in the burgeoning field of bioethics also have treated legal controversies such as the "right to die" in a provocative manner. Leon Kass, in *Life, Liberty, and the Defense of Dignity,* for example, is sharply critical of the Supreme Court's unwillingness to slam the door on organizations that promote euthanasia and PAS. Onora O'Neill's *Autonomy and*

Trust in Bioethics considers how, why, and when the medical community lost so much trust among the public that courts had to devise the notion of informed consent.

Conclusion

Not all topics related to medicine and the courts can be considered in an introductory study of this type. There are many areas of law related to mental illness that are not explored here. The question of involuntary committal to mental-health facilities, for instance, is an important area of legal medicine. Indeed the whole question of how the courts have treated mental illness is worthy of a separate volume parallel to this one.

For experts who deal with medicolegal subjects every day, such as malpractice attorneys, this volume simply scratches the surface of case law. Medical practitioners—especially forensic pathologists—likewise will know about legal aspects of current medical practice in much greater detail than can be presented here. From the nonforensic physician's standpoint, a particularly well-written rumination on certain medicolegal dilemmas faced by modern American doctors can be found in sections of Atul Gawande's *Complications.* As a surgeon, Gawande offers a perspective on medical negligence, for example, that is representative of the view of many medical specialists.

Some topics related to the central themes of this study have been discussed ably in a recent volume in this series—Lynne Curry's *The Human Body on Trial.* Curry approaches several medicolegal subjects more directly than I do; for instance she skillfully describes compulsory vaccination at the beginning of the twentieth century in cases such as *Jacobson v. Massachusetts* (1905). The overall emphasis in the current volume is different from Curry's. Rather than focusing, as Curry does, on the autonomy of the human body, I have considered medicine's role within the legal system. In particular, I concentrate on the roles that physicians have played when medicine was "on trial."

Furthermore, I do recognize that other medical personnel have been key actors in U.S. courtrooms. "Alternative" practitioners, nurses, midwives (both lay and licensed), and even medical administrators have been important participants in legal controversies. Nor has every issue that is medicolegal in nature been included in this volume, since not every controversy has been considered by courts. Human cloning, for example, has not yet been the subject of a court case. Some provocative topics that have been outgrowths of important cases, however, are included in Chapter 4. As that chapter's discussion of foreign approaches to medicolegal controversies suggests, many medicolegal issues rapidly are becoming international in scope. Increasingly, U.S. legal authorities are recognizing that they must take cognizance of other nations' approaches to the medicolegal topics that have confounded U.S. courts. Whether U.S. courts will adopt, adapt, or act in a manner opposite to the actions of foreign nations with respect to difficult medicolegal questions remains to be seen. What is clear, however, is that courts will continue to oversee medicine and its practitioners. Meanwhile, medical personnel will play some role—most likely a decisive role—in shaping the law concerning medicine.

References and Further Reading

Curry, Lynne. *The Human Body on Trial.* Santa Barbara, CA: ABC-CLIO, 2002.

Dworkin, Roger. *Limits—The Role of the Law in Bioethical Decision Making.* Bloomington: Indiana University Press, 1996.

Gawande, Atul. *Complications: A Surgeon's Notes on an Imperfect Science.* New York: Picador, 2002.

Horn, Carl, Donald H. Caldwell, and Christopher D. Osborn. *Law for Physicians: An Overview of Medical Legal Issues.* Chicago, IL: American Medical Association, 2000.

Kass, Leon. *Life, Liberty and the Defense of Dignity.* San Francisco, CA: Encounter Books, 2002.

O'Neill, Onora. *Autonomy and Trust in Bioethics.* Cambridge: Cambridge University Press, 2002.

Porter, Roy. *The Greatest Benefit to Mankind.* New York: Norton, 1998.

Rich, Ben A. *Strange Bedfellows: How Medical Jurisprudence Has Influenced Medical Ethics and Medical Practice.* New York: Kluwer Academic Publishers, 2001.

Rothman, David. *Strangers at the Bedside.* New York: Basic Books, 1991.

Starr, Paul. *The Social Transformation of American Medicine.* New York: Basic Books, 1982.

The Verdict, VHS. Directed by Sidney Lumet. Beverly Hills, CA: Twentieth Century Fox, 1982.

2
Historical Background

Gatekeepers to the Courts: American Coroner and Medical Examiner Systems

For courts to consider cases (either civil or criminal) in which a death is involved, they first must know how those deaths occurred. Without a finding that a death was the result of untoward circumstance rather than natural causes, no one could pursue a legal remedy. The officials who make that determination, therefore, are gatekeepers to the court system—providers of a necessary first step in the judicial process.

Traditionally, both coroners and medical examiners (MEs) have filled this gatekeeper role. In the twenty-first century in the United States, persons who hold offices as coroners and MEs almost always have been trained as specialists in forensic pathology. Although they are not always well known among the American public, forensic pathologists are vital and persistent figures within the U.S. legal system. Once they have investigated the medical causes of death, forensic pathologists must work closely with police and public authorities, such as district attorneys, in gathering evidence for criminal prosecutions. At trials, forensic pathologists frequently give evidence as medical experts. In contrast to the ordinary medical practitioner, who rarely if ever testifies in court, forensic pathologists in large urban jurisdictions can come into court dozens—perhaps even hundreds—of times during their careers. Some of those medical experts have become quite famous among laypeople. They are medical detectives who have inspired dramatic portrayals on television and in novels. How did forensic pathologists (both coroners and MEs) come to play such a vital part in the judicial determination of criminal responsibility?

The modern coroner is an appointed or elected official who investigates unnatural deaths, as well as deaths that occur in public institutions, such as prisons, or in hospitals during the course of medical procedures. Coroners are most often seen in countries that are of English-speaking heritage, including Canada, Australia, South Africa, and the United States. In other areas of the world, the police generally have investigative functions related to unexpected deaths.

The coronership is an office dating at least as far back as the late twelfth century in England. The office arose out of a national fiscal emergency that was caused by King Richard I (the Lion-Hearted) being kidnapped and held for ransom when he was on his way home from a crusade in the Middle East. Desperate to raise what was literally a king's ransom, the officials who were in charge of revenue collection in England commanded that in each county three local residents of wealth and stature, assisted by a clerk, should be "keepers of the pleas of the crown."

In large part, the national administrators undertook this reorganization in local governmental authority to protect royal revenues from sheriffs, who were supposed to be serving the king but (as the Robin Hood legends relate) often were notoriously corrupt. The "crowners" (later coroners), however, also were charged with a variety of other duties designed to uphold national governmental authority. Among these tasks were the oversight of revenues from wrecks and other found treasures as well as the supervision of the catching of certain valuable types of fish. Coroners also were in charge of holding inquests on dead bodies, particularly with a focus on obtaining monies due to the king, as in cases of suicides when all properties were forfeit to the monarch. In addition, any object that "moved to the death" of a victim was forfeit, as a *deodand* or "god-gift" due to the king. Lastly, coroners had the responsibility of administering the Norman law that required communities to pay a *murdrum*—a fine on unsolved killings that originally had been aimed at anti-Norman violence in localities. Thus, taken as a whole, the office of coroner originally was associated with political and fiscal service to the throne. Yet the coronership had a popular dimension as well. The coroner did not reach his conclusions alone; he presided over the examination of dead bodies by a group of jurors. In conjunction with that jury, the coroner's court reached a verdict that could lead to further legal action such as an indictment for murder. And so the coroners' link to legal proceedings—in particular criminal legal proceedings—was established.

The connection became even stronger over time. Sheriffs, the other key royal representative in the counties, recovered some of their lost political clout. Within 100 years or so, sheriffs regained control of tax collection. Meanwhile, coroners remained charged with collecting revenues connected to violent deaths. By the end of the fifteenth century, other local officials, the justices of the peace, were gaining power at coroners' expense, garnering most of coroners' revenue collection duties, although coroners still had the right to exact fees from localities for their services. (Some coroners continued to demand payments for their services with impunity, however, leading to the long-standing reputation of the coroner as not only a political figure but also a corrupt one. Shakespeare even used an actual case of a coroner's inquest on a suicide victim being reviewed by a higher court [*Hales v. Petit,* from 1562] to comment on the irrational findings that came from some coroners' inquests, when in *Hamlet,* act 5, scene 1, the gravediggers marveled at the absurdities of "crowner's quest law.") In 1751, Parliament provided for fees for coroners to be paid through local tax rates overseen by circuit justices rather than the interested parties. The justices, however, proved reluctant to approve fees except in instances where coroners could show that they had strong evidence of the deaths having been related to felonies. Thus coroners had an inducement *not* to investigate more mundane deaths (such as fatalities from mere accident or those that were sudden but arguably natural) but only those deaths likely to be related to a crime.

Interestingly, under the English system coroners did not have to be medically qualified. In fact few coroners were, because in the medieval era they were in charge of determining simply whether a death was felonious or not. In the period prior to the nineteenth century, most coroners were legally trained and were property owners, usually residing within the jurisdiction that they served.

All this changed in the nineteenth century. In the 1830s, because of the new visibility of coroners' inquests concerning industrial and transportation accidents (the numbers of which were rising into the hundreds every year), a campaign for medical qualifications for coroners arose in England. Leading this movement was Thomas Wakley, a coroner elected in the early 1830s for the highly visible area of Middlesex (in and around London). Himself a physician, Wakley had founded the medical journal *The Lancet*, a preeminent medical journal still published today. He employed the journal to advocate the need for medical qualifications for coroners. He argued against both "attorney-coroners" and laypersons serving in the office, contending that neither had the skill to determine causes of death in a world filled with exploding steamships and fast-moving railway engines. A tireless reformer, Wakley was the force behind 1836 legislation by Parliament that required that medical witnesses and toxicological experts at inquests be paid and that fees should be collected for all autopsies performed by coroners.

The campaign for a medical coronership continued long after Wakley's death, fueled by an increasing sense of professionalism among physicians and a long-standing loyalty among the English public to the jury system. Although an important coroners' act was passed in 1887, defining coroners' authority more clearly, only in 1926 did Parliament mandate that coroners be professionally qualified. Interestingly, that act allowed either legal or medical qualification, along with five years' work experience. In fact, in Northern Ireland the old prejudice against medical coroners held sway, and physicians actually were barred from service as coroners unless they also were legally credentialed. Yet in England, before long, most coroners were trained physicians.

So events stood for most of the twentieth century until, in 1977, a new English law allowed coroners even less legal authority than they had possessed, declaring coroners' courts powerless to reach a determination of murder or manslaughter. This, the law informed, was solely the province of the courts. English coroners' courts by the beginning of the twenty-first century thus had three remaining functions: to determine causes of death, to calm public fears that similar deaths might occur, and to be a forum for the expression of public concerns (for instance, about safety issues).

The coronership was one aspect of English law among many that were exported to the British North American colonies in the seventeenth and eighteenth centuries. Historians of the coronership have noted that it came to America at a singularly poor time in its history—when the office was under attack for partisanship and graft, and was characterized by a lack of professionalism, organization, and coordination. Often, local undertakers served as coroners; in other jurisdictions coroners were elected in frankly partisan contests, and they had no training at all in the examination of dead bodies. Many coroners were reluctant to order autopsies because they perceived them as unpopular with voters.

In the second half of the nineteenth century and the beginning of the twentieth century, several U.S. states and localities reexamined their coronerships and found them to be wanting. These investigations of the coronership were just one aspect of the broader reform of local governments to make them less corrupt, more open to employment by civil-service principles, and more efficiently administered. In the United States, as opposed to England, those who sought to reform the coronership agitated for medicolegal investigations that were independent of juries. The National Municipal League (NML), organized in 1894, had as a goal the streamlining of ballots so that voters could be more fully informed about local-government contests and less controlled by political bosses. Coroners were among the local officials whom the league sought to remove from voters' purview.

In 1877, the state of Massachusetts replaced its coroners with medical examiners (MEs). MEs were appointed officials charged with the medical and legal investigation of deaths. They were licensed physicians with expertise in pathology and often microscopy. MEs usually were chosen from among qualified civil-service employees. Some of the early MEs such as those in Massachusetts were allowed to investigate only deaths that clearly were violent in nature. The city of Baltimore created an alternative form of the ME system in 1890, in which professional MEs performed autopsies as ordered by the still popularly elected local coroner or the state's attorney.

An ME system was established in New York City in 1915 after a critical report was published condemning the coroner's office for its partisanship and lack of professionalism. Similar reforms soon followed in coroners' offices across the country. New York City's ME's Office, in fact, came to serve as a prototype for many of these new model systems. Its employees (including forensic pathologists) were part of the civil service. Its equipment was state of the art. New York City eventually required that its ME should be not only a physician but also a fully trained forensic pathologist—a comparatively new medical specialty in the early twentieth century. More significantly, the Medical Examiner's Office in New York City was authorized to investigate a wide range of suspicious deaths, which expanded the role of the ME's office from that of the traditional coroner.

The first statewide ME system was set up in Maryland in 1939. Virginia provided for an ME system in 1946. Although it did not have forensic laboratories in every locality, Virginia made forensic pathologists available in regions throughout the state; its MEs were appointed. The NML again was part of this effort to rationalize post-mortem medical examinations. It was aided by state medical associations, which lobbied for the adoption of changes to coroner-based systems. In 1954, the NML issued a model county charter, which included a model coroner law based on the effective ME systems in Massachusetts, Virginia, and Maryland. State medical associations quickly became interested in obtaining copies of the league's Model Post-Mortem Examinations Act, which had been published by the National Conference of Commissioners on Uniform State Laws. Both the American Medical Association (AMA) and the NML endorsed the model legislation.

In the late 1950s and 1960s, many localities and some states replaced their coroners with MEs, although in a number of states both systems continued to exist side by side. By the end of the twentieth century, there were over 2,000 separate jurisdictions in the United States in which death investigations took place either through coroners or MEs. Almost half of the population of the United States was served by ME systems; 22 states had no coroners at all. In several western and southern states, however, local elected and partisan forces still controlled the coroners. The ME system had not been universally adopted, and its expansion slowed significantly after about 1990. Despite diligent efforts among forensic pathologists' groups to replace coronerships with MEs' offices, the coroner remained a feature of many local governments.

The modern U.S. ME system is not without critics. Some complain, for instance, that its lack of public hearings impedes inquiries into widespread dangers to public health and safety. Critics of MEs also argue that only coroners, as legal officials, can require that witnesses testify about controversial matters. In addition, most MEs, although experienced in matters of forensic testimony, because of their lack of legal training may not be experts at interpreting state statutes regulating their duties. This occasionally causes them problems, for example, in relation to the ordering of autopsies and the transplantation of organs. The relationship between MEs and police and district attorneys, in addition, is a delicate one. For example, the decision by an ME as to whether, when, and to whom to disclose an autopsy report is of great import in criminal prosecutions.

Forensic Pathologists in the Courtroom

By the time reforms began to replace the coronership in the late nineteenth and early twentieth centuries, a new medical specialist had appeared: the forensic pathologist. Experts in forensic pathology transformed the investigations of deaths within the legal system. In many places outside England, forensic pathologists replaced coroners completely. Forensic pathologists also became important figures in courtrooms when they appeared there as expert witnesses. Most surprisingly, the practitioners of that often gruesome science of pathology became celebrities within the larger society in both England and the United States.

Historically, neither medicine nor law was willing to recognize the need for training in the other field. When legal training of doctors and medical training of lawyers did occur, however, it was related to the vital and growing importance of forensic science within nineteenth- and early twentieth-century courtrooms. For most of the nineteenth century, the term *legal medicine* was closely connected with the training of physicians who would serve the needs of justice—that is, forensic specialists. There were two important chairs in medical jurisprudence created in the nineteenth century in the United States—one at the College of Physicians and Surgeons in Philadelphia in 1814 and another at Harvard in 1877. Forensic experts filled both positions. Even when medical schools finally added courses in medical jurisprudence in the middle of the twentieth century, most of those classes focused narrowly on forensic science rather than on a more expansive view of medicolegal subjects (such as medical ethics).

The growth of the pathologist as an expert witness and of pathology as a legitimate part of the legal process occurred slowly, largely in response to a series of notorious cases (mostly involving murders) in which several early twentieth-century specialists in forensic pathology made themselves household names. In doing so, they also greatly enhanced the reputation of their field within both the legal and medical professions. In examining the careers of twentieth-century forensic pathologists Bernard Spilsbury and Keith Simpson of England and Thomas Magrath, Milton Helpern, and Thomas Noguchi of the United States, one can see how in several important respects U.S. and British courtrooms were growing increasingly dependent on medical expertise.

Precisely how did these five eminent forensic pathologists help the cause of medicine when it was "on trial"? Bernard Spilsbury, for example, resuscitated the reputation of the pathologist through his skillful testimony in several poisoning cases—exactly the type of case that had bedeviled his profession in the later nineteenth century. Keith Simpson gained a prominent reputation with the public when he became an expert on certain disturbing causes of death that previously had been mysterious—notably the battered child syndrome. He, like Spilsbury, pioneered in the meticulous and grisly art of reconstructing dismembered bodies; it was a skill that served him well as murders seemed to become more and more gruesome in the early twentieth century. Simpson also advocated the advancement of several specialties within forensic pathology, such as forensic odontology. The use of dental records in a forensic context became a key weapon for pathologists in the twentieth century, in murder cases and in connection with the identification of bodies after mass accidents such as airline crashes.

Thomas Magrath raised the profile of forensic pathologists in part simply because he worked in the well-known jurisdiction of Boston. He also worked outside Boston, however, serving as a consultant in dozens of cases in New England. There, through sheer force of personality, Magrath conveyed to less urban areas the notion that forensic pathologists could be effective crime solvers. Magrath also was skilled in testifying about ballistics, for example in the extremely well-known trials concerning Sacco and Vanzetti in the 1920s. Thus Magrath represented several trends within forensic pathology during the period from 1910 to 1930: the field's becoming even more technical in nature, its broadening appeal among even rural areas, and its increasing presence within the courtroom in high-profile cases.

As the chief medical examiner for New York City for several decades, Milton Helpern presided over the busiest (and one of the best-publicized) ME's jurisdiction in the nation. New York's numerous and vociferous members of the press critiqued his failures and celebrated his successes in a long series of sensational cases. Helpern was the consummate modern ME in many respects; he was beloved by medical peers for his modesty, yet accomplished in a technical sense. He frequently was called upon to be a consultant all over the world in difficult cases. He also was unusually well liked by jurors, who found him forthright and believable. Still, Helpern was not always an unqualified success on the stand. As he himself noted, his more reserved—even gentle—manner sometimes was no match for the no-holds-barred style of advocacy that was emerging in the early 1960s with young attorneys such as F. Lee Bailey.

Among Americans, the pathologist who exemplified the celebrity coroner was Thomas Noguchi, who worked in Los Angeles in the 1960s, 1970s, and 1980s. As the "coroner to the stars," Noguchi not only investigated the deaths of several popular figures (such as Marilyn Monroe), he also endeavored to raise the profile of the coronership within his geographical area, so that he could secure funds for a state-of-the-art medicolegal facility that focused on the "total investigation" of deaths. Such a facility would include a variety of experts (such as ballistics, chemistry, and microscopy) working in modern laboratories and coordinating investigative efforts among themselves. Noguchi's early skill in working with politicians and the public did not preclude him from being well respected among his fellow forensic pathologists. However, he was not able to continue to satisfy all of the demands that were made upon him in running the Los Angeles Coroner's Office, and his detractors accused him of ignoring the everyday operations in his gleaming new facility because he was too involved in world-famous investigations. For Noguchi, fame eventually came at the cost of his job.

The pathologist who served as an ME or coroner and became famous walked a thin line in several respects, especially in regard to his personality and public persona. Since an ME or coroner was a public servant, he could not make a habit of rankling supervisors in government (such as county officials). To be perceived as a self-promoter or too flamboyant, an ME quite literally risked removal from office on charges that he was neglecting the more mundane aspects of his job. If on the stand he shaded too much into arrogance, he was not persuasive with jurors. On the other hand, the ME had the task of testifying under often rigorous cross-examination. In order to be taken seriously, he had to convey a certain amount of assurance in court. That self-confidence served him well, also, in his dealings with other legal officials such as district attorneys. It certainly was necessary for the pathologist to be respected by his peers in the medical profession if he wished to be appointed to office, for obtaining a position as an ME in a large locality was dependent on one's having and maintaining a strong standing in the field of forensic pathology. Furthermore, the forensic pathologist consorted not only with his peers and with legal experts but sometimes also with the public at large. In his interactions with laypeople, the ME needed to communicate with them clearly and yet humanely. For example, he had to explain causes of death in terms that jury members could grasp and in ways that would be neither too clinical nor too graphic for the jurors. He also often had to speak with family members of the deceased persons he was examining when family members identified bodies or gave permission for autopsies. If he was insensitive, those family members could and did complain about him to their elected officials, who had the authority to terminate his employment.

The most successful and well-known forensic pathologists working in a public capacity in the twentieth century managed a delicate balance between the several constituencies they served. Though of very different backgrounds and temperaments, forensic pathologists Spilsbury, Simpson, Magrath, Helpern, and Noguchi managed to be professionally long-lived because they knew how to satisfy those various masters: their medical peers, the legal officials with whom they worked (such as judges and prosecutors), and the public.

Bernard Spilsbury became a forensic pathologist at an inauspicious time for his field—at the very beginning of the twentieth century. In the second half of the nineteenth century, the new field of forensic pathology had been tarnished in several criminal cases when experts in toxicology had mishandled and misinterpreted evidence. Most infamous among these cases was Britain's 1859 trial of Thomas Smethurst (himself a physician), who had been charged with poisoning his wife with arsenic. Between the time of a preliminary hearing and the trial itself, the well-known toxicologist Alfred Swaine Taylor had to change his testimony about the presence of arsenic in the body of the deceased due to flaws in his testing instruments. The accused was not convicted, in spite of strong opinion among the public that he had committed the crime. Taylor, the most esteemed toxicologist in Britain at the time, thus damaged the reputation of his field. By the end of the nineteenth century, several respected pathologists working at major London hospitals had improved the reputation of pathology with the public. Among other physicians, however, pathologists still were seen as practicing a distasteful (and nearly disreputable) form of medicine.

When Spilsbury first began to practice forensic medicine in the early twentieth century, he profited from a close relationship between London's small forensic medical community and the Home Office, which oversaw police investigations in England. In conjunction with Edward Henry (later metropolitan commissioner of police), Spilsbury advocated that forensic pathologists should help the police modernize criminal investigations. Spilsbury contended that England's lack of a centralized crime laboratory contrasted negatively with other nations—particularly France, where there were medicolegal institutes in Paris, Lyon, and Lille. The laboratory at Lyon, established in 1910 by Edmund Locard, was in fact widely admired and influential.

Although he never saw the establishment of such a national laboratory in Britain, that political failure did not halt Spilsbury's growing influence on the evolution of forensic pathology. Because of his pivotal role in several criminal prosecutions in the second decade of the twentieth century, Spilsbury became internationally known. The *Crippen* case of 1910 was a typical example of his skill not only as an investigator but also as a courtroom presence. The defendant, U.S. citizen Harvey H. Crippen, stood accused of murdering his wife and trying to dispose of her body with lime. Crippen almost was successful in getting away with the crime because he nearly obscured the victim's identity. But through careful examination of the crime scene, Spilsbury recovered a small piece of skin from the remains. Luckily for Spilsbury and most unfortunately for Crippen, Spilsbury was able to establish that the skin was from a person's abdomen and that it bore the scar from an operation. That linked the remains to Crippen's missing wife, for her medical records established that in fact she once had undergone abdominal surgery. The jury was dazzled by Spilsbury's forensic prowess; Crippen was sentenced to hang. Due to the American connections in the *Crippen* case—not only Crippen's nationality, but also his effort to flee England by taking a transatlantic steamer to freedom—the trial became well known in the United States. The case considerably raised the profile of forensic pathology as a tool for solving difficult crimes.

Spilsbury was involved in cases other than murders as well. He testified, for example, at several coroners' inquests into the deaths of patients who died while under the influence of anesthesia. In the late nineteenth century, the public viewed the comparatively new use of chloroform and other anesthetics with some skepticism. For their part, anesthesiologists were angry that their practices should be examined at all by laypersons, as some coroners (and all of their juries) still were. By the 1920s, however, even those medical professionals who had resisted scrutiny had to admit that the inquest could be an effective forum for demonstrating to the public that anesthetics usually were safe and that the medical community was capable of policing itself. Among the most prominent exponents of this view—of the inquest as reassuring to the public—was Bernard Spilsbury.

Spilsbury was recognized with a knighthood in 1923; that honor was a tribute to his international reputation as well as his enhancement of the profession in which he worked. For several decades in the early twentieth century, he appeared nearly invincible as an expert witness for the prosecution, in one famous case prevailing over half a dozen well-qualified witnesses for the defense. Newspapers heralded his appearances as turning points in trials. Keith Simpson, Spilsbury's successor as the leading forensic pathologist in England, began his professional career while "Saint Bernard" was at the height of his fame.

Simpson was well aware that Spilsbury had made a name for himself, but he and other younger pathologists remained concerned that the field of forensic pathology still was not well organized or professional in terms of training and standards. One symptom of forensic pathology's enduring lack of reputation was that even in 1926, when the coronership in England was reformed by act of Parliament, medicolegal postmortem examinations still could be performed by any licensed physician. That is, forensic pathologists had not yet established themselves as indispensable to the autopsy process. By the end of Simpson's career in the late 1970s, forensic pathologists were firmly in charge of autopsies in England and the United States, and these professionals were regularly in courtrooms. Simpson had a lot to do with that further advancement of his field.

Simpson, like Spilsbury, frequently appeared as the lead expert witness for the prosecution. He was a favorite witness for the Crown in sensational murder cases because his calm yet self-assured manner played so well with jurors. He had particular talents, like Spilsbury, for reconstructing bodies and making identifications of bodies in difficult physical circumstances. Simpson could withstand the most unnerving cross-examinations with poise. He spoke in terms that jurors easily understood. He got along very well with the police. Simpson was a leader in presenting the scholarship of his field. In spite of his heavy caseload, he made professional contributions to forensic pathology through hundreds of scholarly publications. He enjoyed giving radio and television interviews, and the public was drawn to listen to his explanations of the most grisly crimes because of his lucid and well-prepared speaking style. He did not hesitate to take on controversial topics with which his work had brought him into contact, such as child endangerment and the spread of AIDS. His collaboration with forensic pathologists in many other parts of the world improved his own reputation, and Simpson's use of innovative techniques to help solve notorious crimes increased the prestige of the field as a whole.

Although he never met Bernard Spilsbury, Dr. Thomas Magrath was his American counterpart. Magrath presided as ME in the visible and busy jurisdiction of Boston. In that capacity, Magrath influenced forensic medicine and criminal cases in courtrooms in Massachusetts as well as all over New England and, in certain instances, the entire nation. Magrath had decided to become a pathologist in the late nineteenth century, just after Massachusetts replaced its local coronerships with MEs' offices. Magrath nursed a lifelong suspicion of coroners. He regarded them as unqualified and greedy, largely because many coroners he had seen were morticians who tried to obtain two jobs from the same body. In 1907, Magrath parlayed a career in public health into a stint as the ME for the northern district of Suffolk County. Early in his tenure as Suffolk County ME, several former employees of his office tried to discredit him. With the support of a Boston newspaper, however, he was cleared of suspicions of immorality and incompetence. He retained the Suffolk County ME's position until 1935. Magrath clearly was a medical expert who knew how to deal with the mass media—a vital talent if he was to be successful not only in his medical field but also as a public servant.

An athletic man who also was an accomplished vocal and keyboard musician, Magrath was a formidable expert witness. He always worked for the prosecution, even in cases outside the jurisdiction where he was a consultant. He argued that since his role within the Commonwealth of Massachusetts was to testify at the behest of the state's attorneys, he could not oppose prosecutors elsewhere. His physical size (and a shock of red hair) combined with his fine training and a self-confidence that sometimes shaded into arrogance.

Though opinionated, intimidating to colleagues, and able to state his conclusions convincingly to jurors, Magrath consistently maintained that it was his job to be a scientific witness rather than an advocate.

Like other forensic scientists in the early twentieth century, Magrath saw certain types of cases over and over again, and he developed a familiarity with them that ordinary medical practitioners could not approach. He had performed autopsies on several victims of poisoning, for example, which was a well-known but relatively rare crime, and he could lecture to medical students about the comparative properties of certain poisonous agents. In his line of work, Magrath saw many of the results of domestic violence. His testimony was critical, for example, at a grand jury inquiring into the death of a Yarmouth woman whose husband claimed that she had fallen down stairs in an accident. Magrath established that the woman had been killed not by the fall, but by blows to the head with a rolling pin. The husband broke down and confessed to the grand jury, pleaded guilty, and was sent to prison. Such dramatic episodes were especially important in establishing not only Magrath's personal reputation, but also the viability of the ME as an expert witness in criminal trials. It was one thing for Magrath (the Harvard man) to be believed by a jury in urban Suffolk County; it was quite another for him to gain the trust of a rural Maine or New Hampshire jury. When his personal credibility was accepted, so too was the credibility of his field enhanced in the minds of the public.

The most famous instance in which Magrath was an expert witness was the Sacco and Vanzetti trials, which were held in Boston in the 1920s. The *Sacco-Vanzetti* case was an international cause célèbre, particularly after the guilty verdicts were announced. In the United States and around the world, the trials of the two Italian American defendants were examined closely. Nicola Sacco and Bartolomeo Vanzetti professed leftist political ideals in the years just after the First World War, when radicalism was becoming increasingly unpopular among the general public. As shown through a series of "Red Raids," the U.S. government advocated detention and deportation for persons accused of sympathy with communism. Many critics of the Sacco and Vanzetti trial contended that Sacco and Vanzetti had been convicted more of radicalism than of the commission of a crime.

The two men were accused of participating in an armed robbery in the suburbs of Boston, during the course of which a paymaster and guard had been fatally shot. Despite a mass of data at the trial concerning issues such as the defendants' whereabouts before, during, and after the crime, the case turned on ballistics evidence. It happened that the bullets that killed the victims were distinctive, since they were no longer in current usage and thus relatively rare. Sacco had bullets of the type in question in a loaded gun and in his pocket at the time of his arrest. Therefore the identification of the fatal bullets as having been those actually taken from the bodies of the victims was a crucial link between the crime and the defendants. Dr. Magrath's testimony at a grand jury investigating the fatal robbery was not made public until nearly sixty years after the execution of Sacco and Vanzetti. At that hearing, Magrath noted that the bullets he removed from one victim's body appeared to him to have been fired from a single gun. At the trials of Sacco and Vanzetti, however, the bullets produced in evidence that were said to have caused guard Alessandro Berardelli's death were of at least two types; the bullets produced at trial could not have been fired by the same gun. Magrath's testimony to the grand jury had been thorough; even the most vehement critics of the trial verdicts did not question Magrath's expertise. Magrath's precision in answering the questions put to him, however, leads those scholars who in retrospect are convinced of the defendants' innocence to conclude that the ballistics evidence was tampered with between the autopsy and the trial.

In his autobiography, Milton Helpern reflected on a distinguished career as chief ME for the City of New York. Although Helpern himself was modest and gracious about his accomplishments, many of his contemporaries in the medical profession considered him the foremost forensic pathologist in the middle of the twentieth century. In large part, his reputation had to do with his effectiveness in court; he was a model for others in his field about how to be at once firm, kind, respected, and effective on the stand. Helpern was employed as a consultant, with other eminent pathologists such as England's Keith Simpson, on complex cases. He served as an effective advocate for the establishment and modernization of MEs' offices in the United States and elsewhere in the world. He worked for the professionalization of his field, serving in the 1960s as a founder of the National Association of Medical Examiners (NAME) and as an energetic and active first president of the association.

Not only was the New York City Medical Examiner's Office the busiest jurisdiction in the nation (with about 30,000 autopsies per year by the 1970s), it was one of the oldest locations of a medical examinership and a place often cited as a model for a centralized, well-funded system. Since the office was set up in New York at the beginning of the century, only 2 persons had held the chief examiner's position prior to Helpern. During his more than 40-year tenure at the Medical Examiner's Office in New York City, Helpern became identified among the public as the world's greatest medical detective. In his career, he oversaw over 60,000 autopsies and participated as a principal examiner in 20,000. Among the types of cases that Helpern and his fellow MEs often saw in the middle of the twentieth century were deaths involving botched abortions. Many of those cases involved physicians who made money outside of their regular practices by offering abortions to young women who were desperate to terminate pregnancies in the era prior to legalized abortion in the United States. Helpern did not crusade against abortions as Bernard Spilsbury had; in spite of his condemnation of the actions of doctors who provided abortions illegally, Helpern often evidenced an understanding for the circumstances that drove women to take such grave risks.

As with his fellow forensic pathologists Magrath, Simpson, and Spilsbury, Helpern appeared on the stand as an expert witness many dozens of times, often in scandalous criminal trials. With his gentle and unassuming manner, Helpern was well liked by colleagues. Helpern also was a hit with jurors, who viewed him as plainspoken, careful, and yet often solicitous of jurors' feelings. He was known for describing violent and disturbing case details in a manner that made them less traumatic than they might have been to juries. He objected to the use of the term *morgue,* for example, as too morbid—perhaps reminiscent of Edgar Allan Poe tales rather than descriptive of the modern facility that he oversaw. The many tabloid newspapers in New York City that covered criminal trials in vivid detail helped spread Helpern's reputation as a convincing witness. Thus Helpern was typical of MEs—indeed of public officials in many fields in the twentieth century: he had to do his job under the unrelenting gaze of the mass media.

No episode better illustrated Helpern's contributions to his office—and his formidable celebrity—than the investigation that Helpern considered his most interesting, the *Coppolino* case. Though not particularly well remembered several decades later, the *Coppolino* case was a sensational episode in the mid-1960s. It consisted of a complicated set of allegations that a physician, Carl Coppolino, had murdered his wife (also a physician) and had helped to kill the husband of his female lover. Helpern remarked sharply, in retrospect, about the strong tactics employed by the young and talented defense attorney in the trials, F. Lee Bailey. Among the key public moments in the case were Helpern's dogged and consistent performances under searching cross-examination by Bailey. Helpern recalled Bailey's efforts, which occasionally were underhanded if not unethical, to ferret out information. When Helpern and others in the ME's office would not come forward with details that Bailey hoped would be useful for the defense of Carl Coppolino, Bailey resorted to public criticism of Helpern, along with threats of suits against him. Bailey's threats became more heated when Carl Coppolino finally was found guilty of second-degree murder and sentenced to a long prison term. Helpern considered the case very important in regard to forensic toxicology; it helped to establish the standards for poisoning by a substance called succinylcholine. He also noted the extraordinary publicity concerning the episode. In addition, Helpern argued that the trials were an example of competing legal experts being heard by a jury—a trend that was appearing in criminal and civil cases. In several ways, then, the *Coppolino* case was typical of new developments to which MEs were having to adjust in Helpern's day: more opposition from brash defense attorneys, greater attention from media that fed on scandalous cases, and increasing difficulty among jurors in distinguishing between technical experts from both sides.

One of the most famous instances in which one set of medical experts testified for the defense and another took the side of the prosecution was a Canadian case in which both Milton Helpern and his contemporary Keith Simpson took part. In 1959, a murder charge was leveled against a fourteen-year-old named Steven Truscott, who was accused of sexually assaulting and strangling a twelve-year-old girl named Lynne Harper. An examination of the contents of the victim's stomach placed the moment of death at a time when Truscott was known to have been with her or nearby. Largely on the strength of that forensic evidence, Truscott was convicted. The forensic examination became a focal point for criticisms of the trial, some of which were published in England and attracted the interest of noted forensic pathologists there. Eventually, the Canadian parliament asked that the Supreme Court of Canada hear evidence to ascertain if there were grounds for a retrial. Independent of each other, the U.S. expert, Helpern, and England's expert, Keith Simpson, agreed on the soundness of the original autopsy and, thus, the validity of Truscott's conviction. Armed with their opinions about food digestion as a tool for establishing the time of death, Helpern and Simpson faced down other medical witnesses from England and the United States who argued for Truscott's innocence. The Canadian Supreme Court in 1967 issued a brief judgment affirming Truscott's sentence. The case once again made clear the vitality of forensic pathology as a field and the importance of forensic pathologists as expert witnesses.

By the time of his death, Milton Helpern had become the gray eminence of forensic pathology in the United States. Esteemed by his peers and recognized by foreign investigators, he still could not always escape the politics of being a civil servant in New York City. A young successor to Helpern's prominence in the field of forensic pathology, Thomas Noguchi, likewise found it treacherous to be a public servant. Noguchi's visibility was magnified by the fact that many of his "patients" were Hollywood stars. More than any other forensic pathologist, Noguchi's career illustrated the potentials and pitfalls of fame in his profession. Noguchi was a participant in many courtroom dramas concerning others, and he himself was an example of forensic pathology being "on trial." Noguchi's critics argued that he had so infused his office with sensationalism that it no longer was professional with regard to the ordinary business of death examinations.

Thomas Noguchi came to the United States from Japan in the late 1950s as an intern at Orange County Hospital near Los Angeles. He took a job early in his career as a deputy ME with the Los Angeles Coroner's Office. In 1956, an election among the citizens of the area decided that coroners should be required to have professional qualifications as forensic pathologists. Still, however, the chief ME for Los Angeles was called the coroner; he was a civil servant overseen by political officials. Noguchi was a highly qualified young physician; he had studied law and medicine at the same time while in Japan. Forensic pathology seemed an odd choice for an ambitious and talented young man like him. It was a comparatively low-paying specialty, and as a civil servant he would be answerable to public officials, notably the Los Angeles County Board of Supervisors. Nonetheless, Noguchi was drawn to forensic pathology as a field. He was famously dedicated to his work. He became known for conducting autopsies late at night and seven days a week. He also was committed to the upgrading of the physical facilities of the coroner's office. He envisioned an office where forensic pathology would be a part of total investigation of deaths. Expanding on the concept of laboratories pioneered in France at the turn of the twentieth century, Noguchi proposed that inquiries into deaths be conducted under one roof by a range of medical scientists, who would be assisted by a range of other experts such as criminologists.

When Los Angeles dedicated a new forensic science facility in 1972, its existence was due largely to Noguchi's efforts. Quickly recognized as a state-of-the-art facility, the Los Angeles Coroner's Office drew referrals from all over the world. The bodies of victims of plane crashes, for example, were sent to the Los Angeles County Forensic Science facility for identification. By the 1970s, the Los Angeles Coroner's Office was the second-largest ME's facility in the nation, with nearly 14,000 cases coming under the coroner's authority (that is, requiring autopsies) annually. Of those thousands of instances in which autopsies were performed by Los Angeles MEs, only a small minority—perhaps 10 percent—were related to the possibility that homicidal crimes had caused the deaths. Those cases obviously were ones that brought the Los Angeles Coroner's Office into the legal realm following the autopsy—as part of a criminal investigation by police as well as in any trial affixing criminal responsibility. The other autopsies were on the victims of accidents (for instance, on highways and at harbors) or suicide, or they reflected deaths that were determined to be natural, or they were fatalities of undetermined causes. It was Noguchi's luck—for good or ill—to have been involved as an ME in a number of death investigations that not only resulted in homicide findings but also were connected to the deaths of famous people.

From his earliest days with the Los Angeles Coroner's Office, Noguchi's talent led medical colleagues to request his presence in particularly difficult death inquiries. Noguchi performed the autopsy on Marilyn Monroe in 1962, for example, when he was a young assistant ME. Noguchi recalled in his best-selling autobiography that his supervisor, Coroner Theodore Curphey, telephoned and left a message that Noguchi was to perform the postmortem examination on "Marilyn Monroe." Noguchi, not realizing that the actress had died, assumed that Curphey was referring to the body of another person with the same name. He thought that Curphey had specified his presence because he knew that Noguchi (being a professor with two specialties in forensic pathology) was unusually well qualified to work on difficult cases.

Noguchi recalled that when he saw that it was the body of film star Marilyn Monroe who was lying on the autopsy table, he was emotionally affected for the first time by the prospect of conducting an autopsy. He composed himself, however, in part with the realization that the cause of her death would be a subject of worldwide attention. As a result of Noguchi's meticulous autopsy, Dr. Curphey's official report on Monroe's demise listed her death as a "probable" suicide. Twenty years later, Noguchi was called to testify at another inquiry into allegations that Monroe's death had been the result of a murder rather than an accidental overdose of barbiturates. Despite a host of speculation about Monroe's passing, Noguchi remained convinced that she had ingested the substances that led to her death on her own; in his autobiography, he noted that her death was very probably a suicide.

In those memoirs, published in the early 1980s, Noguchi created controversy when he raised the possibility that despite the arrest and conviction of an assassin, Sirhan B. Sirhan, Senator Robert Kennedy's death remained unsolved. At the time that Robert Kennedy was shot in Los Angeles in June 1968, just following his winning the California presidential primary, Noguchi recently had become Dr. Curphey's successor. Noguchi recalled the intense debate surrounding President John F. Kennedy's assassination by Lee Harvey Oswald in 1963. Even while Robert Kennedy lay in a hospital gravely injured, Noguchi grimly laid plans should he have to oversee an autopsy. He asked advice from Dr. William Eckert, head of the International Reference Organization in Forensic Medicine, a group that stored information from MEs' offices all over the nation.

Eckert warned Noguchi that much of the speculation concerning President John F. Kennedy's assassination was because the president's body was not examined by the Dallas Medical Examiner's Office, which contained well-trained forensic pathologists. Instead, the body was taken hurriedly to Washington, D.C., and examined by military physicians with little forensic experience. Those who later insisted that Oswald had not acted alone as an assassin argued that the autopsy of John F. Kennedy's body was part of a wider conspiracy to keep details of the president's death from the American public. In a 1968 review of the autopsy, a distinguished panel of forensic pathologists stated that their findings did not differ in any significant respects from those of the physicians at the autopsy; the panel also agreed in substance with the Warren Commission's conclusion that

Oswald had been the lone assassin. Among those pathologists was Russell Fisher, who had served as ME in Baltimore for nearly twenty years and was considered a leading American authority in his field. Dr. Fisher's recommendation that there be a standard mechanism for autopsies in the event of political assassinations of important figures never has been acted upon.

Among other contingency measures at the time of the shooting of Robert Kennedy, Noguchi arranged for forensic pathologists from the Armed Forces Institute of Pathology to participate in the autopsy should Robert Kennedy not recover. Despite some bulletins from the hospital that gave Kennedy supporters hope in the hours just after the shooting, Kennedy's wounds were too severe, and he never regained consciousness. An admirer of Robert Kennedy (just as he had been a fan of Marilyn Monroe), Noguchi was so moved by Kennedy's death that he took the unusual step of covering Kennedy's face during the autopsy. Although Noguchi believed that Sirhan had acted alone, his scientific training also would not let him ignore several puzzling details of Robert Kennedy's death that he observed at the postmortem examination. Thus Noguchi wrote in his autobiography that Robert Kennedy may have died by more than one hand; it was an honest argument, but one that stirred more controversy about both the assassination and Noguchi.

Noguchi's high profile with the public earned him international recognition as the coroner to the stars. He examined the bodies of actors Natalie Wood (who had drowned), William Holden (who had suffered a gash on his forehead and bled to death), and Dorothy Dandridge (whose cause of death was difficult to determine). He also performed a postmortem on singer Janis Joplin, who died of a drug overdose. In 1982, Noguchi was present at the investigation scene in a hotel where the body of comedian John Belushi had been discovered. Police and medical personnel initially had assumed Belushi had died of a heart attack, because alternate causes such as weapons and drugs did not seem apparent. Noguchi followed his instincts, however, which told him that Belushi was too young to have suffered cardiac arrest. Noguchi astonished his colleagues at the scene by pinching the skin at Belushi's inner elbow; a telltale drop of blood emerged, indicating that Belushi had been injected with a needle just hours earlier.

Noguchi performed autopsies on the victims of the Charles Manson murders in 1969 and worked closely with prosecutor Vincent

Bugliosi in the complex reconstruction of those crimes. Noguchi and Bugliosi relied on the expertise of a psychiatrist, terrorism specialist Dr. Frederick Hacker, to help them profile the killers. A murder weapon never was recovered—sometimes a huge stumbling block to obtaining a conviction. Manson and his followers were tried and convicted, though, in part due to Noguchi's testimony about how the fatal wounds were inflicted, as well as his wisdom in relying on non-medical crime experts.

Noguchi's fame, however, also cost him dearly in a professional sense. In both 1969 and 1982, the Los Angeles County Board of Supervisors held hearings to inquire into whether Noguchi was using his office for self-aggrandizement. The supervisors, armed with critical articles published in the *Los Angeles Times,* also charged that Noguchi's attention to well-known cases was allowing the more mundane operations in the coroner's facility to falter. Noguchi believed that some of the criticism of him was motivated by racism. In the earlier episode, Noguchi bested his critics with a show of public support. As a result of the 1982 investigation, however, the charges stuck, and he was demoted. Ironically, the year of that embarrassment in Los Angeles was the year in which Noguchi was elected president of NAME, the most prestigious professional organization in his field. Despite certain fundamental divergences in personality and ability, career paths and goals, forensic pathologists such as Spilsbury, Simpson, Magrath, Helpern, and Noguchi became celebrities to a national—even international—public. The person on the street knew of them; more to the point, the ordinary juror was awed by them and implicitly trusted their opinions. In the twentieth century, courts in Great Britain and the United States increasingly allowed the testimony of medical experts—and chief among those was the forensic pathologist in a murder case. All of these forensic pathologists could be and were understood as they spoke in the courtroom. Somewhat surprisingly, given the grisly quality of their work, they also came to be liked and admired by the public at large.

New Developments in Forensic Science

In the latter half of the twentieth century, one of the most important developments in regard to scientific and medical testimony in courtrooms has been the employment of scientific data called DNA evidence. The DNA molecule—formally called deoxyribonucleic acid—

is a part of chromosomal patterns and serves to identify persons in an extremely accurate fashion. Just as fingerprints are unique to individuals and can be employed as forensic evidence, so DNA can pinpoint or exclude individuals who are accused of crimes, especially if they deny any recent contact with victims and then their DNA is recovered at the crime scene. DNA evidence also serves to assist defense attorneys in demonstrating that their clients have been wrongfully convicted. A political furor ensued over capital punishment around the turn of the twenty-first century, for instance, when several death-row inmates were found, through DNA analysis, not to have been involved in the crimes for which they were awaiting death. In a Houston trial, for example, defendant Josiah Sutton was convicted of the rape of a woman largely due to DNA evidence. The Houston police crime lab that tested the DNA samples and sent an expert to testify at Sutton's trial was later audited. The lab was found to have defects in training and techniques for handling evidence, leading to the contamination of samples. Among the cases in which prosecutors requested retesting of samples, seven concerned inmates on death row; prosecutors argued, however, that no one actually had been executed on the basis of evidence from the crime lab. Josiah Sutton, who had insisted at his own trial that he was innocent, later benefited from DNA tests conducted by a private company. Those tests established that DNA samples found at the crime scene could not be his. After serving more than four years of a twenty-five-year sentence, Sutton was released from prison and sought a pardon from the Texas governor.

On a more everyday basis, DNA evidence has been used in courtrooms throughout the United States since 1986 to provide forensic data about the identity of criminals and their victims. DNA evidence may be convincing, but it is not always foolproof as a method for securing convictions for the prosecution. The prosecution in the double-murder trial of O. J. Simpson in 1995, for instance, relied on DNA evidence. Despite the fact that Prosecutor Marcia Clark was considered expert in her wielding of DNA evidence, and in spite of the superior facilities and experience of the Los Angeles Coroner's Office, the jury refused to convict Simpson of the crimes. The trial demonstrated how effective skillful defense counsel could be in undermining even clear scientific evidence and experienced medical testimony.

Other types of evidence that were used in forensic settings also were refined in the later twentieth century, though with results that were less publicized and less controversial than in DNA cases. Forensic odontology (the identification of persons through dental records) was crucial, for example, in the identification of Richard Ramirez, who eventually was convicted of the "night stalker" murders in Los Angeles. In 1979, serial killer Theodore (Ted) Bundy also was linked conclusively to his victims through forensic dentistry. Although at Bundy's trial the defense did its best to discredit the science of forensic odontology, a representative from the well-respected New York City Medical Examiner's Office convinced the court and the jury that the science was well established and accurate.

Other Expert Medical Evidence: The Case of Psychiatry

Forensic pathologists are not the only medical experts to have an impact on court proceedings. More than a century before forensic science gained credibility in criminal trials, another type of physician became important in British and U.S. courtrooms. The field of psychiatry actually developed at the same time that its practitioners were being called upon as expert witnesses to testify about controversial matters such as methods of treatment for the mentally ill, conditions surrounding committal to institutions, and mental conditions that might mitigate responsibility for criminal or tort actions. Of these, the most significant involved testimony over mental competency. Medical testimony was, in fact, a necessary, even vital, component in discussions of mental competence in criminal cases when accused persons tried to plead that they were not guilty by reason of insanity. For if a defendant could not recognize that his or her actions were wrong, by definition no crime had been committed. A series of important criminal trials brought the insanity plea and the medical witnesses associated with it into the public eye.

Physicians first played a key role within U.S. and British courtrooms because of the developing prestige of psychiatry as a medical specialty in the early nineteenth century. Prior to that era, medical doctors had testified in court, of course, in a variety of cases, but were not generally thought of as being experts in any particular area of law, including the law concerning the mentally ill. Those eighteenth-century physicians who concentrated their practices on treating "mad" patients—the so-called mad-doctors—occasionally had appeared in trials concerning their patients who were accused of serious crimes; those appearances, however, were sporadic and not always successful.

Prior to the nineteenth century, even the medical practitioners who treated the mentally ill usually had a bleak view of the prognoses for their patients. Mental illness, they reasoned, was organic and permanent in nature, often hereditary, and resulted in behavior that was easily distinguishable from that of "normal" persons. The genuinely mentally ill, according to eighteenth-century medical (and legal) standards, often appeared maniacal or "furious." These persons thus had to be restrained forcibly and kept away from ordinary society. In the eighteenth century, most of the mentally ill who were very poor and could not be cared for by their own families at home lived in institutions that offered a chaotic and harsh physical environment. Ironically, such conditions often exacerbated any mental illness that patients might have had prior to admission to the "madhouses."

The influential American physician Benjamin Rush (whose life and career spanned the era of the American Revolution and the early nineteenth century) stood squarely between older and newer views of insanity. In his 1812 treatise, *Medical Inquiries and Observations upon the Diseases of the Mind,* Rush contended that "partial insanity" was an observable phenomenon; thus his was a different view than that of many eighteenth-century mad-doctors. He took the view, however, that insanity could be "cured" through physical restraints on patients. Informed by a much different perspective on the causes of and potential treatments for insanity, the psychiatric profession in the early 1800s proposed that mental illness could be controlled—if not cured—through the provision of more supportive physical environments for treatment. The directors of new asylums for the mentally ill thus discarded the notion of physical restraints for patients, preferring instead "moral therapies" such as useful hand labor and the instilling of methods of self-control. In fact, several of the earliest among the new asylums in America and England (circa the late 1700s and early 1800s) were funded and run by Quakers, who stressed that the institutions should be calm, orderly, and familial.

That physicians specializing in mental illness should be considered experts in court was a tribute in part to their efforts at professionalization during the period from 1810 to 1850. Like the rest of the medical profession in the Victorian era, experts on mental disease and treatment began to organize themselves into effective groups that published journals, held conferences, and encouraged professional training. England's Association of Medical Officers of Asylums and Hospitals for the Insane, formed in 1841, lobbied Parliament on policies such as capital punishment. The Association of Medical Superintendents of American Institutions for the Insane (AMSAII) was founded in 1844. It was an auspicious moment to develop a professional profile, for it was exactly at this time that a case arose that tested the standing of psychiatry as a field within the courts.

The case arose out of a context of changing judicial views on the standing of insanity as a defense. For much of the first quarter of the nineteenth century, the courts were receptive to new definitions of mental disease. Informed by more modern conceptions of mental illness and treatment, courts began to accept psychiatrists' view that patients could be temporarily (or "partially") insane. Eminent and well-spoken psychiatrists such as England's Forbes Winslow testified at several well-known trials involving defendants with mental disabilities who were accused of sensational crimes. Psychiatrists argued that madness was a subtle state, one that often appeared and waned in patients. For a time in the early nineteenth century, judges were moved by these arguments. (This type of argument, for example, was employed by psychiatrists who appeared on behalf of defendant James Hadfield, who was accused of trying to assassinate George III in 1799.) So informed, judges encouraged juries to return special verdicts of not guilty by reason of insanity in instances where defendants were ably defended by psychiatric experts. By the 1840s, however, many judges were increasingly uncomfortable with psychiatrists' notion of partial insanity. Partial insanity appeared more and more to judges to be a concept that undermined courts' assumption that defendants exercised free will—a fundamental legal assumption. The stage was thus set for a clash between medical/psychiatric views of insanity and judges' and lawyers' desire to hold defendants accountable and to punish them accordingly when courts found that they had committed illegal acts. The psychiatric construct of partial insanity, moreover, coexisted unhappily with a view among laypersons that defendants who were found not guilty by reason of insanity were escaping punishment, since defendants who successfully pleaded insanity were being sent to newer types of mental institutions that the psychiatrists touted as much more humane than older facilities. Courts, psychiatrists, and the public puzzled over the question of who should determine whether a defendant was sane. Should that decision rest with forensic psychiatrists, through their expert testimony? Or should judges explain sets of legal standards that governed a law of insanity? Or perhaps should juries assess defendants' criminal responsibility through factual determinations in each case?

All this came to a head in the 1843 trial of Daniel M'Naghten in England, where the defendant, an accused assassin, pleaded not guilty by reason of insanity. Largely on the strength of medical testimony from psychiatrists, who argued for an updated definition of insanity, M'Naghten was acquitted but sent to a mental facility. The trial and verdict outraged citizens and lawmakers, who argued that M'Naghten had been handled too gingerly. Britain's parliament asked a group of eminent judges whether there were in fact judicial standards (rather than medical principles) that would govern future adjudications concerning sanity. The M'Naghten Rules were the judges' response to Parliament's pointed questions. The rules held defendants to several tests as to their mental state. In order to claim insanity, for example, a defendant had to be suffering from an identifiable "disease of the mind"; that is, the defendant's mental incapacity had to be physical in origin, or at least had to be a disorder that was widely recognized in the medical community as a whole as causing mental disability. Another of the rules' tests of a defendant's mental state was his ability to distinguish right from wrong—the "right-wrong" test. If he could not make that distinction *and* if he also suffered from a disease of the mind, then he could be insane according to the law. If the defendant could not satisfy the right-wrong test, then there was another option: he might show that at the time of the commission of the crime, he did not know what he was doing. Thus, if that incapacity was due to a disease of the mind, he could claim insanity. Taken as a whole, the M'Naghten Rules made it significantly more difficult to claim mental illness to such a degree that a defendant was legally insane and thus exempted from criminal responsibility.

The M'Naghten Rules were swiftly adapted or adopted outright in England and almost all U.S. states. The rules remained extremely influential in the United States for at least a century, although most psychiatrists along with many lawyers and judges eventually would argue that the rules were outmoded in a scientific sense. Federal courts, in fact, hesitated to employ the M'Naghten standards in all their rigor, but state courts insisted on applying state laws that usually were passed in response to public cries that "the insanity dodge" not be allowed. The law on insanity at the federal level was greatly influenced in 1981 by the attempted assassination of President

Ronald Reagan by a young man named John Hinckley Jr. As when the not-guilty verdict directed M'Naghten to be institutionalized until he was cured, John Hinckley's being sent to Saint Elizabeth's Hospital caused an outcry that federal law was too lenient toward defendants who claimed insanity.

Medical experts, such as psychiatrists and forensic pathologists, who served as expert witnesses underlined the fundamental role of jurors in reaching verdicts. Many criminal prosecutions ultimately turned on jurors' appreciation for the character and personality of the expert witness as an individual. The appearance of expert medical testimony within U.S. courtrooms in the nineteenth and twentieth centuries was of tremendous importance, beginning with psychiatric testimony in the early 1800s. From the 1920s onward, in an array of cases, U.S. courts began to lean heavily on technical information such as medical evidence in reaching their verdicts. In its influence on juries, the growing importance of technical evidence was somewhat at odds with the rise of the expert witness. Scientific evidence could and often did confound lay jurors, who were presented with masses of sophisticated and often contradictory data. Science—and most particularly medicine—had created the types of experts that were appealing and helpful to laypersons (especially jurors) in the courtroom. Technical information at trials, however, too often proved unintelligible, self-serving, or confusing to jurors.

Medicine and the Bureaucratic State

The federal Food and Drug Administration (FDA) enforces regulations that have profound implications for Americans' health, though its authority is not without limits. Although other administrative authorities (such as the U.S. Attorney General, the Surgeon General, and the Department of Health and Human Services [HHS]) at times have a hand in enforcing federal regulations related to medicine and public health, the FDA is the regulatory agency that often is at the epicenter of medicolegal controversy.

The modern FDA regulates drug testing, and controls and authorizes human clinical trials. In all of those arenas, the legal issue of informed consent—developed first by U.S. courts rather than by medical or philosophical experts—has been vital. The FDA also is the first point of regulatory contact between drug companies and physicians (and thus their patients) when new drug products are to be distributed in the United States. Congress passed a series of Food and Drug acts and amendments, notably in 1906, 1938, and 1962, authorizing the FDA to regulate aspects of drug testing and marketing and providing for follow-up of drug trials. In the century of its existence, the FDA often has been caught between being too cautious in approving drugs and medical devices for widespread use and not being watchful enough. Groups such as AIDS activists recently have criticized the powers of the FDA, arguing that the FDA has had too much control over drug approval and that the agency has been overly cautious in allowing drugs to undergo human testing. On the other hand, a series of products and drugs that the FDA once approved for use in patients—from breast implants to drugs for use in pregnant women—turned out to be dangerous after having been on the market for many years. How did the FDA garner such power and create such controversy in the late twentieth century?

One source of the FDA's control over areas such as drug testing—and its pattern of reluctance to release new drugs onto the American market quickly—can be seen in an examination of the thalidomide scare of the early 1960s. In the late 1950s, a German chemical manufacturer named Chemie Grunenthal was touting a newly developed drug that it termed a nonnarcotic sleep aid. That drug, thalidomide, eventually was marketed by Grunenthal's distributors and subsidiaries in 46 countries around the world, including Germany itself, Great Britain, Canada, Australia, South America, and parts of Africa. Several factors held up the U.S. distribution of thalidomide. Initially, Grunenthal had trouble finding a U.S. affiliate. A potential distributor, SmithKline Pharmaceuticals, did not concur with Grunenthal about the effectiveness of the drug in inducing sleep. Another U.S. company, Richardson-Merrell, eventually signed on with Grunenthal. Richardson-Merrell began the process of securing FDA approval for marketing the drug widely in the United States by sending out packets of the drug to physicians as a part of its effort to gather data on the substance's effect on human subjects. Richardson-Merrell, like Grunenthal, viewed thalidomide as a potential gold mine, and its press to get the drug tested and approved echoed that optimism. Thalidomide was distributed to over 1,200 physicians, with enough dosages for more than 20,000 patients. Such a widespread trial distribution of a drug was unprecedented in U.S. history. Never had a drug been tested in more than 5,000 patients, or sent out to more than 200 doctors. For all that relative accessibility of thalidomide among Americans, the drug was much less widely available in the United States than in other areas of the world—particularly third-world countries, where during the late 1950s it often could be obtained without physicians' prescriptions.

Richardson-Merrell, however, ran into difficulty when it submitted a request for FDA approval that included data on human and animal trials supplied by the German parent company, Grunenthal. A young physician at the FDA, Dr. Frances Kelsey, noted troubling aspects in the drug company's reports on previous human and animal trials, and she recalled that European medical journals had mentioned side effects associated with the drug; those side effects were not mentioned in the application from Richardson-Merrell. Although faced with stern warnings from her superiors to let the application go through without further objections, Dr. Kelsey continued to voice concern that thalidomide might not be thoroughly tested yet. She argued that its introduction onto the U.S. market ought to be delayed. Her persistence saved a number of lives.

In the summer and fall of 1961, German and Australian pediatricians began reporting an alarming increase in the number of cases of a previously rare, catastrophic set of disabilities among babies. At hospitals, infants were being born with either no limbs or flipper-like appendages, along with moderate to severe brain damage. That set of disabilities was known as phocomelia. It did not take long for medical experts to associate the problem with one overriding causative factor: the infants' mothers' having taken thalidomide (sometimes as little as one pill) in the early stages of their pregnancies. Richardson-Merrell joined other nations' distributors of thalidomide in withdrawing the drug from circulation, and the company withdrew its FDA application in March 1962. Unfortunately, the drug's dissemination had been so poorly monitored that no party—the drug companies, the FDA, and certainly not the public at large—knew exactly to whom thalidomide had been given. Most patients had received packets of thalidomide that contained only the simplest instructions and few warnings or restrictions on use, and usually no drug name was printed on the label.

Thalidomide's effects became widely known in the summer of 1962. President Kennedy took the unusual step of making a televised plea for all households to check their medicine cabinets for unmarked drugs and to throw away any drugs that could not be identified. The nation breathed a sigh of relief that many more people (especially pregnant women and their children) had not been affected by thalidomide. Other nations were not nearly as fortunate. In Germany, for example, nearly 5,000 thalidomide babies were born, leading to sweeping reforms in Germany's state system for monitoring drugs. Among third-world nations, reporting procedures were so lax that it was impossible to determine how many people had received thalidomide in an over-the-counter setting. In the United States, increased oversight of drug companies by the FDA was a natural response to the near tragedy. In Great Britain and several other industrialized nations, hundreds of children suffered the effects of thalidomide, leading to large numbers of lawsuits that continued for years.

Britain's struggle to resolve those lawsuits was protracted and contentious. In 1976, an article in the *Sunday Times* investigated the fate of the thalidomide children, and commented that the drug company that had distributed thalidomide in Britain (Distillers Limited) seemed to be prolonging legal action in hopes that victims would die before settlements were reached. (This was a point similar to that made by the critics of U.S. tobacco companies; tobacco corporations often successfully delayed suits brought against them until the plaintiffs had died of lung cancer.) Distillers responded with a request for a contempt citation against the *Sunday Times,* claiming that the newspaper had impeded its right to obtain a fair trial in the civil actions that the company still faced. The European Court of Human Rights finally adjudicated the controversy, narrowly ruling against the injunction on publication (*A.G. v. Times Newspapers* 1979). In that ruling, citizens' guarantees of fair trials were balanced against the right to comment freely on issues of great public importance. By a narrow margin, the European court ruled that Britain's laws on contempt of court were an infringement on freedom of speech.

In Congress in 1962, a bill written by Tennessee's senator Estes Kefauver calling for reforms in the marketing and testing of drugs and the expansion of FDA authority over those matters suddenly gained widespread attention and support. That bill—eventually passed as the Kefauver-Harris Act—became an amendment to the Pure Food and Drug Act of 1938, which had made the FDA a prime force in regulating drugs in the United States. The Kefauver-Harris Act required that pharmaceutical manufacturers demonstrate to the FDA the safety and effectiveness of drugs prior to their being approved for mass distribution on the American market. Unlike Germany's postthalidomide policies, the legislation did not provide for compensation for the victims of drugs that had been approved but later were found to be dangerous.

The thalidomide scare in the United States could have resulted in a crisis about abortion law had thousands of women found themselves and their unborn children at risk for severe birth defects. The year 1962 was a time when many states did not allow abortions except to protect the life of the mother. Such was not the case in many other nations where thalidomide was widely distributed, such as Britain, Australia, and Canada. There, abortions were largely a matter not regulated by the state, but to be decided between a pregnant woman and her physician. Abortions in the event of suspected fetal abnormalities were allowed. The few American women who had taken thalidomide and wished to terminate their pregnancies faced great obstacles. The situation of Sherri Finkbine of Arizona became particularly well known. Refused an abortion in her home state as well as in neighboring areas, she eventually underwent the procedure in Sweden.

Despite the higher profile of the FDA in the wake of the thalidomide scare, the agency remained the focus of critics who said that it did not do enough to eliminate risks to the public from dangerous drugs or faulty medical products. The Kefauver-Harris Act of 1962 did not set up an extensive monitoring plan to track the effects of drugs once they were approved for the U.S. market, a plan that Britain had implemented. The absence of such mechanisms became apparent when substances such as fen-phen, redux, and ephedra were allowed onto the U.S. market and resulted in hundreds of deaths and injuries.

Technically, the regulation of diet drugs available by prescription (such as phentermine) and dietary supplements that were advertised as promoting weight loss (such as products including ephedrine) were regulated differently by the FDA. Prescription drugs were subject to a higher standard of review prior to being allowed on the market. Dietary supplements were regulated by a 1994 piece of legislation called the Dietary Supplement Health and Education Act. That law, passed with the support of the vitamin and supplement industry, set rules that made it difficult for the FDA to ban such nonprescription substances. The law was a response to cases such as *U.S. v. LeBeau* (1993), in which a defendant who sold dietary supplements was prosecuted for violation of the Federal Food, Drug, and Cosmetic Act. The FDA charged that Mr. LeBeau and the labels on the products he was selling (made by a corporation called Vital Health Products) claimed that the substances could cure diseases such as cancer, AIDS, and arthritis. In an unpublished opinion in the *LeBeau* case, the U.S. Court of Appeals for the Seventh Circuit granted the injunctive relief that the government was seeking. The judge noted that courts had established in a series of cases that the federal government had the authority to limit "freedom of choice in medicine" (*U.S. v. LeBeau* 1993, 1501). That is, federal authorities such as the FDA could prohibit alternative medical practitioners and drugmakers from taking their claims directly to consumers. The 1994 law on dietary supplements was an effort to skirt that federal authority.

When the FDA was hamstrung in regulating dietary supplements by the 1994 legislation, that lack of authority obviously could and did have an impact on consumers. But the FDA's regulation of prescription drugs had not prevented consumers from being injured by dangerous medicines, even after the agency's powers were strengthened in the wake of the thalidomide tragedy. One key flaw in the FDA's extensive system of testing for prescription drugs and medical devices (such as surgical implants) was that some substances took years to show their dangerous effects in patients—or even in patients' progeny. By the time that the risk to consumers was evident, the drugs or medical products could have been widely available for a decade or more. The filing of product liability cases (often as class action suits) against manufacturers of prescription drugs and devices that had caused harm over a long period of time became big legal business in the 1980s and 1990s. Advertisements on television were common, sponsored by law firms that approached consumers/patients directly: "If you have taken any of the following drugs . . . you may be entitled to damages. Call the law firm of XYZ for more information. Time may be running out to file a claim!"

The FDA's approval of medical devices such as silicone breast implants did not head off product liability claims against manufacturers such as Dow Corning, which had designed the implants. Increasingly, when courts heard product liability claims about drugs or medical devices, they tended to place a burden on manufacturers to label products so as to fully disclose potential dangers. Failure to disclose potential dangers to consumers/patients usually resulted in liability on the part of the product's manufacturer. In spirit and in law, the FDA concurred with such labeling requirements. With respect to drugs, labeling at least could be read by consumers/patients, even if labels included highly technical terms and could not fully be understood by laypeople. Medical devices, however—especially surgically implanted ones—could not be studied in the same manner by consumers; thus courts placed a higher degree of responsibility on physicians and surgeons to interpret manufacturers' materials and disclose to patients the risks associated with the devices.

The FDA had authority for regulating not only manufactured medical devices, but also human tissues that were used in surgery. In orthopedic surgery, for example, tissues such as ligaments taken from human cadavers were employed to repair joints. The FDA took steps to ensure that those tissues were not dangerous products; the agency could and did place limits on the use of products supplied by certain companies when those providers of tissue could not ensure the purity of the tissues from fungi or bacteria. In the first years of the twenty-first century, some critics of the FDA alleged that it was too lax in regulating certain types of soft tissues as opposed to others, for example that it was more stringent about the safety of orthopedic tissues than about heart valves. The only guidelines for handling soft tissues were voluntary and were provided by the industry itself rather than the FDA. The providers who did not belong to industry self-regulatory organizations in effect made up their own rules about procedures to follow to ensure the safety of the tissues that they supply for surgeries. In 2002, the leading U.S. supplier of donated heart valves, Cryolife, delivered heart valves that later were implicated in at least twenty-five serious infections and one death. The FDA, however, merely investigated Cryolife; the agency did not mandate that Cryolife change its procedures for processing heart valves.

New Medical Technology and Patient Control

In the later part of the twentieth century, medicine for many Americans underwent drastic changes. These alterations were as profound as those experienced a few centuries earlier, when institutions that cared for patients began to replace healthcare at home. At the end of the eighteenth century, the "clinic" had appeared as a place where many persons sought help for medical complaints. Receiving treatment in a clinic setting was far different from care within a domestic setting; the birth of the clinic involved a whole new conception of the human body, for example.

By the late twentieth century, most Americans' access to a primary care physician had greatly improved. Many persons at last had "their own" doctors; yet no longer did most citizens believe that they had close relationships with those physicians. Many persons still were uninsured or underinsured for their health, in spite of the appearance of governmental programs such as Medicare and Medicaid. Many Americans who were insured bemoaned the demise of the family physician—particularly one who made house calls. In contrast with the residents of other nations, such as Great Britain, twentieth-century Americans relied more and more on an array of specialists rather than on one general physician.

Other factors undermined the doctor-patient relationship; foremost among these factors was the growing influence that nonmedical institutions had in shaping medical practice. By the end of the twentieth century, for instance, federal and other governmental authorities regulated many aspects of healthcare; decisions by the FDA, for example, could and did have profound effects on patients' lives. Increasingly, other parties intervened in the doctor-patient relationship as well. Insurers, hospitals, employers, healthcare corporations, and even manufacturers (i.e., makers of new technological devices and therapies that physicians prescribed) were becoming increasingly involved in almost every aspect of patient care. The makers of drugs even have tried in some instances to bypass physicians by appealing directly to patients; they advertise on television for patients to "ask their doctors" about new prescription medications in the hope that patient questions and requests will influence the doctors' actions and thus generate more sales. However, at the same time that drugmakers began marketing even prescription medicines directly to consumers, healthcare was becoming so complex and scientific that it alienated patients.

A confusing array of prescription and over-the-counter drugs were becoming so readily available that neither patients nor physicians could distinguish their claims to efficacy. Particularly as the patents on some drug formulations were due to expire, the holders of the original drug formulas sought to distinguish them from recent generic forms. A war of words involving the makers of the widely used and highly profitable thyroid drug Synthroid, for example, demonstrated the high stakes involved in convincing physicians that newer or generic drug substitutes were less effective. In the 1990s, the drug companies that had been developing drugs that would compete with the market leader, Synthroid, began a not-so-subtle marketing campaign to point out that Synthroid sometimes had unpredictable effects on patients. These campaigns alleged that Synthroid was not being manufactured according to the FDA's requirements mandating consistency in potency. Rumors began to circulate among pharmacists and physicians, as well as the public, that the FDA might take Synthroid off the market while it investigated such claims. For patients dependent on daily dosages of the drug, as well as for their healthcare advisors, this presented a dilemma. Should the patients be switched to the newer rivals of Synthroid, in anticipation of a possible shortage of their regular medication? The makers of Synthroid argued that there would be no diminishing of the Synthroid supply and also contended that to change patients' medicines would be to take a risk with patients' health. In the end, the makers of Synthroid were able to convince the FDA that their manufacturing processes were consistent and safe, but not before the newer alternatives had made inroads into the very lucrative thyroid-drug market.

Particularly in areas of medicine such as cardiac care, in the middle of the twentieth century mechanical means for treatment were becoming so advanced that patients and even some providers began to react against that technology. Some persons and groups became committed to regaining control over their own physical health, perhaps working closely with a trusted family physician. This effort was especially the case with medical issues connected to the end of life. In the 1960s, new approaches to death and dying appeared among the public and the medical community. The influential Swiss physician Elisabeth Kübler-Ross promoted knowledge about and acceptance of the stages of dying in her 1969 work *On Death and Dying.* The advocates of a more "natural" approach to dying emphasized the humanizing elements of dying outside of institutions such as hospitals. They advocated de-emphasizing artificial means of prolonging life, such as artificial respiration and defibrillation. Hospice programs aimed to help dying persons be more comfortable both psychologically and emotionally. It was significant that such efforts stressed the value of people ending life in a home setting whenever possible. Despite the vast technological advances that the clinic boasted in saving and maintaining life, it had become a sterile and unkind place in which to die.

Some advocates of "good death" went so far as to argue for either physician-assisted suicide (PAS) or euthanasia. PAS is a doctor's providing a patient with the means to cause his/her own death. A physician might obtain for the patient powerful narcotics, for example, which if self-administered by the patient would be fatal. Although physicians provide the death-inducing substances in such cases, they usually are not present at the time of the patient's ingestion of the lethal materials. It is considered to be euthanasia for a physician or another person to hasten the death of a patient through the actual administration of a lethal substance. Thus for a physician to give an injection that resulted in the patient's death was euthanasia; if the patient had requested the injection, then advocates of euthanasia termed the physician's act "voluntary euthanasia."

Groups such as the Hemlock Society and the Euthanasia Society contended that those measures should be carried out, although only among consenting adults of sound mind. In the face of American medical and legal traditions that did not countenance physicians' or other healthcare providers' hastening patients' deaths, those organizations sought changes in the law so that healthcare personnel would not incur criminal penalties for assisting in a patient's demise. Bills to permit either euthanasia or PAS were introduced in U.S. state legislatures in the 1960s and early 1970s. Sometimes the measures were termed "death with dignity" bills; they emphasized the desire of terminally ill patients to obtain legal medications from physicians so that the patients could end their own lives. Even when a person who had thought about and consented to termination of life was in a permanent or persistent vegetative state, as defined by medical experts, U.S. legislatures and courts were very slow to grant that fundamental change in the law. Euthanasia, or "mercy killing," was not authorized in the United States, although it was allowed under certain circumstances elsewhere—notably, in the Netherlands. In the 1980s and 1990s, other nations instituted procedures for PAS that went far beyond what was permitted in even the most liberal circumstances in the United States.

Several American physicians believed so strongly in the validity of euthanasia or PAS, however, that they risked certain prosecution in order to aid individual patients' efforts to die. In the course of their participation in deaths, these physicians and the groups that supported them also brought great public attention to the moral, legal, and medical questions surrounding euthanasia. The most famous of those "death doctors," Jack Kevorkian, was prosecuted on several occasions for murder. His acquittal in two Michigan cases led directly to Michigan's passage of a law prohibiting PAS. Kevorkian (called by some Doctor Death) in 1998 was sentenced to a long prison term for his part in hastening a patient's demise.

PAS has been more readily put into law than euthanasia, most notably in the state of Oregon's Death with Dignity Act, which was enacted in 1994. Although not often invoked, that statute does provide the opportunity for terminally ill persons to request from their physicians the medications that will allow them (the patients) to commit suicide. The physicians may not administer or participate in the administration of the drugs. The implementation of the act was complicated in 2001, when United States Attorney General John Ashcroft tried to intervene to stop physicians from being able to prescribe medicine that would be used to assist suicides. Ashcroft argued that under the federal Controlled Substances Act of 1970 physicians were prohibited from distributing controlled substances (as many of the death-inducing narcotic drugs were) for the purposes of helping patients to die. Although an Oregon court rebuffed the attorney general, the possibility that the federal government would contravene the pathbreaking Oregon law had been a genuine one.

Conclusion

Largely due to the late nineteenth- and early twentieth-century appearance of both forensic pathologists and psychiatrists in criminal trials, U.S. courtrooms grew to depend on medical expertise to a far greater degree than they ever had prior to about 1800. Besides becoming increasingly accustomed to hearing from medical experts, courts have grown much more concerned with medical issues. As American medicine in the past century has become increasingly tied to technology, corporate influence, and governmental regulation, the courts have been drawn into controversies about how patients are served by those connections. To put it another way, the greater number of parties that enter into a relationship between doctor and patient, the greater the potential for harm—for which courts are asked to apportion blame.

As discussed in Chapter 3, the fact that courts have intervened to resolve medicolegal controversies such as medical-product liability cases, however, does not mean that either patients or physicians will prevail in judicial forums. Sometimes the winners when medicine is "on trial" are third parties, such as the makers of medical products.

In certain instances, courts' adjudication of medicolegal controversies is so complex—as has been the case in multistate lawsuits such as the breast-implant class actions—that patients have difficulty determining whom or even when to sue. Courts' consideration of medicolegal matters has had a still more profound impact as well; it has forced discussion of whether the judiciary is making new policy in regard to explosive topics such as abortion and assisted suicide. In considering particular cases—notably those involving the beginning and end of life—some judges pointedly have warned that they are not the appropriate authorities to resolve the most vexing medicolegal controversies. These judges' discussion about courts' role within U.S. government and society transcends particular legal and medical conflicts and speaks to the place of the judiciary within a democratic society.

References and Further Reading

Ambage, Norman, and Michael Clark. "Unbuilt Bloomsbury: Medico-Legal Institute and Forensic Science Laboratories in England between the Wars," in Michael Clark and Catherine Crawford, eds., *Legal Medicine in History,* 293–313. Cambridge: Cambridge University Press, 1994.

Bix, Amy Sue. "Breast Cancer and AIDS Activism Revolutionize Health Politics," in John Harley Warner and Janet A. Tighe, eds., *Major Problems in the History of American Medicine and Public Health,* 489–498. Boston: Houghton Mifflin, 2001.

Blakeslee, Sandra. "Surgeons Are Warned about Heart Valve." *New York Times,* August 28, 2002, p. 15A.

Blanche, Tony, and Brad Schreiber. *Death in Paradise.* Los Angeles: General Publishing Group, 1998.

Brown, Douglas, and Tom Tullet. *Bernard Spilsbury: Famous Murder Cases of the Great Pathologist.* New York: Dorset Press, 1988.

Bugliosi, Vincent. *Helter Skelter.* New York: Bantam, 1975.

Burney, Ian. *Bodies of Evidence: Medicine and the Politics of the English Inquest, 1830–1926.* Baltimore, MD: Johns Hopkins University Press, 2000.

Cawthon, Elisabeth. "Thomas Wakley and the Medical Coronership." *Medical History* 30 (1986): 191–202.

Childs, Richard. "The Passing of Lay Coroners." *Journal of Forensic Sciences* 19 (January 1974): 8–11.

Cordner, S. M., and B. Loff. "800 Years of Coroners: Have They a Future?" *The Lancet* 344 (1994): 799–801.

Davis, Joseph H. "The Future of the Medical Examiner System." *American Journal of Forensic Medicine and Pathology* 16 (1995): 265–269.

"DNA Retesting Frees Rape Convict." *Dallas Morning News,* March 13, 2003, p. 20A.

Eckert, William G. "Sir Bernard Spilsbury." *American Journal of Forensic Medicine and Pathology* 2 (June 1981): 179–182.

Eigen, Joel Peter. *Witnessing Insanity: Madness and Mad-Doctors at the English Court.* New Haven, CT: Yale University Press, 1995.

European Court of Human Rights. *The Sunday Times Case.* Strasbourg, Belgium: European Court of Human Rights, 1979.

Feegel, J. R. "The Medical Detective." *Trial* 14 (October 1978): 23–25, 46.

Ficarra, Bernard J. "History of Legal Medicine." *Legal Medicine Annual* (1976): 1–27.

Grob, Gerald N. *Mental Institutions in America: Social Policy to 1875.* New York: Free Press, 1973.

Hanzlick, Randy. "History of the National Association of Medical Examiners and Its Meetings, 1966–93." *American Journal of Forensic Medicine and Pathology* 16 (1994): 278–313.

———. "Coroner Training Needs: A Numeric and Geographic Analysis." *Journal of the American Medical Association* 276 (1996): 1775–1778.

Hanzlick, Randy, and Debra Combs. "Medical Examiner and Coroner Systems: History and Trends." *Journal of the American Medical Association* 279 (1998): 870–874.

Helpern, Milton. "The Role of the Forensic Pathologist in the Administration of Justice." *American Journal of Clinical Pathology* 59 (1973): 605–612.

———. *Autopsy.* New York: St. Martin's Press, 1977.

Jennett, Bryan. *The Vegetative State: Medical Facts, Ethical and Legal Dilemmas.* Cambridge, MA: Cambridge University Press, 2002.

Knightley, Phillip, et al. *Suffer the Children: The Story of Thalidomide.* New York: Viking Press, 1979.

Kübler-Ross, Elisabeth. *On Death and Dying.* New York: Macmillan, 1969.

Larsen, Richard W. *Bundy: The Deliberate Stranger.* Englewood Cliffs, NJ: Prentice Hall, 1980.

Mintz, Morton. *The Therapeutic Nightmare.* Boston: Houghton Mifflin, 1965.

Noguchi, Thomas, and Joseph DiMona. *Coroner.* Boston: G. K Hall, 1984.

Picton, Bernard. *Murder, Suicide or Accident—The Forensic Pathologist at Work.* New York: St. Martin's Press, 1971.

Presswalla, Faruk B. "Historical Evolution of Medico-Legal Investigative Systems." *Medico-Legal Bulletin* 25 (1976): 1–8.

Rich, Ben A. *Strange Bedfellows: How Medical Jurisprudence Has Influenced Medical Ethics and Medical Practice.* New York: Kluwer Academic Publishers, 2001.

Robinson, Clement. "Of Magrath, Spilsbury and Homicides." *Journal of the Maine Medical Association* (June 1959): 202–214.

Rothman, David J. *The Discovery of the Asylum.* Boston: Little, Brown, 1971.

Rush, Benjamin. *Medical Inquiries and Observations upon the Diseases of the Mind.* Philadelphia: Kimber and Richardson, 1812.

Shakespeare, William. *Hamlet,* ed. G.B. Harrison. New York: Harcourt Brace, 1968.

Shapiro, E. Donald, and Anthony Davis. "Law and Pathology through the Ages: The Coroner and His Descendants—Legitimate and Illegitimate." *New York State Journal of Medicine* 72 (April 1972): 805–809.

Simpson, Keith. *Forty Years of Murder.* London: Granada Publishing, 1980.

Spitz, Werner, and Russell Fisher. *Medicolegal Investigation of Death: Guidelines for the Application of Pathology to Crime Investigation.* Springfield, IL: Charles C. Thomas, 1980.

Stevens, Rosemary. *In Sickness and in Wealth: American Hospitals in the Twentieth Century.* New York: Basic Books, 1989.

Taylor, Blaine. "The Case of the Outspoken Medical Examiner, or an Exclusive Interview with Russell H. Fisher, MD, Chief Medical Examiner of the State of Maryland." *Maryland State Medical Journal* 26 (March 1977): 59–77.

Wadee, Shabbir Ahmed. "Forensic Pathology—A Different Perspective: Investigative Medicolegal Systems in the United States." *Medicine and Law* 13 (1994): 519–530.

3
Cases

How have medicolegal controversies affected medical practice, the law, and public debate? This chapter explores that multipart question by examining a number of famous and less celebrated cases decided by modern U.S. courts. Judicial decisions concerning medicine (and shaping its course as a profession) have ranged over a variety of areas of American life far beyond specialized medical subjects. At the beginning of the twenty-first century, medical science, medical principles, and medical experts are integral parts of a variety of courtroom discussions, including criminal prosecutions; determinations of mental competency and child custody; assignments of disability benefits; questions concerning assisted reproduction (AR), abortion, and euthanasia; and inquiries into hospital and nursing home care. This extensive intersection of medicine and the courts was far from the norm in the early history of the United States.

Although the very term *medicolegal* is in common usage in the twenty-first century, it would have been foreign to both medical and legal professionals 150 or 200 years ago. In the first half of the nineteenth century, medicine and the law were distinct specialties that did not often mix in practice. Each field generally disdained to offer training in the other, with almost no medical schools providing courses in legal matters, even for pathologists, and only the rare law school teaching legal medicine. Furthermore, medicine was not a leading element of most trials, in terms of the issues under contention, the evidence presented, and the experts relied upon as witnesses.

Though there were a handful of medical professionals who argued that medicine should play a greater role in legal arenas, including the advocates of medical training for coroners in the 1830s and 1840s, those who had a vision of medicine and law as closely linked were very much in the minority. Few people, even among the advocates of a more powerful coronership, would have predicted that within the next century medicine as a field and medical personnel themselves would become a vital presence in courtrooms in the United States. Yet this is exactly what happened. Some of medicine's expanded legal presence in the later nineteenth century was due to gradual changes in the practice of forensic medicine so that the field had a higher and better-respected legal profile. As has been discussed in Chapter 2, however, the greatest rise in stature among forensic pathologists (beginning with figures such as Bernard Spilsbury) did not occur until the twentieth century.

Meanwhile, what developments caused medicine as a field and medical professionals as experts during the late 1800s to be much more widely known and accepted within courtrooms? The answer is a somewhat unlikely one: practitioners of a medical specialization that was itself new in the early nineteenth century seized the opportunity to make themselves experts in the courtroom. Those practitioners, psychiatrists, were still in the process of forming themselves into professional groups during the early 1800s when they provided expert testimony in several spectacular and well-publicized trials. Fully aware of the high profile of the cases in which they were engaged as expert witnesses, they advanced the cause of not only the clients on whose behalf they testified, but also their field. Judicial authorities, legislators, and even the public did not always welcome that new medical presence—the psychiatrist as expert witness. Trials in the middle and late nineteenth century were full of examples of skepticism that any doctors could or should play a key courtroom role, especially in regard to the controversial insanity defense. By the early twentieth century, however, judicial decisions were bearing out the belief that medical knowledge—and medical experts themselves—could play a constructive role in the resolution of cases.

At the same time that medicine began to have a vital presence in court, the late nineteenth- and early twentieth-century judiciary began to take a more critical view of medicine. This was new; judicial attention to the medical field had not long been the rule. Aside from discrete court cases involving individual doctors such as those accused of medical malpractice, as late as the first half of the nineteenth century the law had not exercised much influence on the medical community. By the twenty-first century, on the other hand, physicians are well advised to remain informed about litigation involving their specialties. (How could a modern plastic surgeon not be aware of the Dow-Corning breast-implant litigation, for example? How could an obstetrician not pay attention to the trends in jury awards for injury-at-birth suits?) Like it or not, medical professionals were forced to pay attention to the law—ironically at the same time that the law was beginning to pay more attention to medicine.

What has caused the courts to intrude upon the practice of medicine? In part, it has been medicine's promise of ever-more complex and expensive techniques and remedies. The science of medicine underwent vast changes in the twentieth century. For example, medicine was increasingly associated with technology, and medicine placed much greater reliance on therapeutic cures. Although technology and drug therapies held out the promise of cures and a higher quality of life for many patients, those innovations also raised alarms. Could individual patients' personal autonomy be compromised by medicine's overreliance on machines that were too complicated and drugs that were dangerous? Courts often decided that patients were put at risk by the very medical techniques and therapies that were designed to prolong and enhance lives.

In addition, courts were drawn into the oversight of medical institutions and personnel due to concerns that the complexities of modern patient care might imperil patients' safety. In particular, the process of corporatization of medicine (that is, the growing connection between medical practice and hospitals, and the takeover of medical management by corporate entities) caused courts to intervene in a variety of medical cases. For example, in the beginning of the twentieth century, with many more persons than before seeking treatment in hospitals, often for surgeries, courts took it upon themselves to define more clearly the notion of informed consent for medical procedures, a legal process described in more detail later in this chapter. In the later part of the twentieth century, courts increasingly considered cases involving *a variety of parties* who made decisions that could harm patients—not only doctors, but also medical management companies, for example, that set policies followed by physicians.

So in the past 150 years, medicine and medical experts came into court, and the courts intruded into medicine—two vital historical developments. Yet a third process may have been still more important: the spilling over of medicolegal controversies into the larger society. At the same time that medicine currently pervades many courtroom dramas, it is becoming commonplace for medicine to be "on trial" outside courtrooms as well, especially in the political arena. Because the actions of powerful regulatory agencies such as the Food and Drug Administration (FDA) affect Americans, as well as people around the world who consume American products, those agencies themselves have come under scrutiny when they are embroiled in medicolegal controversies. Questions about the power of government agencies to regulate public health necessarily envelop more than just the matter of doctors' or patients' rights; they encompass a consideration of the relative powers of various institutions, such as legislatures, state versus federal authorities, and even social institutions such as the family. Courts' widely publicized resolutions of the exceptionally difficult issues that arise in medicolegal debates (notably in beginning-of-life and end-of-life cases) even have inspired renewed consideration of the judiciary's proper role in a democratic society.

Thus this chapter will focus on three major historical developments from the past 150 years: how medicine and medical practitioners (particularly physicians) became a usual and important presence in courtrooms; the ways in which the law has shaped medical practice; and the impact of medicolegal controversies on broader public concerns within American society. The mixing of law and medicine in courts has been an increasingly well-known process. It also has been a productive one, for medicolegal controversies, as played out in a rich variety of cases, have forced public consideration and discussion about fundamental issues of grave public concern.

Medicine Shapes Trials: The Doctor as Expert in the Courtroom

Psychiatry and the Insanity Defense

In the nineteenth century, the single greatest element in medicine gaining more clout in the courtroom was the participation of medical professionals in sensational insanity trials. By virtue of the fact that two of these cases concerned the assassination or attempted killing of heads of state (one in England and another in the United States), every aspect of the trials received enormous attention from the public as well as medical and legal authorities. In the trials of Daniel M'Naghten (1843) and Charles Guiteau (1881) the key testimony of the medical experts who only recently had claimed for themselves professional authority to diagnose and treat mental illness—psychiatrists—was for the first time very openly under consideration.

In 1843 in London, Daniel M'Naghten shot a man who he thought was Prime Minister Robert Peel. The victim, who in fact was Peel's secretary, subsequently died; Peel was unhurt. Thus M'Naghten was accused of murdering the secretary. M'Naghten singled out Peel for his anger because he believed that he was being persecuted by the police. (Peel was the founder of a modern police force in London.) The M'Naghten trial of 1843 helped to bring medicine into English and American courtrooms in a key area of the law—the so-called insanity defense, in which a defendant argued that a lack of reason excused a criminal act. Widely publicized, the controversy surrounding the M'Naghten trial's verdict had implications in U.S. as well as English law for over a century. For in M'Naghten's trial, psychiatrists were the witnesses who made the difference between the defendant's conviction and his acquittal.

M'Naghten's lawyers argued that M'Naghten suffered from "partial" or temporary insanity—a contention highly representative of many psychiatrists' views by the mid–nineteenth century. Prior to the nineteenth century, most English and U.S. courts had held to the view that true insanity must have totally deprived the person of his or her human character; thus the classic test for insanity was whether one acted as "a wild beast." In several well-known trials around the year 1800 that involved potential assassins of the British monarch, this view began to modify somewhat. Psychiatrists suggested that it was simplistic to argue that insanity necessitated that a patient should be totally deprived of reason. Still, just before the *M'Naghten* case, psychiatrists generally argued that accused persons might be insane only if they had no moral compass at all—that is, if they never had the ability to distinguish right from wrong.

In M'Naghten's case, however, psychiatric experts maintained an even more modern view that a person might be insane if he or she could not tell right from wrong *at the time that an illegal act was committed.* The newer version of the "right-wrong" test provided for the possibility that insane persons could move into and out of mental incapacity. Such a view was consistent with the building of more humane facilities for the housing and treatment of the mentally ill. In those more modern asylums, patients could be observed as exhibiting gradations of mental illness, whereas in older institutions patients might be so traumatized that they never seemed to act in a "normal" fashion.

Several famous psychiatrists testified at M'Naghten's trial, and the works of others were read into evidence. Among the most influential proponents of a modernization and broadening of the right-wrong test was American physician Isaac Ray, whose 1838 book, *A Treatise on the Medical Jurisprudence of Insanity,* had been both controversial and influential in England and the United States. Some commentators on Ray's work noted that as an American who was writing about the use of English common law on insanity, Ray could be more critical of England's judicial rulings on insanity, contrasting them unfavorably with continental laws such as the Code Napoleon. M'Naghten's counsel, Alexander Cockburn, skillfully employed Ray's contentions about the possibility that a person could be partially insane. In his diplomatic and effective defense of M'Naghten, Cockburn argued that if earlier judges had had the benefit of the newer asylums, they too could have grasped that patients confined there could seem insane at times, while at other junctures the mentally ill might act in a more contained (or normal) fashion.

When M'Naghten was found not guilty by reason of insanity and committed to Bethlehem Hospital rather than executed, loud protests ensued. The verdict itself and M'Naghten's fate were under fire, and the influential testimony of psychiatrists itself had stirred up a storm of controversy. In the wake of the trial, Britain's parliament demanded that leading judges draw up a set of legal standards for insanity. That is, Parliament balked at the idea that medical experts could prescribe the legal parameters for insanity; it preferred to hear those ground rules from the mouths of jurists.

The judges were under pressure to rescind the relative liberality of the *M'Naghten* trial verdict. They responded accordingly, enunciating a set of guidelines to be applied in British courtrooms for determining a defendant's insanity—guidelines that, if they had been in force at his trial, would have convicted M'Naghten. The judges summarized English law as they believed it to be valid, in the following way: a person was legally insane (and thus not responsible for his criminal act) if, at the time the act was committed, he suffered from a disease of the mind that caused him either not to know what he was doing or not to realize that what he was doing was wrong. The person, in other words, could not be merely eccentric or perverse, and his disease had to be one that could be identified and widely recognized by mental-health experts. Those principles, or tests for insanity, soon became known as the M'Naghten Rules (1843). They influenced the law on insanity in both England and the United States for many decades.

In the mid–nineteenth century, most American states adopted a version of the M'Naghten Rules as their standard for the legal definition of insanity. A few states modified the M'Naghten Rules with a principle called the irresistible impulse doctrine. That principle reflected the opinion among psychiatrists that a person might be insane on a temporary basis when he or she was seized by an overwhelming impulse to commit an act that he or she would otherwise realize was wrong and illegal. Thus the notion of irresistible impulse satisfied those who argued for stern definitions of insanity (along the lines of the M'Naghten Rules), yet allowed psychiatrists to argue that *some* individuals could not maintain control over their own emotions. Interestingly, the only state that clearly did not base its judicial decisions on the M'Naghten Rules was Isaac Ray's home area, New Hampshire. In the influential case of *State v. Pike* (1870), the Supreme Court of New Hampshire considered the case of a man who had been convicted of first-degree murder. The defendant, Joseph Pike, had argued that since he wished to plead insanity, New Hampshire could not then presume that he was sane, but had the burden of proving beyond a reasonable doubt that he was sane. The court found that argument too strong but, in the process of making its decision, put forward a method for deciding cases of alleged insanity that was both distinctive from other states and different from the M'Naghten Rules.

The New Hampshire Rule, as enunciated by Justice Charles Doe, presumed that mental disease was at the root of insanity and that defendants who claimed insanity might be no more responsible for their illness than persons who were suffering from other physical ailments. Further, New Hampshire courts placed the determination of the validity of a claim of insanity into the hands of the jury, with only a minimum of legal instruction from the bench. The question of insanity, Doe ruled, was a matter of fact—to be determined in each case by jurors—rather than one to be decided on the more abstract basis of legal tests. Justice Doe, furthermore, preferred that jurors, in assessing whether the defendants were insane, rely on the evidence of laypeople who had observed defendants in everyday situations. In other words, he somewhat devalued the expert medical witness.

Despite the sensational nature of these cases, the insanity defense actually was relatively rare in U.S. and English courtrooms in the nineteenth century, as it remains in a more modern era. Even as courts relied on the M'Naghten Rules, there was considerable variation in exactly how they were applied from state to state and between state and federal jurisdictions. In fact, throughout the twentieth century, the insanity defense was notable for its rarity. In most states, there were only a handful of insanity pleas per year and sometimes no successful ones. Yet the insanity dodge—as it was known among many members of the public—was extremely well known and much discussed, largely because insanity was an issue raised in a handful of famous cases of attempted assassination. One of these earlier U.S. cases was the trial of Charles Julius Guiteau after the assassination of President James Garfield in 1881.

Guiteau was described in his own time and has been described since as a disappointed office seeker. In the days before civil-service requirements for federal and state officeholders, elections were an occasion for the distribution of jobs as a reward for political loyalty. To expect a job in the early days of a new U.S. president's administration would not have been unusual. To be bitterly disappointed when a position was not forthcoming also would have been a typical reaction for many individuals. Guiteau took his anger much further than most, however, by committing homicide against a symbol of his frustration. (With no irony or apology, Guiteau said that he bore no particular grudge against Garfield as an individual, just as the president.)

Unlike the assassination of President Lincoln just a few years before, the death of President Garfield was a tragedy that seemed easy to address through the criminal justice system. Whereas the leader of the plot against Lincoln, John Wilkes Booth, had been killed on the run and Wilkes's coconspirators tried by a military court, Guiteau gave himself up to police immediately after the shooting of Garfield. Guiteau appeared ready to have his case considered by ordinary civilian authorities. Guiteau's prospects of being considered legally insane, despite the magnitude of his offense, initially were good because President Garfield had survived the shooting, thus lessening the gravity of the crime in many people's eyes. When Garfield took a turn for the worse, however, and after several months of suffering succumbed to his wounds, opinion in the press and among legal experts turned against the assassin.

One aspect of the M'Naghten Rules that had been clear in most U.S. and English courtrooms was that the rules' emphasis on the defendant having a disease of the mind in order to show insanity virtually required the use of expert medical testimony in trials. But those experts were far from unanimous in their opinions about the causes, symptoms, and effects of insanity. Was insanity hereditary? That was the argument of many eminent anatomists who were influenced by European psychological theorists. Was a tendency to commit crimes caused, instead, by "moral depravity"? So argued several experts on crime, including some physicians. Nor were medical professionals such as psychiatrists the only ones concerned with these questions. Insanity also was an important topic among prison and asylum superintendents, who had their own professional organizations in the United States by the 1880s and whose growing professionalism theoretically challenged the dominance of psychiatrists as sole experts in these matters.

The Guiteau trial was a showdown between competing visions of insanity in relation to crime. A set of expert witnesses who testified for the defense about Guiteau's state of mind were led by the young, talented Edward Spitzka, a physician and the head of the New York Neurological Society. Trained in Europe and optimistic about the potential for physiology to unlock the secrets of mental disease, Spitzka held to the view that insanity was primarily organic in origin and was hereditary. On the side of the prosecution was the powerful superintendent of the large Utica Asylum in New York, John Gray. Gray also was the editor of the *American Journal of Insanity.* He used that journal as an organ for his view (widely shared) that insanity was a recognizable but rare phenomenon. Most of the persons who claimed insanity in court, Gray believed, were merely sinful or eccentric. They acted illegally out of depravity, which carried with it the connotation of moral failing. Truly insane persons, to Gray, looked much like the persons who would have fit within the old English "wild beast" test. They not only tended to be "furious" in the archaic sense of the word, but they had a lifelong history of mental disease. Insofar as Gray's views recalled the first one or two decades of the nineteenth century in English law, they were compatible with an application of the M'Naghten Rules (which in 1843 had turned back the clock to that earlier era).

Guiteau's conviction surprised few Americans and disappointed even fewer. Guiteau's self-aggrandizing conduct during the trial, along with his record as a somewhat shady lawyer prior to his criminal act, certainly hurt his case with the public. But his execution took some of the venom away from his critics. Guiteau's behavior had continued to be bizarre, even long past the point at which it could have served Guiteau's purpose in deliberately acting insane. At his execution, he sang a plaintive and peculiar song that he had composed; that act alone convinced some observers that he was not sane. Anatomists made much of their finding, upon an autopsy of his body, that Guiteau had suffered from syphilis—a disease known to cause mental decline. For the most part, however, the *Guiteau* case solidified the insanity defense in the minds of many citizens as a crafty device that was employed by conniving defendants and their lawyers to try to evade the death penalty. Still, inspired by the use of the M'Naghten Rules in the District of Columbia court that had convicted Guiteau, most state courts that had not yet adopted the rules in some form now did so.

Another well-publicized insanity case followed the 1901 assassination of President William McKinley. The lawyers for defendant Leon Czolgosz raised the question of their client's sanity in an interesting, if halfhearted, manner. Their argument was that to commit such a brazen act, for which the death penalty was so sure as a punishment, Czolgosz must have been insane. The New York court hearing the case refused to consider that contention as a formal insanity plea, however, and reminded the jury that the law in New York required a presumption of sanity for the defendant. Czolgosz swiftly was convicted and executed.

Even in New York State, however, the insanity defense was capable of being stretched to accommodate an exceptionally persistent—and wealthy—defendant's claims. In the trials of Harry K. Thaw, a millionaire son of a prominent Pittsburgh family, Thaw's defense team tried two approaches to the insanity defense. Thaw was on trial for shooting eminent architect Stanford White; the fact of the shooting was admitted by the defense. Thaw argued, in justification for his act, that he had been momentarily blinded by rage (that amounted to insanity) when he heard from his wife that White had sexually assaulted her prior to her marriage. The case was dubbed the murder of the century when it made headlines in 1906. The trials were a national sensation, not only because of Thaw's wealth and White's prominence, but also due to the beauty and fame of the alleged assault victim, former actress and Gibson Girl Evelyn Nesbitt. In the first trial of Thaw, the defense argued that Thaw's momentary insanity should be called "dementia Americana"—the righteous anger that any American male supposedly would experience upon learning of his wife's injury. Such an approach, though not completely novel in a murder trial of an angry husband, proved divisive among the jurors. Eventually the judge had to declare a mistrial. Fearing a similar result, in Thaw's second trial the defense lawyers took a more conventional approach to demonstrating Thaw's insanity. They called medical witnesses to attest to a Thaw family history of mental illness. The jurors, who already were sympathetic to Thaw, were ready to accept that argument, and they consigned Thaw to a mental hospital rather than death row.

After several years' confinement, Thaw was released from the mental institution. The grounds for his release ostensibly were that he was cured of his temporary insanity. Many among the public, however, speculated that a generous donation by his family to the mental hospital had in fact been the determining factor in his diagnosis of good mental health. After his release, Thaw engaged in numerous episodes of erratic and violent behavior—particularly toward women—that considerably damaged the sympathy he had remaining among laypeople from the time of his trial. Meanwhile, in an ironic twist, mental-health professionals who at the time of his trials had doubted Thaw's insanity concluded from his postrelease behavior that he might indeed be mentally unstable. The case and its aftermath therefore had a complex effect on perceptions of the insanity defense. Thaw's trials helped make the insanity defense known among the public as a strategy employed by wealthy defendants. In particular when defendants were found to be not guilty and were sent to mental facilities, the popular view was that those patients with influential families easily could secure privileges such as the ability to leave the institutions' grounds or even could obtain early release. Thus there was the fear that violent persons (whether one accepted the fact of their mental illness or not) were being treated too leniently on the basis of their class connections.

Thaw's fate (both in a judicial forum and in his subsequent life experience) also piqued the interest of the psychiatric community, which was increasingly concerned at the degree to which public opinion about a defendant could impact a trial's outcome. Quite literally, of course, a jury verdict was a reflection of public views on insanity. Thus some psychiatrists, as well as the lawyers representing persons who claimed insanity, began to pursue the strategy of asking for judges' rather than jury verdicts whenever possible, under the reasoning that judges were less emotional and less easily swayed by popular prejudice against an unsympathetic defendant.

Although it was not formally raised as a defense in the 1924 trial of the "thrill killers" Nathan Leopold and Richard Loeb, the insanity defense loomed large in the background of this case as well. Defense counsel Clarence Darrow stopped short of employing an insanity plea in his effort to secure a verdict other than death for his clients. Darrow, however, did rely on voluminous reports from medical experts to demonstrate the mental abnormality of Leopold and Loeb. In essence, Darrow was betting on the expert opinions of medical experts to establish the unusual mental state of the defendants as a mitigating factor in assessing punishment for their guilt—a factor that justified allowing the defendants to live. It was medical testimony on the mental state of Leopold and Loeb that lay at the heart of Darrow's case. Yet Darrow was canny enough to realize that pressing for an insanity defense would have been an unpopular, perhaps fatal, tactic. In addition to his walking a fine line with respect to his clients' mental state, Darrow made a brilliant calculation that the judge rather than a jury might hear him out as to a mitigation of the crime. The life sentences imposed by the judge on Leopold and Loeb were one of the greatest victories of Darrow's career. Thus Darrow, like many psychiatrists, correctly perceived that the insanity defense would play very poorly with a jury, particularly in the case of these sons of extremely wealthy families.

From the 1920s onward, medical authorities argued that the M'Naghten Rules were hopelessly out of step with a modern medical understanding of mental illness. Psychiatrists said plainly to courts that they no longer even employed the terminology of *sanity* and *insanity* but instead used much more specific terms such as *psychosis* and *schizophrenia* to refer to types of mental illness. Many psychiatrists began to argue that the M'Naghten Rules were an unwieldy apparatus for deciding insanity cases and that the New Hampshire standards, which had been the exception among states for almost a century, would be preferable. Several prominent judicial figures agreed. Mr. Justice Cardozo, for example, in 1928 gave a speech to the New York Academy of Medicine, in which he argued that "the present definition of insanity has little relation to the truths of mental life" (*Durham v. United States,* 214 F.2d 864). In 1953, Mr. Justice Frankfurter testified before Britain's Royal Commission on Capital Punishment that he did not "see why the rules of law should be arrested at the state of psychological knowledge of the time when they were formulated" (*United States v. Currens,* 290 F.2d 765).

Interestingly, it was another District of Columbia verdict (as the *Guiteau* decision had been) that was the first major repudiation of the M'Naghten Rules in the United States. The case of *Durham v. United States* (1954) offered an excellent example of a defendant whom most medical authorities believed to be mentally ill but who would not fit within the M'Naghten (that is, legal) standards for insanity. Consequently, the U.S. Court of Appeals for the District of Columbia Circuit not only remanded the case for a new trial but also declared that the existing tests of criminal responsibility—the M'Naghten Rules—were "obsolete and should be superseded" (*Durham v. U.S.* 1954, 862).

Monte Durham had endured the problems of mental illness his whole life. Suffering from hallucinations and other symptoms of mental incapacity, Durham was discharged by the navy at the age of seventeen as being unfit for military service due to his mental condition. He subsequently was in and out of mental institutions (including Saint Elizabeth's Hospital in Washington, D.C.) for several years, receiving diagnoses that he was psychotic and psychopathic. He also was periodically in trouble with the police for petty crimes. In 1951, he was arrested on a charge of housebreaking and spent time again at Saint Elizabeth's before psychiatrists would certify him as able to participate in his own defense. At his trial, the judge appeared unsympathetic to the argument that Durham might not be mentally competent and rejected expert evidence by psychiatrists who had examined Durham that the defendant had been of unsound mind on the date of the commission of the crime.

In reviewing and ultimately reversing the trial court's decision (to require Durham to serve out the remainder of a jail sentence that he had previously received), the court of appeals gave a brief history of insanity law in England and the United States, focusing on the District of Columbia's courts. The right-wrong test, a key element in the M'Naghten Rules, had been employed in the District of Columbia since 1882, when it was first used in the *Guiteau* case. Efforts to soften the impact of M'Naghten were rejected by D.C. courts in two cases at the turn of the twentieth century: *Taylor v. United States,* in 1895, and *Snell v. United States,* in 1900. In both of those instances, the courts refused to recognize a defense called emotional insanity, which was similar to Isaac Ray's concept of temporary insanity. In 1929, however, the application of M'Naghten standards was supplemented by the irresistible impulse test in the case of *Smith v. United States.*

The appeals court judges, writing in the *Durham* case in the 1950s, noted that learned writers for years had argued that legal practice was far behind medical science in regard to insanity cases. Psychiatric authorities, along with judges and law professors, branded the right-wrong test as obsolete. Rather, psychiatry in the middle of the twentieth century recognized that the ability to reason and thus distinguish right from wrong was only one aspect of a person's complex personality. To base an appraisal of a person's mental state on his or her "knowledge" was to grossly underestimate the other factors that could determine an individual's behavior. With this in mind, the *Durham* appeals court judges decided that the question of whether a defendant suffered from a mental disease was central to the disposition of such cases, for in cases where criminal acts stemmed from mental disease, neither moral blame nor criminal responsibility legally attached to the defendant. The determination of insanity, in turn, was up to jurors who would weigh all the available medical evidence, including expert medical opinion.

The *Durham* appeals court ruling came very close to an adoption of Dr. Ray and Justice Doe's New Hampshire Rule. Mental-health experts praised the decision as a desperately needed modernization. The legal acceptance of *Durham* was not universal, however; in fact some courts went out of their way to note that they disagreed with it. In *Feguer v. United States,* for example, a U.S. Court of Appeals justice sniffed that "every court that has considered *Durham* has rejected it" (243). Still, the need that had motivated the *Durham* judges to rule as they had remained strong. If M'Naghten was an inadequate standard, then what should replace it? Where could a proper balance between medical and legal definitions of insanity be found?

One answer to the dilemma of providing a workable legal measurement for mental disability in criminal cases was proposed in the *Currens* case of 1961. Although the defendant, Donald Currens, was, like Monte Durham, a petty criminal with a penchant for stealing cars, *Currens* provided a more representative model for the courts than *Durham* because it involved a defendant who was more of a borderline case than Monte Durham had been. That is, in numerical terms, more defendants tended to be like Donald Currens than like Monte Durham. Durham clearly had had psychotic episodes that had been well documented for years by psychiatric experts at hospitals. Currens, on the other hand, was a person who, according to mental-health experts, suffered from a disease, but a disease whose specifics were difficult to classify. Currens was variously described as hysterical, hypochondriacal, disturbed, and unstable. Whether he should be called psychotic or sociopathic was a matter of debate among physicians who examined him. His crimes included passing bad checks as well as auto theft, and he frequently seemed to be under the influence of alcohol. To most mental-health professionals by the middle of the twentieth century, abuses of alcohol and drugs often were understood as efforts to self-medicate, and addictions to these substances could provide evidence of chronic mental illness. Among psychiatric professionals, therefore, Currens was representative of many people with mental disorders who ran afoul of the law. That is, he engaged in small-time offenses rather than violent or spectacular acts such as assassinations, and although his mental instability was difficult to classify in an exact sense, he exhibited behavioral characteristics that sometimes were symptomatic of mental disease.

The U.S. Court of Appeals for the Third Circuit, in deciding the *Currens* case, clearly believed that the time was ripe for throwing out the M'Naghten Rules. Like the judges in *Durham* before them, the court members here reviewed the application of the rules in the United States, as well as the history of their adoption in England. They then sought to apply the lessons of this historical record in determining an appropriate legal standard of insanity. Interestingly, the court in *Currens* chose as a fitting analogy in their present case—and hence a ready source upon which to base the standards they sought—the trial of the British would-be assassin James Hadfield in the early nineteenth century. Hadfield was a former soldier who had suffered a severe head injury during the Napoleonic Wars. Since his discharge from the army on medical grounds, Hadfield had identified himself as a Christ-like figure. In 1812, he tried to assassinate King George III. Hadfield declared that he knew that his act was wrong according to the law, but he thought himself morally justified nonetheless. Charged with both attempted murder and treason, Hadfield, through his lawyers, argued that he was mentally unfit and hence not legally responsible for his actions. The judge agreed. Clearly Hadfield had a physical basis for his mental state; consequently, the trial judge instructed the jury to acquit him, and it did. (It did not hurt Hadfield's position with judge and jury, of course, that he had sustained his brain injury while in battle.) Under the M'Naghten Rules, however, Hadfield would have been convicted.

In making that analogy between defendants Hadfield and Currens, the judges of the third circuit demonstrated their acceptance of current medical arguments about the complexity of mental disease. The question so often posed to psychiatrists who were appearing as expert witnesses in insanity cases, according to the M'Naghten standard, was "Did the defendant know the difference between right and wrong?" The court in *Currens* commented: "How, conceivably, can the criminal responsibility of a mentally ill defendant be determined by the answer to a simple question placed on a moral basis? To state the question seems to us to answer it. All in all the M'Naghten Rules do indeed . . . put the testifying psychiatrist in a strait-jacket" (*United States v. Currens* 1961, 767).

In place of M'Naghten's Rules, the *Currens* court proposed that a simpler test for criminal responsibility should be applied. The components of that test were medical rather than either moral or legal: (1) What was the defendant's mental condition at the time of the act? (2) Was the defendant suffering from a mental disease or defect? (3) At the time of the alleged crime, could the defendant conform his or her actions to the requirements of the law that was violated? The *Currens* court, however, did give an important nod to public opinion skeptical of "the insanity dodge." The court recommended that hospitalization in a secure mental-treatment facility should be *mandatory* for persons who were acquitted of crimes by reason of their mental state.

In 1962, the American Law Institute (ALI) drafted a set of principles for courts to use in insanity cases. The ALI standard, as it came to be called, was very close to what the court had recommended in the *Currens* case. The ALI standard included the requirement that a defendant had to lack the "substantial capacity" to conform his or her conduct to the "requirements of the law" for an insanity defense to succeed (quoted in Steadman 1993, 46). Thus the ALI standard adopted the *Currens* requirement that the defendant's mental disability had to be in effect only at the time of the commission of the crime (not for years previously); yet it also included the M'Naghten Rules' requirement that the defendant had to suffer from a mental disease or defect. Many state courts adopted the ALI standard after 1962.

In spite of the efforts of psychiatric organizations to ensure that more sophisticated standards such as those in *Currens* and *Durham* were implemented, the combination of the right-wrong test from M'Naghten with the irresistible impulse test remained in wide usage in many states in the 1960s and 1970s. At the 1979 trial of Dan White for the murder of San Francisco Mayor George Moscone and City Supervisor Harvey Milk, for instance, White's lawyers offered a form of the irresistible impulse test as a mitigation of White's crime. White, they argued, had been so unbalanced by a steady diet of sugary foods that he suffered a chemical imbalance that led him to commit the murders. Although they also may have been influenced by White's all-American image and biased against victim Milk because of his open homosexuality, the jury chose to accept the mitigation and convicted White of manslaughter instead of murder.

As had occurred in previous high-profile cases, in the early 1980s another potential assassin brought new scrutiny to the insanity defense. John Hinckley Jr. was obsessed with film star Jodie Foster and had shown signs of mental instability for years. Convinced that only a grand gesture would win Foster's attention, in March 1981 Hinckley shot President Ronald Reagan and several other persons while the president was on his way into a hotel in Washington, D.C. Several of the victims were seriously wounded, including Press Secretary James Brady; the president's injuries were less severe. Hinckley's family, who admitted to feeling guilty for having practiced "tough love" toward their son rather than getting him psychiatric help in recent months, hired talented and experienced defense lawyers.

The case quickly became a rallying point for those who insisted that the M'Naghten Rules should be modernized so that a broader definition of mental illness would allow a defendant to escape criminal responsibility. Hinckley's trial attracted equal attention from those who supported the abolition of the insanity defense altogether. It was the first trial of a presidential assassin (or attempted assassin) since Guiteau where the defense made a concerted effort to argue that the assassin was insane. Besides the case of Leon Czolgosz, where the insanity defense was muted at best, there had not been another effort to claim insanity for a presidential assassin. (In the 1933 trial of Joseph Zangara for the attempted assassination of President-

Elect Franklin Roosevelt and the murder of Chicago Mayor Anton Cermak, for example, no insanity defense was offered.)

When Hinckley's case went to trial, the defense was helped by the decision of the trial judge to hear the case under federal standards for proof of insanity. Federal courts had adopted the burden of proof used in the New Hampshire Rule. In federal courts, once an insanity plea had been entered, the prosecution had the burden of demonstrating that the defendant was sane. In most state courts, however, the burden was reversed, with the defense having to prove insanity. The trial quickly became a contest between medical experts for each side. The defense emphasized Hinckley's recurring mental difficulties and his fixation on Jodie Foster. The prosecution noted Hinckley's actions preceding the assassination attempt, which pointed to his calculating state of mind.

Like M'Naghten, Hinckley was found by the jury to have been insane at the time he committed the attempted murders. Like M'Naghten, Hinckley was sent to a mental hospital for an indeterminate—perhaps unlimited—period of time. Hinckley was committed to Saint Elizabeth's Hospital in Washington, D.C., which was the place where Monte Durham had been treated. Hinckley's acquittal, like M'Naghten's, proved extremely controversial in a political sense. Public reaction was swift and critical; polls indicated that many among the American public thought Hinckley's rich family had secured preferential legal treatment for him through their highly paid counsel. Even Hinckley's stay at Saint Elizabeth's inspired comment. Several years after his committal, when hospital administrators considered allowing Hinckley to travel beyond the grounds of the facility for a few hours at a time, they encountered public criticism of relaxed confinement rules. As with the case of Harry Thaw in the early 1900s, critics of the insanity defense argued that any special privileges given to Hinckley had to do with his family's financial status rather than with Hinckley's progress toward recovery. More importantly, critics contended that any such relaxation in supervision endangered the public.

Some in Congress proposed abolishing the insanity defense altogether (as a few states, namely Montana, Idaho, and Utah, either had already done or did in the immediate aftermath of Hinckley's acquittal). The Insanity Defense Act, passed by Congress in 1984, was a direct result of that sharp criticism of the insanity defense by public and policymakers alike. The legislation for the first time set a federal standard through codified law for the insanity defense. According to the new law, a defendant could be successful with the insanity defense only if he or she suffered from a severe mental disease or defect that made him or her unable to understand what he or she was doing or that it was wrong. The defense had the burden of showing that the defendant was insane. Medical witnesses could be employed by both sides, but they could not state opinions as to the sanity or insanity of the defendant. At least nine states patterned revisions of their laws on insanity after the Insanity Defense Act, with seven states also shifting the burden of proof to the defendant. Shortly after *Hinckley* and the federal law's enactment, about two-thirds of the states had laws that placed the burden of proof on the defense. In addition, several states added an alternative verdict of which juries could avail themselves—the formal finding of guilty but mentally ill. The states' standards for demonstrating insanity generally were somewhat lower than at the federal court level; most states required that the showing of insanity be by "a preponderance" of evidence rather than by "clear and convincing evidence" (as was the federal mandate).

The insanity defense, therefore, remained a topic that stirred controversy in the late twentieth century, in part due to its discussion in exactly the types of cases where it had proved explosive in the early 1800s—assassinations of well-known figures. The insanity defense was employed in other types of cases as well, of course, including some instances where it raised criticism. In particular, the insanity defense appeared in the trials of several mothers accused of murdering their children in the first decade of the twenty-first century. The 2002 case of Houston resident Andrea Yates, who drowned her five children in a bathtub, was especially widely publicized. Yates's lawyers argued that a severe form of postpartum depression amounted to her being insane by legal standards at the time of the commission of the crime.

The treatment of those persons who pleaded mental disorder as a justification in their effort to escape legal sanction continued to be a highly disputed subject not only among courts but also among the medical community and the public at large. As in the nineteenth century, legislators sometimes saw fit to try to tighten judicial standards for insanity when courts did not move quickly enough to suit public demands that "the insanity dodge" be either eliminated or at least drastically narrowed. But if psychiatrists had not succeeded in convincing policymakers or the public that they, rather than courts or legislatures, should be the sole authority on mental illness, psychiatrists at least had inserted themselves into courtrooms as an indispensable presence.

Psychiatric testimony had become a vital but highly controversial aspect of many types of trials by the end of the twentieth century. Psychiatric expertise had become so widely accepted in courtrooms that mental-health experts were employed not only in those rarer, high-profile cases where a defendant pleaded not guilty by reason of insanity to a charge of murder, but also in more everyday cases such as ones involving child custody. Psychiatrists clearly had an important role as expert witnesses in cases inside courtrooms, but they also functioned within the legal system in more subtle ways. They worked with prison populations on a daily basis, for example, treating persons for mental illness.

In serving the mental-health needs of incarcerated persons, psychiatrists had conflicting loyalties. On one hand, they were often prison officials, holding positions such as associate warden within the penal system. On the other hand, they had duties of care toward their patients. Those responsibilities—to preserve authority on one hand and to provide care on the other—sometimes brought prison psychiatrists into medicolegal controversies. The increasing availability of new types of drugs to treat mental illnesses and an increasing willingness among the medical community to apply drug therapies to mental disorders such as psychosis, for example, brought complaints by prisoners that drugs were being employed not merely for therapeutic purposes but to ensure inmate control. Courts thus sometimes had to examine psychiatrists' authority to recommend that prisoners receive drug therapies—particularly antipsychotic drugs—that were against a prisoner's wishes. In the 1990 case of *Washington, et al., Petitioners v. Walter Harper,* for example, the U.S. Supreme Court ruled that the state of Washington's procedural safeguards for the involuntary administration of antipsychotic drugs were adequate. The state had set up a special unit in its Corrections Department for diagnosing and treating mentally ill state prisoners. It had a written policy providing for hearings to be held on decisions about involuntary medication of prisoners. After reviewing that policy, the Supreme Court held that it did not violate the Fourteenth Amendment guarantees of due process. Justices Stevens, Brennan, and Marshall, while agreeing in part with the majority, also voiced concern that to force a prisoner to take drugs against his or her will on the basis of "purely institutional concerns" was an unwarranted intrusion on the "integrity of the inmate's body and mind" (*Washington v. Walter Harper* 1990, 249–250). To maintain order inside the prison, the doctor (a psychiatrist) might have to force his patient to accept treatment; courts would bow to that necessity, but with reservations.

This decision and others concerning the rights of prisoners to obtain or refuse psychiatric treatment in the 1990s brought judges to a reexamination of a key question concerning the authority of medical professionals. It is a question that is considered later, in the section entitled "The Law Shapes Medical Practice: Court Decisions and Medicine": At what point should courts limit medical practitioners' scope of actions toward their patients when patients' bodily autonomy is compromised? The answer that courts historically had given to that query was a complicated response that changed over time during the twentieth century. Courts' regulation of the medical decisions of healthcare providers at first was deferential; that is, courts recognized physicians' growing ability to organize themselves as professionals and deferred to their professional judgment on certain issues, such as the administration of anesthesia. But courts did not grant medical authorities—particularly physicians—unlimited discretion in relation to their medical treatment of patients. In a series of decisions in the early and mid-twentieth century, judicial rulings warned physicians that courts would oversee the medical community to make certain that patients gave informed consent to medical procedures, including not just surgeries and drug therapies but also tests and other medical actions that involved patient autonomy.

At about the same time in the late nineteenth and early twentieth centuries that courts were first recognizing medical authority in a legal setting, they also were grappling with a more technical question: Exactly how should medical testimony be admitted and assessed within courtrooms? As we have seen in Chapter 2, at the turn of the twentieth century, the proponents of an expanded medical examinership were just beginning to have an impact in making their own courtroom testimony credible. And although psychiatric testimony already had established itself as important in judicial settings by the early twentieth century, other forms of medical expertise were by no means inevitable in trials in that era. Medicine did not have a regular place within courtrooms as a field that commanded respect. In particular, courts had no bias toward the testimony of medical experts (except perhaps psychiatrists and some forensic pathologists) and no mechanisms for distinguishing between conflicting testimonies from medical experts. Even more importantly, courts generally heard arguments that were legal in nature, rather than contentions based on the experiences and principles of medical or scientific professionals. Medicine, that is, was only sporadically important within the courtroom. That situation changed beginning with a rather unlikely episode—a case involving the working hours of women, in which a young attorney attempted a novel strategy when presenting his arguments before the Supreme Court.

New Uses of Medical Evidence

A key moment in the use of medical evidence in U.S. courtrooms was the development and acceptance of the "Brandeis brief" in 1908. In challenging the practice of allowing women workers to be employed for long periods of time while performing physically demanding tasks, young attorney Louis Brandeis pursued a novel strategy. Following Justice Oliver Wendell Holmes's philosophy that the life of the law was not logic, but experience, Brandeis hoped to convince the U.S. Supreme Court that Oregon's regulations on the working hours of female workers were constitutional. He had to make his case in spite of recent Supreme Court decisions that seemed to point to the Court's disapproval of such progressive legislation. One of those decisions, *Lochner v. New York* (1905), had undermined the operation of a New York law regulating bakers' hours on the grounds that the law was an interference with workers' freedom of contract under the Fourteenth Amendment. Brandeis found a way to distinguish his case, *Muller v. Oregon,* from *Lochner.* He made a pithy argument that the Fourteenth Amendment forbade states from interfering with liberty of contract only in instances when the state could not demonstrate that it had reasonable concerns about workers' health or safety—the very concerns that had inspired the regulatory legislation. Brandeis proposed to show the Supreme Court that Oregon was acting in a reasonable fashion when it limited women workers' hours (whereas presumably New York had not in *Lochner*). Backed by a group of dedicated researchers who scoured library records for two weeks prior to his appearance before the Supreme Court, Brandeis marshaled evidence from historical and contemporary sources that purported to prove women were harmed by working too long in physically demanding settings.

The section of Brandeis's brief that included medical and scientific findings about the deleterious effects of work on women's health ran to about one hundred pages. This was in contrast to his legal argument on the distinction between *Lochner* and the present case, which consumed only about two pages. Much of Brandeis's evidence was from physicians who had testified before Britain's parliament at the time of the passage of the factory acts of 1833 and 1844. Again and again in that testimony, physicians affirmed their observation that working for long hours at repetitious tasks was harmful to women and children. One hundred years later, such observations would appear simplistic to both physicians and social reformers; factory work was deleterious to persons of both genders. But in England in its heyday of industrial growth in the 1830s, as well as in the United States in Brandeis's day, in order to demonstrate the physical strain caused by factory labor, factory reformers first had to show labor's effects on presumably the most vulnerable members of the population.

Highly innovative, Brandeis's brief also proved convincing. Not only did the high court decide in favor of Brandeis's clients, but Brandeis's method of arguing his case, with great reliance on medical, scientific, sociological, and economic data, became widely accepted. In a variety of subsequent cases (including landmark decisions such as *Brown v. Board of Education of Topeka, Kansas* in 1954), lawyers relied on masses of data to support their arguments, and the Supreme Court endorsed such "fact-based" jurisprudence.

Courts refined their trust in such evidence, however, in several subsequent decisions. The case of *Frye v. United States* (1923) established the requirement that medical and scientific authorities recognize the methods used to arrive at any conclusions used in testimony in order for that testimony to be taken as expert. That is, the Supreme Court set up a test for the validity of scientific expert testimony—the *Frye* standard—that was based on the general acceptance within the general scientific community of the science being relied upon. This requirement would remain in force for half a century. Not until the end of the twentieth century, in *Daubert v. Merrell Dow Pharmaceuticals* (1993), were judges allowed much discretion in going beyond the word of expert witnesses. Under the "sound methodology" test enunciated in *Daubert*, however, federal judges might examine the evidence themselves to determine its validity, rather than relying on an assessment of general scientific acceptance.

In a series of cases in the late nineteenth and early twentieth centuries, then, medicine made inroads in U.S courtrooms, especially because of courts' recognition of the value of psychiatric testimony in insanity trials and the judicial acceptance of fact-based (and often medicine-based) jurisprudence as a form of argument. By the 1920s, the question was not whether medicine would be employed within courtrooms but exactly how medical knowledge was to be utilized and assessed. Courts' widespread acceptance of the Brandeis brief and the adoption of the *Frye* standard indicated that courts henceforth would be employing the terminology of medicine and would rely heavily on medical experts and medical data in a variety of cases.

The Law Shapes Medical Practice: Court Decisions and Medicine

We already have seen in Chapter 2 that in the twentieth century, medicine became a crucial aspect of criminal trials, chiefly because of the role of forensic pathologists as gatekeepers to the trial process. In the argument presented in the previous section of this chapter, we also have pointed to medicine's impact on courtroom testimony and evidence. But what impact did medicine's exposure to the legal system have upon medical practice and the medical profession? The answer changes with the time period being considered. The early nineteenth-century American medical community was known at the time, and has been considered by historians since, as poorly trained, disorganized, and held in low esteem by the public. In the later nineteenth century, therefore, courts appeared simply to support a medical profession that was reforming itself from a rather unimpressive history. As the twentieth century progressed, however, courts took an increasingly critical view of medicine and its practitioners. Ironically, that criticism—and courts' increasing willingness to take an active role in regulating medicine—were partially grounded in medicine's own successes. That is, as medicine purported to discover more answers to problems of disease and injury, those supposed remedies and cures in turn created dilemmas for courts and for American society at large.

Licensing

The medical profession was growing more self-aware, professional, and organized in the second half of the nineteenth century. In part, this change was based on new perceptions of physicians' social status, as well as their professional achievements. In the eighteenth and early nineteenth centuries, American doctors were notably similar to their patients in socioeconomic background, and they emphasized that similarity with an attitude of circumspection and modesty toward their patients. By the end of the 1800s, however, medical practitioners were drawing upon a new sense of prestige that affected other professional groups (such as lawyers). That prestige came out of a realization that in a complex and rapidly changing society—especially one that was becoming quite urban—citizens had to rely on the talents of specialists rather than the goodwill of their communities and the healing skills of their neighbors to serve their physical needs. In addition, medical practitioners basked in the favor of the public toward new technology and scientific advancement in general. When they were seen as representatives of science, physicians appeared to many to be agents of progressive change as well as experts in medical matters—in contrast to other types of practitioners such as faith healers, herbalists, and midwives. Increasingly, physicians were separating themselves from their patients in terms of family background, educational experience, and wealth. Ironically, while they now tended to see their physicians as less approachable, patients perceived doctors as more respectable and knowledgeable.

One key method of announcing their new focus on scientific training and methodology, as well as touting their superiority to other forms of healthcare providers, was for physicians (newly organized into professional groups such as state and local medical societies) to approach state governments and request licensing as medical practitioners. Licensure of professionals was not a new concept. In fact, licensing had been a feature of eighteenth-century governmental regulation of many fields, including law and medicine. Not simply professionals but many other occupational groups (some of them occasionally in competition with medical personnel, such as barbers and embalmers) asked for and got state licensing for their own trades in the 1700s. Licensure had fallen into disrepute in the Jacksonian era (1828–1850), however, for several reasons—among them a popular distrust of favoritism toward not only medical specialists, but also any other "monopolies" on trade or knowledge. In addition, the public looked upon medical licensure for a time with some cynicism because obtaining a medical license in the early nineteenth century often was automatic for anyone who managed to graduate from a medical school, and most medical schools in that era were notorious for their poor quality of medical training. Thus many states actually repealed or took all of the teeth out of their licensure laws during the second quarter of the 1800s.

But from the 1850s and 1860s onward, medicine was beginning to establish itself as a profession and a science, and state licensure was one way of announcing a new commitment to enhancing medicine's prestige with the public. Physicians' groups were keen to set their own standards for licensing; these groups saw state licensure as a means to set themselves apart from (and above) other medical professionals, such as nurses and pharmacists. Of course licensing was not the only means to the goal of physicians' asserting dominance as medical practitioners. Simply within their institutional settings (such as hospitals, where they increasingly were in residence), physicians proved successful in making clear that they expected deference from nursing staffs. As professional rivals, physicians faced greater resistance from pharmacists, who had been accustomed to prescribing medications for patients for years and disliked handing that authority to doctors. Still, the trend toward professional dominance by doctors was clear.

It is important to note that the state licensure requirements generally were initiated and drafted neither by the public nor by state authorities per se, but rather by the medical groups themselves. Self-definition of licensure rules was, in fact, a key component of nineteenth-century medicine's drive for professional recognition. And yet the very fact that the state was formally in charge of licensure meant that states in theory were exercising authority over the health and welfare of their citizens through regulation of medical practitioners. In the late nineteenth and early twentieth centuries, that state oversight of citizens' physical well-being was the constitutional basis of a series of state and federal courts' rulings favoring licensing.

In the case of *Dent v. West Virginia* (1889), the U.S. Supreme Court affirmed West Virginia's law that required physicians to obtain a certificate from the state. Eleven years later, Wisconsin's Supreme

Court—like courts in many other states—issued a similar ruling in *The State ex rel. Kellogg v. Currens and the Wisconsin Board of Medical Examiners* (1901). The *Dent* and *Kellogg* cases involved challenges to those states' certification laws, with plaintiffs arguing that states really were establishing licensure requirements. This proved a hard argument to sustain. Most early licensure laws set certification rules that were hardly burdensome. In West Virginia, for example, the state certificate was issued to mark a physician's graduation from a medical school, his continuous practice within the state for ten years, or his receipt of certification from a medical board of examiners of his competency to practice medicine. Wisconsin required physicians to pass a licensing examination given by a state medical board and to pay a small fee.

This trend of licensure constituting merely a superficial requirement began to change as the turn of the century neared. In the U.S. Supreme Court decision of *Hawker v. New York* (1898), the Court ruled that a state board of medical licensure could enforce a "character" requirement for medical certification, thus giving state licensing authorities even broader powers to limit entry into the medical profession. As is evident in data cited by the Court in that decision, many states already had implemented a regulation that persons who had been convicted of a felony (like the plaintiff in the *Hawker* case) were barred from the practice of medicine.

By the end of the first quarter of the twentieth century, state medical licensure requirements were much more substantial and meaningful than the earlier, superficial qualifications. Courts allowed states to set medical licensing requirements that included graduation from an accredited medical, pharmacy, or nursing school. In turn, medical schools set their own standards for admission, continuation, and graduation, and courts upheld those requirements in most cases. The courts, that is, supported the state's allowing the medical profession control over its own membership. That control by the medical profession extended not only to medical schools in the strict sense, but also to training facilities in general.

With the growth of hospitals as institutions that provided places for doctors to practice and learn, many nineteenth- and twentieth-century physicians (particularly specialists) found that being associated with those institutions was not only advisable but also necessary for their professional success. As with medical training in educational programs, courts generally viewed hospitals (institutions that provided continuing professional training for physicians) as fully capable of setting their own rules about physician affiliation. Thus, physicians' control of their profession was extended by the courts to include hospital settings. Doctors not only maintained authority over entry into their profession, they also dominated the physical setting in which they worked, and courts supported the physicians' governance.

The early twentieth century, therefore, was an era when physicians were increasingly flushed with their success. For not only were they earning much larger incomes and greater respect as specialists in healthcare, but medical doctors increasingly were equated in the public's mind with science and professionalism. Furthermore, states' licensure requirements and the courts' upholding of the rules of professional licensing affirmed and protected their new status. This latter benefit—protection—was especially important to the growing dominance of medical practitioners over healthcare. Scientifically trained doctors were not the only healthcare option available. Throughout the nineteenth century and even the twentieth century, alternative forms of medical practice vied with traditional medicine for acceptance and influence. It was therefore particularly important in the short term that physicians' licensure requirements made their own qualifications appear superior to those of competitors—chiefly practitioners of the so-called alternative forms of medicine.

Alternative Medical Practices

When states regulated the health and welfare of their residents by setting up licensure requirements for medicine in the late 1800s, they inevitably made choices as to acceptable and hence unacceptable forms of medical training and practice. Those preferences by the state in turn inspired suits by persons who wished to engage in nontraditional (or, in more modern parlance, alternative) medical practices. Both practitioners and patients of alternative approaches challenged state licensure laws, not only in the era in which those laws were implemented, but also throughout the twentieth century, as newer forms of alternative medical practices were developed.

In part, the courts' handling of cases concerning alternative medical practices was a by-product of a debate about the "duty of care" that physicians owed their patients (a debate that is discussed in more detail in the next section of this chapter, concerning standards of care for physicians). In another respect, however, courts heard cases concerning alternative practitioners simply under the rubric of defining and enforcing the states' police powers.

In the late nineteenth and early twentieth centuries, when most states set up their licensing requirements for medical practitioners, courts considered cases involving unlicensed practitioners. In the leading Supreme Court case of *Dent v. West Virginia* (discussed previously in this chapter), for example, the appellant, Frank Dent, was challenging West Virginia's licensure requirements that, he argued, unfairly prohibited him from practicing medicine. Dent's difficulty with the licensing board was that he had obtained his medical degree from a nontraditional medical school—one that taught a form of medicine called Eclecticism. The Eclectics shared with traditional medical doctors most ideas about the functioning of the human body, although they tended to rely more on herbal remedies and less on manufactured drugs. But the Eclectics also had a reputation as politically and socially radical; their medical schools admitted women, for example. When the state's Board of Health refused to recognize Dent's diploma from an Eclectic medical college, he took his case before the courts, arguing that the licensure laws unfairly kept him from earning an income in his chosen (and legal) profession. The courts, citing the necessity of states' being able to protect the public health, affirmed Dent's right to make a living, yet ruled that that right was outweighed by the state's interest in citizens' welfare.

Other alternative practitioners found their scope of practice severely limited by states' licensure laws. Thus, when confronted with tougher licensing requirements, many alternative medical providers either had to move to a state that had more lax requirements, or they had to obtain traditional medical qualifications in addition to their unorthodox training. Besides the Eclectics, practitioners of homeopathy and osteopathy were especially hard hit by licensure. Homeopaths, who advocated treatments for disorders with small quantities of the substance that was causing the affliction, also placed emphasis on close communication between patient and care provider. Homeopathy, therefore, went against the grain of late nineteenth-century medical science in two respects. More mainstream medicine was then focused on "curing" diseases through medicines that counteracted the effects of disorders rather than underlining them as homeopathy did. Homeopathy's focus on close contact with patients by practitioners also was in conflict with the trend for regular physicians to be less interactive with patients on a daily basis; physicians were acting more in the role of consultative specialists. In the late nineteenth century, there were two other well-known types of alternative practitioners: osteopaths and chiropractors. Those healers focused on the understanding of the human body as a mechanism. They argued that good health could be achieved by successful "manipulation" of that machine's various parts. To regular medical practitioners, osteopathy and chiropractic were too mechanistic and did not rely enough upon drug therapies and surgeries.

Some of the alternative practitioners eventually tried to make their peace with traditional medicine. Despite their early opposition to licensure laws, Eclectics and homeopaths eventually decided that, instead of challenge licensing requirements, they would join with regular physicians on state boards and seek to influence regular medicine to adopt some of their principles. That tactic was only partially successful. In many states by the end of the twentieth century, homeopaths still were fighting for recognition of the legitimacy of their ideas. Homeopaths could not obtain licenses in some states; in *State v. Hinze* (1989), for example, the Supreme Court of Nebraska ruled that state regulations against a homeopath practicing any medicine at all could stand. Furthermore, if a regularly licensed physician leaned toward homeopathy in his or her practice, that traditional doctor might find himself or herself censured or even removed from medical practice by a state medical board for diverging too far from current medical practices. In the case of *In re Guess* (1992), the U.S. Supreme Court ruled that it was within the state's police power to safeguard public health by holding its medical licensees to certain standards of professional practice. (Dr. Guess was a regularly licensed physician who was accused by North Carolina of in effect becoming a homeopath; the state took away his license to practice medicine.) The *Guess* case was an important decision because it underlined state regulatory power over medicine in spite of the fact that no harm had been inflicted upon the allegedly erring physicians' patients—several of whom supported the practitioner in legal actions against the state.

Chiropractors and osteopaths chose to remain outside the licensure system in the early twentieth century; it was a decision that carried risk, for most states took a long time to grant licensure privileges to nonmainstream practitioners. (Chiropractors, interestingly, gloried in their "illegality," and for a time the very term *chiropractic* was associated with rebellion against the status quo.) And although many states in the late twentieth century eventually did expand the types of medical personnel who could be licensed, the states still retained control over the licensing procedures and the practices of alternative and "complementary" practitioners such as massage therapists, acupuncturists, practitioners of Eastern medicine, and homeopaths. Increasingly, these alternative forms of medicine were becoming very popular with the public, not usually as the only forms of medical treatment employed by patients, but as a supplement (hence the term *complementary*) to traditional medical care.

Alternative medicine's popularity was reflected in legal changes in licensure. By the late twentieth century, many states allowed persons trained in alternative medicine to obtain licenses. Even chiropractic was legal in every state by the year 2000. When states regulated alternative practitioners, however, they often made clear that nontraditional medical personnel had to stay strictly within their specialties. This could be a difficult rule for alternative practitioners to adhere to in practice, for unconventional healers often acknowledged the efficacy of other nontraditional approaches. Ultimately, licensing did empower alternative practitioners and give more freedom to patients who sought such nonmainstream treatments. But at the same time, states still remained in control over entry into medical practice, even in the instances when they allowed alternative forms of medicine to exist.

Still another type of alternative medical practitioner that emerged during the late 1800s presented an interesting quandary for the licensing process and thus for the states that oversaw licensure and the courts that heard cases about it. Christian Science was an organization founded by Mary Baker Eddy in Boston in 1879. Eddy and her followers taught that healing could not be effected by regular medicine because disease was caused by sin. Thus Christian Scientists believed that, rather than depending on regular physicians, they should consult healers who employed faith and prayer. Christian Science "practitioners" received training in prayer rather than in medical technology. Christian Science health facilities provided physical care such as room and board for persons in those facilities, but they did not rely on medicines, surgeries, or modern medical devices for healing. Here, clearly, was a fundamental conflict for states as they regulated citizens' physical welfare. How could a state prohibit the practice of healing when that practice also was grounded in the free exercise of religion?

It was very fortunate for Christian Science that it developed at exactly the same time that licensure for medicine was becoming an issue in state legislatures—in the second half of the nineteenth century. Many states did decide, in instituting or strengthening their medical licensing requirements in the late 1800s, that they could not interfere with the Christian Scientists' First Amendment right to practice their religion, in which the power of healing through spirituality was a key principle. Thus most states early on set up a special category for Christian Science practitioners as healthcare providers, effectively placing them outside the requirements that medical practitioners had to be trained and certified in certain traditional ways.

Courts in turn allowed such a distinction, but this caused further legal complications. The exemption from regular medical licensing requirements for Christian Scientist practitioners created demands for exceptions by other "faith healers." The courts, however, generally allowed the states to distinguish between Christian Science (which had its own requirements and qualifications for authorized practitioners) and various other persons who wished to obtain drugless practitioner certificates. In the 1917 case of *Crane v. Johnson,* for example, the U.S. Supreme Court refused to acknowledge that the plaintiff (a non–Christian Scientist who employed "prayer and hope" in the treatment of disease) had been denied equal protection under the Fourteenth Amendment by California's requirement of drugless healing certification.

And yet despite its special (some would argue privileged) status with state authorities and courts as a faith-based type of medical practitioner, a status that has lasted over a century, the Church of Christ, Scientist continues to be a party to cases involving the states' regulation of medical treatment. Since the late nineteenth century, representatives of Christian Science have argued successfully in court that their beliefs (centered on healing) constitute a religion and thus are deserving of First Amendment protection as a formal religious organization. And yet although many states did allow exceptions for Christian Science healers under their licensure requirements, these states did not exempt Christian Scientists from other aspects of state law. For example, how should Christian Science practices be viewed by the state when they appear to place the health and welfare of citizens at risk? Such a question often put Christian Science firmly in opposition to conventional medical practitioners, who argued that Christian Science was not only unwise but often dangerous in failing to take advantage of modern medicine. Courts and state authorities generally approached such situations with a light touch. Both state officials and judges were reluctant to interfere with the freedom of citizens to practice their religious beliefs. They hesitated to interfere with the practice of faith healing, especially in connection with a religious group with a long history of defending those beliefs in court.

But there were situations when states did intervene in Christian Science medical practice and where courts upheld that intervention. States stepped in to protect the physical welfare of children whose parents invoked Christian Science in shunning conventional medical treatments; in such cases, the states and the courts once again made clear their preference for regular medical practices and practitioners over alternative medicine (in this case Christian Science). In a controversy with wide implications for other states, the Court of Appeals of Florida, Second District, heard the appeal of a married couple who had been convicted of causing the death of their daughter when they employed Christian Science healing techniques rather than resorting to modern medicine. The child had diabetes, a disorder that medical experts at the parents' trial testified was easily treatable and rarely fatal if treated in a timely fashion. Medical testimony also established that the child had been ill for months, and that even within hours of her death she might have been saved if the parents had taken her for mainstream medical treatment. The parents, William and Christine Hermanson, both were well-educated persons who readily would have had access to good conventional medical care.

When the State of Florida first accused them of child abuse and then prosecuted them for the child's death, the Hermansons claimed their right to practice their religion superseded the state's interest in protecting their daughter from death. The Florida appeals court noted that the Hermansons were sincere in religious belief but nonetheless upheld their convictions for murder. Their beliefs were defensible, the court held, but their conduct under Florida law endangered the life of the child. As that case, *Hermanson v. Florida* (1990), made clear, Christian Scientists might practice faith healing freely as adults, but the state could require that parents avail themselves of medically conventional treatments for children.

The status of Christian Science treatment facilities that received Medicare and Medicaid funds came under scrutiny in the case of *Children's Healthcare is a Legal Duty, Inc., v. Vladeck* (1996). The plaintiff was an organization that had been founded to challenge the many exemptions in state laws implemented throughout the twentieth century that had been granted to Christian Science practitioners and institutions. (The group's founders included a man whose estranged wife was a Christian Scientist who wanted to rear their children according to her beliefs.) In the case at hand, the plaintiff went after an even larger target; Children's Healthcare challenged a set of exemptions for Christian Science sanitoria that were found in the federal Medicare and Medicaid laws. For example, Christian Science facilities were not subject to reviews of their practitioners' professional performance. They also were not required to assure patients that treatment was being performed in a cost-effective manner or only when medically necessary, whereas other hospitals and skilled nursing facilities had to make those assertions to their patients.

Although it was sensitive to the arguments made by the defendants on behalf of their free exercise of religion, the court concluded that the Medicare and Medicaid acts impermissibly accommodated the religion of Christian Science by singling out Christian Science for exemptions not given to other religious groups that operated healthcare facilities. The court reminded lawmakers that there was a "basic constitutional requirement of neutrality in religions" (*Children's Healthcare v. Vladeck* 1996, 1485). In spite of the sincerity of a religious group's beliefs about the healing power of faith, for lawmakers to bestow special privileges upon one sect was unconstitutional. That decision was a very serious blow to the status historically enjoyed by Christian Science as an alternative medical practice.

Thus despite several spirited challenges to licensure laws throughout the twentieth century, the U.S. Supreme Court, as well as courts at state and lower federal levels, has generally upheld licensing requirements by states that favor traditional medical practitioners, such as physicians and licensed nurses. The courts have strictly enforced state laws mandating that only licensed practitioners can offer medical treatment and have refused to accept arguments by alternative practitioners that licensure damaged their right to earn a living. In general, although courts recently have permitted state licensing and regulation of alternative medical practices and have allowed a key exception for Christian Science practices among individual adults, judicial rulings have shown a preference that more traditional medical authorities should remain firmly in control of American medicine.

Standards of Care: Informed Consent and Malpractice

The professionalization of medicine under state authority came with a cost for medical practitioners. As experts who were licensed by the state, physicians in the twentieth century were held to increasingly higher standards of behavior and practice. (Suits for malpractice by patients were not new in American society. In fact, historians have argued that there was a "malpractice crisis" in the 1840s caused in part by the very poor reputation of the medical profession in the early part of the nineteenth century.) But licensure—which was initiated by physicians as a means of winning the public's trust—actually seemed to provoke more malpractice suits than ever.

There also was a more technical basis for malpractice suits against physicians continuing at a high level, even after licensure became better accepted. The use of anesthetics beginning in the mid–nineteenth century allowed physicians to perform more skilled surgeries on badly injured limbs—limbs that previously would have been simply amputated. Thus patients began to have the prospect of saving their limbs through a doctor's action. In the recent past, most patients would have accepted the loss of limbs and would have been grateful to be alive at all. Now, raised expectations about medical success caused some patients to sue physicians for malpractice when surgery on limbs did not yield perfect results—and most surgeries still did not, in part due to problems of infection. Suits concerning injured limbs that did not heal properly after surgery were a large category among malpractice actions in the late 1800s and were the basis of several leading judicial decisions concerning the standards of care that courts said the physicians ought to exercise toward their patients.

In the second half of the nineteenth century, courts began to demand that physicians demonstrate that they were acting within commonly accepted professional standards of care in treating their patients. If physicians did not come up to those standards, courts said they might be sued successfully for malpractice. At first glance, this may have appeared to create a wide opening for successful malpractice actions against physicians, and in fact courts' theoretical stance in enforcing professional standards of care did encourage some patients to sue. But those suits increasingly were thwarted when they reached court because of another judicial principle connected to malpractice actions: the locality rule.

In the late nineteenth century, courts articulated a local standard of care for physicians known as the locality rule. According to the locality rule, doctors were expected to exercise the skills and engage in the practices that were common in local communities similar to their own. A rural physician, for example, would be held to a different (usually lower) standard of care in serving his patients than a practitioner in a large and wealthy community such as New York or Boston. The locality rule first was expressed in state court decisions—among them the highly representative *Gramm v. Boener* (1877) and *Small v. Howard* (1880), argued in Indiana and Massachusetts, respectively, but soon adopted across the nation. (Those two cases were based on fact situations that were common as the genesis of malpractice actions in the nineteenth century—improper healing after an injury to a limb.)

The locality rule had important implications for the success of malpractice actions, for it meant that the most direct way to assemble evidence against a physician whom one was suing would have been to obtain testimony from his colleagues within the immediate vicinity. Because the late nineteenth century was a time when physicians placed emphasis on joining with one another in local and state medical societies (in part to get the state to pass licensure laws!), physicians were quite likely to know and associate with one another and to identify strongly with their peers. Thus, gathering evidence from physicians against their allegedly negligent colleagues became increasingly difficult for patients who alleged that doctors had departed from the usual standards of care. The patient's task in proving malpractice became even more challenging when local and state medical organizations put together legal-defense funds that were dedicated to opposing malpractice suits. Those funds proved extremely successful in defending doctors in state after state. Probably without intending to do so, the courts had articulated a rule that worked very much to the benefit of physicians defending themselves against malpractice actions.

In the influential case of *Pike v. Honsinger* (1898), for example, a New York court heard an appeal concerning the case of a rural physician who (like so many physicians in this era) had failed to ensure the complete healing of a broken limb—in this case, a part of the knee. In their decision, the judges affirmed the locality rule. To defend themselves against malpractice charges, the court in this case ruled, doctors had to demonstrate that they did not depart from usual standards of good care among the local medical profession. In this case, the "reasonable care and diligence" expected of a physician—a usual phrase in such cases—referred not only to the physician's treatment of his patient for a broken patella, but also to his warnings to the patient about subsequent use of the injured knee. The court added a corollary to the locality rule as well, one that had the effect of making malpractice actions still less likely to succeed. Discussing the concept of reasonable care and diligence, the judges noted that physicians did not have to exhibit extraordinary skill or talent in order to be providing adequate care to patients. Doctors, in other words, did not have to be geniuses at their job to effectively provide reasonable care; merely making a good-faith effort was all that reasonably could be expected.

For courts to mandate that doctors should exercise reasonable care seemed a sensible standard. It was a standard that was easy to enforce when physicians fit the profile of the physician/defendant in *Pike v. Honsinger*—that is, when doctors were treating their patients in uncomplicated settings such as homes or local offices. But as many physicians in the later nineteenth century began to focus their practices within hospitals, the relationship between doctors and patients became much more complicated. Within hospitals, patient care involved additional parties beyond merely the physician himself, including particularly members of the hospital's nursing staff, as well as other physicians and surgeons. Those other medical personnel were not only serving as supplemental healthcare providers beyond a patient's personal physician, they also were performing much more complex procedures within the institutional setting than could be offered in an individual doctor's office.

The medical procedure most closely associated with hospitals, then as now, was surgery. Until the nineteenth century, surgery had been extremely dangerous and almost unbelievably painful, but that was beginning to change during the 1800s. The first negative aspect of surgery to be eliminated, through the development of anesthesia, was the pain of the operation itself. Anesthesia was an exceptionally promising medical innovation. But anesthesia also posed a number of interesting and difficult issues for the courts when patients sued in cases involving its use. In several anesthetics controversies that will be discussed later in this chapter, courts made important rulings concerning physicians' duties of care toward their patients as well as patients' consent to medical procedures.

The most common inhaled anesthetics, ether and chloroform, were fairly new and poorly understood in the late nineteenth century. Hence, despite some of the terrible surgical experiences endured by patients in the days before anesthetics, nineteenth-century physicians often hesitated to employ anesthesia for major surgeries. Their reasons were sound. Physicians knew that to open the body was to expose patients to terrible risks of infection. This was particularly the case when operating on the chest, abdomen, and head—sections of the body where internal organs would be exposed and thus put at risk. Given doctors' limited understanding of antisepsis and asepsis at that time (knowledge that only became widely acknowledged following Joseph Lister's work in the late nineteenth century), physicians were justified in their nervousness about the major surgeries that anesthesia theoretically had made possible.

But if anesthesia worried physicians, it terrified many members of the public. Far from providing the assurance of a pain-free operation, anesthesia conjured up for some patients the spectacle of surgeries that were far too risky (in more modern terms, even "experimental") and that carried with them the real threat of postoperative infection. Furthermore, the public perceived anesthetics as medical tools so fully within the control of physicians that their misuse easily could be covered up. When deaths under anesthesia occurred within hospital operating rooms in the course of surgeries, the only witnesses to the operations often were medical personnel, individuals who tended to close ranks and refuse to testify against their colleagues in cases of malpractice. Raising fears about the dangers of anesthetics at an inquest and alleging a cover-up by medical doctors in hospitals are minor tasks compared to proving medical negligence in the trial of such a case.

Despite those difficulties, or perhaps because of them, during the late nineteenth and early twentieth centuries, courts did decide several cases concerning anesthesia, but those cases were not usually concerned with deaths. Rather they arose over issues of patient control in regard to surgical procedures being performed. Some of these cases were related to allegations that doctors had used anesthesia without patients' consent. Other suits stemmed from charges that physicians had failed to secure patients' permission for additional procedures, beyond those authorized, that were performed once patients were under the influence of anesthesia. In either case, during the time when anesthesia still was comparatively new, U.S. courts reinforced the paternalism that inspired physicians to operate without patients' knowledge or full consent.

In the case of *Bennan v. Parsonnet* (1912), for example, the Supreme Court of New Jersey decided that a surgeon who had operated to repair a patient's hernia should not have been penalized for malpractice. The surgeon had told the patient that he was going to repair a hernia on one side; while the patient was anesthetized the surgeon discovered a much more serious hernia on the other side and decided to repair it first. In the face of a common-law tradition that seemed to demand patient consent, the judges noted that anesthesia had altered medical practice so much as to require a change in the judge-made law. The court dismissed as irrational the notion that a surgeon should refuse to take lifesaving action because he could not obtain the patient's consent to the specific operation that the surgeon was undertaking:

> The question, however, is one to be settled not by authority but by reason, and its importance is such that it touches at a vital point the interests of the entire public, any member of which may at any time suffer in life or health by the establishment of a rule that will paralyze the judgment of the surgeon and require him to withhold his skill and wisdom at the very juncture when they are most needed, and when, could the patient have been consulted, he would manifestly have insisted upon their being exercised on his behalf. (*Bennan v. Parsonnet* 1912, 27)

In making that determination, the judges in *Bennan v. Parsonnet* unquestionably came down on the side of medical discretion in emergency surgical situations.

In the 1920s, courts still were granting physicians considerable authority to make decisions about the need for surgical procedures when time was a factor and when patient consent could not be obtained. For instance, in the case of *McGuire v. Rix*, a Nebraska court echoed the conclusion from *Bennan v. Parsonnet* that anesthesia had created a change in the older common-law rule that surgeons always had to secure consent. In *Rix*, the court considered the case of a woman who was operated upon for a severe leg fracture. The patient thought she was under anesthetic merely for the purpose of having the leg set; instead the surgeon performed a far more complex operation, for which the recovery time and the complications were much greater. The appeals court decided that patient McGuire could not recover the $100,000 in damages that she initially was awarded by the trial court. The appeals court remarked that if such a malpractice verdict were allowed to stand, it would considerably dampen the enthusiasm of surgeons for operating in emergency situations. It also would be a serious curb on medical discretion, the court reasoned, for a surgeon not to be able to rely on his best medical judgment. Once a patient was unconscious and the surgery had begun, the surgeon might discover circumstances that he had not first anticipated when he initially had obtained consent for a less complex procedure.

Such decisions about emergency situations involving obtaining patients' permission for surgery, however, were not the norm in medical practice. It was much more usual for surgeons to be able to predict what they would find once a patient was on the operating table. In those normal situations, courts held to a much simpler standard: they insisted on informed consent to the procedures. The judicial reasoning was straightforward: as medical knowledge became more specialized, courts decided that doctors had an increasingly greater burden of making patients aware of the aspects of care that patients could not, as laypeople, know about.

In the early twentieth century, that is, courts began to insist that since medical treatment was becoming more scientific, physicians had a greater responsibility for securing consent from their patients for all medical procedures, including surgery. In the well-known case of *Schloendorff v.The Society of the New York Hospital* (1914), the U.S. Supreme Court made a strong statement about the necessity of surgeons obtaining informed consent. The decision also was a ringing declaration of patients' rights to the autonomy of their bodies—a clear message to the medical profession that their professional authority had real limits, which courts could prescribe.

Mary Schloendorff, already a patient in a hospital, was told by a staff physician that she had a fibroid tumor that must be examined and that the examination had to be performed while she was anesthetized. She consented to receive ether and undergo the examination, but said plainly that she did not want to be operated upon. A surgeon removed the tumor while she was under the anesthetic. Schloendorff claimed numerous health problems developed as a result of complications from the unauthorized surgery, and she sued the hospital for damages. The court did not allow Schloendorff to recover damages from the hospital, noting how detrimental such a finding would be to charitable institutions' financial welfare. The court did state in the strongest terms, however, that Schloendorff's attending physician was liable not only for negligence, but for committing an assault.

Within a few years after the *Schloendorff* decision so forcefully warned physicians about the limits of their discretion in performing surgical procedures, courts added another twist to suits for medical malpractice. They enunciated standards for the acceptance of expert testimony of a scientific nature. Those judicial principles governing scientific and medical testimony (as discussed earlier with respect to the *Frye* decision of 1923) were predicated on the idea that among the scientific and medical communities there was an identifiable body of knowledge that many physicians across the nation shared. Thus, as a result of *Frye*, medical practitioners could and did begin to testify in court about the generally accepted standards of care in their particular specialties. Those national standards of care were limited to standards within specialties, because courts as well as physicians agreed that although *medical knowledge* could be imparted to most practitioners, certain *skills* in the performance of medical duties could not. Such testimony by doctors about national standards within specializations, of course, in time had the effect of undermining the locality rule.

As medical practitioners came into court as expert witnesses more frequently in the twentieth century, courts in turn relied on generally accepted standards in deciding whether to admit expert testimony. Additionally, courts required that healthcare providers conform themselves to those standards. Eventually, courts went still one large step further. Beyond recognizing the existence of medical standards and then enforcing those standards, courts finally reserved the right to override those standards in favor of *judicial* determinations of appropriateness of medical care. Such was the ultimate effect of the *Daubert* principle for the acceptance of scientific evidence. (In the 1990s, *Daubert* partially superseded the *Frye* rule.) But well before *Daubert* became the norm in courtrooms, judges already were making key decisions about physicians' treatment of their patients. Particularly in trials where the question of patient consent was at issue, courts were taking a very active stance with regard to the authority of doctors. Plainly put, by the middle of the twentieth century, courts were putting physicians on notice that they were required to secure patient consent not just in obvious circumstances when patient autonomy was at risk—such as surgeries—but also in grayer areas such as testing and other medical procedures.

With a paternalistic model of the doctor-patient relationship in mind, some physicians argued that they served most faithfully by withholding information from their patients. For example, keeping a malignancy from the patient was very much the norm through the beginning of the twentieth century. That withholding of crucial information about a patient's prognosis remained widespread in the late twentieth century in several other countries, such as Japan.

Of course some instances of physicians' withholding of information amounted to scandalous or even criminal conduct. These cases created firestorms when they became known. In U.S. history, the best-known example of physicians keeping key details about medical treatment from their patients was the Tuskegee experiment, in which African American men were followed by physicians for forty years—without appropriate treatments—in a study of the effects of unchecked syphilis on the human body. Some denials of information to patients, of course, were criminal acts rather than medically justifiable on any level. There have been instances of health workers such as nurses who suffered from disorders such as Munchausen's syndrome by proxy, which caused them to injure patients and then seek care for them. Anyone who lived through the years of World War II (particularly in Europe) was aware of the extent of Nazi physicians' participation in live human experimentation and other "eugenical" efforts, such as the sterilization of "unfit" persons and the involuntary "euthanasia" practiced on individuals with physical or mental disabilities.

Most rationales for the keeping of secrets from patients were much less venal, however, and some actually *could* have had benefits for patients' well-being. Doctors maintained, for example, that patients might forgo needed procedures if every dire possibility were laid out before them concerning the perils of surgeries or other treatments. Still, in the twentieth century, U.S. courts increasingly were unwilling to accept arguments in favor of the withholding of medical information from patients. The notion of informed consent was built on early twentieth-century cases such as *Schloendorff.* Especially after the Nazi horrors and notorious examples such as Tuskegee became well known (in the 1940s and the 1970s, respectively), courts broadened the notion of informed consent to encompass surgeries and many other medical procedures, including medical testing and human experimentation.

By the last quarter of the twentieth century, the doctrine of informed consent had been applied to so many aspects of the physician-patient relationship that that connection was much less a dependent one on patients' part. Patients expected—and courts encouraged them to demand—that they should be given sufficient information by physicians to make fully informed decisions about their physical condition. It was a far cry, in other words, from the beginning of the twentieth century, when doctors were presumed by most patients and many courts to be the possessors of specialized knowledge that enabled physicians even to decide when to perform surgeries without patients' consent.

As the technology of medicine became more widely available (and, in some instances, cheaper), courts imposed on physicians a duty to make patients aware of medical procedures that could be beneficial. In the case of *Helling v. Carey* (1974), the Supreme Court of the State of Washington went so far as to say that physicians no longer could rely on the standards of care that were customary among their medical peers to defend themselves against charges of negligence. The case under consideration involved a woman who, suffering from vision problems, had gone to an ophthalmologic practice. For nearly ten years, Dr. Thomas Carey treated the patient for nearsightedness, prescribed contact lenses for her, and consulted again with her on at least nine other occasions. It was on the ninth visit that Dr. Carey decided to test the patient's intraocular pressure and her ability to see across a field of vision—a "field vision test." Both tests indicated that the patient was and probably had been suffering from a form of glaucoma (increased pressure inside the eye) that had led to the loss of a considerable part of her peripheral vision.

The patient sued Dr. Carey, arguing that if the glaucoma had been detected earlier, she would have retained much of her sight. Dr. Carey maintained that the accepted standard of care among ophthalmologists was not to give an eye pressure test to patients such as the plaintiff who were under age 40, since among young people the incidence of glaucoma was quite low (about 1 in 25,000). After age 40 the incidence was much higher, so the test was routinely given. In the appeal of the patient's case to the Washington Supreme Court, the court agreed with the patient that Dr. Carey had been negligent. The court's reasoning was that the eye pressure test was harmless, widely available, and relatively inexpensive. Even though patients under age 40 who might benefit from it were rare, there was no excuse for the test not being offered. In making that determination, the court indicated that professional standards among ophthalmologists were not the appropriate legal standards of care. Thus the decision had two very important elements: (1) The court considered the accessibility and cost of medical detection as a factor in determining medical negligence. (2) More importantly, the court said that judicial authority rather than medical custom (that is, the usual standards of care among medical specialists such as ophthalmologists) would determine which standards of care were appropriate.

In another tragic case, a court warned physicians that they bore the responsibility for informing patients about tests that could prove lifesaving. Indeed, doctors had to tell patients of the consequences of not undergoing certain tests that were appropriate for their circumstances. Cases of this type reminded physicians that providing such information to patients was part of medical professionals' duty to secure their patients' informed consent. The children of Rena Truman sued their mother's family physician, Dr. Claude Thomas, for the wrongful death of their mother. Mrs. Truman saw Dr. Thomas for about six years, including during the time she was pregnant with her second child. When Mrs. Truman consulted a urologist about a complaint that first had been treated by Dr. Thomas, the urologist discovered a large cervical tumor. The tumor proved malignant and inoperable; Mrs. Truman died at age thirty of the cervical cancer. Mrs. Truman's survivors contended that Dr. Thomas never had performed a pap smear on their mother, although that test was well known as a screening device for cervical cancer. The plaintiffs also argued that within the medical community (and in Dr. Thomas's own locality), it was standard practice for physicians to recommend to their female patients that they have an annual pap smear. Dr. Thomas testified that he had recommended a pap test to Mrs. Truman several times, but that she was concerned about its costs. Dr. Thomas did not push the issue. Specifically, he did not set out for Mrs. Truman the possibility that failure to have the test could be very dangerous, while having the test could detect cervical cancer at a stage when it could be treated. As in *Helling v. Carey*, the court held in *Truman v. Thomas* (1980) that the physician was liable. In both of these cases, the basis of the doctors' liability was their failure to secure informed consent.

Obviously such judicial outcomes had important implications for physicians' conduct. In ophthalmologists' offices all across the United States, physicians after *Helling* became more aggressive about suggesting that even younger patients undergo eye pressure examinations. Particularly in the event that patients had family histories of glaucoma or if they suffered from any complaints that might be attributable to glaucoma, physicians ignored *Helling* at their peril. In the parallel case, gynecologists or other physicians who treated women of childbearing age began to recommend pap smears even more routinely than they had before *Truman*, and they were wise to inform their female patients of childbearing age of the consequences of not undergoing that screening test.

A case from 1972 illustrates how far courts had come toward equalizing doctor-patient interaction through their broadening of the doctrine of informed consent. In *Canterbury v. Spence*, the U.S. Court of Appeals for the District of Columbia considered the case of a man named Jerry Canterbury who had agreed to undergo surgery by a neurosurgeon (Dr. William Spence) because of pain between his shoulder blades that had been unrelieved through medication. (The case was decided thirteen years after the surgery in question; Canterbury had been nineteen years old at the time that he initially consulted with doctors about his condition.) After a laminectomy—a procedure to remove a portion of one vertebra—Canterbury was recovering in the hospital, being largely confined to bed. He slipped out of bed, however, and was injured further; that injury caused some paralysis of his legs and necessitated another operation. Besides finding that Canterbury was entitled to a new trial in order to ascertain whether the hospital along with Spence was negligent, the appeals court determined that Dr. Spence had owed Canterbury the duty to disclose all of the possible risks of the laminectomy prior to performing the procedure. In Canterbury's situation, Dr. Spence had not divulged all of the operation's dangers either to Spence (who, it might have been argued, was too young to appreciate the risks) or to Spence's mother, a woman of limited means who arrived from West Virginia after the surgery had been performed. With regard to its requirement that consent be informed, the court said that it would allow exceptions only in cases when a patient was unconscious and thus unable to respond *and* a close relative could not be told of the risks in order to act in the patient's stead.

Could informed consent have been stretched much further to circumscribe physicians' authority than it was in *Canterbury v. Spence?* With a well-known ruling in 2001, the Supreme Court did expand informed consent as a concept, even beyond its previous applications. That 2001 case reaffirmed the importance of informed consent with respect to medical personnel and their patients. In underlining the value of informed consent, however, the court placed physicians in an even more awkward position than they had been, for it put doctors at odds with public law-enforcement authorities. In the case of *Ferguson v. City of Charleston,* the court considered informed consent not in the context of medical malpractice but within a discussion of law-enforcement officers' right to search for and seize evidence that could be used against patients. In *Ferguson,* two women who had received obstetrical care at a Charleston hospital (affiliated with the Medical University of South Carolina, or MUSC) sued the city, law-enforcement officers, and officials at MUSC. The women maintained that they had given urine samples as a part of their usual obstetrical examinations. Their urine had been tested and found positive for the presence of illegal drugs; the results had been shared by MUSC with local law-enforcement and antidrug authorities. Those positive drug tests had caused some of the patients to be arrested. Other women who had received similar care had been referred to drug-treatment programs and in some cases prosecuted for child neglect. With dissents by Justices Scalia, Rehnquist, and Thomas, the majority of the court found that the hospital's diagnostic tests on the urine did constitute an unreasonable search, since the patients had not consented to the procedures with full knowledge of how the urine samples would be used. In the course of his dissent, Justice Scalia observed that the police actions were designed to protect not just the pregnant women but also their children; he also noted that South Carolina (like other states) did not recognize a doctor-patient privilege. The court majority, however, agreed with the plaintiffs that they had a valid Fourth Amendment claim against the city, law-enforcement officials, and the medical center.

Clearly, courts at the end of the twentieth century were warning medical professionals that their duty to secure patients' informed consent overrode many other vital concerns—even (as shown in the *Ferguson* case) the need to enforce the law prohibiting illegal drug use. Thus courts might and did infringe upon the physician-patient relationship (if indeed one did exist) at many junctures.

But increasingly in the twentieth century, medical malpractice cases did not just involve doctors and patients. As more and more physicians agreed to associate with managed-care corporations in the second half of the twentieth century, both physicians and patients complained that doctors were compelled to make treatment decisions based on monetary or at least insurance-related considerations. To what extent could physicians be sued for malpractice when the doctors could argue that they were pressured by third parties to make certain decisions in the interest of cost containment? Emergency-room physicians, for example, often refused to test their patients for the presence of alcohol and drugs in their blood. The physicians feared that patients would be denied medical insurance coverage for the hospital visits if illegal substances were found to have caused the accidents that brought them in for medical attention.

An even more widespread fear among doctors and patients was that uninsured persons would be refused treatment for their injuries or illnesses when hospitals discovered their lack of insurance. The federal Emergency Medical Treatment and Active Labor Act (EMTALA) was passed by Congress in 1986 to prevent the passing along to other hospitals of patients who were uninsured. (That practice of transferring uninsured patients to other facilities sometimes was referred to by the slang term *dumping.*) The legislation made it mandatory for hospitals that saw emergency cases, including women in active labor, to assess and treat, regardless of the patient's ability to pay, each emergency case that came through their doors. Only when patients were medically stable could they be transferred to other facilities.

Although some patients and their families tried to bring federal cases under EMTALA, courts generally were reluctant to make the law broad in reach. In cases such as *Phillips v. Hillcrest Medical Center* (2001), federal courts suggested to persons who believed that they had received substandard medical care in emergency rooms that they should rely principally on medical negligence claims pursued through state courts. Thus, interestingly, federal courts seemed to encourage further malpractice suits against individual physicians rather than recommending recourse to federal law.

At the time he appeared at an emergency room at the Hillcrest Medical Center (HMC), Martin Shane Phillips complained of chest pains. Accompanied by a coworker, Phillips could not produce his medical insurance card; his colleague presented a card just like Phillips's card, since they were employed at the same business and had the same health coverage. Later, Phillips's family claimed that the hospital made a notation on Phillips's records that he was lacking health insurance. After Phillips's consultation with a hospital triage nurse, he saw a physician on the "minor care" side of the emergency room. Although doctors prescribed some medicines for Phillips and recommended that he visit a medical clinic, he returned to work. By the end of the week, Phillips was faring poorly; his family took him to Tulsa Regional Medical Center. He was admitted but died there, five days after his initial visit to HMC. The federal claim by Phillips's family did not succeed; the U.S. District Court of Appeals for the Tenth Circuit reminded the plaintiffs that EMTALA was designed chiefly to prevent poorer and uninsured patients from being "dumped" before they were stabilized. A failure to diagnose or treat a patient appropriately (even if he were presumed by the medical facility not to be covered by insurance) was not in and of itself evidence that the medical authorities had run afoul of EMTALA. It was a sad footnote in the Phillips case—which was an important decision in regard to EMTALA—that the patient who died as a result of allegedly improper treatment actually *was* insured!

Although the *Phillips* case is most easily understood in the context of EMTALA (or, rather, federal courts' reluctance to allow claims against hospitals under that legislation), it also illustrates another point with regard to a key group of medicolegal controversies—suits involving medical negligence. The court of appeals in *Phillips* denied the family's claim under EMTALA, but seemed to encourage the family to take judicial action against individual medical center employees who may have erred in Phillips's diagnosis and treatment. (Of course it generally would be much more lucrative to win a case against a medical center than against an individual physician or other medical practitioner; that may have been part of the reason that Phillips's family pursued the EMTALA claim.) The appeals court, in noting that the family could embark on a medical malpractice case, also was in line with decades of legal history, for in the twentieth century, as we have seen, suing physicians had become very popular with the public. Malpractice suits had grown to be a very big business for lawyers, as well, as is clearly shown in the story of several medical-product liability controversies from the late twentieth century.

Medical-Product Liability: Patients, Courts, and the FDA

As discussed previously, in cases concerning standards of care and informed consent, courts made decisions reminding physicians of a duty to provide up-to-date care for their patients and to inform the patients fully about that care. However, in the mid–twentieth century, the courts' task in overseeing certain aspects of medical care became a great deal more complex for two reasons that went beyond courts' expanded oversight toward medical standards of care and patient consent: (1) Medical malpractice actions were ever more crowded with new concerns and additional players. That situation reflected the changing face of medical practice as a whole, for in American medicine generally the doctor-patient relationship had gained several new participants in the later twentieth century, notably the federal bureaucracy and businesses that specialized in health management. (2) Another important series of medical developments had a key impact on medicolegal controversies: the discovery of new forms of treatment for medical complaints.

In the twentieth century, an enormous numbers of treatment alternatives became available to healthcare providers. Medical historians speak of Western medicine—and the U.S. medical system in particular—as undergoing a "therapeutic revolution" in the decades following World War II. As a part of that growth, business enterprises (many of them multinational in scope) saw tremendous profit potential in producing therapeutic drugs—particularly prescription drugs—for distribution on a mass market. These drug companies consequently responded with an ever-growing catalog of drugs. More to the point, using their political clout within the United States, they pushed hard for their products to be tested and distributed rapidly. Meanwhile, episodes such as the thalidomide controversy (discussed in Chapter 2) drove home the necessity of external regulations, such as those promulgated by the FDA, to prevent dangerous medical products from getting to market. Thus the story of the therapeutic revolution goes hand in hand with a chronicle of the changing regulatory powers of the FDA.

Most drugs (unlike thalidomide) proved both reasonably safe and well accepted by medical professionals and the public. Accordingly, a large number of drugs were developed and eventually adopted into general usage for a variety of ills: antibiotics to treat infections, antipsychotic drugs to control mental illnesses, anticancer agents, new formulas to be used as anesthetics, and even the wildly popular contraceptive commonly known as the pill. The potential for curing ailments through drugs seemed unlimited. Another closely related event—the marshaling of increasingly sophisticated scientific technology for medical purposes—accompanied and extended beyond the therapeutic revolution. With the development of computers and microtechnology, as well as new chemical advances, medical devices seemed to carry the enormous potential for improvement in patients' physical welfare, as the new drugs also had promised.

Unfortunately for the manufacturers of new drugs and medical devices, the vast expansion in treatment options in the second half of the twentieth century inspired numerous and complex courtroom discussions. Despite their obvious benefits in most instances, some of those medical panaceas proved harmful to patients who had trusted in them. These failures, in turn, raised difficult questions for the courts. Where did a physician's responsibility end and a drug company's begin, for example, if a physician prescribed treatments or medications that later were discovered to be dangerous? Was the drugmaker responsible for alerting, through labeling, both physician and patient to potential dangers? What should the courts' response be when there was a significant lapse of time between the ingestion of a medication or placement of a medical device and the point when the injury was detected? Did delayed symptoms negate or enhance the liability of those who manufactured and distributed dangerous drugs?

Again and again, in handling product liability cases that were connected to such medicolegal questions, the courts had to make reference to the FDA. The FDA, after all, was the governmental agency that first gave a stamp of approval for the marketing of drugs and medical devices that later were alleged to be dangerous. As we shall see in the following discussion, although theoretically the public should have been shielded somewhat from faulty or dangerous products by FDA regulations on medicines and medical devices, in fact the activities of the agency often only muddied the waters in some of the courtroom showdowns concerning medical-product liability. Thus the FDA figured prominently in court cases and the public discussions surrounding those cases; legal controversies over medical-product liability also were, in effect, commentaries on the scope and efficacy of the FDA.

It is instructive in this context to consider the massive national and even international adjudication over two medical treatments that once had been thought safe but later were shown to be dangerous: the drug diethylstilbestrol (DES) and silicone breast implants. DES was a drug developed for use as a preventative for miscarriages; years after its administration, however, the drug proved to have been extremely hazardous for the children who had been in utero. In another tragic irony, breast implants, which were supposed to enhance the quality of life for the patients who received the devices, often did exactly the opposite by causing disfigurement and discomfort. In the cases of DES and breast implants, tens of thousands of persons were affected directly as victims. Thousands of those victims, in turn, availed themselves of opportunities to sue for damages, sometimes individually but usually through class actions. Judicial resolution of the DES and breast-implant cases proved enormously complex and consumed years.

At the center of these litigations were the drug companies. Not only had they been the ones to develop the drugs or devices in question, but they also had deep pockets that promised the possibility of a sizable payoff. (Actually, although injured patients ultimately would collect some monetary payments, the persons who profited most from the settlements of the cases were trial lawyers involved in the class actions—but this is an issue beyond the scope of the present discussion.) Yet while individual physicians usually were not being sued for prescribing DES or implanting silicone into patients' bodies, the cases raised many issues related to doctors' roles as caregivers. Specifically, given how well known these litigations became, they heightened public discussion and expectations about related medicolegal issues central to the provision of medical care in modern America. Such medical-product liability controversies in the courtroom underlined issues such as the premarket testing of drugs and medical devices, the authority of the FDA, physicians' responsibility to warn patients of dangerous medical products, and even patients' duty to protect themselves.

DES had seemed a drug with enormous therapeutic potential when it was approved by the FDA in the early 1940s. DES was approved at first for treating a variety of medical problems. Later in the decade, the agency also approved for DES new drug applications (NDAs) for the drug's most promising use—preventing miscarriages. By the late 1960s, however, alarming reports began to surface that some of the daughters of DES users were suffering from forms of gynecological cancers and precancerous conditions, as well as infertility. In 1971, the FDA banned DES use among pregnant women. By that time, however, hundreds of young women had been affected, and many of them attempted to sue the makers of the drug.

In the case of *Hymowitz v. Eli Lilly* (1989), the Court of Appeals of New York wrestled with several aspects of the product-liability law raised in the DES cases. The court also struggled to meet objections by the defendant that a New York State statute, which in 1986 had revived the possibility of filing suits for DES exposure, violated the defendant's right to due process. That statute allowing DES suits to be filed for a one-year period in effect suspended the statute of limitations. The decision reviewed the history of DES as a drug and the subsequent litigation that spanned many states. The court eventually did decide in favor of the plaintiffs who were suing DES-maker Eli Lilly. Part of the court's reasoning was that the legislature had created an exception to the statute of limitations in order to allow women a period in which to file cases. (Within its decision, the New York court even allowed recovery in the absence of the exact identification of particular manufacturers as having made particular batches of DES. Other jurisdictions—Iowa, for example, in the case of *Mulcahy v. Lilly*—had required that the state legislature modify legal doctrine to permit recovery in nonidentification DES cases.) Based on its examination of how DES cases had been handled in other courts (such as in California and Wisconsin), the New York judges decided to apportion the mass claims based on a market-share theory predicated on a national market.

The New York court referred to DES litigation as a "singular" case, which required unusual remedies:

> Indeed it would be inconsistent with the reasonable expectations of a modern society to say to these plaintiffs that because of the insidious nature of an injury that long remains dormant, and because so many manufacturers, each behind a curtain, contributed to the devastation, the cost of injury should be borne by the innocent and not the wrongdoers. This is particularly so when the Legislature consciously created these expectations by reviving hundreds of DES cases. Consequently the ever-evolving dictates of justice and fairness, which are the heart of our common-law system, require formation of a remedy for injuries caused by DES. (*Hymowitz v. Eli Lilly* 1989, 507)

The courts and the public may have hoped that DES injuries were a tragedy that could occur only once. Unfortunately, there arose other instances of medical-product liability that presented many of the same challenges for patients, the courts, and the FDA. Chief among those instances was the case of silicone breast implants. As with DES, the dangerous aspects of silicone breast implants became apparent to physicians and consumers only months and sometimes even years after "consumption." In another similarity to the DES controversies that were heard in courts, the FDA often was invoked in breast-implant litigation, for the FDA had allowed silicone implants onto the market after only minimal research into their safety. Thus the litigation over breast implants was both a trial of drug companies and a commentary on the effectiveness of the FDA's regulatory process.

The first silicone breast implants were created in the early 1950s. Implants made of saline already had been used, but many patients complained that saline implants had an unnatural look and feel. At first, silicone—like DES—had promising medical applications. The FDA regarded silicone as a safe substance that already had been used in other medical devices implanted in the body and (based on the safety record of other silicone implants) approved silicone to be employed in breast implants through the FDA's "grandfathering" process. This meant that the manufacturers did not have to provide safety studies or continuing information on the product's safety. By about 1991, at least 750,000 patients had the implants. Most of the implants were surgically placed in the course of cosmetic breast surgery; a significant minority, however, were implanted in reconstructive procedures that followed mastectomies.

In 1991, the FDA began to respond to a large number of complaints about the silicone implants leaking. The leaks allegedly contributed to breast disfigurement, but patients and physicians linked silicone to several additional health problems, from weakness to memory loss. The FDA asked breast-implant manufacturers for studies on the safety of the devices; the agency considered the makers' responses inadequate. The FDA reacted by taking silicone breast implants off the market for public use, although they still could be used in clinical trials.

Litigants who sought damages from breast-implant makers faced a variety of hurdles. Some courts, for example, insisted that there had not been enough scientific studies to establish common understanding among the medical and scientific communities as to the physical effects of silicone implants. In suits of this type (where plaintiffs were alleging harm from a product about which courts basically had not heard cases in the past), the legal rules concerning the admissibility of scientific evidence were of crucial importance. In *Toledo v. Medical Engineering Corp.*, a Pennsylvania case from 2001, the Court of Common Pleas of Philadelphia County ruled that expert testimony by the plaintiff's medical experts was not admissible. The court cited *Frye v. U.S.* (1923) (that is, the *Frye* standard), which barred the use of novel scientific evidence. The plaintiff had tried to introduce evidence that silicone implants (placed in her body in 1986) had caused localized pain. The court, in looking at a medical study cited by the plaintiff, concluded that the study had argued that the surgery to implant the devices, rather than the devices themselves, could have caused the symptoms about which the plaintiff complained. Thus to maintain that the silicone gel, rather than scarring after the surgery, had created complications for the patient was to apply scientific evidence in a way that contradicted *Frye.*

As with the DES suits, by the time that courts began hearing large numbers of breast-implant cases, state legislatures also had gotten involved in breast-implant litigation. Some states in the 1990s had passed laws allowing plaintiffs to file suits within a specified time, thus bypassing the statute of limitations for a limited period. If plaintiffs chose not to avail themselves of the opportunity to sue, or, more commonly, if they could not understand the complex regulations surrounding those limitations on bringing suit, then they were without judicial recourse. In the case of *Michals v. Baxter Healthcare Corp.* (2002), the U.S. Court of Appeals for the Sixth Circuit ruled against a Kentucky woman who believed herself to have been injured by a succession of silicone and saline implants. Sherry Michals first had breast augmentation surgery in 1974. She complained of discomfort, however, and subsequently underwent several more surgeries in which the implants were replaced with devices made by different manufacturers. The court ruled that Michals knew that the initial complaints she had were attributable to the first set of implants and that therefore the statute of limitations on her injury had run out in 1978—a considerable time before she filed a lawsuit in 1993 and opted out of a class settlement action in 1996. The U.S. Supreme Court denied certiorari in the *Michals* case.

In an unreported decision of the Superior Court of Connecticut in 2002, the court discussed the complexity of breast-implant litigation in the past decade. The court noted that the case before it, *Barbour et al. v. Dow Corning et al.*, was but one of hundreds of similar filings. Some of those cases had traveled in Connecticut courts and then gone to the northern Alabama federal court that was handling the multistate litigation, only then to be sent to U.S. District Court for the District of Connecticut and then to the Connecticut Superior Court. Several of the suits at hand had named several companies as being liable. One of those manufacturers of breast implants, Minnesota Mining and Manufacturing Company (3M), had made breast implants in the 1970s and 1980s, but had sold its interest in breast implants to McGhan Medical Corporation in a series of arrangements between 1977 and 1984. Since the plaintiff, Anna Barbour, complained that her implants were manufactured after 1984, she could not recover damages against 3M under Connecticut's applicable product-liability statute. The court granted 3M's motion for a summary judgment since 3M did not manufacture the device that was claimed to have caused Barbour's injury.

As is apparent from those three examples (among many others that could be cited), plaintiffs suing breast-implant makers for damages had a difficult and long task ahead of them. The U.S. government, however, fared better than the average defendant. The federal government became involved as a party to the breast-implant claims as a result of its financing of procedures to remove or replace faulty implants through programs such as Medicare, Medicaid, the Department of Health and Human Services (HHS), the Departments of Defense and Veterans Affairs, and the Indian Health Service. The U.S. government argued that it should be reimbursed for those payments by Dow Corning and the other implant makers that had been named in the mass litigation. In September 2002, the government was awarded $9.8 million in damages by the judge who was overseeing the Dow Corning bankruptcy proceedings. Although Dow Corning's bankruptcy certainly delayed the payment of claims to successful litigants in ongoing or future litigation, ironically the enormous government claim also held up payments to injured persons who already had won claims against Dow Corning before the bankruptcy. Despite that settlement of what the government believed it was owed by Dow Corning, the United States had to pursue separate claims against other breast-implant manufacturers, including 3M, Bristol

Myers Squibb, and Baxter Healthcare. It was ironic that the government should have accepted the settlement at the same time (late 2002) that the FDA was considering the premarket approval applications of several implant makers to sell silicone implants again on an unrestricted basis. Once again, the FDA was about to become embroiled in controversy over its approval of a medical product, but this time it was a product that already had a long history of litigation concerning its safety.

Another well-known medical-product liability controversy in the late twentieth century involved diet drugs. The courtroom discussions about diet drugs, a type of product that resulted in hundreds of suits in courts across the United States, illustrated the precarious position that physicians could be in as new drugs and medical technologies were being developed. Doctors found themselves confronted with rapidly changing drug therapies coupled with inconsistent FDA oversight of those therapies, as well as poor communication from drug companies to prescribing doctors coupled with increasing patient demands for more-effective drug treatments.

A number of lawsuits arising from physicians' prescriptions of weight-reducing drug therapies appeared in U.S. courts beginning in the 1990s. The suits concerning diet drugs, as well as the doctors who prescribed them and the drug companies that manufactured them, were different in one key respect from suits over medical products such as DES and breast implants: diet drugs often were given to patients in "off-label" circumstances. That is, the drugs were prescribed to persons who did not fit the scientific profile of patients for whom the drug originally had been developed and tested, and for whom the drug had been labeled. Another form of off-label usage was when the drugs were dispensed by physicians to patients for conditions other than those recommended by the makers of the drugs. (A well-known off-label practice in the 1950s and 1960s was the prescribing of amphetamines for their weight-reducing qualities.) Even drugs that had been manufactured specifically for use as diet aids could be misused if doctors prescribed them for patients who were not *overweight* by a medical definition of that term. That is, certain diet drugs had been developed and labeled only for use among persons who were very overweight, so persons with only mild weight problems who took those substances did so at their peril.

The danger posed by diet drugs being prescribed for off-label use was made still greater because of precisely who was administering the drugs. Any physician might set himself or herself up as a "diet doctor" and begin to prescribe drugs to patients. Diet doctors, that is, were not a recognized medical category, but rather simply were physicians who claimed that they could treat obesity. Many practitioners who called themselves experts in dietary matters or obesity in fact were not trained at all in the formal specialty of bariatric medicine (the treatment of obesity and weight-related problems). Thus diet doctors may not have had much background at all in managing drug treatments for obesity.

When such self-proclaimed experts began prescribing weight-reducing drugs such as the combination of fenfluramine and phentermine—popularly known as fen-phen, a medical tragedy was only a matter of time. Those powerful drugs when taken individually and together eventually were shown to cause serious—perhaps fatal—health problems. By the time such adverse reactions to fen-phen became known, however, the FDA for years had been relatively lenient in allowing physicians to prescribe the drugs as weight-loss tools for overweight persons. To wit, the agency had not been zealous in keeping fen-phen out of the hands of diet doctors, generally; nor had the FDA alerted either the public or the medical profession about the adverse reaction reports that it received about the drugs; nor had the FDA cracked down on the off-label use of fen-phen.

Harmful consequences were bound to follow such a loose approach to the regulation of diet drugs. Similarly, the courts were inevitably drawn into charges that patients had been harmed by drugs such as fen-phen. In the fen-phen cases, as with certain other drug-liability cases such as the DES suits, courts generally were sympathetic to patient claims against drugmakers; judicial decisions put much of the burden on manufacturers to inform patients and their physicians about product dangers.

But what liability did courts assign to the diet doctors? The response by courts was somewhat mixed. On one hand, many suits were aimed at the drug manufacturers' substantial financial resources, thus doctors were not always the objects of the legal actions. On the other hand, when they *were* named as defendants in fen-phen suits, it was difficult for diet doctors to escape the charge that they were practicing in an unethical fashion if they had prescribed diet drugs to patients who did not meet the strict medical criteria for obesity.

A case from West Virginia illustrates the usual judicial approach in apportioning blame to physicians for the harm that diet drugs could cause: although courts usually preferred not to hold individual physicians responsible for injuries caused by such new drugs, sometimes courts could not escape the conclusion that diet doctors had acted negligently. About seven weeks after the birth of her third child, Mrs. Teddi Wilkinson consulted Dr. W. Rexford Duff, who was associated with Bariatrics, Inc., which specialized in "medically supervised weight loss." Dr. Duff examined Mrs. Wilkinson briefly and prescribed phentermine for her. Apparently the physician never ascertained from Mrs. Wilkinson that she recently had given birth and had been breast-feeding. After taking the drug for only four days, Mrs. Wilkinson had severe chest pains and shortly afterward went into full cardiac arrest. She died as a result of the brain damage that occurred from the heart attack she had suffered. An autopsy revealed spontaneous dissection of one of Mrs. Wilkinson's coronary arteries.

Mr. Wilkinson sued three parties—the hospital where it was not initially recognized that Mrs. Wilkinson was in cardiac distress; the emergency physician (Dr. David Life) who had decided that her EKG, although abnormal, was within normal limits and had discharged her from the hospital; and Dr. Duff, the doctor from the weight-loss clinic. Dr. Life and the Montgomery County Hospital settled out of court with Mr. Wilkinson. Dr. Duff persisted in fighting the claim. Dr. Duff maintained that Mrs. Wilkinson, who was a professor of nursing, possessed enough medical knowledge to have recognized that she should tell Dr. Duff that she recently had borne a child. In addition, Dr. Duff argued that he did not have enough information from the maker of the drug phentermine to have warned Mrs. Wilkinson to avoid using the drug if she were immediately postpartum or breast-feeding. (Dr. Duff was seeking to make the manufacturer of the phentermine—Eon Labs and Calvin Scott—rather than himself liable for Mrs. Wilkinson's death.)

In the decision in *Wilkinson v. Duff* (2002) the Supreme Court of Appeals of West Virginia would have none of Dr. Duff's contentions. The court ruled that the manufacturers were not liable as a third party in the suit against Dr. Duff, and it commented at several junctures about Dr. Duff's superficiality in examining and prescribing phentermine for Mrs. Wilkinson. The physician, in other words, still was being held by the courts to a certain minimum standard of care in regard to his patient's welfare, despite the fact that other parties certainly also contributed to the harm that had occurred.

The product-liability issue with the largest scope of all as a medicolegal controversy in the later twentieth century was the case against tobacco makers. Although tobacco was not a medical product in the sense that a medicine, such as DES, or devices, such as breast implants, were (tobacco had not been used for medicinal purposes for centuries), the tobacco lawsuits certainly raised medicolegal questions. There were several clear connections between the medical community and tobacco-related lawsuits. For example, scientists and physicians had known of studies establishing a connection between cigarette smoking and cancer as early as the 1920s (and had suspected links between tobacco and other cancers even earlier), but there was not wide publicity about those dangers prior to the early 1960s. In 1962, the U.S. surgeon general began investigating cigarette manufacturers as distributors of a product that scientific studies increasingly condemned as both harmful and addictive. In 1966, the federal government required that labels be placed on cigarette packaging. Voicing concern about the impact of tobacco advertising on young people (who were taking up tobacco use at an early age), eventually the government went beyond restrictions on the sale of tobacco to minors and imposed limitations on tobacco advertising in the broadcast media. By federal law, increasingly sharper warnings stating that tobacco use was dangerous to one's health were required for tobacco packaging.

Plaintiffs suffering from tobacco-induced illnesses (especially lung and oral cancers) who sued tobacco companies found that they faced an arsenal of defenses from those manufacturers. Important among the tobacco makers' justifications in court was the argument that consumers had been warned for years, via the surgeon general's statements, that tobacco was a dangerous product. The companies contended that if consumers continued to smoke or otherwise use tobacco products, they did so at their own risk. It was a powerful argument, but it sat uncomfortably with the companies' long-standing position that scientific studies did not conclusively link tobacco use with harm to the human body. The tobacco companies also pursued strategies of delay in allowing cases to come to trial at all; clearly they hoped that plaintiffs would either tire of waiting for a court date or (as did happen in several cases) die of their ailments before trials could commence.

The case of *Cipollone v. Liggett Group, Inc.,* heard in the 1980s, was a milestone among suits against tobacco companies. In the first place, it was one of the first few cases of its type actually to come to trial. In addition, at an early point in the case, the judge issued a key ruling: the tobacco maker would not be able to get the suit dismissed on the ground that federal warnings about the dangers of tobacco shielded the company from tort liability. Between the time that the original plaintiff, Rose Cipollone, was diagnosed with lung cancer (1981) and the time that the judge in U.S. District Court for the District of New Jersey made that ruling (1984), Rose Cipollone had been in declining health. In October 1984, the plaintiff died. Although her husband took the case forward, it took almost four more years for the case to go to trial. The attorneys for Antonio Cipollone introduced evidence that the tobacco maker, Liggett Group, Inc., had known of tobacco's injurious effects even prior to the government's warnings but had failed to alert consumers. (Rose Cipollone, like many Americans of her generation, had begun smoking as a teenager.) The trial ended with a victory for the plaintiff's estate; the jury required Liggett to pay $400,000 in damages to the Cipollone family, even though the panel also found that Rose Cipollone bore the majority of responsibility for her smoking addiction.

In its ruling on the appeal of the case, the U.S. Supreme Court in 1992 affirmed the earlier ruling that tobacco companies could not rely on governmental warnings about tobacco's dangers to shield them from liability. The Supreme Court did require, however, that plaintiffs meet higher standards of proof concerning how tobacco was promoted and advertised in order to obtain damages. In the interim between the original verdict and the Supreme Court decision, Antonio Cipollone had died. The Cipollones' children could have carried on the legal battle with Liggett, but they decided not to pursue the case. Thus although the Cipollone family appeared on the way to winning their battle, the cost of the fight was too great and the time spent in contention was far too lengthy; in a sense, therefore, the tobacco companies had outlasted another individual plaintiff.

But tobacco had another, more powerful adversary in the courts. In 2003, a suit filed by the U.S. government itself accused tobacco makers of deceptive advertising of a dangerous product. The Justice Department began proceedings to file the suit, seeking damages of $289 billion, claiming that tobacco companies knew of the dangerous and addictive nature of their product at least as early as 1954. The government contended that the makers colluded to sell tobacco to minors, in hopes that the young people who had tried cigarettes, for example, would continue smoking for a lifetime because of their addiction. If the case of *U.S. v. Philip Morris et al.* went forward and damages were collected, that award would surpass the $206 billion settlement that tobacco companies reached with forty-six states in 1998 as a result of a previous set of suits by the states. The federal suit was initiated under the administration of President Bill Clinton, with the direction of Attorney General Janet Reno. Since the George W. Bush administration has been in office, Attorney General John Ashcroft has downplayed the importance of the proposed action, warning that, in his opinion, such a suit would not be successful. Attorneys working within the Justice Department, though their budget for the project is limited, are proceeding with the plans for the suit. The case has a trial date of September 2004.

In deciding cases concerning medical negligence, against either individual doctors or other parties such as drug companies, courts are facing ever-more complex fact scenarios. It is no longer the norm for a medical malpractice case to involve merely the rural physician who attempted to set a badly broken arm and a dissatisfied patient who then sued the doctor when the arm did not heal cleanly. Instead, suits for medical harm in the modern era typically concern medical products that are newly developed and only recently available to physicians. Furthermore, such medical liability cases test courts' insistence that physicians should provide acceptable standards of care, for individual physicians (however competent or well trained) still might not manage to be well versed in the use of new drugs and medical products.

Physicians' competence to treat their patients is being tested, as well, by consumer demand. Patients (who see direct-to-consumer advertising in the mass media, which is discussed in Chapter 4) increasingly are requesting off-label applications of medicines and devices. And doctors sometimes are concurring in that prescription of medical products for conditions that had not been the basis of the products' development and testing. If harm results to the patients, then courts have to sort out liability. Cases involving medical injuries might not be individual suits at all, but rather class actions involving hundreds of patients. This vastly increases the complexity of courts' considerations of medical liability, especially when legislatures see fit to intervene in the controversies, for instance by creating "windows of opportunity," during which suits can be brought, years after injury initially had occurred.

Finally, the presence of the FDA in controversies concerning medical-product liability has been decidedly a mixed blessing for patients when their cases go to court. On one hand, the FDA unquestionably performs a valuable function by enforcing laws requiring that drugs and medical products be safe, adequately tested, and properly labeled for physician and patient use. On the other hand, the agency, through insufficient enforcement of several of its own standards, has failed to prevent several very large and well-known medical tragedies. Thus in many medical-product liability suits, courts have to ascertain the fault of medical manufacturers and physicians, as well as the FDA.

Nonmedical Oversight of Medical Care

As the twentieth century wore on, courts took account of a more-complex relationship between physicians and patients, and of the presence of still other parties within that medical relationship. In obtaining medical care in the later twentieth century, patients increasingly had to interact not only with their personal physicians but also with government officials as well as hospital authorities and insurance providers. How have the courts decided cases that have arisen concerning the government's role and the presence of managed-care organizations (MCOs) within healthcare? Several judicial decisions addressing patient concerns about MCOs and the denial of patient claims by federal agencies illustrate that courts usually have allowed considerable latitude to nonmedical parties in overseeing medical care.

In contrast to several other Western and industrialized nations, the United States does not have a nationalized healthcare system. Indeed, despite periodic political pressure for a national healthcare plan, many Americans (including key physicians' groups such as the American Medical Association [AMA]) long have prided themselves on the fact that medical care in the United States is provided through private enterprise and individual doctors rather than any government agency. And yet government has been closely involved in healthcare in the United States, certainly since the 1960s when Congress set up the federal programs Medicare and Medicaid. Poorer persons and those in certain legally defined categories, such as the elderly, for instance, found that payment for their medical treatment would be allowed or denied by government authorities that administered Medicare and Medicaid. A physician's determination that medical treatment was needed was no longer sufficient to secure financial coverage for the patient. Oversight by governmental agencies concerning physicians' treatment decisions obviously has occurred in regard to the care that patients receive in doctors' offices and hospitals; it also has taken place in regard to other facilities, such as nursing homes. That is, through programs such as Medicare and Medicaid, governmental agencies have had broad control over doctors' discretion and thus over patients' physical welfare.

In the case of *Wood v. Thompson* (2001), the U.S. Court of Appeals for the Seventh Circuit denied the appeal of Floyd Wood, a Medicare patient who was suing the U.S. secretary of HHS. The HHS (which oversaw Medicare claims) had denied Wood's claim for dental care. The HHS argued that Wood's dental procedures were not within the few exceptions to a Medicare policy that generally refused treatment for dental work. Wood's cardiac surgeon had told his patient that Wood needed to have extensive dental extractions done prior to a heart-valve replacement procedure; to perform the dental work after the heart operation would have created a serious risk of cardiac infection. In a hearing before an administrative law judge (ALJ), Wood argued that the medical necessity of the dental procedure should have created an exception to the Medicare rules. Both the ALJ and the appeals court, however, were reluctant to overturn the discretion of the secretary of HHS in interpreting the relevant Medicare Act. The appeals court recommended crisply that "Wood should lobby Congress or the Secretary; the judicial branch can be of no use to him" (*Wood v. Thompson* 2001, 1036). Thus in a case where it appeared that the timing of a patient's medical procedures was of critical importance to the patient's welfare, the courts allowed a nonmedical authority to gainsay the recommendation of the patient's physician.

It was not unusual for cases concerning Medicare and Medicaid to be heard before an ALJ. In addition, the court of first instance in many cases of medical-disability claims filed under other federal statutes often was an ALJ. ALJs heard appeals of claim denials related to the Social Security Act, for example. In the case of *Nabours v. Commissioner of Social Security* (2002), the U.S. Court of Appeals for the Sixth Circuit considered the situation of a woman who had been denied social security and supplemental-income benefits after a hearing before an ALJ. The court made several important points concerning both the form of the "trial" that the plaintiff received and medical evidence presented concerning her case. (At administrative hearings, persons seeking benefits could and often did waive legal representation. That was what Linda Nabours had done, and she apparently represented herself effectively in many respects, although the ALJ had ruled against her in the end.) The ALJ heard medical evidence concerning Nabours's argument that several disabilities prevented her from engaging in even the light work that she previously had performed. All of the medical experts who appeared as consultants in the case testified that they would have certified Nabours as fit for light work duties. A physician who actually treated Nabours was the only medical expert who stated that Nabours was incapable of work on an indefinite basis. Thus the court had to weigh the relative merits of "competing medical experts," several of whom were consultants only, versus one doctor who had treated the patient but was alone in his opinion about the severity of her disability.

In the appeal of the denial of benefits, Nabours had counsel; the attorney representing her raised the question of whether the medical evidence on her behalf had been adequately considered by the ALJ. The appeals court rejected several specific contentions from the plaintiff about medical aspects of her case. The court decided that Nabours bore the ultimate burden of proving (and presenting sufficient medical evidence to prove) that she was entitled to benefits. Even though she was not represented before the ALJ by counsel, the court of appeals decided that the initial hearing officer did not have the responsibility to "ferret out" medical information that would have helped her case. Most importantly, the court ruled that although the opinions of a treating physician were entitled to some deference, they were not entitled to carry the day when other medical opinions contradicted the plaintiff's claim. The *Nabours* decision, therefore, had important repercussions for the doctor-patient relationship, especially when the appeals judges ruled that courts would not always regard a personal physician's knowledge of her or his patient's condition as the final word.

Medicare and Medicaid, therefore, had an impact on *who could decide* what medical treatment was appropriate for patients. Those federal programs also had an effect on decisions about *where patients could go* for medical treatment or care. Nursing homes might make use of programs that assessed whether patients were receiving care in appropriate levels of facilities. According to those utilization reviews (by Utilization Review Committees, or URCs), patients sometimes were transferred to institutions called health-related facilities, where they received care that was not as highly skilled as the care received in skilled-care facilities. Such lower-level facilities were less expensive. Although the requirement for URCs was a federal mandate, and in spite of the fact that Medicaid had been set up by Title XIX of the Social Security Act, a state might decide to discontinue benefits to patients who did not consent to recommended transfers. The Supreme Court said in the decision of *Blum v. Yaretsky* (1982) that such a determination by the state was not a violation of patients' due process rights under the Fourteenth Amendment.

But patients did not have to fall within the purview of Medicare and Medicaid in order to find that their access to and choices about treatment were circumscribed by outside parties (parties other than themselves and their physicians). Chief among those new participants in healthcare were businesses that "managed" healthcare based on the profit motive. As both patients and doctors chafed at the control over medicine increasingly exerted by those businesses, the courts more and more were called upon to decide cases involving these additional parties.

Many—if not most—malpractice claims in the late twentieth century involved physicians who were associated with either health-maintenance organizations (HMOs) or MCOs. These for-profit organizations attempted to control the rapidly rising costs of healthcare through incentives to physicians to contain costs. For example, physicians within some networks of MCOs had to obtain prior approval from the management organization before ordering certain medical procedures for their patients, and doctors were promised financial incentives for keeping costs low by not recommending costly treatments. This represented a fundamental shift in how medical services were compensated. The older fee-for-services model, critics said, created incentives for physicians to prescribe treatments as long as patients (and their insurers) continued to pay for those treatments. With the shift to a model of healthcare based on fixed fees, MCOs sought to limit treatments in order to contain costs. The newer model had real disadvantages, however. For example, it easily could put physicians in the difficult position of having to limit tests or treatments that they believed were most effective for patients in order to protect their own self-interest in remaining on an HMO's or MCO's "preferred provider" list.

Although occasionally recognizing the awkwardness of this situation for physicians and patients, the U.S. Supreme Court has not entered into many such controversies. In most instances, the court has not provided a remedy for either physicians or their patients, but has let lower court decisions (usually state court decisions) stand. For example, in spite of a spirited dissent by Justice White, the Court refused to grant certiorari in the California case of *Fein v. Permanente Medical Group* (1985). Mr. Fein had sued an affiliate of Kaiser Health Foundation because physicians and a nurse practitioner who were associated with Kaiser's HMO had failed for several days to diagnose his heart attack. The jury award in Fein's case was substantial—including over $1 million as compensation for pain and suffering, as well as intangible damage to his future health. (Although the court refused to hear the case, thus allowing the large jury award to stand, the Fein lawsuit had important effects on California legislative policy, as discussed later in this chapter.)

In *Pegram v. Herdich* (2000), the Supreme Court refused to allow a malpractice claim against an HMO to be pursued through ERISA (the federal Employment Retirement Income Security Act of 1976). The case involved a fact scenario that was not uncommon: a physician's implementation of an HMO policy to delay expensive diagnostic testing whenever possible, in hopes that the patient's symptoms would subside before those tests were necessary. The plaintiff/patient, Cynthia Herdich, had complained of abdominal pain. Her physician, Dr. Lori Pegram (who was affiliated with an HMO), told Herdich that she should have an abdominal ultrasound to determine the cause of the discomfort, but that the test could be performed only after eight days had elapsed. While waiting for the diagnostic ultrasound, Herdich suffered a ruptured appendix and developed peritonitis. In its ruling, the court decided that the plaintiff had not demonstrated that the HMO was acting illegally (as defined in ERISA) when its physician treated the plaintiff so as to cause an injury. The court maintained that the HMO was engaging in "mixed treatment-and-eligibility" decisions concerning patient care rather than breaching a fiduciary obligation to patients. That is, the court reasoned that an HMO-affiliated physician could make determinations about diagnosis and treatment within HMO guidelines and, in recommending treatment, even could consider whether the HMO would cover certain procedures without those medical decisions being a breach of the obligation set out in ERISA for healthcare providers to "perform their duties solely in the "interests of plan participants" (*Pegram v. Herdich* 2000, 216). Although the 1985 judicial rulings in the *Fein* case had seemed to encourage suits against HMOs, *Pegram v. Herdich* pointed in another direction. That later decision encouraged injured plaintiffs to pursue claims in state courts and pushed patients toward suits against individual physicians rather than HMOs.

Yet patients currently are having a slimmer chance of success with malpractice suits, both in winning the suits and in garnering large awards. The political climate has contributed to aggrieved patients' current lack of success in court. As a result of a proliferation of malpractice claims against not only individual physicians but also HMOs and institutions such as nursing homes, many states have considered and even implemented laws that limit awards in medical malpractice cases. The sponsors of such legislation, often physicians' groups and representatives of nursing home associations, argue that the cost of malpractice insurance is driving doctors and institutional healthcare providers to either limit or get out of healthcare entirely. In response to cases such as *Fein,* in 1998, California passed Proposition 103, which limited insurance premiums. California also imposed a $250,000 cap on damages (such as punitive damages) that are "noneconomic," or not tied specifically to a monetary loss by a plaintiff. In the face of what has been termed a malpractice crisis, several other states have implemented or considered such limitations. Meanwhile, a few states followed the example of other nations (including Sweden and New Zealand) that operate under limited types of no-fault systems for medical malpractice. In those systems, injured patients are compensated regardless of who (or, more specifically, which healthcare provider) is at fault.

Attorneys' groups such as the Association of Trial Lawyers of America (ATLA) doggedly lobby against those several types of tort reform at the state and national levels. Critics of the ATLA, on the other hand, have looked at this controversy as yet another example of the mercenary bent of lawyers. They charge that lawyers who oppose tort reform are interested only in collecting contingency fees, which sometimes amount to 40 percent of medical malpractice settlement amounts. Consumer advocacy organizations have weighed in on the debate over tort reform, and they contend that medical malpractice premiums are rising because the insurance industry has managed itself poorly and that medical malpractice lawsuits are a useful protection against incompetent physicians.

In 2002 and 2003, there was discussion among members of Congress and President George W. Bush about writing a federal law that would limit nonmedical awards. That debate promises to be ongoing and contentious. If past medicolegal controversies about medical-product liability and medical malpractice are any guide, the discussion will be an expansive one—probably including arguments about patient care, physicians' autonomy, courts' activism, and even lawyers' role within American society.

Refusal of Treatment

Historically, much of the courts' attention to medicine has been directed to cases in which doctors are accused of acting inappropriately or inexpertly. And yet medicolegal controversy also occurs under a very different scenario: when patients have wished to be left alone and *not* treated by medical professionals but medicine has intruded onto their bodies anyway. That is, in some instances when physicians have provided care, patients did not desire medical action at all or would have preferred only limited intervention. When these situations have occurred, patients sometimes have alleged in court that their personal rights (to bodily integrity, privacy, and even religion) have been violated. Cases related to the right to refuse treatment are often quite complicated for courts to resolve. The easiest of the refusal-of-treatment controversies for courts to decide involve fully conscious adults; in such instances, judicial authorities generally give great leeway to adults to make medical decisions that affect only themselves. But what if courts must determine the fates of patients who *cannot clearly express* their refusal of medical treatment, say when the patient is unconscious or is a child? There, the dilemma for the legal system can be acute.

During the middle of the twentieth century, as the doctor-patient relationship became much more crowded with additional parties, even those physicians who recently had enjoyed the trust of their patients' families and the courts—forensic pathologists—found themselves under fire for intrusiveness. Some of the most interesting controversies of this type, in fact, concerned the authority of medical examiners (MEs) and coroners to order autopsies on the bodies of "their patients"—that is, persons who died under circumstances that the MEs believed to be questionable. In several difficult cases, the courts examined regulations by state and local governments of MEs' and coroners' actions. Many states and localities in the early to mid–twentieth century gave MEs and coroners the authority to order autopsies (although in some instances other officials such as district attorneys also were responsible for authorizing postmortem examinations). In most cases, therefore, suits did not succeed against individual medicolegal officials when they performed autopsies without the consent of family members. Courts only required that MEs and coroners needed to be performing their duties in good faith and acting within their recognized statutory authority.

In a suit against the New York City Medical Examiner's Office, for instance, the husband of a woman whose body had been autopsied against the husband's wishes failed to convince the court that the ME was acting inappropriately. In a case titled *Cremonese v. City of New York* (1966), the plaintiff alleged that he had refused to consent to an autopsy on the body of his wife, in spite of the fact that the physicians who had attended the deceased could not decide why she had died. Upon his refusal, the ME's office at first issued a death certificate but listed the cause of death in such vague terms that the certification was refused by the Board of Health. Due to that refusal, the ME went ahead and performed an autopsy without permission from the family. Ultimately, the court supported the ME's action, based on its reading of the ME's responsibility to act in compliance with the authority of the Board of Health.

In another case from the same era, however, an ME discovered that his misreading of the controlling state law put him at risk for legal censure. The associate ME for Broward County, Florida, understood state law to read that he could perform an autopsy if a death were due to violence or had occurred in unusual circumstances, *or* if he was authorized to perform a postmortem by the county prosecutor. In the case at hand, that of an eighty-two-year-old woman who had died in a hospital, the associate ME believed that the patient's death had been unusual enough to justify an examination of her body despite the family's explicit refusal to consent to an autopsy. In fact, the state had required both that the death be violent or unusual *and* that the prosecutor request an investigation in order for an autopsy to proceed without the consent of next of kin. In the resulting case of *Jackson v. Rupp* (1969), the court ruled that the ME had acted without authorization from the state and the family, and found against him. In consequence, the Florida court reminded the ME that his power to override a family's wishes was not absolute. The decision in *Jackson v.*

Rupp placed MEs on notice that they had to act within state law, particularly in regard to the delicate question of performing an autopsy without the family's consent.

In certain cases, however, courts will refuse to allow the niceties of individual conscience to interfere with the protection of public health. In particular, courts have long upheld the notion that the police powers of states include taking action to combat communicable diseases. In *Jacobson v. Massachusetts* (1905), for example, the Supreme Court allowed Massachusetts to implement a mandatory smallpox vaccination program. In *Compagnie Francaise v. State Board of Health* (1902), the court upheld quarantine restrictions as constitutional and not an infringement on citizens' Fourteenth Amendment rights. In more recent instances, courts have allowed municipal authorities to enact "hold and treat" ordinances for persons who carried venereal diseases. The case of *Reynolds v. McNichols* (1973) concerned one such local regulation in Denver. Although the plaintiff (an admitted prostitute) argued that the city's injection of her with penicillin without her consent was unconstitutional because her male sexual partners were not similarly treated, the U.S. Court of Appeals for the Tenth Circuit denied her claim. States had the authority to protect the public (including the clients of prostitutes) against sexually transmitted disease, the court ruled, even if that protection meant compulsory treatment for the potential carriers of disease.

Yet in contrast to courts' rather firm stance regarding compulsory protections against communicable diseases, many other controversies concerning refusal of treatment have proved troublesome to courts. Several cases involving the charge of intrusion into patients' privacy or contravention of their wishes by medical practitioners have been made more complicated by the fact that, when decisions about medical intervention reach a crisis state (that is, when courts must be invoked to settle a controversy), there often is an element of time involved. A decision about whether medical care should be given in the face of a patient's objections sometimes must be made very quickly. By the time that courts can be petitioned and cases heard, the practical matter already has been decided and the issue is no longer a live legal controversy—meaning that for many courts it is no longer justiciable.

This has never been illustrated more clearly than in the famous case of *Georgetown College v. Jones* (1964). When Mrs. Jesse Jones was admitted as a patient at Georgetown College Hospital, she was gravely ill due to loss of blood from a bleeding ulcer. The chief resident at the hospital, Dr. Edwin Westura, determined that Mrs. Jones had to have a blood transfusion immediately in order to save her life. Mrs. Jones's speech could not be understood easily in her weakened state, but she seemed to indicate that she would not accept a transfusion. Her husband, who accompanied her, told attending staff that his wife and he were members of the Jehovah's Witnesses religious sect, and that they had religious grounds for refusing the blood products from animals from entering their bodies. In vain, doctors tried to persuade Mr. and Mrs. Jones to allow the transfusion.

Lawyers for the hospital applied to Judge Edward Tamm of the U.S. District Court for the District of Columbia to authorize the transfusion. When Judge Tamm refused (probably because the request was oral rather than written), within hours the hospital applied to Judge J. Skelley Wright of the U.S. Circuit Court of Appeals. Wright went to the hospital and attempted to interview Mrs. Jones himself. Faced with a life-threatening emergency, Judge Wright granted the hospital's request. The physicians who were attending Mrs. Jones administered a transfusion, and she recovered rapidly. Mrs. Jones and her family then asked for judicial determination of whether the hospital's action had been constitutional.

The case and its appeals had obvious implications for the constitutional guarantee of freedom of religion. It touched, as well, on important questions such as the control by adults over their own medical treatment and physicians' and hospitals' scope of action in case they were in dispute with patients and their families. As Judge Warren Burger phrased it in his dissent from the court's decision to refrain from revisiting the controversy on appeal:

> The episode presents on one hand an example of a grave dilemma which confronts those who engage in the healing arts and on the other hand some very basic and fundamental issues on the nature and scope of judicial power. We can sympathize with the one but we cannot safely or appropriately temporize with the other; we have an obligation to deal with the basic question whether a judicially cognizable issue is presented when a legally competent adult refuses, on grounds of conscience, to consent to a medical treatment essential to preserve life. (*Georgetown College v. Jones* 1964, 1015)

The majority of the appeals court, however, rested its decision on the nonjusticiability of the matter. They reasoned that Mrs. Jones was out of danger (indeed she was out of the hospital), and therefore to hear her case was to argue an abstraction. The U.S. Supreme Court refused to grant certiorari; it indicated, though, that its decision against certiorari was not related to the merits of this particularly dramatic and important case.

Georgetown College v. Jones became a well-known precedent not only in courts, but also among hospital administrators, for it illustrated the fact that judges would consider making emergency medical decisions that went against deeply cherished beliefs of patients. But the medical prognosis had to be grave and the remedy clear-cut for courts to intervene. Thus a more practical alternative for medical authorities was to head off the crisis at a much earlier stage. By presenting patients who were being admitted to hospitals with a list of procedures to which they might have conscientious objections, healthcare providers could protect themselves from legal actions of the type that Mr. and Mrs. Jones had initiated. Either the medical providers would obtain patient consent for those procedures before there was a life-threatening incident, or they would reassure themselves and the courts that patients had considered in advance the potentially harmful effects of refusing the procedures. As a result of Mrs. Jones's particular situation, preadmission forms allowing patients to consent to or decline the use of blood and blood products came into wide usage in hospitals across the nation.

If courts have struggled to decide when to permit involuntary medical intervention for adults, they have agonized over decisions involving the medical treatment of children. Courts generally have protected parents' rights to make medical decisions for their children, although they have been at pains to point out that parents' control over their children's health is not absolute. In the 1979 case of *Parham v. J. R.*, for example, the U.S. Supreme Court held that parents should be presumed to have their children's best interests at heart when the parents made medical decisions for those minor dependents. *Parham* was concerned with the rights of children who were committed by their parents to mental-health facilities without benefit of a hearing at which there was a neutral third party. The dissenters on the Court were troubled by the denial of due process to minors; thus they saw a deprivation of liberty to children under the U.S. Constitution's Fourteenth Amendment. It was significant in a historical sense that the mental-health facilities in question had been built in the second half of the twentieth century; they were considered up-to-date and humane institutions, rather than throwbacks to the eighteenth century's asylums for the mentally ill. It was not the institutions themselves but rather the lack of a formal, adversarial hearing before committal of the children that drew criticism and served as the basis for the suit.

In 1992, the Supreme Court of Georgia decided *In re Jane Doe*—another controversy that centered on parents' rights to make crucial medical decisions for their children. The case concerned a thirteen-year-old patient who had been admitted to a hospital with neurological problems that recently had become severe. Jane's parents could not reach an understanding between each other about whether their child should be resuscitated through measures such as the application of an electric shock and chest compressions if she went into cardiac arrest. The parents also could not concur about whether Jane's medical treatment should be "de-escalated"—that is, for example, whether a ventilator should be discontinued. Susan Doe, the mother, generally was in favor of the entering of a Do Not Resuscitate (DNR) order and the initiating de-escalation of treatment; Jane's father, John, opposed those measures. In the face of the parents' disagreement, the hospital asked its Bioethics Committee to consider Jane Doe's situation. Eventually, the hospital's working position (following a Georgia law that set up a presumption of consent to resuscitation) was that until there was a judicial resolution of the case, one parent's objection to a DNR order meant that that order could not stand.

The court, therefore, was faced with the difficulty of choosing from among several parties who claimed to speak for the patient: her mother, Susan, and father, John, who disagreed among themselves about the proper course of their daughter's treatment, and the hospital at which Jane had been treated, which was asking the judicial system for guidance on how to proceed. Although Jane Doe had died before the Supreme Court of Georgia heard the case, the court considered the controversy not to be moot. In contrast to the appeals court's ruling in *Georgetown College v. Jones,* this court decided that the case at hand was "capable of repetition yet evading review"— a principle that the U.S. Supreme Court had enunciated in *Gerstein v. Pugh* (1975).

The court in the *Doe* case decided to take a middle ground in regard to Jane's care, conferring an exclusive right to make decisions for an incompetent patient (such as a child) neither to parents or other family members, nor to medical authorities, nor to the courts. Rather, the court looked to legislatures for some guidance, and it leaned heavily on parental and medical decision making. The *Doe* decision thus reserved for courts the right to intervene in unusually controversial cases involving refusal of treatment for children. As the court expressed it: "Under certain circumstances, the parents of an incompetent child may exercise the child's right to refuse medical treatment without prior judicial approval. We have never held, however, that parents have an absolute right to make medical decisions for their children" (*In re Jane Doe* 1992, 393).

During the decade following *In re Doe,* courts continued to struggle with parental authority in refusal-of-treatment cases, especially in situations when hospitalized children needed resuscitation or other lifesaving measures. Even when there were detailed state statutes supposedly defining the authority of hospitals, physicians, and parents, courts still were asked, in effect, to mediate conflicts among the parties. The 2000 Texas case of *Miller v. Columbia/HCA,* for example, provided a heartrending example of the dilemmas that parents and medical care providers faced, for example, in either mandating or denying care to critically ill newborns.

In 1990, a pregnant woman named Karla Miller was admitted to a hospital with both an infection and signs of premature labor. Mrs. Miller's doctors estimated that the baby she was carrying was of twenty-three weeks' gestational age. Staff at the hospital told Mrs. Miller and her husband, Mark, that if labor proceeded, there was only a slight chance that the baby would be born alive. Babies at that early age not only had a small chance of survival, but they were at grave risk of severe mental and physical defects if they did live. Ironically, some of the heroic resuscitation measures that often were employed to save the lives of extremely premature babies at birth themselves could contribute to the babies' having further impairments. The Millers, fearing that such intense resuscitation efforts would create terrible physical problems for their child, expressed to the doctors and staff that they did not want resuscitation to be performed on the baby when she was born.

Texas state law pointed in several directions as to the duty of the hospital to resuscitate the baby. On one hand, according to several relevant judicial decisions, parents had a legal duty to provide necessary medical care for their children. The state (for example, child-welfare authorities) might step in, as *parens patriae,* in cases when parents acting on their religious convictions refused to take a child to a hospital, as in the case of *Mitchell v. Davis* (1947). But on the other hand, parents were allowed to refuse medical treatment for their terminally ill children, according to the Natural Death Act passed by the Texas legislature in 1989. Also pointing to parents' ability to refuse treatment was a Texas precedent that doctors had a duty to obtain parents' consent for lifesaving medical procedures except in cases that were too urgent for consent to be procured. In addition, a physician who operated without a patient's (or his or her parents') consent risked liability for assault and battery, as was decided in the case of *Gravis v. Physicians and Surgeons Hospital* (1968).

In the hours between Mrs. Miller's admission and the baby's birth, the hospital held several meetings concerning the situation. The facility eventually decided that it was bound to abide by the policy from its parent company (Healthcare Corporation of America—HCA) that it must perform resuscitation—even if that was in violation of the Millers' wishes. At that juncture, the hospital staff and the Millers' doctors informed them that if, at the time the baby was born, the child weighed more than 500 grams, she would be resuscitated. Interestingly, the hospital did not seek a court order to perform resuscitation, although it would have had time to do so.

The baby (a girl named Sidney) was delivered alive; in terms of her weight, she met the hospital's criteria for resuscitation and received that treatment. As a result of the resuscitation, she was severely impaired both physically and mentally. Her doctors agreed that Sidney would require lifelong care to meet her basic needs. The Millers sued both the hospital and HCA on behalf of Sidney, asking for past and future medical expenses, punitive damages, and interest. The heart of the Millers' case was that the hospital had provided treatment without their consent, and that the healthcare corporation had implemented a policy requiring treatment (of infants born above a certain weight) regardless of consent. The trial court was extremely sympathetic to the Millers' arguments, rendering a judgment of $29,400,000 in past and future medical expenses, $13,500,000 in punitive damages, and $17,503,066 in prejudgment interest.

The Court of Appeals of Texas considered the difficult issues raised in the *Miller* case and, although divided, ruled against them. According to the court, HCA was not liable for its policies regarding resuscitation of premature babies, and the Millers were entitled to no damages from the healthcare provider. The court placed particular stress on several points of law. It noted, for example, the important Supreme Court decision of *Cruzan v. Director, Missouri Department of Health* (1990). In *Cruzan,* the Supreme Court had said that only an individual patient could exercise his or her right to refuse medical treatment and that states were not required to authorize anyone else to refuse such treatment on the patient's behalf. Thus, the court reasoned, the Texas legislature, in passing the Natural Death Act (and then amending it ten years later, in the Advance Directives Act of 1999), had expressly provided a right for parents to refuse medical treatment for their terminally ill children. The state had *not* carved out other instances, however, in which parents could exercise that right—for example, for children who were severely disabled but not terminally ill, which was Sidney Miller's situation. The court also reasoned that *Cruzan* had determined that the state had the greatest interest in preserving life when that life was most capable of being saved—in Sidney's case, in the minutes immediately after her birth, when a decision had to be made about whether to perform resuscitation and if so, which type. Finally, the *Miller* decision reminded litigants that federal law did not preempt state laws concerning parents' consent to medical treatment for children. Such cases, the court said, should continue to be governed by state rather than federal law.

The Law Informs Public Debate: Current Medicolegal Controversies

The *Miller* case illustrates how much medicine had changed in the twentieth century, not just with respect to malpractice actions but also in general. Medicine in the twentieth century became almost unbelievably more expert; 100 years earlier, the saving of a baby of twenty-three weeks' gestation would have been nothing short of miraculous. And yet medicine also was unquestionably more complex and undeniably more affected by the law. Now, the delivery room included not just the Millers' physician, but also—at least in effect—hospital administrators and healthcare system policymakers. That is, medicine had become a corporate venture in many respects. Finally, in a figurative but no less real sense, when Sidney Miller was born, the courts were on hand as well, warning healthcare personnel that if they did not save the baby's life through heroic means, they could be sued. Medical malpractice suits had become so usual and so feared in American society that they informed and necessitated medical decisions once the province of only the family and the attending doctor.

Sidney Miller's situation was exceptionally awkward for judicial authorities in part because it involved the two most difficult categories of decisions courts could face: beginning- and end-of-life issues. When they considered controversies concerning life and death, courts confronted the fact that medicine's great technical advances did not guarantee agreement about the implications of lifesaving measures. Furthermore, merely in deciding cases that tapped into citizens' deeply cherished beliefs about life and death, courts were guaranteed to spur further debate. Even in instances when courts managed to reach a short-term solution in a life-and-death dispute, they often created additional problems, for short-term judicial remedies could be outmoded quickly by changing medical technology or practice. And in the thorniest cases involving the beginning and the end of life, courts brought down the full wrath of the public, which condemned them as arrogant and antidemocratic.

Reproduction and Abortion

Nowhere has the courtroom debate about life-and-death issues been fiercer than with regard to matters connected with reproduction, birth control, and abortion. Those issues evoke cherished ideas connected to privacy, family, and religious belief, and of course they certainly involve questions about the medical profession and medicine as a science. Courts have been especially involved in reproductive issues as medicine has changed its own understandings of human reproduction, the medical techniques related to it, and the medical community's role in providing reproductive care.

Prior to the twentieth century and for some time in the new century, both states and certain federal agencies were allowed to regulate not only the sale of contraceptive devices but also the distribution of information about contraception even by medical professionals. In 1872, for example, Congress passed the so-called Comstock Act, prohibiting the mailing of obscene materials. The legislation was named for Postmaster General Anthony Comstock, who was a leading critic of what in more modern terms would be called pornography. (Comstock's efforts to purge books of information that he deemed inappropriate were termed *Comstockery,* just as the English moralist Thomas Bowdler gave rise to a term meaning censorship: *bowdlerization.*) Comstock had a very broad definition of obscenity, which included any information about artificial birth control. Thus, physicians in Comstock's time were greatly hampered in even dispensing birth control information because they could not order books or pamphlets about it or request contraceptive devices to be sent through the U.S. mail without fear of prosecution for obscenity. Those regulations were left to stand by the Supreme Court largely until the 1960s and 1970s.

The career of birth control advocate Margaret Sanger illustrated the sweeping effects of the Comstock laws. Sanger, a nurse, had worked for years among poor communities and was convinced that many of the economic challenges faced by persons in need were due simply to the large number of children in their families and the crushing burden of work that many children in a household created for their mothers. Sanger also based her views on the need for birth control on her discussions with birth control advocates in Europe, who had views rooted in feminism. In 1917, Sanger was tried under a New York statute that prevented the dispensing of birth control information to anyone for any reason. (The New York law was a Comstock-inspired policy, but it also had the support of the Catholic Church.) The single exception to the prohibition was for physicians, who were allowed to discuss contraceptives—such as condoms—with their patients, but only for the purpose of preventing the spread of venereal disease.

Sanger believed that women should have access to information about contraception in order to protect their health, and she was determined to challenge the law as a violation of the Constitution's equal protection clause. The Court of Appeals ruled against Sanger in its 1918 decision. The court's reading of the New York law was that Mrs. Sanger was a nurse, rather than a physician, and thus was not allowed to discuss birth control with her patients. The court did broaden the New York statute, however, in terms of its provisions for doctors to discuss contraception. The decision in *People v. Sanger* included the holding that physicians could act to prevent diseases or health threats to women by prescribing contraceptives for them.

Thus states continued to regulate citizens' decisions about when and if they should reproduce, albeit with some recognition of physicians' role as healthcare providers in regard to contraception. Although Comstock-era laws that regulated contraception devices and information did impinge upon citizens' reproductive behavior, another type of state law intruded even further. Several states created programs of forced sterilization, aimed at persons who were classified as mentally handicapped. In the infamous case of *Buck v. Bell* (1927), the U.S. Supreme Court reviewed the state of Virginia's laws that allowed sterilization of the "weak-minded." Carrie Buck, an eighteen-year-old unmarried mother, was sterilized at the Virginia Colony for the Epileptic and Feeble-Minded. The Court's decision in *Buck v. Bell* permitted Virginia to proceed with sterilization without the consent of institutionalized persons. The decision also forcefully endorsed the policy of using sterilization to rid the nation of later generations of persons who, in the memorable opinion of Justice Oliver Wendell Holmes, "[sapped] the strength of the State" (*Buck v. Bell* 1927, 207). Justice Holmes saw a clear analogy between state-mandated vaccination programs and sterilization for the purposes of "good birth" or "eugenics." The courts were endorsing strong measures in pursuit of eugenics.

By the 1920s and 1930s, however, the scientific and medical communities were beginning to reject eugenical ideas. (Even as eugenics was proving extremely controversial, however, it remained the basis of many states' laws for decades. Virginia's laws allowing involuntary sterilization were on the books until 1974.) The first case in which the Supreme Court backed away from its support of eugenics occurred in 1942. Even the Court, as strongly as it had spoken in *Buck v. Bell,* could not fail to be influenced by a worst-case scenario that appeared abroad in the 1930s and 1940s: Adolf Hitler's program of forced sterilization of those persons whom the Nazi regime considered "unfit" or "degenerate." In the case of *Skinner v. Oklahoma,* the Supreme Court declared that Oklahoma could not escape the strict scrutiny of the high court, for Oklahoma presumed to interfere with a basic civil right by involuntarily mandating a vasectomy for convicted felon Jack Skinner. Although some of the majority justices' opinions were narrow in scope and drew little distinction between the criminal Jack Skinner and the "feeble-minded" Carrie Buck, Justice William O. Douglas did delineate a broader application for the case. He foresaw that the Court would mark off and protect procreation as a key function of human beings.

Douglas was proven correct in the mid-1960s. The Court in *Griswold v. Connecticut* (1965) held that reproduction was a fundamental right, safeguarded through the U.S. Constitution. *Griswold* was the culmination of a decades-old effort to broaden the discussion of birth control beyond the confines of a doctor and patient. After *Griswold,* states could not interfere with the right of married persons to obtain birth control devices and information. The Court's ruling in *Eisenstadt v. Baird* (1972) broadened that right to minors. For physicians concerned about the scope of their authority, such rulings were both good and bad news. In one sense, the Supreme Court had freed physicians from worrying about how (indeed sometimes whether) they communicated with their patients on the controversial topic of birth control.

In another respect, however, physicians no longer were the only parties who could dispense birth control information, advice, and devices. Although some medical devices (notably the birth control pill, which was new in the early 1960s) remained available by prescription only, many others could be or soon would be bought over the counter. The privacy/contraception cases also demonstrated the power of groups such as Planned Parenthood (the plaintiff in the challenge to Connecticut's 1879 law that *Griswold* overturned). Obviously an organization that had legal and political skill, Planned Parenthood also aimed to offer birth control advice outside of the traditional medical framework by providing advice through its own physicians at times, as well as through nurses and lay birth control counselors. Thus courts' enunciation that reproductive choices were rights that were protected under the U.S. Constitution had the effect of increasing physicians' scope of authority while at the same time leaving doctors with new rivals—other parties who legally could dispense birth control information and services.

In the early 1970s, the Supreme Court took on an issue of great political interest when it agreed to hear cases having to do with abortion. Abortion had been made legal by four states in the late 1960s, as a result of efforts by women's rights groups to abolish state statutes holding abortion providers criminally liable. Those statutes had been of fairly recent historical vintage. Until about the middle of the nineteenth century, most American jurisdictions held to the English common-law view that any abortion performed "before quickening"—that is, when a woman could feel movement in the womb—was legal. In the later nineteenth century, however, particularly as physicians tried to establish themselves as the primary providers of healthcare for pregnant women (edging aside midwives), states began to regulate abortion much more strictly. Abortions at any time during pregnancy were banned, with stiff penalties for both unlicensed medical practitioners and regular doctors who performed the procedure. A few states allowed exceptions only if the life of the mother was at stake; others permitted exceptions in case of rape or serious threat to the mother's physical health.

By the late 1960s, judges in some jurisdictions were declaring state bans on abortion unconstitutional, usually citing the right to privacy that had been enunciated in the contraception case of *Griswold v. Connecticut* (1965). In a pair of cases in 1973, *Roe v. Wade* and *Doe v. Bolton*, the U.S. Supreme Court considered the constitutionality of antiabortion statutes from Texas and Georgia, respectively. (In both cases at the time, the name of the woman who had sought an abortion was kept secret. Subsequently, at her own request, the name of the *Roe* petitioner, Norma McCorvey, was made public.)

The two cases were slightly different in factual content, but each contained similarities in terms of the laws they tested. "Jane Roe" was an unmarried Texas woman who claimed that she had been raped. Ironically, she said that the location of the rape was Georgia; it was in Texas, however, that she sought an abortion. Plaintiff "Mary Doe" was married and already the mother of three children. Desperate to remain married to her husband, who had threatened to leave her if they had another child, she sought an abortion. The Texas law (written in 1859 and amended in 1879) was so strict that it did not allow a woman to have an abortion even if she had been raped; only if her life were in peril from carrying the pregnancy to term was an abortion permissible. The Georgia law, conversely, was considered one of the more liberal antiabortion statutes among the states because it provided not only a rape exception, but also an exception based on danger to the mother's health rather than her life. Still, that requirement was a standard that Mary Doe could not meet.

Based on earlier rulings, the Supreme Court in both the *Doe* and *Roe* decisions easily found a compelling interest, on the part of states, in protecting both the life of the unborn child *and* that of the mother. But how could those rights be weighed, one against the other, when abortion seemed to put them in direct conflict? In answering that dilemma, the Court looked to medicine for answers. Medical authorities believed that human beings could not live on their own outside the uterus any earlier than the very end of the second trimester. Thus the Supreme Court marked out a time within pregnancy when the state's interest in the life of an unborn child had to be balanced against the right of a woman to make a private decision about the disposition of her own body. In consultation with her physician, a woman might choose to have an abortion in the first trimester of pregnancy, and that right would be constitutionally protected from state intervention. In the third trimester of pregnancy, however, babies could be and were being delivered alive. Moreover, at that point in a pregnancy, abortion was a medical procedure that was relatively dangerous for the mother. The Court (led by Justice Blackmun) argued that the third trimester of pregnancy was a time that states could devise regulations on abortion—especially having in mind the state's interest in regulating unlicensed practitioners. The second trimester presented the greatest dilemma for the Court. During the second trimester, it was not clear that abortion was safer than a full-term pregnancy. Nor was medical science prepared to state at exactly which moment in the second trimester an infant was viable. The Court decided that states might enact reasonable restrictions on second-trimester abortions, providing authorities could justify those restrictions as protecting the health of the mother. (Justice Blackmun had the difficult task of spelling out and justifying the trimester divisions, largely because he was the Court's resident expert on medical law. He had served for several years as legal counsel to the Mayo Clinic.)

The *Roe* and *Doe* decisions were a victory for those who advocated a liberalization of state abortion laws and for the medical profession, for which the decisions represented a high watermark of the profession's prestige in courts. The Supreme Court paid close attention, for example, to the opinions of both the American Bar Association [ABA] and the AMA, organizations that had filed *amicus curiae* briefs challenging the state laws. In its decision, the Court also noted the safety of abortions that were provided in hospitals as opposed to "abortion mills"; thus in a sense the Court was congratulating medicine on its antiseptic techniques and modern facilities. In making the contention that medicine was much improved from the Victorian era, the Court referred to medical data from the plaintiffs that abortion was a fairly safe medical procedure. That safety record was in contrast to the hazards of abortions in the era when Texas and Georgia had written their antiabortion statutes. In making its judgment, the Court, that is, relied heavily on the powerful voices within the medical community.

As much as any other decisions rendered by the Court in its history, *Roe* and *Doe* unleashed enormous controversy. In the wake of the decisions, members of Congress proposed a number of restrictions on abortion that, if passed, would have limited the widespread application of *Roe* and *Doe*. At least eighteen congressional proposals set forth constitutional amendments that would have severely restricted abortions—usually mandating that abortions be allowed only under rules similar to Texas's or Georgia's pre-*Roe* and -*Doe* statutes. Although none of the amendments to the federal Constitution were enacted into law, the Hyde Amendment of 1976 added to a Medicaid-appropriations bill the provision that an abortion would be funded by that federal program only if the pregnancy was life-endangering to the mother. The Hyde Amendment was reenacted several times subsequently. In a key test of federal funding restrictions for abortions—the case of *Harris v. McRae* (1980)—the Court ruled that such limitations were permissible.

It was important for those interested in the judicial disposition of abortion cases that the Court had divided 4 to 5 in *McRae*, whereas the decisions in *Roe* and *Doe* were by a majority of 7 to 2. Encouraged by *McRae*, those who sought greater restrictions on abortions than had been allowed by the Court in 1973 took their fight first to state legislatures. Antiabortion groups sought state restrictions on abortions that might be allowed by a Supreme Court that obviously was changing in both composition and mood. Those opposed to "liberal" abortion laws, for instance, sponsored state legislation that mandated waiting periods before women could obtain abortions, during which time women might have to undergo counseling about pregnancy. Other state regulations imposed parental-notification requirements on teenagers seeking abortions. A few states required married women to notify their spouses prior to obtaining abortions.

Such state requirements were challenged in the case of *Planned Parenthood of Southeastern Pennsylvania v. Casey* (1992). Although a U.S. Court of Appeals had declared unconstitutional the spousal-notification provision of a Pennsylvania law, it let stand various other restrictions on abortion that Pennsylvania had imposed. In a complex and heated decision, the Supreme Court could manage no basic agreement on the constitutionality of Pennsylvania's law. The Court maintained that states must not place an "undue burden" on women's right to secure an abortion, but that warning pleased almost no one, because it was vague and difficult to interpret. *Casey* left the door open for more challenges to state notification laws and for other areas in which states regulated abortions.

Casey also certainly signaled the depth of division on the Court itself about how and by whom the abortion controversy ought to be addressed. Justice Blackmun's rebuke to his fellow justices who, in the *Casey* decision, had been critical of *Roe* was stinging:

> I fear for the darkness as four Justices anxiously await the single vote necessary to extinguish the light. . . . [T]he Chief Justice's criticism of *Roe* follows from his stunted conception of individual liberties. . . . In the Chief Justice's world, a woman considering whether to terminate a pregnancy is entitled to no more protection than adulterers, murders, and so-called sexual deviates. . . . I am 83 years old. I cannot remain on this Court forever. (*Planned Parenthood v. Casey* 1992, 923)

It was not surprising that the Supreme Court remained deeply divided on the issue of abortion, especially with the replacement of some of the justices who had heard *Roe* and *Doe.* Whereas the members of Court in the 1970s had been appointed mostly in the 1950s and 1960s and were influenced by the leadership of Chief Justice Earl Warren, retirements and deaths in the years after *Roe* and *Doe* had given subsequent U.S. presidents (especially in the era of President Ronald Reagan) the opportunity to replace those relatively liberal justices with jurists who took a more conservative stance on a number of issues, including abortion. In several cases at the very end of the twentieth century, the Court denied certiorari in well-known abortion cases, and yet the voices on the Court that wished to overturn *Roe* and *Doe* were growing stronger. The justices who dissented from those denials made strong arguments demonstrating the fervency of their beliefs about the issue.

For example, in the case of *Voinovich et al. v. Women's Medical Professional Corporation,* from 1998, the Supreme Court refused to hear an appeal from a decision of the U.S. Court of Appeals for the Sixth Circuit. The circuit court had affirmed a district court decision that enjoined an Ohio law as unconstitutional. The 1996 Ohio statute had made abortions illegal if the fetus was viable, allowing exceptions only if the physician who performed the abortion determined that the procedure was necessary to save the life or preserve the major bodily functions of the mother. Thus, under the statute, a physician could perform an abortion to preserve the health of a woman whose heart function was seriously (and irreversibly) threatened by carrying the pregnancy to term; but the physician could not do so using the argument of preserving the mother's mental health.

The lower courts that had deemed the statute unconstitutional criticized its lacking an exception for the mental health of the mother. They also found the Ohio law's provision for how the physician should make the determination of medical necessity (that is, "in good faith and in the exercise of reasonable medical judgment") to be so vague as to expose physicians to both criminal and civil liability, even when they acted on their best-informed medical judgment. In their dissent from the denial of certiorari, Justices Thomas and Scalia took issue with the appeals courts' interpretation of recent Supreme Court decisions such as *Doe v. Bolton* (1973), *Coulatti v. Franklin* (1979), and *Planned Parenthood v. Casey* (1992). In particular, Thomas and Scalia emphasized the holding in the *Doe* case. There, a statute prohibiting abortions had been allowed because it had provided for exceptions when physicians considered the entire well-being of the patient, including her physical, emotional, psychological, and even familial health, and determined that the pregnancy ought to end in an abortion. Thomas and Scalia argued in *Voinovich* that *Doe* had not *required* physicians to consider all of those factors, but only had *permitted* them to be considered. They pointed out that the majority of states limited the performance of abortions during late pregnancy and that most of those did not provide a "mental health" exception. The dissenters were worried that the Supreme Court's failure to review the appeals decisions would "cast doubt on the validity of other state statutes" (*Voinovich et al. v. Women's Medical Professional Medical Corporation et al.* 1998, 1040).

In *Cloer v. Gynecology Clinic, Inc.* (2000), Scalia and Thomas again dissented from the Court's refusal to review an abortion case. The *Cloer* case involved a common fact scenario at abortion providers' facilities: clashes between antiabortion activists and clinic staff and patients in the immediate vicinity of an abortion clinic. The leading members of the antiabortion group—as was often the case—were persons who had religious objections to abortion. In this instance, the protestors were a group called Pastors for Life, headed by the Rev. Michael Cloer. The South Carolina State Supreme Court had allowed an injunction to stand that had barred antiabortion protestors from approaching physicians, going into the clinic as trespassers, obstructing traffic, protesting inside a twelve-foot buffer zone near the clinic, or making noises that could be heard inside the clinic. That type of injunction was very common in many localities throughout the United States. For violating the injunction, the South Carolina court allowed the protestors to be penalized under a civil conspiracy claim. Justices Scalia and Thomas (this time with Scalia writing the dissent) again had wanted the U.S. Supreme Court to grant certiorari. They were alarmed that the Supreme Court of South Carolina would decide that peaceful activities of protest (for Cloer and his followers never were accused of violence or destruction of property) constituted a civil conspiracy. The appellants had maintained that, as peaceful protestors who sought to change people's minds about abortion by lawful words and actions, their First Amendment rights precluded a civil conspiracy claim.

The depth of the Supreme Court's division became even more readily apparent in the decision of *Stenberg v. Carhart* (2000), in which the Court considered state regulations of partial-birth abortions. Although the Court voted, 5 to 4, to uphold the lower court decisions that had held a Nebraska statute strictly regulating abortions to be unconstitutional, the four dissenters all voiced deep reservations about the majority opinion. Three of the dissenters also took the opportunity to express their dissatisfaction with several major Supreme Court decisions on abortion, signaling their willingness to overrule those decisions should the right moment arise. Some of their arguments were unusually frank and broad in scope.

The case went right to the heart of physicians' legal role as abortion providers. A Nebraska statute made criminal any medical procedure that involved a "partial birth abortion." A *partial-birth abortion* was defined to mean a termination of a pregnancy in which a vaginal delivery occurred and a fetus or body parts of the fetus were extracted so as to kill the child. In one sense, the Nebraska law was a conventional one. Nebraska was doing what several other states did in the wake of the *Roe* decision, which was to outlaw abortions in the third trimester of pregnancy, when the assumption was that the fetus was viable. This particular statute, like many other state laws of its type, provided an exception when the life of the mother was in jeopardy. It did not, however, allow for exceptions if the mental or physical health of the mother would be compromised by continuing the pregnancy. By placing such stringent restrictions on the circumstances in which abortions could be performed, Nebraska incurred the wrath of the medical profession. Nebraska's law also earned the censure of the members of the Supreme Court who wished to protect the physician-patient relationship, just as the Supreme Court had done in *Roe.*

By far the most common method of abortion (almost 90 percent of all abortions performed) in the United States at the time of the *Carhart* decision was a method known as "vacuum aspiration," in which a vacuum tube sucked out the contents of the uterus. Vacuum aspiration almost always was performed at less than twelve weeks into a pregnancy. Another method of abortion, known as dilation and evacuation (or D&E), was the usual method of abortion in the second trimester of pregnancy. Abortions in that part of pregnancy amounted to about 10 percent of all abortions performed. D&E replaced the saline injection method of abortion that had been used until the 1970s. When the Supreme Court decided cases such as *Planned Parenthood of Central Missouri v. Danforth* (1976), saline injection—a nonsurgical procedure—was safer than a vaginal birth. In *Danforth* as in *Roe,* in the course of describing why states had a right to regulate them, the court discussed the relative safety of abortion as a medical procedure. By the 1980s, D&E was considered safer than saline injection, although it did carry some risks. It amounted to a vacuum aspiration of the fetus, combined with cervical dilation and the use of surgical instruments to remove pieces of the fetus. The entire fetus at that (second-trimester) stage of gestation could not fit through the internal structure of the uterus, and when instruments were used to pull the fetus out of the cervix, the body of the fetus was pulled apart.

The Nebraska lawmakers may have supposed that they could answer the call from antiabortion groups in their state to ban partial-birth abortions without stirring up intense controversy. After all, the statute at first appeared to prohibit only one abortion procedure—a type known as dilation and extraction (or D&X). Usually D&X was performed in the late part of the second trimester or the third trimester. It was a relatively rare procedure. Estimates ranged from there being several hundred to several thousand D&X procedures performed nationally in a year. D&X was distinguished from D&E in medical textbooks, because of some technical differences between it and D&E. Most important among those differences was the fact that in the D&X procedure, the contents of the fetus's cranium were emptied by the surgeon after extraction of the rest of the body. This made D&X particularly appropriate in cases where the pregnancy was being aborted because of hydrocephaly (or abnormal fluid accumulation on the brain)—a situation that was incompatible with the fetus surviving outside the womb. In a political sense, however, that aspect of D&X caused it to be a procedure that, when explained in detail among the public, was horrifying and graphic.

Physicians' groups such as the American College of Obstetricians and Gynecologists (ACOG), however, quickly supported a challenge to the Nebraska law. They argued that D&X, although rare, sometimes was the most appropriate procedure in a medical sense for a patient requesting an abortion. They pointed out that D&X was a procedure often preferred in instances where the fetus was not viable, as with hydrocephaly. They also noted that, since D&X was so medically similar to D&E, the statute's failure to distinguish between them amounted to a lumping of them together. Thus, they contended, the Nebraska statute infringed on women's right to choose to have an abortion in the second trimester, which was when D&Es characteristically were performed.

The Supreme Court's majority opinion accepted both of those objections to the Nebraska partial-birth abortion law as valid. The Court decided that the state had not allowed an exception to the abortion restriction for the health (rather than just the life) of the mother. The Court had required this type of exception in *Planned Parenthood v. Casey* (1992). In addition, the Court ruled that the Nebraska law interfered with women's right to choose abortion prior to fetal viability, due to the statute's muddying of the line between the D&X and D&E procedures; thus Nebraska's partial-birth abortion ban was contrary to *Roe v. Wade.*

As in the *Roe* case, the arguments put forward by physicians and professional medical organizations carried great weight with the Supreme Court. The majority opinion in *Stenberg v. Carhart* relied on medical evidence (especially by a panel of the ACOG) to emphasize the D&X's appropriateness in certain circumstances. It also noted that, despite some risks to the patient, the D&X was considered by abortion providers to be safer than the D&E. In the D&E, which was performed without significant cervical dilation, pieces of the fetus's body—especially bone—might become lodged in the uterus and create "horrible complications" for the mother (*Stenberg v. Carhart* 2000, 932). Therefore the majority of the Court argued that Nebraska actually might be making abortions more dangerous by banning the D&X procedure (if indeed the state did distinguish adequately between D&X and D&E, which it did not). The majority cited several cases from federal trial courts in 1998 and 1999, in which medical evidence pointed in the same direction. Finally, the majority opinion maintained that it was beside the point for the critics of partial-birth abortions to argue that a ban on the procedure would limit the choices of only a few patients. The question, the majority posited, was not how rare a procedure was, but "whether protecting women's health requires an exception for those infrequent occurrences" (*Stenberg v. Carhart* 2000, 934).

The dissents in *Stenberg v. Carhart* were exceedingly strong—even passionate—in language. Justice Scalia, for example, began his dissent on an emotional note:

> [O]ne day, *Stenberg v. Carhart* will be assigned its rightful place in the history of this Court's jurisprudence beside *Korematsu* and *Dred Scott.* The method of killing a human child—one cannot even accurately say an entirely unborn human child—proscribed by this statute is so horrible that the most clinical description of it evokes a shudder of revulsion. And the Court must know . . . that demanding a "health exception" . . . is to give live-birth abortion free rein. (*Stenberg v. Carhart* 2000, 953)

Justice Scalia went on to assert that *Planned Parenthood v. Casey* (in which he had dissented) had been incorrectly decided and should be overruled. Scalia (joined by Justices Rehnquist and Thomas) also contended that even if *Planned Parenthood v. Casey* were to remain valid law, there were ways of distinguishing the Nebraska statute so that it did not fall under *Casey*'s rubric. Justice Thomas, who frequently had been critical of the *Roe* decision, argued outright that although states might permit abortions, he saw nothing in the Constitution that required them to do so. He was prepared to overturn *Roe.*

Most interesting among the dissents were the remarks of the members of the Court who had not been as visible as Justices Scalia and Thomas in criticizing the *Roe* and *Casey* decisions, in particular Justice Kennedy. In a joint dissent, Justices Kennedy and Rehnquist reminded the Court that the *Roe* decision had allowed states to retain a "critical and legitimate interest" in regulating abortions. They feared that many decisions of the U.S. Supreme Court in the wake of *Roe,* however, had not given states much leeway in exercising that interest. To Kennedy and Rehnquist, *Carhart* was a decision that again went too far in denying a state's scope of legislation. As they put it in their dissent, the "political processes of the State are not to be foreclosed from enacting laws to promote the life of the unborn and to ensure respect for all human life and its potential. The State's constitutional authority is a vital means for citizens to address these grave and serious issues" (*Stenberg v. Carhart* 2000, 957).

During their dissent, Justices Kennedy and Rehnquist made another important argument about the effect of partial-birth abortions on the medical profession as well. The justices cited, in graphic detail, both eyewitness accounts of the procedure and the testimony of physicians who were proponents of D&X to argue that partial-birth abortions could prove desensitizing for even abortion practitioners. In that sense, Kennedy and Rehnquist echoed the *Casey* decision, which noted that abortion "is fraught with consequences for . . . the persons who perform and assist in the procedure [and for] society which must confront the knowledge that these procedures exist, procedures that some deem nothing short of an act of violence against innocent human life" (*Stenberg v. Carhart* 2000, 852).

Kennedy and Rehnquist contended that the medical profession (as exemplified by Dr. Carhart, the abortionist in the case before them) might be losing sight of some of medicine's fundamental purposes. Recalling an argument that they had made in an end-of-life case—*Washington v. Glucksberg* (1997)—the dissenting justices maintained that states might "take steps to insure the medical profession and its members are viewed as healers, sustained by a compassionate and rigorous ethic and cognizant of the dignity and value of human life, even life which cannot survive without the assistance of others" (*Stenberg v. Carhart* 2000, 962). Clearly, there were members of the Supreme Court in the first few years of the twenty-first century who were willing to take physicians individually and collectively to task for their support of abortion.

The decision in *Stenberg v. Carhart* demonstrated that the abortion decisions by courts could create as many quandaries as they solved. For example, abortion was an issue that clearly illustrated how much medicine had been affected by technology. Medicine had devised ways to save extremely preterm infants in the same era in which fetuses of the same gestational age could be aborted. But was a fetus that was below a certain age alive? Was that being a person, with a right to life that should be constitutionally protected? Such were some of the fundamental questions that the courts increasingly found themselves addressing in abortion cases in the twenty-first century. It was no wonder that those questions were both insoluble and inflammatory.

The question of when life begins, in particular, had powerful implications for additional fields of practice, such as obstetrics, beyond those fields of medical practice concerned with abortion. Beginning-of-life issues were of crucial importance, for example, for persons who were seeking not to terminate a pregnancy, but to initiate one. And in the second half of the twentieth century, medicine increasingly was deeply involved in the business of assisted reproduction (AR)—helping patients who sought to have babies but could not on their own do so. First through artificial insemination, and then using techniques possible through laboratory insemination, microscopy, and even microsurgery, medicine made huge advances in its ability to solve problems of infertility. But even as the possibilities of AR appeared promising, so its pitfalls began to loom large.

When artificial insemination had become widely used, for instance, in the 1940s and 1950s, both medical and legal authorities were unprepared for the numerous issues that would arise in courts as to the rights and duties of donors, children, parents, and physicians. In the case of *Strnad v. Strnad* from 1948, for example, the New York Supreme Court considered the custody of a child who was conceived through artificial insemination between the wife and another party. The child had been cared for lovingly by the husband (who was not the biological father), even though he knew that he was not the biological parent. Thus the court decided that the estranged husband was entitled to visitation rights to the child, just as he would be if he had adopted a child from a wife's previous marriage. The court rejected the wife/mother's argument that the child's conception through artificial insemination placed the child in a different category in relation to her stepparent or adopted parent.

As in vitro fertilization (IVF) and other methods became more widely employed as means of AR in the 1980s, questions arose regarding the legal standing of parties who participated in such techniques. The very-well-known *Baby M* case from that decade, for example, illustrated how difficult it was for legislatures and courts to keep abreast of developments in reproductive technology. That case, plus several others discussed later in this section, also showed how vitally involved in the legal system physicians had become. Physicians developed and oversaw AR technologies; they were the persons who performed many of the procedures by which persons conceived children through AR. Physicians also testified as expert medical witnesses when cases were filed in court. In addition to courts calling upon AR physicians, psychiatrists were an integral part of such cases, for the divisive questions that were raised in court often meant that experts on mental health had to assess which resolution would be in the best interests of the children of AR.

In 1985, William and Betsy Stern had not been successful in conceiving a child. They turned to a surrogacy agreement in which a third party, Mary Beth Whitehead, would be inseminated with William Stern's sperm and bear a child. According to the terms of the surrogacy contract, Whitehead would allow William Stern to have custody of the baby. Although Betsy Stern was not named in the surrogacy agreement, it was understood that she would be in the same household with William Stern as he reared the child. In return for her serving as the surrogate mother of the Sterns' potential child, Whitehead's medical and legal expenses were to be covered and she would receive another $10,000 in payment. The surrogacy was arranged by attorney Noel Keane, who drew up the contracts and made most of the other medical and legal arrangements. Whitehead eventually changed her mind about giving up the baby she was carrying. After the child—a daughter—was born in March 1986, Whitehead gave the baby a name of her own choosing and asked the Sterns to let her keep the baby for about a week. During that time, Whitehead took the child out of state (from New Jersey to Florida). She later decided that she wanted custody of the child, whom she had named Sarah Elizabeth Whitehead, and entered into a lengthy battle with the Sterns. The Sterns, for their part, tried to enforce the surrogacy contract and gain physical custody of the child they called Melissa Stern.

The Superior Court of New Jersey found itself without much precedent to rely upon, because surrogacy contracts were very new in 1987 when the case of *In re Baby M* came to court. The judge hearing the case, Harvey Sorkow, found a privacy basis for the constitutionality of surrogacy agreements. Since courts had reasoned that a right to privacy meant a right to procreate, he inferred that a right to procreation included the ability to choose how to procreate. Sorkow did not find any of Whitehead's objections to surrogacy contracts to be compelling enough to allow state restrictions on those agreements. Thus having determined the validity of the contract between William Stern and Mary Beth Whitehead, the judge tried to order specific performance of the contract. But in considering whether to compel Whitehead to give up the child, the judge by state law had to be convinced that that outcome was in the best interests of the child. Sorkow ordered testimony from a number of witnesses—including psychologists, psychiatrists, and social workers—who offered their opinions on the fitness of Mary Beth Whitehead as a parent. Those experts commented at some length on Whitehead's efforts to flee with the baby at several junctures and referred to conversations with William Stern in which Whitehead had threatened to kill herself and the baby if she had to give up parental rights. Judge Sorkow decided to award custody to William Stern, to allow the Sterns to adopt the baby (immediately), and to terminate Whitehead's rights as a parent.

The decision created a furor in public opinion and inspired a quick appeal. Advocates for women's groups, in particular, saw in Whitehead a woman who had been employed as a "womb for rent." They argued that commercial surrogacy contracts devalued the intense feelings that biological mothers experienced toward their infants. Advocates for infertility support groups, on the other hand, perceived the Sterns and the baby as being manipulated by an unstable surrogate mother. In the 1988 decision of the New Jersey Supreme Court in the case involving the Sterns and Whitehead (which was known almost universally as the *Baby M* case), the court invalidated surrogacy contracts as contrary to public policy. The court reasoned that children usually profited from being reared by both biological parents; thus surrogacy agreements that bartered away the right to know both biological parents were contrary to laws that forbade the selling of babies. Whitehead in essence was promised visitation with the child, although William Stern was awarded custody.

As a result of the *Baby M* case, many states made commercial surrogacy contracts, of the type that Mary Beth Whitehead had signed, illegal. The case of *Stiver v. Parker*, though decided in 1992, involved a surrogacy arrangement that was entered into before the state of Michigan revised its laws in that manner. The plaintiffs in the case were Judy and Ray Stiver. Judy Stiver had agreed to be inseminated with the sperm of a man named Alexander Malahoff. The person who made the surrogacy arrangements involving the Stivers and Malahoff was once again attorney Noel Keane. The surrogacy contract that Judy Stivers signed was a rather one-sided document. In return for monetary payments totaling about $8,500 to Judy Stiver, she agreed to undergo the insemination and to carry any resulting pregnancy to term, unless the donor of the sperm wished her to have an abortion because the fetus was found to be suffering from an abnormality. Judy Stiver bore all of the risks of the surrogacy attempt, including the risk of death. She also agreed to forgo all visitation rights to the child, who was to be in the custody of Malahoff.

Judy Stiver did become pregnant shortly after being inseminated with Malahoff's sperm. The child who was born, a boy named Christopher, was found to have an infection known as cytomegalovirus (CMV). CMV, which is contracted in utero due to the mother's becoming infected, causes numerous serious medical problems, including mental retardation, hearing loss, and neuromuscular disorders. Neither Judy Stiver nor her husband was infected with CMV prior to the artificial insemination; the CMV almost certainly came from Malahoff's sperm, which was live and untested at the time of insemination. Malahoff decided that he did not want to keep the child, and the Stivers assumed the care of Christopher. Malahoff argued that he was not responsible for the baby's problems for two reasons: (1) A test revealed that Ray Stiver, rather than Malahoff, actually had fathered the child. (2) Malahoff contended that he had relied on the expert advice of Keane and the physicians and lawyers who had arranged the surrogacy. Therefore even though he had caused the infection that afflicted Christopher, Malahoff maintained that he was not to be blamed for that turn of events.

The Stivers sued Malahoff, Keane, and the physicians and lawyers involved for negligence. The U.S. Court of Appeals for the Sixth Circuit decided that surrogacy was no ordinary situation of obstetrical practice. Those who made money from the surrogacy brokering—including the physicians and lawyers—were under a heightened duty to protect all of the parties from harm. The failure to test Malahoff's sperm certainly raised a question of negligence. The case bore out the wisdom of strict regulations on surrogacy contracts. As the court said: "Because surrogacy contracts create a high degree of risk of injury or loss, we conclude that the programs under which these contracts are arranged—when not outlawed as against public policy—create affirmative duties of care" (*Stiver v. Parker* 1992, 270).

The case of *Kass v. Kass* (1998) demonstrated once again that family law was being greatly affected by the advances in AR technology. Maureen Kass suffered from infertility as a result of her exposure to diethylstilbestrol (DES). Maureen and her husband, Steven Kass, had gone through a number of high-tech attempts to produce offspring from their marriage, including trying to conceive a child through a surrogate mother and several efforts at IVF. In some of those attempts, Maureen Kass had produced more pre-embryos than were implanted in her (or the surrogate's) body. According to established procedures in their IVF program, the Kasses had to sign consent forms specifying what was to happen to the pre-embryos if for some reason the couple decided not to implant them. If the Kasses no longer wanted them, were the embryos to remain in frozen storage? If so, a fee had to be paid annually to cover the storage cost. Were the pre-embryos to be destroyed, donated to another couple, or used for research purposes? The Kasses committed for retention and short-term storage each set of pre-embryos that were not implanted. At that same time, the Kasses indicated on the consent form that they wished the unimplanted pre-embryos to be used in scientific research rather than kept in long-term storage. (As a result of cases such as the Stivers' and Mary Beth Whitehead's, most contracts involving AR were much more specific and carefully drawn by the 1990s than they had been in the 1980s.)

The Kasses' marriage did not survive the emotional turmoil of their prolonged, expensive, and unsuccessful efforts to produce a child through AR. When they divorced, Maureen Kass wanted to regain the pre-embryos so that she could continue to try to have a child with them at some future time. Steven Kass opposed that effort and asked the court to enforce the agreement (that the pre-embryos be donated for research) that the Kasses had signed with the IVF program. The Court of Appeals for New York placed great weight on the informed consents that the Kasses signed with the IVF program while they still were married. The court refused to accept Maureen Kass's argument that she should retain the pre-embryos because of her constitutional rights to privacy and reproductive choice. The court ordered that the pre-embryos be donated for research to the IVF program. In addition, the court ruled that the pre-embryos were not "persons" under the U.S. Constitution. The pre-embryos (sometimes termed *prezygotes*) were eggs that had been penetrated by sperm, but in which certain genetic changes had not yet taken place. That determination, of course, touched on an extremely emotional issue raised in such cases: when life begins. The case was troubling to some who heard about it, because the idea of the pre-embryos being used by researchers conjured up images of human experimentation. That is, if the pre-embryos were to be considered alive and having the character of persons, then it might be immoral to use those pre-embryos for the purposes of research.

Courts often were asked to resolve disputes about payment for AR medical services. Treatments involving IVF, for example, easily could involve patient outlays of over $10,000 per cycle of treatment; patients might decide to try several times to get the desired result—a viable pregnancy. (The Kasses had spent over $75,000 and had not had a live birth.) That very expensive technology was not covered by many employees' health plans. Courts generally were not willing to approve coverage for infertility treatments if insurance schemes denied coverage, even when insurance plans were regulated through federal statutes such as ERISA. In the 1996 case of *Krauel v. Iowa Methodist Medical Center*, for example, a woman suffering from endometriosis who had undergone fertility treatments including artificial insemination and gamete intrafallopian tube transfers (GIFT) was denied coverage for the AR treatments that had resulted in a pregnancy. The U.S. Court of Appeals for the Eighth Circuit let that denial stand, ruling that the plaintiff's health insurer had not discriminated against her under the Americans with Disabilities Act, the Pregnancy Discrimination Act, or Title VII of the Civil Rights Act. The denials of benefits for infertility treatments such as plaintiff Krauel experienced effectively placed AR technology out of the financial reach of the great majority of Americans.

Clearly, courts were finding themselves increasingly drawn into and bogged down with cases that were related to the beginning of life. Particularly with the development of very complex and extremely expensive technologies for artificial reproduction, medicine has offered tantalizing "fixes" for infertility, but with a high practical and ethical price tag. Parties to cases concerning the beginning of life often discover that they have unearthed issues that have profound ramifications unconsidered just a few years before—such as the creation of "excess" embryos that must either remain stored cryogenically, be destroyed, or be used for some other purpose if they are not to be implanted in potential mothers' bodies. Courts at best only lag behind technology in such matters; at worst their decisions incite terrible controversies that involve not only legal but also ethical, religious, and even psychiatric considerations. Much the same can be argued about medicolegal controversies concerning the end of life.

(Abortion, of course, can be said to involve both the beginning and the end of life; not surprisingly it is thus doubly vexing for courts.) End-of-life controversies as heard in the courts are like beginning-of-life matters in three key respects: (1) They have been irreversibly affected by vast changes in medical technology. (2) They have agitated and divided the medical community. (3) They have provoked great public interest and action.

End-of-Life Issues

Particularly since the middle of the twentieth century, courts at all levels have struggled with questions raised in cases concerned with end-of-life issues. Especially as technology has made it possible for medicine to keep severely injured or ill persons alive through artificial means (such as respirators and cardiac devices), there have arisen cases in which courts have had to decide whether sustaining life through artificial means was in the patients' best interest. In addition, the practice of medicine has become an enterprise where doctors and patients are not alone; patients who face difficult prognoses are attended by not only their personal physicians but also other specialists. Healthcare corporations may manage patient care, and the financial decisions related to patients' treatment might rest in the hands of governmental authorities. So who will decide the fate of desperately ill persons who face either connection to or disconnection from a machine? In end-of-life decisions, as in other areas of medicolegal dispute, courts must untangle responsibility for patient care. But the stakes are even higher in end-of-life cases than in most other medical legal disputes, for in such circumstances courts literally are making judgments about whether patients will live (and under what circumstances) or die.

For courts as well as medical and religious authorities, determining when life ends has been an endeavor fraught with problems. A key dilemma for courts has been the degree to which physicians might intervene in the dying process. When the patients had no hope of recovery, could medical personnel disconnect feeding tubes and other "artificial" or mechanical means by which patients were being sustained? Would it make a difference in such cases if a person had indicated a preference not to be kept alive through certain methods such as artificial respiration? What if the patient were incapable of communication? Could anyone else speak for her or him to medical authorities? At the far end of the spectrum in end-of-life cases, courts even might be confronted with cases of physician-assisted suicide (PAS), which were defended by certain parties but illegal according to state laws. Thus courts had to consider whether there was a right to die that would encompass the hastening of death. Could doctors provide drugs for patients who were physically able to commit suicide themselves, but who preferred a gentler method than weapons? Could physicians be present at the suicides of their patients? Courts had to resolve such contentious issues, even in the face of a lack of agreement on end-of-life matters among the medical community, religious authorities, ethical experts, and the public at large.

In the 1970s, the case of Karen Ann Quinlan focused attention on just those questions about the end of life and the medical and legal fields' responses to dying persons. At issue were the roles that medical personnel, family members, and courts ought to play in making decisions for patients—for unlike many persons who actively and clearly voiced a wish to commit suicide with physicians' assistance, Karen Ann Quinlan was incapacitated and unable to express her own preferences. Before April 15, 1975, Karen Ann was a healthy young woman from a loving family. On that date, she attended a party and consumed drugs and alcohol. The mixture of substances put her into respiratory distress that caused irreparable brain damage. She did not regain consciousness.

Since her electroencephalogram (EEG) indicated some brain activity, according to accepted criteria among medical experts she was not dead. Her doctors concluded, however, that neither did she have any hope of recovery. She appeared unable to breathe on her own; each time doctors tried to remove her from a respirator she did not sustain respiration independently. After agonizing about their daughter's condition and consulting with religious advisors (the Quinlans were Roman Catholics), Karen Ann's father, Joseph, asked the hospital to turn off her respirator. Joseph Quinlan argued that Karen Ann would not have wanted to be kept alive through artificial means and recalled conversations in which Karen Ann had commented on cases involving "brain death." She had indicated that she would not want her family to be put through the process of keeping her alive should a catastrophic medical event deprive her of consciousness.

The hospital and its physicians, although not completely unanimous in their opinions about a course of action, took the position that they could not disconnect Karen Ann's breathing apparatus without a court order to do so. According to current medical criteria on brain death, Karen Ann still was alive; the hospital and doctors feared that to disconnect the respirator might expose them to charges of murder. Mr. Quinlan argued that as Karen Ann's guardian, he was entitled to make the decision to discontinue life support. The Quinlan family endeavored to get a court's authorization to remove their daughter from artificial respiration. A New Jersey Superior Court that heard the case initially clearly recognized immediately its profound implications.

That court found in favor of the hospital. It removed Joseph Quinlan as Karen Ann's guardian and appointed another person to serve as her guardian *ad litem* (the caretaker of an infant or incompetent person). Despite its ruling against Mr. Quinlan, however, the court was at pains to note the sincerity of the Quinlans' religious and moral beliefs and the love that they evidently had for their daughter.

The Quinlans next took their case to the Supreme Court of New Jersey. Joseph Quinlan argued that Karen Ann should be removed from the respirator because to allow her to exist in her current state violated her free exercise of religion, intruded on her right to privacy, and interfered with the Constitution's protection against cruel and unusual punishments. Arrayed in opposition to the Quinlans were Karen Ann's physicians, the hospital, her newly appointed guardian *ad litem,* the local prosecutor, and the state of New Jersey.

The decision that came from that higher court, like the earlier disposition, was notable for its awareness of the grave legal, moral, and medical issues at stake. The New Jersey Supreme Court judges, like their colleagues at the lower-level court, also demonstrated great sensitivity to the emotional nature of the case for the Quinlan family and for others among Karen Ann's caregivers. The court referred to no less than the Declaration of Independence to establish as a key principle in U.S. law the importance of the preservation of human life. The *Quinlan* case involved matters of "transcendent importance," the court said (*In re Quinlan* 1976, 10). In its decision, the court noted that because of vast and recent changes in the ability of medicine to save and prolong lives through mechanical means, it was inevitable that cases such as Karen Ann's should come before the courts.

In its review of the medical evidence concerning Karen Ann's condition, the court noted an interesting aspect of medical practice.

There were many instances when physicians would not institute artificial respiration in patients. Among medical personnel, it was common to have an understanding that certain patients were not to be resuscitated. On the chart of a patient with metastatic cancer, for example, a physician might simply pencil in the initials "DNR." Others at the hospital would understand that those letters meant "do not resuscitate," and they would implement the implied order if the patient ceased breathing. Sometimes DNR orders were not written down at all, but simply passed along orally among the medical staff for fear that physicians would be sued or even prosecuted for hastening their patients' deaths. The Quinlans argued that the existence of DNR orders was an open secret among the medical community.

Those who opposed the discontinuation of respiration, however, countered that the medical profession had developed stringent standards for "brain death." Some patients who did fit the medical definition of being in a "permanent" or "persistent vegetative state"—as Karen Ann certainly was—still remained alive by medical standards. Particularly when such persons could not speak clearly for themselves, medical personnel argued that they would be acting with grave impropriety to allow them to die. The medical parties to the *Quinlan* case also emphasized that they, with their long experience with cases of comatose and terminally ill patients, were better fitted than courts to make case-by-case determinations of a proper course of action. As they had argued in the lower court's consideration of the *Quinlan* case, the physicians maintained that "doctors . . . to treat a patient, must deal with medical tradition and past case histories. They must be guided by what they do know. The extent of their training, their experience, consultation with other physicians, must guide their decision-making processes in providing care to their patient. The nature, extent, and duration of care by societal standards is the responsibility of a physician" (*In re Quinlan* 1975, 137 N.J. Super. at 259).

In terms of the constitutional issues raised by the Quinlan family, the New Jersey Supreme Court was most concerned with the claim of a right to privacy. It noted that courts recently had considered certain areas of family life worthy of judicial protection, for example in the contraception and abortion cases *Griswold v. Connecticut* (1965) and *Roe v. Wade* (1973). But could Karen Ann's family assert a right to privacy for her? The court decided that it could: "If a putative decision by Karen to permit this non-cognitive, vegetative existence to terminate by natural forces is regarded as a valuable incident of her right to privacy, as we believe it to be, then it should not be discarded solely on the basis that her condition prevents her conscious exercise of the choice" (*In re Quinlan* 1976, 70 N.J. at 10).

The court ruled that if the Quinlan family continued to believe as they did, their wishes would be respected. Karen Ann's physicians were advised to consult with the hospital's Ethics Committee; if the physicians and the committee continued to maintain that Karen Ann still had no hope of recovery, then the hospital should remove her from the respirator according to her family's wishes. The court promised that such an action would be immune from prosecution, even if it caused Karen Ann's death. Although the Quinlans did pursue that course and Karen Ann was taken off the respirator, she was kept on a feeding tube. To the surprise of most of the medical experts, she was able to breathe on her own. She remained in a vegetative condition until 1985, when she died from pneumonia.

The *Quinlan* case caused many states as well as hospitals and medical and legal professional organizations to examine their policies concerning "the right to die." Many healthcare facilities, for example, began to allow patients to create and maintain at the facility "advance care directives" that specified whether certain life-sustaining techniques should be employed in the event of a catastrophic medical situation. Some facilities concluded that lifesaving mechanisms would not be used if two physicians concurred that a patient was "brain dead," or even if the patient was in an irreversible coma and had indicated opposition to advanced care. Healthcare facilities also indicated that they would accept patients' statements about artificial respiration and other technological means of maintaining life in the form of patients' "living wills."

The role of the physician in authorizing the removal of life-sustaining treatment only rarely came into question in U.S. courts. One of the very few examples of a physician being prosecuted for withdrawing life-prolonging treatment occurred in the wake of the *Quinlan* case. In 1981, a patient named Clarence Herbert had abdominal surgery. There was a cardiopulmonary event just after the surgery that caused him to have irreversible brain damage. When his condition was disclosed to his wife, she, armed with clear instructions from Herbert that he did not want to be kept alive by artificial means, asserted that she did not want Herbert to be connected any longer to a respirator. Herbert continued to breathe on his own, however, even after the respirator was removed; his family therefore requested that all feeding and fluids be stopped. Before those tubes were removed, however, a nurse who was among Herbert's caregivers had a disagreement with one of the physicians on the case. The nurse wanted to use a humidifier in the room in order to allow the tubes to work more effectively; the doctor thought this merely prolonged the patient's discomfort. Though the patient did die shortly, the nurse took her case to the Los Angeles government authority that oversaw healthcare workers. The District Attorney's Office pursued a murder case against two of Herbert's physicians. The case of *Barber v. Superior Court* (1983) eventually was decided by the California Court of Appeals, with the charges against the doctors being dropped. At one court level down, however, a superior court judge had taken the charges quite seriously, largely because of conflicting medical opinions about whether the patient had been in a coma long enough to justify withdrawal of life-sustaining treatment. The court of appeals, in its final resolution of the case, emphasized both the proper professional standards that physicians should apply in making a decision to withdraw treatment and the necessity of securing clear instructions from the family in such a case.

In 1990, another case again focused attention on the right of gravely ill persons and their families to determine whether they should receive advanced care. The case involving patient Nancy Cruzan was slightly different from that of Karen Ann Quinlan because Cruzan, as an adult, had spoken fairly clearly of her wish not to be kept alive by artificial means; Karen Ann Quinlan was a teenager when she made similar remarks to her family. Further, the specific question before the court in Cruzan's case was whether a feeding tube rather than a respirator should be removed. Still, many of the issues were the same. Cruzan was comatose and unable to recover from brain injuries; her family was pursuing court action to allow discontinuation of her feeding. The state of Missouri contended that only in the presence of "clear and convincing evidence" of a patient's wishes could medical personnel discontinue treatments that kept the patient alive. Without written proof of her views on the subject, the state was unwilling to follow the family's wishes. The U.S. Supreme Court decision in *Cruzan v. Director, Missouri Department of Public Health* (1990) affirmed Missouri's position.

Cruzan was, therefore, a kind of rejection of *Quinlan* at the national level. In the absence of a clear mandate from a patient like

Quinlan or Cruzan, the Supreme Court favored the interest of the state in preserving life. On the other hand, the Supreme Court recognized that in the years since the *Quinlan* decision, many patients had made the choice to draw up directives for scenarios in which they were unable to communicate their own wishes. The Court in *Cruzan* seemed to say that if patients had prepared such lucid and well-considered instructions, then states and medical authorities were bound to recognize them; failing this, however, the doctors and the state were required to preserve the patient's life. The Patient Self Determination Act of 1990 was Congress's effort to require healthcare facilities (including hospitals and nursing homes) to inform patients of their right to file advance directives and living wills.

Following the lead of Congress, several states soon enacted legislation that called for "death with dignity." The statutes set forward scenarios in which caregivers might be allowed to remove life-supporting mechanisms from critically ill persons. Such laws, for example, provided for patients to be able to set out contingency plans in living wills; they also permitted persons to appoint guardians of their persons who would have "medical power of attorney." But what standards were to be followed if a patient's guardian requested the end-of-life support and no written instructions were on file from the patient her/himself? In that most problematic third scenario, courts often required—before allowing respirators or feeding tubes to be disconnected—that there be a "clear and convincing" demonstration of evidence that a patient would have wanted to be removed from life support. (In a legal sense, the "clear and convincing" standard was considered an intermediate requirement; it was harder to meet than a "preponderance" of the evidence, but less demanding than "proof beyond a reasonable doubt." The U.S. Court of Appeals for the Second Circuit, for example, reiterated its reliance on the clear and convincing nature of such evidence in its decision in *Quill v. Vacco* [1996, 727].)

In a case from Delaware's Supreme Court in 1995, the court considered what to do about the situation of a woman who had left no legal documents expressing her wish not to be kept alive through mechanical means. Mrs. Charlotte Tavel was being sustained by a feeding tube after having suffered a stroke several years before. She was confined to her bed in a nursing home and gave no sign of recognizing anyone who came to visit her. Mrs. Tavel's daughter asked the courts to allow her mother to die by discontinuing the feeding tube that was attached to her stomach. She presented a number of witnesses—from former employees of Mrs. Tavel to Mrs. Tavel's rabbi, who supported the request on the grounds that Mrs. Tavel had previously been vivacious. In addition, she had expressed a wish not to be kept alive through artificial means, like many of the persons whom she had visited in nursing homes. Mrs. Tavel's daughter specifically cited a conversation in which she and her mother had discussed the actions of Dr. Jack Kevorkian, the "death doctor" who had been in the news because of his controversial assistance in the suicides of several terminally ill persons. She recalled that her mother had called Kevorkian's assisting with suicides "a blessing." Even the guardian *ad litem* who had been appointed by a lower-level court joined in the request from Mrs. Tavel's daughter. In its decision in *In the matter of Charlotte F. Tavel,* the Delaware Supreme Court ruled that Mrs. Tavel's daughter had satisfied the burden of proof that her mother would decide to be allowed to die "naturally"—that is, of the natural course of disease and without additional feeding through a tube.

But what about the rare case in which a patient actually could express her or his wishes to hasten the end of life, yet for physical reasons (such as an inability to control his or her hands) could not actually commit suicide? That is, the courts had enunciated for patients a right to express a preference that their deaths be allowed to occur in a manner that minimized heroic medical measures. (In addition, committing suicide brought no legal penalties, such as England's former rule that the property of suicides could be forfeited to the state.) Could that right to control the manner of one's death be extended so that patients legally could have the assistance of a physician, for instance in obtaining a deadly dose of narcotic drugs? The Supreme Court's response to PAS was negative. The Court made clear in *Cruzan*—and would continue to maintain—that the right to refuse unwanted medical treatment was not the same as a right to commit suicide with the assistance of a physician. This was another side to the right-to-die debate. Assuming that a patient had the right to refuse treatment, many argued that doctors also should be able to provide the means of death. In both instances, the decision to die rested with the patient. The end results were the same. Yet the Court disagreed. The right to refuse unwanted medical treatment was grounded in a long line of cases that allowed competent adults to object to medical care, for example on religious grounds. The right to end one's life and to have assistance from medical personnel, with a promise by the state not to prosecute, went against an American legal tradition that frowned on physicians' hastening of death.

Nonetheless, the issue of PAS was debated throughout the United States in the 1970s, 1980s, and 1990s. States responded to those discussions with laws addressing assisted suicide, which had not so much been directly as obliquely at issue in the previous judicial decisions. Most new state laws reflected the opinion that assisted suicide should be criminalized. As of the end of the twentieth century, at least thirty-five states had statutes that made assisted suicide illegal; nine states allowed courts to use the common law to make assisted suicide illegal; one state (Virginia) imposed civil sanctions on persons who assisted with suicide. Three states—North Carolina, Utah, and Wyoming—had no statutes making assisted suicide illegal, while in Ohio there was a judicial ruling indicating that PAS was not criminal. Only Oregon, according to its Death with Dignity Act (enacted in 1994 and put into effect in 1997), actually supported its physicians in assisting with suicides. By the middle of the 1990s, the Supreme Court—faced with such state laws—confronted the issue of PAS even more directly than it had in *Cruzan.*

The twin cases of *Vacco v. Quill* and *Washington v. Glucksberg,* decided by the U.S. Supreme Court in 1997, reaffirmed the policy of the Court that America had a recent history of honoring patients' control over their own bodies even to the point of allowing patients to decide to let themselves die. The Court, however, refused to acknowledge any *inherent* right to PAS. Indeed, in *Glucksberg,* Chief Justice Rehnquist warned that states owed a duty to their citizens to protect them from euthanasia—a particular danger to vulnerable groups such as the elderly and the disabled. He also noted that the medical profession had a responsibility not to participate in the taking of patients' lives—exactly the position that Karen Ann Quinlan's doctors had taken in 1975.

Although the decisions were unanimous, there was far from universal understanding among the justices of every specific question raised about assisted suicide and the right to refuse medical treatment. Justice Stevens, for example, in his *Glucksberg* opinion, reminded the Court that physicians might be faced with situations in which, to minister to the needs of their terminally ill patients, doctors would have to consider dispensing powerful pain-relieving medication that also might hasten their patients' deaths. To help the patient might be to alleviate unbearable pain. The right-to-die cases thus forced a consideration of physicians' role before the law, as well as in relation to medical institutions and with respect to individual patients and their families. The spectacle of Dr. Jack Kevorkian rigging up a "suicide machine" so that a patient could self-administer a lethal dose of medicine seemed to some a heroic act and to others (including some members of the Supreme Court) nothing short of murder. To its advocates, PAS was a compassionate act; to its critics, it evoked images of Nazi euthanasia programs. The decisions in *Vacco v. Quill* and *Washington v. Glucksberg*, as well as several others related to end-of-life issues, placed a burden on individual states to come up with laws that could survive a test before the high court, and they challenged the medical profession to examine their fundamental place as healers in American society.

Conclusion

It was by no means a given in the early nineteenth century that medicine belonged in the courtroom. Medical personnel did not routinely participate in trials, even in cases where medical testimony would have seemed germane—such as in cases where causes of death were in dispute or the defendant's mental health was in question. This absence of medical personnel from the courts happened, in part, because there was no mechanism for paying for or compelling expert testimony. Yet more importantly, the courts in the early nineteenth century did not recognize many fields of medicine as being *expert.* After all, most areas of medical practice were poorly organized as specializations, medical training often was slipshod, and professional connections between medicine and law were few.

In two key areas of medicine in the 1800s, however, medicine began to demonstrate that it could and should have a presence within trials: with regard to insanity pleas in criminal cases and with respect to the practice of forensic pathology. With the increasing professional development of psychiatrists and forensic pathologists, courts began to take medical experts and medical testimony seriously. The insanity cases heard by courts both in the United States and England in the 1800s were of paramount importance, not only for the areas of the law relating to mental health, but also for the prestige of the medical profession generally. Over time, insanity cases showed courts' increasing trust in psychiatrists' advice about patients' competency and guilt. Though in any given case, courts' faith in psychiatric testimony was not always complete—and jurors and the public certainly did disagree with certain psychiatric definitions of sanity and insanity at times—courts' growing reliance on psychiatry as a field was unquestioned.

Forensic pathology took longer than psychiatry to establish itself as an authoritative voice in courtrooms—arguably until the very end of the nineteenth century. But at some point before the turn of the twentieth century, several prominent jurisdictions in the United States and England boasted of the presence of medical specialists who were in charge of forensic investigation of suspicious or violent deaths in localities. Gradually, in the early twentieth century, those forensic experts began working with police and winning over the trust of the public. By the middle of the twentieth century, forensic pathologists not only were gatekeepers to the judicial system in instances of unexplained or suspicious deaths, but they also were usual participants in trials.

As more and more areas of medical practice became self-conscious (for example, forming professional associations such as state medical societies and insisting on more rigorous training and licensing procedures for medical practitioners), they became groups to be reckoned with in a political sense. During the late 1800s, medical organizations successfully lobbied state legislatures to allow them (the medical professionals) to determine licensing requirements and to enforce those requirements against competing groups, such as alternative and unlicensed practitioners. The courts supported traditional medical groups, such as physicians' organizations, in medicine's effort to enhance the credibility of the medical profession with the public.

The stature that physicians had gained among courts by the 1900s, however, was challenged by the increasing sophistication and complexity of medical practice. As medical personnel associated themselves with hospitals, courts looked upon medical professionals differently than in the past. Physicians were considered so much more educated than their patients about medical matters that the doctors increasingly were required to inform patients about the dangers of potential treatments. Patients, the courts further reasoned, needed even greater protection than before against medical misconduct when they were in more complex relationships with their medical caregivers. This was especially the case, for instance, in hospital settings when practitioners other than primary physicians might perform surgeries, and when persons such as nurses—acting under not only physicians' but also hospital administrators' orders—carried out patient care. Thus the early and middle twentieth century was a time when courts took pains to spell out the conditions in which informed consent could occur.

In the early twentieth century, medicine was changing in another way, beyond its growing association with hospitals. Technology increasingly was being merged into the practice of medicine. The X-ray machine was the precursor of sophisticated medical technologies in the years just prior to World War I; that machine rapidly was joined by a number of expensive medical devices for testing and treatment. Some of those devices were large enough that they needed to be housed in institutions (like CT-scan machines); some were small enough that they could be implanted in patients' bodies (like cardiac pacemakers). Large or small, however, those devices usually exhibited such a degree of complexity in design and operation that courts had to take a deep look at exactly who was liable for their safe placement and operation. Medical technology thus bred a series of court decisions on medical-product liability—decisions that were made still more complicated by the national (and indeed international) extent of such technologies' distribution. By the middle of the twentieth century, in turn, the advanced technologies of medicine were joined by a "therapeutic revolution," when businesses that long had been involved in chemical manufacture saw the potential for the development of medicines (both prescription and over-the-counter varieties) that would find a mass market. Courts again had to address that medical development, and they did so in a series of lawsuits involving the dissemination of harmful drugs by U.S. and multinational companies.

Those controversies that reached courts concerning faulty medical devices and damaging drugs brought into high relief the position of regulatory agencies—notably, the FDA. Authorities such as the FDA were supposed to help protect the public against the shoddy development and manufacture of medical products. With regard to product after product, however, the FDA's critics said that it regulated too little, too late. Still other critics accused the agency of being overzealous about premarket drug testing, thus denying desperately ill patients access to experimental treatments.

The FDA was only one among a number of nonmedical authorities that had become a part of medical care for most patients by the mid-twentieth century. Other governmental agencies, such as the Surgeon General's Office and the Department of HHS, had a hand in the regulating of Americans' health because of a variety of laws and regulations that had been promulgated by Congress in the mid-1900s. While payment for medical care was not acknowledged to be a universal right for Americans, *access* to care was increasingly being mandated by federal, state, and local authorities. Medicare and Medicaid—programs initiated by Congress in the 1960s—were key examples of federal standards concerning healthcare that caused federal courts to become even further involved in medical controversies.

Medicine also became corporatized in the twentieth century as insurance providers and other business organizations entered the business of healthcare. MCOs insisted on medical decisions being made with an eye (if not a whole focus) on the bottom line: profit. Insurers argued that healthcare professionals should either manage their costs, or they, the insurance providers, would do the managing for them—for example, through programs that offered incentives for fewer referrals to specialists by primary care physicians or that promised rewards for physicians who kept the number of prescriptions low. The place of MCOs and insurance plans within the physician-patient relationship thus has been a major concern of modern courts as patients bring cases alleging that MCOs have compromised not only their health but the decision-making authority of healthcare practitioners.

Finally, as medicine has grown to involve both big business and big government, courts have been concerned about the potential for medicine and medical practitioners to interfere with patients' autonomy. Cases such as the *Quinlan* decision have forced courts to grapple with the growing ability of medicine to keep patients alive through artificial and heroic means; they also have inspired provocative discussions about the roles that patients, physicians, government authorities, family members—and courts themselves—should play in the most personal matters imaginable. Late twentieth-century judicial decisions about privacy (encompassing both beginning- and end-of-life issues such as abortion, reproduction, and the right to commit suicide) have been made possible not just because of the consciousness of judges about individual liberties. In several high-profile cases involving personal autonomy (such as the *Roe* case and prosecutions involving PAS), the agitation of patients'-rights and other groups that have been alarmed by the impersonality and bottom-line mentality of "corporate medicine" has been crucial. In emotionally charged cases such as the "wrongful life" suit brought by Sidney Miller's parents, courts must confront the question of whether a business model is working in American medicine.

American justice—and medicine—have come a long way from the time when medical testimony appeared in courtrooms only haphazardly and American doctors were barely considered professional, much less expert. U.S. courts now are addressing medical controversies on a regular basis. But the consideration of medical matters in U.S. courtrooms is not as simple a story as might be expected. It is not merely a matter of courts taking increasing cognizance of medicine and medicine being more influential within courtrooms. Far from courts being able to resolve the conflicts that they hear related to medicine, the airing of medicolegal issues in courtrooms is serving to broaden and deepen certain controversies within American society as a whole.

References and Further Reading

Battin, Margaret P., Rosamond Rhodes, and Anita Silvers. *Physician Assisted Suicide: Expanding the Debate.* New York: Routledge, 1998.

Begley, Sharon. "Ban on 'Junk Science' Also Keeps Jurors from Sound Evidence." *Wall Street Journal,* June 27, 2003, p. B1.

Cawthon, Elisabeth A. "Public Opinion, Expert Testimony, and 'the Insanity Dodge'," in John W. Johnson, ed., *Historic U.S. Court Cases,* 36–39. New York: Garland Publishing, 1992.

Chesler, Phyllis. *Sacred Bond: The Legacy of Baby M.* New York: Times Books, 1988.

Cohen, Michael H. *Complementary and Alternative Medicine: Legal Boundaries and Regulatory Perspectives.* Baltimore: Johns Hopkins University Press, 1998.

Curry, Lynne. *The Human Body on Trial.* Santa Barbara, CA: ABC-CLIO, 2002.

DeVille, Kenneth. *Medical Malpractice in Nineteenth Century America.* New York: New York University Press, 1990.

Gawande, Atul. *Complications: A Surgeon's Notes on an Imperfect Science.* New York: Picador, 2002.

Gostin, Larry. "Tobacco Liability and Public Health Policy." *Journal of the American Medical Association* (December 11, 1991): 3178–3182.

Johns, A. Wesley. *The Man Who Shot McKinley.* South Brunswick, NJ: A. S. Barnes, 1970.

Kennedy, David. *Birth Control in America.* New Haven: Yale University Press, 1970.

Langford, Gerald. *The Murder of Stanford White.* London: V. Gollancz, 1963.

Lichtblau, Eric. "U.S. Wants $289 Billion from 5 Cigarette Makers." *Dallas Morning News,* March 18, 2003, p. 1A.

Marty, Martin, and Kenneth Vaux. *Health/Medicine and the Faith Traditions: An Inquiry into Religion and Medicine.* Philadelphia: Fortress Press, 1982.

Milbauer, Barbara. *The Law Giveth—Legal Aspects of the Abortion Controversy.* New York: McGraw-Hill, 1983.

Mundy, Alicia. *Dispensing with the Truth: The Victims, the Drug Companies, and the Dramatic Story behind the Battle over Fen-Phen.* New York: St. Martin's Press, 2001.

Numbers, Ronald. "The Fall and Rise of the American Medical Profession," in Nathan O. Hatch, ed., *The Professions in American History,* 57–67. South Bend, IN: University of Notre Dame Press, 1985.

Pernick, Martin. *A Calculus of Suffering: Pain, Professionalism, and Anesthesia in Nineteenth Century America.* Bloomington: Indiana University Press, 1985.

Ray, Isaac. *A Treatise on the Medical Jurisprudence of Insanity.* Boston: C. Little and J. Brown, 1838.

Rich, Ben A. *Strange Bedfellows: How Medical Jurisprudence Influenced Medical Ethics and Medical Practice.* New York: Kluwer Academic, 2001.

Rosenberg, Charles. *The Trial of the Assassin Guiteau.* Chicago: University of Chicago Press, 1968.

Scherer, Jennifer M., and Rita J. Simon. *Euthanasia and the Right to Die: A Comparative View.* Lanham, MD: Rowman and Littlefield, 1999.

Shilts, Randy. *The Mayor of Castro Street.* New York: St. Martin's Press, 1982.

Simon, Rita J., and David Aaronson. *The Insanity Defense: A Critical Assessment of Law and Policy in the Post-Hinckley Era.* New York: Praeger, 1988.

Steadman, Henry J., et al. *Before and after Hinckley: Evaluating Insanity Defense Reform.* New York: Guilford Press, 1993.

"Yates Found Guilty." *Houston Chronicle,* March 13, 2002, p. A1.

4
Impact and Legacy

In this study, we have considered several ways in which medicine and the courts have changed each other. On one hand, American medical practitioners, chiefly physicians, increasingly have played a very important role in shaping certain areas of law. Their impact is especially noticeable in two areas: the law concerning psychiatry and the impact of forensic pathologists as gatekeepers for criminal trials in general. Courts also have grown to depend on medical expertise in regard to a variety of cases involving diverse fields of legal controversy.

And yet in the very same 150 years that medicine has come into U.S. courtrooms as an influential presence, the courts have made an indelible impact on medicine. Judicial rulings concerning medicine as a field and medical personnel as practitioners have altered the ways in which physicians and their patients interact. This especially has been the case as courts have taken account of parties other than doctors who claim to exercise authority over healthcare, such as insurance companies and government agencies.

Finally, we have examined several medicolegal controversies that have spilled over to the larger society, in large part *because of* the judicial handling of those matters. Especially in regard to beginning- and end-of-life issues, these debates have been ongoing and intense. Largely because the airing of life-and-death issues in judicial settings has proved so divisive for the larger society, neither medicine nor the courts have prevailed, one over the other, in shaping the outcome of these debates.

This study has not emphasized the history of the American medical profession as a whole. Still, it is important to keep in mind that U.S. medicine is different in many respects from medicine as practiced elsewhere in the world. What characteristics typify U.S. medicine in the twenty-first century? As an outgrowth of many of the developments described earlier, one recognizes U.S. physicians' history of professionalism, their independence from state control, their increasing association with corporate healthcare management, and their links to science and technology. Many of those key aspects of U.S. medicine, interestingly, often differentiate it from medicine in other nations—even other industrialized, democratic, and Western nations. Canada and England, for example, have very different healthcare systems and attitudes toward and among physicians. And central to the difference between these nations is the role that is played by U.S. courts in shaping the evolution of U.S. medicine. One means of appreciating the extreme distinctiveness of the U.S. approach to legal controversies concerning medicine is to consider how other nations have addressed similar medicolegal problems. American judicial handling of the diverse issues connected with medicine has parallels in other areas of the world, and yet there are some vast differences.

Another postscript to this study of medicine on trial is how medicolegal discussions continued to play out in the United States, even after concerted efforts at courtroom resolution. What are the prospects for eventual resolution of those controversies, in legal or other forums? As we have seen in Chapter 3, courts in some instances have successfully "solved" certain medicolegal problems in the short term. As medical technology changes, however, and public awareness of the controversies grows, courts often have to reconsider their previous decisions.

For example, the *Quinlan* decision was in response to the much greater ability of medicine to keep persons alive, though in a vegetative state, for years on end. That decision inspired medical experts and legal authorities, as well as the public, to develop fresh approaches to long-term unconsciousness, such as the writing of advance care directives and living wills, so that courts would be able to understand patients' wishes in regard to heroic measures. But then, just when courts seemed to offer the possibility that persons could predetermine their fates if faced with the possibility of living "connected to a machine," the courts' "solution" opened up a discussion of other vexing problems. In the United States and all over the world, individuals facing the prospect of terminal or chronic diseases asked courts to examine their situations. Could those persons exercise a "right to die"? Could medical personnel assist them in that effort? Would courts stand in the way? Judicial interposition in cases such as Karen Ann Quinlan's, therefore, inspired consideration of several other extremely difficult matters connected to the end of life. Those matters not only proved thorny to resolve in a legal sense, but also caused some critics of right-to-die decisions to charge that judicial solutions in such instances were inadequate, if not positively harmful.

Thus in pondering the legacy of medicolegal controversies in the United States, we turn first to the question of other nations' handling of medicolegal questions. We start with a discussion of the medical controversy that was perhaps the most corrosive of all in the United States—abortion—but with a focus here on the English experience. For despite great depth of feeling on that issue in Britain (in current times as well as historically), the British legal responses to abortion have spurred far less venom than those in the United States.

We then consider another clear contrast with the U.S. experience—several other nations' permitting of physician-assisted suicide (PAS) and euthanasia. The remainder of this chapter is concerned with several particularly troublesome legacies of the medicolegal controversies previously considered in Chapters 1 through 3: the impact of the current medical malpractice crisis, here discussed in regard to obstetrical care in the United States; ongoing criticism of the Food and Drug Administration (FDA); and a handful of current arguments concerning the states' police power to combat communicable diseases. Although these legacies in some ways are discrete examples, they do reflect certain themes that already have been considered in earlier chapters. They show, for instance, the uncomfortable legal and ethical position of physicians when they encounter new medical technologies, the increasing connection between medical practice and hospital care in modern America, doctors' uneasy relationship with drugmakers on one hand and patients on the other, and the position of medical expert witnesses in court. Thus they demonstrate that some of the changes experienced by medicine and the law, as they interacted with one another in the past 150 years, still are occurring.

Abortion, Expert Testimony, and the British Parallel to *Roe v. Wade*

Abortion has been a divisive issue in U.S. courts, just as it has been a polarizing topic in American society at large. The discussion of abortion in Chapter 3 focused on U.S. case law in the second half of the twentieth century, particularly at the Supreme Court level. But in considering where the abortion controversy is headed, in the near and distant future, it is useful to discuss briefly two topics besides those recent judicial decisions on a constitutional right to abortion: (1) the ways in which U.S. courts addressed abortion before it had constitutional protection, and (2) another nation's judicial handling of abortion.

Historically, abortion has not come before the courts simply in challenges to state laws of the type that inspired *Roe v. Wade* and *Doe v. Bolton* in the 1970s and subsequent cases in the later decades of the century. Throughout U.S. history, there have been legal discussions of abortion in connection with a variety of courtroom dramas, but most were cases in which persons were accused of performing abortions illegally. In such episodes, the abortionists might have been unlicensed medical practitioners or even laypeople, or they could have been physicians who acted outside of the confines of state rules concerning the circumstances in which abortions could be performed lawfully. Such prosecutions resulting from illegal abortions obviously involved medical testimony, sometimes from forensic pathologists and coroners concerning the cause of death of a pregnant woman or her baby. Abortion cases involving criminal charges were in some respects much more clear-cut than those where constitutional rights were at issue. And yet even criminal prosecutions that touched on the question of abortion could prove extremely emotional and thus difficult to adjudicate. A brief discussion of some of the difficulties faced by courts and medical experts in such prosecutions serves to highlight the emotional quality of the abortion debate prior to the time that courts considered it a constitutional question.

One aspect of the abortion controversy that scholars have not fully discussed is the role of forensic experts in this sort of courtroom showdown, where esteemed forensic pathologists found their judgments to be questioned in cases involving abortion and the closely related crime of infanticide. As the medical examiner (ME) for a busy metropolitan area, Thomas Magrath of Boston occasionally was involved in the medical investigation of suspicious infant deaths. Magrath's years in office, in the early twentieth century, were a time when young and unmarried women still had real reason to fear giving birth outside of wedlock. In the case of a young female domestic worker accused of murder in a small New England town, Magrath was called on to examine the body of an infant who had been found in springtime in an outdoor toilet. (An attempted late-term abortion easily might end in the killing of a near-term infant. Thus abortion might be difficult to differentiate from infanticide.) Despite the forensic challenges associated with the case, Magrath concluded that the baby had been strangled in the autumn, prior to being left in the privy. He thus damaged the alleged mother's defense that the birth had been a surprise to her and that she had panicked, leaving the infant where it had fallen. It was typical of such cases, however, that even expert forensic testimony did not ensure a conviction for infanticide. In that episode, Magrath had provided compelling testimony, yet the jury was sympathetic to the young household worker's plight. The jurors refused to conclude that the dead baby belonged to the accused woman. Scholars who study infanticide argue that such jury equity often was practiced in infanticide cases. What was unusual in this episode, however, was that the venerated Dr. Magrath was gainsaid just at the moment when he in particular and MEs in general were consolidating their authority over expert forensic testimony in U.S. courtrooms.

Magrath was not alone in discovering that abortion was a vexing issue for the courts to address. At about the same time that Magrath suffered that rare rebuff to his formidable reputation, Bernard Spilsbury was offering his expert opinion in British controversies concerning abortion. Spilsbury used his position of leadership in the British Medico-Legal Society to comment publicly on abortions by unlicensed practitioners and emphasize the dangers of death from shock that women faced when they underwent abortions illegally. He also had no qualms about alerting the police and the Home Office (which prosecuted such offenses) to persons whom he believed to be performing unlicensed procedures. He assisted in several prosecutions, including actions against physicians who he thought were performing too many abortions. At the 1933 trial of a physician in Jersey charged with performing an abortion, Spilsbury, appearing for the prosecution, argued that the infant had not been dead before the abortion. Other physicians who appeared for the defense, however, dealt a rare setback for Spilsbury when they convinced the jury that the baby had not been alive, thus clearing the physician of the charges. Spilsbury, like Magrath, rarely saw his expert opinion rejected by jurors; clearly the jurors were sympathetic to the physician in the case—who was licensed—and were not as zealous as Spilsbury in condemning all abortions.

Based on their fairly frequent contact with the adult female victims of botched abortions by unlicensed practitioners, medical leaders Magrath and Spilsbury, as well as forensic pathologists as a group, tended to oppose abortion. Obstetricians and gynecologists, however, took another view: if they, as licensed specialists, were authorized by law to be abortion providers, then abortion should be a safe and relatively rare procedure.

In the 1920s, a fledgling obstetrician named Aleck Bourne had been Bernard Spilsbury's student when Spilsbury was at the height of his crusade against abortion. In the next decade, Bourne went on to become an eminent practitioner in his own right and to challenge Spilsbury's expert opinion in several cases. Bourne testified for the defense, for example, in the Jersey case in which Spilsbury's views were rejected by the jury. As a practitioner who not only spoke about the subject as an expert witness but also performed abortions himself, Bourne thought himself at risk from prosecution under the applicable criminal law at the time. In the 1930s, the British law governing abortion dated from 1861—exactly the same era as the American state statutes that so severely limited the performance of abortions in the United States. (Many state laws from the mid–nineteenth century allowed abortions only when the life of the mother was at stake. It was such a law in Texas that Jane Roe challenged in *Roe v. Wade.*) Section 58 of Britain's Offences against the Person Act of 1861 provided that anyone who tried to procure a miscarriage through the unlawful use of an instrument or other means could be guilty of a felony and might be sentenced to a lifetime prison term.

Bourne and several of his medical colleagues sensed that most prosecutions for abortions were being put forward against unlicensed abortionists, and even those cases were being pressed mostly when the patients died. He and his obstetrical colleagues had performed abortions on women whose health or lives were threatened by pregnancy, and yet most never had been prosecuted. Still, Bourne and others—notably the British Medical Association (BMA)—sought a clarification in the law. In 1938, a case came to Bourne's attention that he believed would be an excellent test of the judicial waters. He heard about a thirteen-year-old girl, "Miss M," who had been lured into an army barracks in London and raped by a group of soldiers. The assault resulted in the girl becoming pregnant. Her parents, anxious to procure an abortion, got in touch with London obstetricians, who alerted Bourne.

Before proceeding to perform the abortion, however, Bourne was careful to make sure that the girl fit certain criteria. He wanted to ascertain that the procedure was in her best interests, and he also wished to be sure that she would serve as a good example from which to argue, should he be prosecuted. In seeking a good medical outcome for the girl, Bourne examined her for signs of infection; an abortion would have been dangerous if it had the opportunity to spread an infection further in her body. He also tried to find out whether she had any mental disability, for he reasoned that carrying a pregnancy to term could be emotionally dangerous for an average person of her age, but not for someone of limited mental capacity. Finally, both in the interest of the soundness of his case and due to his concern about the psychological impact on the victim of continuing the pregnancy, Bourne hoped to assess if she was in any way prone to prostitution. (Bourne in that regard was distinctly judgmental.) Having satisfied himself that Miss M was physically able to undergo an abortion and that she was of such a character that she *would* be emotionally scarred by carrying the pregnancy to term (that is, she was not promiscuous), Bourne decided to perform the abortion.

He did so in a public hospital with other staff present, thus seeming to invite prosecution. In a matter of days, he was notified that the director of Public Prosecutions would be filing a case against him under the 1861 act. Although he raised other issues in *Rex v. Bourne* (1938), the most important element of Bourne's defense was his contention that within the terms of the 1861 act, a physician might lawfully perform an abortion. (The act, after all, had referred to the "unlawful" procurement of a miscarriage, thus intimating that there was a category of lawful abortions, and those would not be prosecuted.) Bourne's challenge was to set out before the conservative British judiciary an argument about why and when abortions ought to be legal.

Bourne and his counsel proposed that the Offences against the Person Act had been aimed primarily against unlicensed abortionists and was not intended to intrude upon the professional judgment of physicians who were acting in good faith to preserve the health of their patients. Even if the judge was prepared to accept that argument, though, the defense still had another hurdle to clear: Bourne had not encountered any serious medical condition (such as diabetes or heart disease) in Miss M that would have provided him with the justification that her life was threatened by the pregnancy. He could argue that pregnancy would be physically dangerous for a girl of thirteen, but medical opinion was divided about exactly how dangerous it would be; and at any rate that was not the crux of his case. Bourne was most concerned about how a girl below the age of consent who had been raped might be affected psychologically by carrying a pregnancy to term. (Here, Bourne had the backing of a BMA committee, which had made a similar recommendation in a 1936 report on the medical aspects of abortion.) Thus the defense contended that abortions ought to be permitted when a physician, using his best judgment, determined that continuing a pregnancy would cause either serious physical or psychological harm to the patient. The judicial decision in *Rex v. Bourne* endorsed exactly that view.

Between the 1938 *Bourne* decision and the time that British law again commented directly on abortion, in 1967, British physicians usually were allowed to perform abortions within hospitals at their discretion, but they and legal authorities were severe toward unlicensed abortionists. Only when licensed physicians seemed to be specializing in abortions—as sometimes was "shown" by evidence of their charging very high fees for the procedure—did abortionists find themselves in court. After *Bourne,* the next major statement about abortion law in Britain—Parliament's Abortion Act of 1967—was a recognition of how widely *Bourne* had been accepted among the public and the legal and medical communities. The 1967 legislation allowed physicians to perform abortions as long as they did so within hospitals, were acting in good faith, and could argue that the procedure promoted the good physical or mental health of the patients. In addition, there was one other provision in the more modern law that had been considered but not made a requirement in *Bourne:* that the physician act in consultation with at least one medical colleague. Aleck Bourne's reputation was so distinguished, and his motives for performing the abortion in 1938 so well known, that in his case there was never any suspicion of his having acted out of greed. Other physicians, however, did well to consult with at least one peer to remove any possibility that they were driven by mercenary goals. In the situation of a doctor contemplating performing an abortion for the psychological welfare of a patient, that other colleague very well might be a psychiatrist.

British legal, social, and medical attitudes about abortion were greatly affected by the *Bourne* case. Like *Roe v. Wade* and *Doe v. Bolton* in the United States (1973), *Bourne* was the judicial affirmation of a right to abortion. In one sense, both *Roe/Doe* and *Bourne* tested the continuing validity of a nineteenth-century prohibition on abortion. In both instances, the courts found the Victorian-era laws to be too restrictive. In both England and the United States, courts allowed medical practitioners considerable scope, in deciding to perform an abortion, to make judgments about the health and welfare of their patients. On both sides of the Atlantic, the prestige of the organized medical profession (and its official position in favor of the liberalization of abortion) carried much weight with the courts.

The factual circumstances that created the leading case in England, however, were far different from the fact situation in *Roe* (which was the better known of the *Roe/Doe* twin cases). Most important in the *Bourne* case was the undisputed nature of the patient's injury: she was pregnant as a result of a rape to which she could not have consented because of her age. She was, therefore, a particularly sympathetic central figure in a test case. Although the woman who was at the center of the *Roe* case also claimed to be a victim of rape by multiple perpetrators, Jane Roe had led a more eventful life than Miss M. It was possible to argue (as some critics of *Roe v. Wade* did in 1973 and have ever since) that Jane Roe had placed herself in a situation that had put her at higher risk for sexual assault. Some critics of Jane Roe and the *Roe* decision even argued that Roe was not raped at all, but had consented to sexual contact. The public perception of Jane Roe also was dimmed by the fact that Roe had not insisted on a prosecution of the alleged rapists. By contrast, Miss M's parents pressed for prosecution, and the rapists were convicted in a trial that was well publicized.

Another key difference between *Roe* and *Bourne* was the participation of Dr. Bourne. A leading figure in the English medical establishment in 1938, he was willing to put his freedom and professional standing on the line in order to clarify the law. The court in *Rex v. Bourne* could not fail to note his courage and impeccable reputation. There was no parallel medical figure in the *Roe* case, not because of a lack of medical luminaries with strong opinions on abortion, but due to the fact that Jane Roe never had an abortion. The controversy was played out in the abstract, for before *Roe v. Wade* could be adjudicated, Jane Roe had progressed too far into the pregnancy to have an abortion. That is, in many respects, *Roe v. Wade* lacked the sympathetic defendant that Aleck Bourne had been; in addition, Jane Roe herself was a divisive figure.

Finally, the *Bourne* case took place much earlier than *Roe.* The 1930s were unquestionably a different time than the early 1970s. The medical profession in that earlier time was more the object of deference, for example. The waters of public opinion were not muddied with the argument that abortion was just another form of birth control that was being countenanced by the courts, for artificial birth control still lacked the mass appeal that it had after the introduction of the pill. That the *Bourne* case occurred when it did left many years prior to the action of Parliament in 1967 for the medical profession and the courts to see how and whether the law should be enforced. When Parliament did act, it did so with information in mind from decades of the operation of *Bourne* as law. And that judge-made law, as it was enforced between 1938 and 1967, operated fairly smoothly, with support from the public and medical authorities. After 1967, antiabortion groups in England had a much more difficult time in attacking the legality of abortion than U.S. antiabortion groups did after *Roe,* for in England, abortion had been legalized through judicial and legislative action. Several generations of the English public were familiar and comfortable with the workings of a liberal abortion policy, presided over by physicians.

In England, therefore, the courts were the key institution that made abortion legal at a national level. When the courts set out a legal sphere in which abortions could take place, they did so in close connection with the medical profession. Scholars of modern English medical history thus refer to the medicalization of abortion in that nation. Medicalization refers not only to doctors' influence in the judicial process (for example the *Bourne* judges' clear deference to the reputation of Aleck Bourne), but also because after *Bourne,* doctors were given the monopoly on the performance of abortions and because abortions had to take place in hospitals, which were the province of physicians.

In the United States, by contrast, the legalization of abortion also occurred through a court case, but the specific grounds for that leading decision were quite different. *Roe* balanced states' interests in regulating the abortion procedure against the potential for human life that might be destroyed by abortion. The decision in *Roe* took into account the medical community's opinions about how dangerous abortion was for the mother as a pregnancy progressed when *Roe* marked off points during the pregnancy (using trimesters) at which a state legitimately might regulate the performance of abortions. Most importantly for the present discussion, throughout the *Roe* decision, the justices relied on medical standards about the relative danger of pregnancy at various points in its course. *Roe*, therefore, was in several respects an example of both making abortion more legal and causing abortion to be more "medical" than it had been. In future, abortion in the United States would be associated less with unskilled, dangerous, or untrained practitioners and much more with trained and skilled physicians in open practice.

But the medicalization of abortion in the United States was not nearly as thorough as it was in England. As we have seen, the U.S. judiciary did not simply turn abortion over to doctors—which very nearly was what was done in England. In the United States, the courts since *Roe* have been reluctant to give total control over abortion to the medical profession. For one thing, medical progress has cut several ways with regard to the abortion debate. For example, although some medical experts could argue that abortion was much safer in the twentieth century and thus it should be legalized, other medical professionals could point out that science now could deliver babies at a far earlier moment in pregnancies than ever before, thus increasing the stake by the state in preserving fetal life. Although such arguments have not thus far held sway with the U.S. Supreme Court, they have been powerful contentions when presented to state legislatures and the public at large.

U.S. courts have listened closely when doctors and medical organizations such as the American College of Obstetricians and Gynecologists (ACOG) have testified about abortion, but the judiciary also has allowed considerable scope for action on abortion by state legislatures. Furthermore, other organizations besides professional medical groups have been influential in U.S. court cases—notably Planned Parenthood and other groups that either provide or encourage abortions outside hospital settings. Thus in the United States, abortion is not as closely associated with hospitals as it is in England. In the United States as well, abortion often is connected in the public's mind with specialized abortion providers who, although they are physicians, are not as respected as obstetrical or gynecological specialists like Dr. Bourne. In fact, insofar as they are medical care providers who, like Dr. Leroy Carhart, specialize only in abortions, American abortionists actually suffer in public opinion and (as *Stenberg v. Carhart* demonstrates) judicial esteem.

Like abortion, end-of-life questions have come before U.S. courts in a series of highly controversial cases at the end of the twentieth century. As with abortion, many end-of-life cases have been impelled by tremendous changes in medical technology. In end-of-life cases, U.S. courts have given the medical community some authority, but not without strings attached. Chief among those strings is the courts' pointing to state legislatures as proper arbiters of many end-of-life issues; courts have encouraged states, for example, to push for the provision of living wills. Also (as we have seen in Chapter 3), courts do not merely remind states to take action; courts sometimes reserve the right to resolve end-of-life questions themselves (that is, judicially) on a case-by-case basis. And as with their handling of abortion controversies, courts have had to use every bit of diplomacy they can muster to avoid bringing down the ire of the public on judicial institutions when courts presume to decide on matters as vital as the right to die. How has such an American approach to the right to die contrasted with other nations' handling of end-of-life questions?

Euthanasia and Physician-Assisted Suicide (PAS) in Other Nations

End-of-life issues have been debated in many other nations besides the United States, due to some of the same factors that have brought those questions to the fore for Americans in the second half of the twentieth century. In particular, the ability of medical technology to prolong life has led to concern over the quality of life for patients. If persons *can* be kept alive through mechanical devices, improved medications, and more advanced understandings of medical care, then *should* those individuals continue to be kept alive? What should the role of the medical profession be in cases where patients desire to end their lives with lethal medicines or when patients request the cessation of heroic measures to continue life? Does the state have any motives for either supporting or opposing individuals' efforts to engage in assisted suicide or euthanasia? The responses to those questions have varied around the world, in connection with the place of the medical professions within each society and the structure of healthcare systems as well as certain historical traditions within each country. (Interestingly, although religion has played a part in some nations' responses to the debate over the right to die, other countries with strong religious traditions that would seem likely to argue against PAS and euthanasia in fact allow those practices. The full discussion of such a paradox is beyond the scope of this project, but one example might be mentioned. In Colombia, a nation with a long Roman Catholic heritage, euthanasia for terminally ill patients has been openly permitted, via a series of judicial rulings, since 1997.)

The case of Sue Rodriguez helped direct the attention of Canadians to the question of PAS. Rodriguez suffered from Lou Gehrig's Disease (amyotrophic lateral sclerosis, or ALS). Only recently a healthy young person, she suddenly had a gloomy prognosis. Within months, her doctors predicted, she would lose her mobility and the ability to care for herself; soon after that she would even lose the ability to breathe and swallow on her own. She was determined to choose the manner and time of her own death, or at least to obtain physician assistance if she could not herself commit suicide because of physical limitations. She challenged the part of Canada's criminal code that made assistance to a suicide (though not the suicide itself) illegal. In the case of *Rodriguez v. Attorney General of British Columbia* (1993), Rodriguez made a powerful argument for her right to commit suicide with the assistance of a physician. Although she lost her case on appeal, the Canadian Supreme Court agreed to take up discussion of the controversy; that court, too, ruled against Rodriguez.

The Rodriguez case was an important challenge to Canadian law because it involved fundamental human rights that were guaranteed in the Canadian Charter of Rights and Freedoms. In particular, Rodriguez hoped to convince courts to recognize a right to be in control of one's own body as one died. The case also was of great interest because Canada has a health system in which care is funded by the state but provided by private practitioners. Thus there is considerable physician autonomy, but within a system of healthcare that in other nations would be called socialized. Although Canadians do not rely on advanced medical technology to the extent that Americans do, and in spite of the fact that they often must wait for long periods before undergoing elective medical procedures, Canadians are accustomed to extensive social services.

Rodriguez's fight galvanized several groups who were interested in the issues raised by her case. For example, the Coalition of Provincial Organizations of the Handicapped (COPOH) joined in Rodriguez's effort with a subtle and persuasive set of arguments related to the rights of persons with disabilities. The COPOH asserted that denying the right of persons affected by disabling diseases to obtain help in ending their lives was to discriminate against them vis-à-vis able-bodied persons under Canadian law. Persons without physical disabilities were permitted to commit suicide; it was the provision of assistance for a suicide that was illegal in Canada. The COPOH recognized, however, that individuals with disabilities also were vulnerable to abuse by those who sought to end their lives prematurely without their consent. In that sense, the COPOH anticipated some of the points made by Not Dead Yet, an organization representing persons with disabilities that was one of the groups filing an *amicus curiae* brief in *Washington v. Glucksberg.*

After the Rodriguez controversy, the Canadian Senate set up a Special Committee on Euthanasia and Assisted Suicide. In 1995, the committee delivered its formal report. It recommended that PAS and euthanasia remain illegal in Canada, though it also signaled that the legislature might countenance judges' relaxation of criminal penalties for those who violated the strictures on assisted suicides in particular circumstances. The committee called for the medical profession to study the alleviation of pain. Particularly if palliative measures could be undertaken in cases where patients were experiencing terrible pain, then perhaps the need for PAS would be lessened. The committee also seemed to indicate that if the administration of pain-reducing medicines had the effect of shortening patients' lives, then physicians' actions in giving such medications might be tolerated by the law. The committee considered the idea of creating a third category of murder in the criminal code, a type called "compassionate homicide," but that proposal was not made into law.

The Canadian debate about assisted suicide highlighted the lack of a coordinated effort by the medical profession to address the needs of persons with physical disabilities, like Rodriguez, and also terminally ill individuals. Patients like Rodriguez who were experiencing physical conditions that left them able to think and even speak but not otherwise care for themselves presented a terrible quandary for medicine, for those patients were not technically in the process of dying, and yet they had a quality of life that they themselves sometimes described as very poor. Advocates for disabled persons in Canada, the United States, and elsewhere have followed episodes like the *Rodriguez* case with great interest. Some organizations for persons with disabilities took inspiration from Rodriguez's fight for physical autonomy. Others predicted that in a worst-case scenario, the establishment of a right to PAS would create discrimination against persons with physical challenges.

But though the Canadian debate over PAS has been newsworthy in the United States and other nations, the experience of the Netherlands has been even more attention-getting. That both euthanasia and PAS are practiced in the Netherlands is well known. What is less widely recognized is that neither euthanasia nor PAS is authorized by statute. They are allowed through interpretations of the law by judges. The medical community's stature and role in the Netherlands are a key element in the permissiveness of the Dutch toward physician participation in patients' deaths. Nazi programs of euthanasia of elderly and disabled persons in the 1930s and 1940s were vividly recalled in the Netherlands. Although the Dutch remember such Nazi activities with horror, they also reflect upon their own physicians' heroic efforts to undermine Nazi eugenical policies. Rather than reveal the names of their vulnerable patients, many Dutch physicians chose to go to concentration camps themselves. The Dutch doctors who were able to remain in practice during World War II shielded their patients from Nazi efforts at extermination of the physically or mentally disabled. In the Netherlands, therefore, there is a sense (based on recent history) that the medical community can be trusted in matters concerning the end of life. In addition, the medical culture in the Netherlands is quite different from that in the United States in other respects. Dutch physicians generally have close, long-term relationships with their patients, for example; they also still make house calls. In an environment where healthcare is universally available and standards of living are very high, there are no financial incentives for either physicians or family members to want to cut healthcare costs for the vulnerable members of the population by resorting to euthanasia or PAS.

A series of cases in the 1970s and 1980s established the legal arena in which physicians could act to shorten the lives of their patients, either by assisting with suicides or by committing euthanasia. One of the most important of those cases involved a physician named Geertruida Postma. In 1973, Dr. Postma administered a lethal dose of morphine to her mother, who was suffering from the effects of a stroke. Her mother had indicated a wish to die; she was in unbearable pain and was literally tied to a wheelchair by nursing home authorities. After giving the morphine to her mother, Dr. Postma reported to the police what she had done. She was charged with mercy killing. At her trial, she argued that she had been placed in an impossible position: as a physician, she was committed to alleviating her patient's pain, but the law forbade her to kill.

The court convicted her, but found her motivation (the relief of physical pain) to be both commendable and a part of her responsibilities as a physician. Dutch courts in subsequent years ruled that doctors who committed similar acts were operating under what was called *force majeure.* That is, physicians were able to use the argument that they were compelled by their duty as physicians to honor their patients' requests for pain relief, that "irresistible force" of their duty to alleviate pain was a defense to the charge of murder.

In the early 1980s, both a leading Dutch criminal court and the Royal Dutch Medical Association prepared standards for voluntary euthanasia and PAS. The medical group and the courts agreed on certain criteria for allowing PAS and euthanasia: the request for physician involvement had to be voluntary and consistent; the patient had to be mentally competent; the physician involved had to obtain concurrence from another physician; and the patient had to be in unbearable pain that had no method of treatment; but the patient did not have to be suffering a terminal illness. A study by the Remmerlink Commission in 1991 followed the operation of those standards. Although in general the study indicated that the Dutch guidelines were operating as advocates of the "right to die" hoped they would, there was one troubling finding: some physicians admitted committing euthanasia in the absence of recent or clear requests from patients to do so. Although the physicians who made that admission were a small minority, the study indicated that there were circumstances in which a few physicians took it upon themselves to decide for patients the appropriate time to die. In the majority opinion in *Washington v. Glucksberg* (1997), Chief Justice Rehnquist of the U.S. Supreme Court explicitly referred to that aspect of the Remmerlink report: "this study suggests that, despite the existence of reporting procedures, euthanasia in the Netherlands has not been limited to competent, terminally ill adults who are enduring physical suffering, and that regulation of the practice may not have prevented abuses in cases involving vulnerable persons" (734). The potential for abuse of physicians' authority was very real, in other words, in the Netherlands. That lesson was not lost on those who watched the operation of PAS among the Dutch—including American courts.

The use of PAS in other nations (even the Netherlands' European neighbors) varies from the Dutch experience in certain key respects. In Switzerland, there is a tension between forces that on one hand would tend to encourage PAS and euthanasia and on the other hand make it ineffective from a cost standpoint. Swiss healthcare is privatized, so it is expensive for families to pursue high-technology treatments that can prolong life for months and years. At the same time, a private healthcare system encourages physicians and other healthcare providers to perceive an economic benefit in extending patients' lives; the longer a patient lives, the greater the revenue for the care facility and physician.

The Swiss Academy of Medical Sciences has set forth guidelines for the administration of euthanasia and PAS. Those two practices are neither sanctioned nor outlawed in Swiss legal codes, but according to Swiss courts since the 1930s, both are permitted to exist. By the 1990s, Switzerland had become the destination of choice for many Europeans who wished to end their lives because of medical concerns. Organizations such as EXIT Suisse Romande and Dignitas have lobbied for positive statements from lawmakers that will recognize the situation that exists in fact—that is, toleration among judicial authorities for suicide, PAS, and euthanasia. In 1996, the canton of Geneva adopted a policy that patients' living wills and advanced directives should have legal force. That the Swiss, with a strong democratic tradition, should recognize the right of persons to make important decisions about their own bodies is not surprising. That the Swiss also should refrain from explicitly authorizing such controversial practices, in light of their observation of Nazi euthanasia policies at close geographical range, also is understandable.

Groups in the United States that either advocate or oppose PAS and euthanasia have paid close attention to the experiences of other nations. For one thing, the groups that agitate for legal changes in regard to the end of life often are international in membership. Also, as discussed in Chapter 3, the policies of other countries in regard to end-of-life issues often are evoked in court cases, particularly by critics of PAS, to demonstrate the pitfalls of an expansion of the right to die. Thus when end-of-life issues are on trial in the United States, the medical and legal responses of other nations have been quite relevant to American courtroom discussions.

In beginning- and end-of-life issues, nations in the world besides the United States have made great changes in policy in the past century. In the United States, judicial decisions about abortion and the end of life are very much bound up with medical practice and opinion, and with rapidly changing medical technology. Despite their willingness to take on many aspects of right-to-death and right-to-life issues, U.S. courts have recognized some authority by the medical profession in those extremely controversial spheres of debate. And yet in other nations, due to a variety of factors, beginning- and end-of-life issues are even more medicalized than in the United States. In other countries, medical practitioners (especially physicians) have much greater control over medical decisions concerning the beginning and end of life, and have far less reason to expect censure from either courts or other state agencies for their actions in caring for patients than practitioners in the United States. The medical community's relative power over such matters is sure to be one of the factors that is considered, as U.S. courts look abroad (and vice versa) in future debates about the beginning and end of life.

Medical Malpractice in the United States: The Problem of Obstetrics

A major theme in recent U.S. medical history has been the sense among medical practitioners that they are under a state of siege. Managed-care corporations and governmental agencies are limiting the authority of medical personnel, and practitioners are being told by the courts how to interact with their patients, through doctrines such as informed consent. There is an even more tangible respect in which the medical community—particularly physicians—complains of being under fire. They are paying more money for insurance, which is a major expenditure for most practitioners.

The soaring cost of medical malpractice insurance in the United States has had a striking effect on certain areas of medical practice. Obstetrics has been keenly affected. Faced with suits alleging medical errors during childbirths, many obstetricians are either moving to jurisdictions where they perceive that suits are less common or are refusing to accept new patients.

Although there are a number of examples of malpractice actions being undertaken, some of the obstetricians' fears about malpractice awards are unfounded. That is, although it is easy to file a suit, courts do not always allow recovery in cases where obstetricians' negligence is alleged. In the case of *Gonzalez v. U.S.* (2002), for example, the plaintiff brought suit on behalf of her infant daughter, who allegedly was injured because of a lack of appropriate care by four physicians and a nurse-midwife at the child's birth. The plaintiff sued the hospital employees as workers for the federal government because the hospital was funded through the Federally Supported Health Centers Assistance Act of 1992. The federal statute of limitations was two years; Gonzalez had waited nearly three years after the birth to file her claim. The U.S. Court of Appeals for the First Circuit decided that Gonzalez had not filed a timely claim, according to the provisions of the Federal Tort Claims Act.

The *Gonzalez* case illustrates two related points: suits for birth injuries are a popular course of action among parents whose children are disabled, yet courts seem to be limiting such claims perhaps precisely because they are proliferating. In spite of the fact that courts often do find ways to deny recovery for malpractice, however, the *perception* that such suits are proliferating *is* a powerful influence on malpractice insurers, obstetricians, potential plaintiffs, and their lawyers.

With obstetricians leaving their practices and some pregnant women facing long drives to get to physicians who will oversee their deliveries, midwives are gaining new popularity. Almost driven out of the birthing process by physicians at the beginning of the twentieth century, midwives are stepping in to assist with births. Midwives are in many ways appealing to families: they are less expensive than obstetricians; they often prefer home birth settings; and they rely less on drugs and technologically sophisticated medical devices such as fetal monitors, preferring low-key techniques in helping women give birth. Ironically, however, many midwives are sharing some of the difficulties that physicians face, including demands by insurers that the births take place in institutional settings, preferably hospitals. Like obstetricians, midwives also have seen the costs for their malpractice insurance rise dramatically. Several groups of midwives in the beginning of the twenty-first century lost their insurance coverage, and had difficulty in obtaining new insurance. In addition, midwives still see resistance from some physicians' groups and state regulators, who charge that midwifery (particularly in home births) exposes mothers and babies to dangers that could be easily addressed by physicians in hospital settings.

Although some midwives are licensed nurses who also have received special training in obstetrical care (called "certified nurse-midwives"), other midwives (called "entry level" or "lay midwives") are not certified by the states in which they practice. At the great majority of perhaps 40,000 home births in the United States each year, women are attended by lay midwives. That is a striking figure, because there are actually fewer lay midwives than certified midwives. Such an apparent contradiction reflects the difficulty that certified nurse-midwives have in abiding by state regulations. Most states, for example, require that midwives have a backup obstetrician to call in the event of emergency complications at a home delivery, and yet many obstetricians are reluctant to add to the already high cost of their malpractice insurance by working with midwives. At least 19 states allow lay midwives to attend at births, and some even allow them to administer certain drugs at births; other states, however, do not license lay midwives.

Thus lay midwives practice in a gray area, both medically and legally, despite the fact that they are very much in demand. Increasingly, their uncertain status lands lay midwives in court, even as many patients continue to value their services. A lay midwife named Abigail Odom was prosecuted in 1997 in San Luis Obispo, California. Among the charges against her were felony child endangerment and practicing medicine without a license. Odom was convicted on six counts. After serving two years in state prison, she vowed never to go back to assisting at births, although she believed that she had been following a calling as a midwife. Another midwife, Freida Miller, was prosecuted in 2002, after Miller administered the drug Pitocin to a woman who just had given birth in a home setting. The drug helped control the woman's heavy bleeding and probably saved the patient's life, but state authorities in Ohio charged Miller with administering the medicine without a license. She was given probation on the charge of administering Pitocin, yet served time for contempt of court because she refused to reveal the name of the physician who gave her access to the prescription drug. Miller for years had assisted at births in Ohio's Mennonite and Amish communities—groups of persons who often shunned conventional medical care but who eventually were won over by Miller's low-tech approach to birthing.

Thus Miller's jail stay deprived those families of much-needed medical assistance.

And so the malpractice crisis has reached beyond doctors. It has begun to affect midwives—practitioners who historically have been undervalued by many physicians, but who recently have stepped in to assist with births when physicians could not or would not participate in obstetrical care. Midwives have been prosecuted for unlicensed participation in births ever since the licensing of physicians was stepped up in the late nineteenth century. At that time, physicians were attempting to shut down unlicensed competitors. The environment of current prosecutions is different. In the twenty-first century, more and more patients are turning to midwives because physicians simply are not available. State legislatures (which set the rules on licensing) may have to recognize that new reality. If history is any guide, the impetus for changing state licensure laws to make them less hostile to lay midwives may need to come from within the medical community itself, just as the nineteenth-century licensure laws emanated from physicians themselves.

Reproductive Cloning and the Stem Cell Debate

As discussed in Chapter 3, in few areas of medical science has technology outstripped the courts' ability to keep pace with that technology faster than infertility research and practice. The ability of reproductive scientists to retrieve, store, and manipulate human embryos outside the human body has raised matters of grave import beyond the issues connected with infertility cases. Through their work with artificial reproductive technology, researchers found methods of producing stem cells, which could be used in medical research. In areas such as the regeneration of nerves and tissues after major spinal injuries and the treatment of degenerative diseases such as Parkinson's, stem cells offer promise for researchers and hope for patients.

But the use of stem cells is fraught with moral, legal, and ethical dilemmas. The stem cells come from a procedure known as somatic cell nuclear transfer (SCNT), which has its roots in infertility treatment methods. A human egg is infused with the nucleus of a cell from a fully developed person; the egg then undergoes divisions to become a blastocyst, which is a collection of cells. When the blastocyst is implanted in a woman, she can become pregnant, with some of the blastocyst becoming the fetus and other parts forming the placenta. Keeping the blastocyst within the "test tube," however, allows the cells to grow and be used for research purposes but never to develop on their own into human beings. Are the stem cells that are in vitro "alive"? Are they future human beings? Some lines of stem cells already exist. Should they be continued simply for research purposes, or is their existence to be tied only to human reproduction? Could they be used to produce a clone of a human being?

In 2002, a distinguished panel affiliated with the National Research Council (including the National Academy of Sciences, the National Academy of Engineering, and the Institute of Medicine) issued a report on its study of the issues of reproductive human cloning and the development of stem cells. The panel recommended that human reproductive cloning be banned for at least five years while further studies explored the potential dangers to human subjects (that is, the women who would carry to term the results of cloning) of these projects. Animal studies involving cloning indicated high fetal mortality in animal-cloning projects. The studies indicated that a large number of embryos were necessary in order to achieve satisfactory results. The panel expressed fears that large numbers of human eggs would need to be used in a human-cloning attempt—itself a barrier to human-cloning experimentation. The panel did recommend that stem cell research be continued. This put them on a collision course with the George W. Bush administration, which in August 2001 had banned researchers with federal support from working with new stem cell lines. According to the administration's directive, only existing stem cell lines could be used in research. The scientific panel, however, did encourage further discussion among the public as well as the scientific community of the many ethical and social issues raised by the stem cell controversy—a recommendation that surely will come to pass.

Continuing Controversy Involving the FDA

The role of the Food and Drug Administration (FDA) in regulating drugs and medical devices continues to be controversial. A large portion of the FDA's authority concerns the regulation of prescription medicines and medical devices that can be authorized only by physicians, and yet the agency's standards for the development, use, and follow-up of those products often are not internally consistent. As has been discussed earlier, for example, heart valves are regulated by a different group in the FDA than orthopedic connective tissues, though both are materials that may become contaminated by fungi and cause harm to patients.

Although the FDA has fairly broad powers to regulate the sale of prescription drugs, the advent of direct-to-consumer marketing has made the agency's oversight of prescription drugs and devices much more complex. Even the FDA admits that it is overwhelmed by demands on its time. The agency has considered allowing the developers of new products to pay fees that would cover the cost of testing by third parties (outside the FDA). Such a scheme would assist in getting drugs and other medical products tested more rapidly and thus approved for human use in a more efficient fashion. It would have the disadvantage of allowing testing by persons with ties to industry rather than government, the result being that the neutrality of evaluators would be much more difficult to ensure. Even those nations that have patterns of drug marketing similar to those of the United States have tried alternative models of drug-industry regulation. New Zealand, for example, is the only other nation in the world with direct-to-consumer drug marketing. New Zealand has adopted an approach to drug-marketing regulation in which the drug industry is self-policing; its system is viewed as responsible, ethical, and effective.

The FDA has some authority over other substances that affect patients' welfare—notably over-the-counter formulations that consumers/patients may purchase and use without a physician's permission. Historically, the FDA's control concerning nonprescription (or over-the-counter) medications is limited to suppressing false advertising or inflated or misleading claims by the makers of nonprescription drugs. Occasionally, in cases where harm has been egregious, the FDA will pull nonprescription medications from public dissemination.

In the later part of the twentieth century, a huge industry sprang up in vitamins, minerals, and formulations termed dietary supplements. Many consumers purchased dietary supplements and vitamins for health-related reasons, and yet the FDA's authority to regulate these supplements was limited. Nonetheless, the FDA took a fairly active role in policing dietary supplements for several years, particularly in the 1980s and early 1990s. In reaction to that attention from the government, the dietary supplement industry lobbied hard for the FDA to take a more laissez-faire approach. The FDA's oversight of dietary supplements was hampered by the 1994 congressional legislation governing those nonprescription substances—the Dietary Supplement Health and Education Act (discussed in Chapter 2), which was bankrolled by the dietary supplement industry itself. As a result of that act, the regulatory powers of the FDA over dietary supplements currently are circumscribed. Now, to pull dietary supplements off the market, the FDA must not only demonstrate the medical risks that the products entail, but must meet a high legal standard in so doing. The agency must show that the products pose a "significant risk of illness or injury" in order to enforce a ban on their sale; the FDA also has to show that the substances are either an "eminent hazard" or a "significant or unreasonable risk to public health and safety."

In early 2003, the death during spring training of baseball pitcher Steve Belcher focused new attention on the FDA's actions concerning one particular ingredient in certain dietary supplements: ephedra. A substance aimed at persons interested in losing weight, ephedra also is regulated by the FDA as an ingredient in nonprescription medications such as over-the-counter decongestants. Critics of the FDA charge that the agency has been delinquent in removing ephedra from the market. There have been at least 1,000 reports of adverse drug experiences (ADEs) from the substance, including heart attacks and deaths; by contrast, the FDA pulled fen-phen from the market after only about 100 reports of adverse experiences. The makers of ephedra, on the other hand, note that it is a substance that has been used widely for years by many persons in the United States and other nations (such as China, where it is derived from the ma huang plant) with no ill effects. The FDA points to the guidelines of the 1994 Dietary Supplement Health and Education Act and notes that that legislation at present permits the agency only to issue a warning (and perhaps order a warning label) about ephedra.

The FDA is in a difficult position because it faces criticism from those who allege harm from substances that it has not banned or regulated tightly enough. The agency responds that many of the guidelines under which it operates are legislative. The 1994 legislation that effectively called for the FDA to regulate dietary supplements less stringently than prescription medications was the product, after all, of the democratic process. On the other hand, the agency recognizes that many Americans are not satisfied with traditional medical therapies and will continue to pursue alternatives. Americans regularly avail themselves of alternative or complementary therapies, particularly when they face serious health problems such as cancer. (In terms of numbers of patient visits to practitioners, visits to alternative practitioners vastly outnumber office consultations with primary care physicians.) Thus those who argue that the FDA should have broader powers to regulate alternative medicines contend that if the FDA does not have authority over nonmainstream medical products, then those substances essentially will be unregulated and it will be consumers who will suffer.

But as discussed in Chapter 3, even long-standing regulation of medical products by the FDA does not guarantee those products' safety. In a sense, the FDA's authority or lack thereof is an issue that affects nations beyond the United States. American-made products—including medical products—currently are sold all over the world. When medical products that are developed in one nation are sold abroad and those products later are found to be dangerous, the legal determination of liability can be complicated. The first major instance during the therapeutic revolution in which drugs caused terrible harm—the thalidomide scare—actually was not the result of a U.S. parent company's actions. And the thalidomide cases generally could be and were resolved within the legal system of each nation where patients resided. The thalidomide controversy, however, as described in Chapter 2, did have a major effect on medical-testing regulations and drug-damage compensation systems in many different countries, including the United States. The thalidomide issue also had ramifications for the powers of the FDA; it greatly increased the agency's authority.

Breast implants were a medical product that proved dangerous for many patients all over the world; they were a device that was developed and manufactured first in the United States. The FDA, while not giving many assurances that the devices were safe, at least had declined to regulate them. So how should U.S. courts have responded, when foreign consumers claimed that the United States should provide them relief when they were injured by a product initiated in America and allowed to be marketed by the FDA? In the case of *Kerr v. Inamed* (2002), several British women attempted to avail themselves of U.S. state laws that allowed recovery for breast-implant injuries. The women who were suing had had implants that had been developed by a researcher at Washington University in St. Louis, Missouri, in partnership with Collagen Aesthetics, a company from Palo Alto, California. Those implants had contained triglyceride, a soy-based oil that at one time was thought to be a promising substitute for silicone in implants. The developers applied for FDA approval in the United States, and they secured permission to market the implants in Europe; 10,000 women received the implants, 5,000 of whom were in the United Kingdom.

When a number of women reported problems with the implants, the United Kingdom's Medical Devices Agency issued a warning that use of the implants filled with triglyceride oil should be discontinued. In 1999, several makers and distributors of the implants, including Collagen Aesthetics and Dr. Young, became part of a large settlement with British patients who had been injured by the implants. Under the settlement, the injured persons each would receive a sum of money (around $500.00 each) to help them replace or remove the implants; in return, they would agree not to pursue individual lawsuits in British courts. The potential plaintiffs would not have the option of "opting out" of the settlement. When several plaintiffs tried to sue in California courts, they were rebuffed. The Ninth Circuit Court of Appeals, in its unpublished decision of the *Kerr* case, reminded the plaintiffs that the courts of the United States did not have to defer to the plaintiffs' choice of a forum for a resolution of the controversy. The U.S. court argued that there was an opportunity in the United Kingdom for the plaintiffs to receive "adequate" compensation. In addition, the Ninth Circuit Court maintained that most of the applicable materials in the case (such as health warnings from the British government) were located abroad; trying such cases in the United States would be cumbersome.

Faced with many similar cases of patients being injured by breast implants, the European parliament considered banning silicone breast implants for patients who were under eighteen years old. European groups, such as an organization called German Self-Help Group for Women Damaged by Silicone, noted that in the United States silicone was banned in implants by the FDA in the early 1990s, but that it was still used in Europe after that date. Even ten years after the FDA restriction on silicone in implants, only France among all the European Union (EU) nations had any restrictions on the use of silicone breast implants. Those who favored regulations on silicone implants in Europe noted that makers of the devices often attested to their short-term safety, but the U.S. experience demonstrated that many effects did not become apparent until years after the implants were inserted. Although there was some disagreement among member states about exactly how to do so, the EU in late 2002 did decide to adopt a more strict classification of breast implants. In the future, they would be considered "high-risk" products. Although the change did make their job more complicated, because it could mean altering the standards for other medical devices (such as hip implants), the European lawmakers clearly believed that breast implants were overdue for more stringent regulation.

Meanwhile, in the United States, medical-product liability cases continued to be brought under the federal laws that governed food, drugs, and cosmetics manufacture and marketing. Although some of these cases did not involve the FDA directly, they did relate to questions that the FDA handled routinely, such as the labeling of medical products. In the case of *Ellis v. C. R. Bard and Baxter Healthcare Corporation* (2002), the U.S. Court of Appeals for the Eleventh Circuit considered whether medical manufacturers were under an obligation to inform only doctors and nurses, or patients as well, of the dangers of their product. Mary Ruth Brown had been hospitalized for knee replacement surgery. After the operation, she was given a morphine pump (manufactured by Baxter) that allowed the patient to self-administer dosages of pain-relieving medication. The pump was available by prescription only. An anesthesiologist prescribed the pump and a nurse programmed it according to the doctor's instructions. On her own, however, the nurse told the patient's daughter that she might administer the morphine to her mother during the night by pressing the button on the pump, so that her mother would not be awakened in pain. When someone who was not the patient pressed the pump, however, its programming was overridden. Mrs. Brown received too much morphine and went into cardiac arrest. As a result of Mrs. Brown's death, her daughter alleged that Baxter had not labeled its product correctly; there were no warnings on the pump about what would happen if third parties pressed the delivery button. On several grounds, the court ruled that Baxter was not liable; the fault lay with the nurse who had told Mrs. Brown's daughter to press the button on her own. According to the courts, neither Baxter's labeling of the product nor its explanation to medical personnel of how the product was to be used had caused Mrs. Brown's death.

What does such a case—an increasingly common type having to do with medical-product labeling—say about medicolegal controversies and the courts? In the first place, it reminds Americans that the practice of medicine still continues to grow in complexity. Medicine involves more and more parties—not just the physician and the patient, but also the manufacturer of medical products, other hospital staff members such as nurses who must operate those products or instruct others on how to do so, and even family members who have a hand in patient care when institutional staffs are overburdened (as they increasingly are). *Ellis v. Baxter Healthcare* illustrates, in fact, that the physician has become less central in many patients' care. Secondly, the case presents another increasingly common scenario, in part because of the fact that hospital staffs are shorthanded: medical products are being designed with the consumer/patient in mind. The physician and other healthcare personnel are being skirted as medical manufacturers seek to make their products more patient-friendly. Ultimately, such an approach fits in well with direct-to-consumer drug-marketing efforts by medical-product makers and drugmakers. Furthermore, this approach underlines the growing lack of authority of the physician in treatment decisions—a lack of authority often encouraged or at least allowed by the courts.

Police Powers and Communicable Diseases

The development of preventive measures against communicable diseases would seem to be one of the great advances of medicine in the past two or three centuries. But the prevention of disease through methods such as vaccination and the curing of diseases with other medicines (such as the curing of some sexually transmitted diseases with penicillin) have contributed to legal controversies. Since the beginning of the twentieth century, U.S. courts have recognized states' authority through the police power to protect their residents' physical welfare. As discussed in Chapter 3, states can implement compulsory vaccination programs, for example, that require persons to receive protection against diseases such as smallpox. (Interestingly, although smallpox appeared to have been eradicated at midcentury from the United States, the spectre of bioterrorism suddenly made it a real threat again at the beginning of the twenty-first century. It very well may be that courts again will have to consider cases related to compulsory smallpox immunization.) A more ongoing controversy, however, is in regard to compulsory vaccination for more ordinary diseases.

Diseases such as measles, mumps, pertussis (whooping cough), and diphtheria used to strike with alarming regularity in vulnerable populations, especially infants and children, throughout Western society. One of medicine's proudest achievements in the past century has been the development of vaccinations against such childhood diseases. And yet the diseases have not been eradicated, even among societies (such as the United States) that have widespread access to healthcare and knowledge about the potential for vaccines to prevent communicable diseases.

That these diseases continue to appear and that some children are not vaccinated are clearly not the result of a lack of support for compulsory vaccination in the twentieth century by the courts and state legislatures. Vaccinations against common childhood diseases are mandatory in states for children who enter the public schools. The Supreme Court recently has commented on mandatory childhood vaccinations for schoolchildren, in fact, as one of the ways in which the privacy of schoolchildren may be intruded upon by the state in its use of police powers. Such exceptions to the privacy of children may be undertaken, the Court has said, in instances of mandatory drug testing by school authorities; this was a ruling in the widely watched Supreme Court case of *County v. Earls* (2002).

In spite of the assurances of medical researchers that such vaccinations are generally safe, adverse reactions have been known to occur. In fact, a vocal minority of parents continue to insist that vaccines are responsible for a host of problems, including conditions such as autism; this has led to refusals by some parents to have their children vaccinated at all. In turn, disease experts point to a failure to vaccinate as being responsible for the continuation of childhood diseases such as measles, which could be practically wiped out through widespread vaccination. In view of the fact that childhood vaccinations were compulsory and yet questions about their safety persisted among the public, the federal government proposed and Congress passed legislation in 1994 setting up a fund to compensate persons who did suffer reactions from the vaccines.

Although most cases of adverse reactions proved mild and transient, a few were serious or even fatal. In such instances, victims' families found it difficult to recover compensation from the fund according to the terms of the National Childhood Vaccine Injury Act. Under the terms of the vaccine act, a special master hears cases in which victims or their families ask for compensation from the vaccine fund; appeals are to the Secretary of Health and Human Services (HHS).

The case of *Helms v. Secretary of Health and Human Services* (2001) illustrates the difficulty that plaintiffs in such cases have faced in satisfying the burden of proof concerning vaccine deaths. The mother of Zachary Helms tried to recover damages from the fund concerning the death of her son two days after he received a vaccine for polio, diphtheria, pertussis, tetanus, and other diseases (a vaccine known as polio/DPT/HIB/MMR) around the time of his second birthday. An autopsy identified a general cerebral edema, but listed the cause of the swelling as undetermined. A medical expert in neuropathology who, on behalf of the family, examined slides from the autopsy believed that the vaccine caused Zachary's death, and he ruled out other causes of death such as suffocation. The Department of HHS called its own witness, who was an expert in pediatric neuropathology; she told the special master that she thought Zachary could have asphyxiated. She further testified that the vaccine in question had not been shown to cause toxic encephalopathy (which was the immediate reason for Zachary's death).

At a higher level of review, the Court of Federal Claims vacated the decision of the special master that Zachary's mother was not entitled to compensation from the vaccine fund. That court took seriously Ms. Helms's contention that the special master had not applied the *Daubert* standard (discussed in Chapter 3) correctly in assessing the weight of expert witnesses. When the special master considered the evidence again, on remand, and came to a conclusion similar to his first decision, Ms. Helms again appealed to the Court of Federal Claims. This time, that court decided that the special master had weighed the expert findings correctly. Ms. Helms had not satisfied the requirement that she show by a preponderance of the evidence that the vaccine had caused Zachary's death. Ultimately, in order to overturn a decision of a special master in such a case, courts would require that a plaintiff show that the special master had been arbitrary or capricious in coming to a decision—obviously a difficult task to undertake.

Thus the state can require vaccination, and the courts will enforce that requirement. Although there is a means for obtaining compensation when vaccines cause harm, it is a difficult one to access and obtain relief from, especially when the harm charged is severe. In this particular area of medicolegal controversy (compulsory vaccinations), that is, the courts have given a certain authority to medical professionals: medical opinion informs legislatures on the need for mandatory vaccination programs, and medical witnesses are key participants in trials involving alleged harm from vaccines. And yet, in the end, it is courts that hold the ultimate power to decide how and when vaccines should be required and indeed what weight should be given to expert medical testimony in trials about vaccines' effects. In such cases, as in others involving alleged harm from drugs, the *Daubert* standard has had a noticeable impact since that case was decided in 1993. Applying *Daubert,* many judges have required such high standards of scientific proof to demonstrate the causation behind injury from drugs that plaintiffs cannot provide sufficient evidence to satisfy the courts. Thus judges' authority to be gatekeepers for scientific testimony has worked considerably to the benefit of drugmakers in the years since *Daubert.*

Individuals who are incarcerated may find their privacy rights violated by the state, for reasons similar to those used by courts to justify compulsory vaccination. Inmates, that is, like schoolchildren, can be required to undergo certain medical procedures in the interest of the more general population's safety and health. Compulsory medical treatment also is justified with an eye toward maintaining order in certain institutions, including schools and prisons. As discussed briefly in Chapter 3, courts have ruled that inmates in prisons may be forced to take antipsychotic drugs; they also may have to undergo mandatory testing and treatment for drug addictions or for the management of communicable diseases. But can state authorities go one step further and actually put inmates in harm's way?

With many prisons having populations where there are widespread infections of serious diseases such as hepatitis and HIV, the right of prisoners to be protected from infection has come before the courts at several junctures, such as in the case of *Rish et al. v. Sally Johnson et al. and the U.S. Government* (1997). David Rish was one of a group of plaintiffs who were inmates at Butner Federal Correctional Institute in North Carolina. Sally Johnson was a physician who was an associate warden and represented the U.S. Public Health Service at Butner. Rish and his fellow plaintiffs challenged the policy of Butner and its managers that required inmates to perform cleaning duties that exposed them to the bodily fluids of other inmates who were infected with contagious diseases. The prison had provided neither training nor appropriate gear (of the types that healthcare workers used) to shield them from contagion while they worked as orderlies in the mental-health unit. The inmates claimed that their Eighth Amendment rights were being violated; that is, that being exposed to infectious agents in the blood and bodily fluids of other inmates violated the right to be free from cruel and unusual punishment.

It was an interesting argument, but the inmates faced a legal difficulty that they could not overcome. In order to sue officials such as Dr. Johnson, plaintiffs had to demonstrate why the officials should not be shielded by the immunity that attached to government workers. In examining the "qualified immunity" of officials such as Dr. Johnson, the court asked: at the time that the inmates' constitutional rights allegedly were violated, could Dr. Johnson reasonably have known that her conduct was infringing on the plaintiffs' rights? The U.S. Court of Appeals for the Fourth Circuit ruled that Dr. Johnson could not have foreseen in the period from 1988 to 1992 (the time when the prisoners complained that violations of their rights had occurred) that the policies she oversaw would be termed an example of cruel and unusual punishment. For prison officials' conduct to fall afoul of Eighth Amendment standards, the court said that the officials' conduct must be unmistakably harmful. That the prison did not use all of the precautions that were recommended by authorities such as the Centers for Disease Control did not put the inmates at such grave risk that they could recover damages from the prison doctors and wardens.

Such cases involving inmates' medical safety are important in part because they highlight the awkward position in which medical caregivers in prisons find themselves. Physicians like Dr. Johnson are both medical doctors, who owe a duty of care to their patients, and officers of the prison system. As such, they have the dual and possibly contradictory responsibilities of protecting patients' health and maintaining order within an institution. Courts generally fell in on the side of order. In addition, such rulings ultimately have had the effect of making clear to the medical community that it is the courts rather than physicians who are the final arbiters on patient care.

Conclusion

In the past 150 years of U.S. history, medicine has become a normal part of court proceedings. This study began with a discussion of a lesser-known role played by physicians within the U.S. judicial setting—being gatekeepers through their participation in forensic investigations. MEs and coroners have a vital place within a system that increasingly emphasizes scientific evidence such as DNA in the criminal trial process. As skilled collectors of physical evidence about fatalities, forensic pathologists literally make or break criminal and civil cases at early stages. Questions about the extent to which MEs and coroners should be controlled by local and state governments have bedeviled forensic pathologists for many years. Despite the drawing of a higher profile for forensic pathology in the past century among the public and the legal and medical professions, MEs and coroners remain public servants. As such, they can be severely hampered by budget cuts and overzealous regulation.

That forensic pathologists should become associated with the scientific solving of crimes should surprise no one who has read the adventures of Sherlock Holmes. In the late nineteenth and early twentieth centuries, Arthur Conan Doyle was a keen admirer of both new police laboratories and the skill of eminent pathologists such as Bernard Spilsbury. Conan Doyle imbued his fictional crime solver with the knowledge of scientific fields such as chemistry that medical experts increasingly were employing to solve real cases. The public acceptance of forensic scientists as celebrities in the twentieth century, on the other hand, is a somewhat unlikely development. The making of popular celebrities from forensic experts could have taken place only when leading forensic pathologists were media-savvy and the mass media was hungry for sensational news from trials—such as in Bernard Spilsbury's era in the early twentieth century. After well-known pathologists like Keith Simpson, Thomas Magrath, and Milton Helpern had become familiar figures in a series of notorious criminal cases, it was a short step for pathologists into American living rooms. That the television programs popularizing the work of forensic pathologists should have emanated from Hollywood in the 1970s also was to be expected: Los Angeles was the home of the "coroner to the stars," Thomas Noguchi.

Although forensic pathologists play a fundamental role in the criminal justice system, however, they represent a specialized type of medical practitioner. Among the medical profession in general, the most public role played by most physicians in court is when they are called upon to justify their conduct in suits for malpractice. As Americans grow more accustomed to high standards of healthcare, they increasingly voice disappointment when those standards are not met. When babies are born with disabilities, Americans sue their obstetricians. When breast implants turn painful or misshapen, they sue surgeons or the makers of the implants. Malpractice claims, further, are fueled by a contingency-fee system that encourages plaintiffs and their lawyers to seek deep pockets. Therefore, individual doctors are not the only entities under fire; the objects of many claims are the financial resources of hospitals, insurers, and the manufacturers of medical products. Such a situation underscores the fact that physicians are not alone in being responsible for patient care.

In the early twenty-first century, doctors are only one of several participants in healthcare, rather than medicine's pivotal force. American physicians share the provision of healthcare with other medical professionals such as nurses, nurse practitioners, physicians' assistants, midwives, and practitioners of alternative medicine, as well as the makers and dispensers of medicines and medical devices, the administrators of hospitals, government regulators, judges and juries, and—through the medium of informed consent—patients themselves. Due to the crowded nature of medicine these days, U.S. courts currently must sort through an immense tangle of parties to ascertain responsibility in medicolegal cases. Ironically, during the same 150 years that medicine has become an inevitable part of American trials, courts have helped make physicians less omnipotent as providers of healthcare.

Technological advancements have pervaded every area of medicine within the past few generations, and medical technology has impelled courts to take account of a variety of cases that are controversial. Medicine has provided extraordinary opportunities for assisted reproduction (AR). Medical developments in areas such as advanced care for critically ill persons have led to the saving of many lives, but they also have created huge difficulties for courts in the realm of right-to-die issues. Medical technology can prolong the end of life to a much greater extent than ever before, but what kind of life is being extended? Likewise, medical advances have made prebirth issues much more difficult in recent years. Embryos can be formed in vitro, but are those embryos alive? More to the point, are they persons under the Constitution? To confront such questions brings courts into extremely emotional arenas where religion, morality, cost containment, personal autonomy, and other divisive issues are raised.

Yet courts persist in intervening in medicolegal controversies, even when the eventual judicial response is to refer matters to legislators for further action. And judicial forums do not always pass the buck. U.S. courts in the late twentieth century have developed and broadened the concept of informed consent to protect patients from mistakes by physicians and intrusions by other authorities (such as the state). In right-to-die cases, courts recently have underlined the fundamental right of patients to live. Thus one of the greatest contributions that the judicial system recently has made within the democratic society of the United States is to support the role that patients play in their own physical welfare.

References and Further Reading

Begley, Sharon. "Ban on 'Junk Science' Also Keeps Jurors from Sound Evidence." *Wall Street Journal,* June 27, 2003, p. B1.

Bichenbach, Jerome E. "Disability and Life-Ending Decisions," in Margaret P. Battin, Rosamund Rhodes, and Anita Silvers, eds., *Physician Assisted Suicide: Expanding the Debate,* 123–132. New York: Routledge, 1998.

Bourne, Aleck. *A Doctor's Creed.* London: Gollancz, 1962, 21.

Brookes, Barbara, and Paul Roth. "*Rex v. Bourne* and the Medicalization of Abortion," in Michael Clark and Catherine Crawford, eds., *Legal Medicine in History,* 314–343. Cambridge: Cambridge University Press, 1994.

"Complementary and Alternative Medicine: Cancer-Fighting Powers of Herbs, Natural Compounds to Be Tested at UCLA." *Cancer Weekly* (February 18, 2003): 38.

Dietary Supplemental Health and Education Act, 1994, 103 S. 784.

"E.U. to Reclassify Breast Implants Despite Dissent." *Devices and Diagnostics Letter* 29 (November 25, 2002).

Hoek, Janet, and Philip Gendall. "Direct-to-Consumer Advertising Down Under: An Alternative Perspective and Regulatory Framework." *Journal of Public Policy and Marketing* 21 (Fall 2002): 202.

Horton, John. "Midwife: 'I Will Go to Jail' for Source." *Cleveland Plain Dealer,* October 21, 2002, p. 1.

Kemper, Vicki. "Health Warning Label Proposed for Ephedra: The Government Cites 'False and Misleading Claims' but Says the Law Prohibits a Ban." *Los Angeles Times,* March 1, 2003, p. 1.

Lee, Henry, and Jerry Labriola. *Famous Crimes Revisited.* Southington, CT: Strong Books, 2001.

McCullough, Marie. "Financial Pressures Bringing Changes to Midwifery." *Philadelphia Enquirer,* March 11, 2003, p. 1.

Mendoza, Martha. "Prosecutions, Jailings Highlight Debate on Safety and Choice." *Associated Press* (November 23, 2002).

Naik, Gautam. "The Grim Mission of a Swiss Group: Visitors' Suicides." *Wall Street Journal,* November 22, 2002, pp. 1, 6.

National Academy of Sciences. *Scientific and Medical Aspects of Human Cloning.* Washington, DC: National Academy Press, 2002.

Scherer, Jennifer M., and Rita J. Simon. *Euthanasia and the Right to Die: A Comparative View.* Lanham, MD: Rowman and Littlefield, 1999.

Smith, Sydney. *Mostly Murder.* New York: D. McKay, 1959.

Thiessen, Tamara. "Clampdown on the Britney Effect." *Straits Times* (Singapore), July 1, 2001, p. 7.

Thomasma, David C., Thomasina Kimbrough-Kushner, et al., eds. *Asking to Die: Inside the Dutch Debate about Euthanasia.* Dordrecht, The Netherlands: Kluwer Academic Publishers, 1998.

Van der Maas, P. J., G. Van der Wal, et al. "Euthanasia, Physician-Assisted Suicide, and Other Medical Practice Involving the End of Life in the Netherlands." *New England Journal of Medicine* 335 (1996): 1699–1705.

Part Two

Documents

The Authority of Medical Examiners: *Jackson v. Rupp* (1969)

By the middle of the twentieth century, medical examiners (MEs) were a regular presence in localities throughout the United States. With increasingly sophisticated medical training in forensic pathology and related areas such as microscopy, MEs were in a key position to help police and other authorities investigate suspicious or unexpected deaths. Still, many people were uneasy with the idea of postmortem examinations being performed on their relatives' bodies and resisted granting permission for autopsies. Occasionally such resistance was based on religious principles; more often it simply demonstrated distaste for the postmortem examination process. Many state laws evidenced sympathy for that popular dislike of autopsies. Statutory limitations on MEs usually required either relatives' permission or some compelling legal reason (affirmed by the participation of a legal official such as a district attorney) before an autopsy could be performed. When an ME did not comply with the applicable state laws, he could find himself, like defendant Dr. Rupp, in serious legal difficulty because of anger among the patient's family. (The Florida statute in question in Jackson v. Rupp *required both a suspicious death and the concurrence of the county prosecutor.) If Dr. Rupp had performed the autopsy and determined that there was some untoward reason for the patient's death (such as a medical malpractice or violence), then perhaps the family might have been grateful for his intervention. But when an unauthorized autopsy uncovered only routine or expected causes of death, then the family was likely to view it as an invasion of privacy. The courts, likewise, usually would censure the ME in such a case.*

COURT OPINION BY CHIEF JUSTICE CROSS. Plaintiffs-appellants, James W. Jackson, Ethel B. Jackson and Ruth Adamson, appeal from a final judgment entered by the trial court on a directed verdict for the defendant-appellee, Joseph C. Rupp, M.D., in a cause of action for damages for performance of an unauthorized autopsy. We reverse.

Clara B. Jackson, deceased, was admitted to Holy Cross Hospital by her treating physician, one Dr. F. A. Osterman, on September 17, 1966. She was then 82 years of age. When admitted she was in a highly agitated state with tentative diagnosis listing Mrs. Jackson's illness as abdominal pain, dehydration and an impression of an intra-abdominal carcinoma.

Upon her admission to the hospital, Dr. Osterman performed an examination which disclosed an impacted colon. The doctor ordered a removal of the fecal impaction and placed Mrs. Jackson on demerol and phenergan for abdominal pain. She was also put on a liquid diet, given a blood transfusion and a lower G.I. series of x-rays was ordered. Later Mrs. Jackson was placed on intravenous fluids, given vitamins, a soft diet and ordered to get out of bed each day and move around.

On September 30, 1966, Mrs. Jackson fell out of bed and sustained an intertrochanteric fracture of the right hip. Orthopedic surgeons performed an open reduction and insertion of Jewett Nail to repair the hip. After the surgery on her hip, Mrs. Jackson gradually went downhill and expired on November 4, 1966. Mrs. Jackson died without giving authority to anyone to perform an autopsy on her body after death.

Following Mrs. Jackson's expiration, Dr. Osterman, the treating physician requested permission of Mrs. Jackson's next of kin to perform an autopsy. The permission was refused.

The defendant, Joseph C. Rupp, who is both a pathologist at Holy Cross Hospital and an Associate County Medical Examiner of Broward County, requested permission of James W. Jackson, one of the plaintiffs and the son of the deceased, to perform an autopsy on Mrs. Jackson's body. Permission was denied.

Thereafter without any request of the Prosecuting Attorney of Broward County, Dr. Rupp made the determination that Mrs. Jackson's death fell within the ambit of his jurisdiction as an Associate

County Medical Examiner, and on November 4, 1966, performed an autopsy on the body of Mrs. Jackson. The autopsy revealed that the cause of Mrs. Jackson's death was intestinal obstruction and adenocarcinoma of the ascending colon.

On June 28, 1967, the plaintiffs filed their complaint against Dr. Rupp alleging the performance of the unauthorized autopsy. Dr. Rupp answered and alleged therein the affirmative defense of authority under law by reason of his position as Associate Medical Examiner.

Thereafter the cause was set and came on for trial, and at the conclusion of the plaintiffs' case the defendant moved for a directed verdict. The trial court granted the motion and entered final judgment. This appeal followed.

We have for our determination whether the testimony presented by the plaintiffs at the time they rested their case was essentially so devoid of probative evidence that the jury could not as a matter of law find a verdict for the plaintiffs. The cause of action for an unauthorized autopsy has not heretofore been dealt with by the courts of the State of Florida. This being so, the necessity of investigating the background of a cause of action of this nature appears evident.

The early English common law recognized no property or property rights in the body of a deceased person. . . . this being due undoubtedly to the fact that the ecclesiastical courts exercised jurisdiction over the affairs of decedents. This doctrine found its way through early American case law. . . . The logic behind these early cases was that a living person could not suffer any legitimate recognizable damage from an act of mutilation on a corpse.

As the American society progressed and became more sophisticated, its courts have held there is a cause of action for an unauthorized autopsy. The basis for recovery is found in the personal right of the decedent's next of kin to bury the body rather than any property right in the body itself. . . . An autopsy is said to be an interference with this right. . . . because the very act of dissecting a body prevents its burial in a proper manner. This personal right to bury a body falls on the person or persons who are in closest relationship to the deceased. . . .

In those jurisdictions recognizing the cause of action for unauthorized autopsy, the courts are not primarily concerned with the extent of the physical mishandling, injury or mutilation of the body, per se, but rather with the effect of the same on the feelings and emotions of the surviving relatives, who have the right of burial. . . .

In an action for an unauthorized autopsy founded solely in tort in order for recovery to be effected for damages resulting from mental pain and anguish unconnected with physical injury, the wrongful act must be such as to reasonably imply malice or such that from the entire want of care or attention to duty or great indifference to the person, property, or rights of others such malice would be imputed as would justify assessment of exemplary or punitive damages. . . .

In spite of the fact that an exclusive right does vest in the surviving spouse, relative, or next of kin to dispose of a corpse, autopsies may be authorized by public authorities for the protection of health or the discovery of crime. . . .

At the time of the performance of the autopsy in question, the legislature of this state had promulgated ch. 27439, Laws of Florida, Special Acts of 1951. This act authorized and empowered the Board of County Commissioners of Broward County, Florida, to employ and appoint a County Medical Examiner. It authorized and empowered the Board of County Commissioners to fix the County Medical Examiner's term of employment, his compensation, and it empowered the County Medical Examiner to investigate deaths of persons resulting from criminal violence by casualties, by suicide, suddenly when in apparently good health, when not attended by any physician, in prison, or in any suspicious or unusual manner.

We glean from the record of testimony elicited from Dr. Rupp as to why he performed this autopsy:

> So I simply as a matter of courtesy called the Jackson family, explained the circumstances that with this hip fracture there was a possibility that death was directly the result of this accident, that for reasons of insurance or possible litigation or for simply an accurate determination of the cause of death in the role that this hip fracture played in this case that it was necessary in my opinion that an autopsy be performed, that Dr. Osterman was in error not to consult our office first, but he had already consulted them and that I was merely calling to ask that an autopsy be done with their permission, implying that it would be done, but that as a matter of courtesy I wanted them to change their minds, do away with their objections to the autopsy and that it be done with their permission.

It is patently obvious from Dr. Rupp's testimony that he might have performed the autopsy not because Mrs. Jackson died in any of the specific circumstances to bring the autopsy within the ambit of § 3, ch. 27439, but because of circumstances far removed from the language embodied in § 3.

. . . The evidence thus far produced at trial with proper inferences that could be deduced therefrom is that Dr. Rupp lacked the request of the Prosecuting Attorney of Broward County to perform the autopsy, and that Dr. Rupp was intent in performing the autopsy irrespective of great indifference to the plaintiffs and their refusal to grant permission. Such is sufficient to withstand the thrust of a motion for a directed verdict.

Accordingly, the final judgment is reversed and the cause is remanded with directions for further proceedings consistent with this opinion.

Reversed and remanded with directions.

The Mind of an Assassin: The *Hinckley* Case (1981)

Before he could stand trial in a formal sense for the attempted assassination of President Ronald Reagan and the wounding of several other persons, it was apparent that John W. Hinckley Jr. would avail himself of the insanity defense. How, then, should Hinckley be handled between the time of his formally being charged and his actual trial? How and when would the court utilize findings of court-ordered examinations to determine Hinckley's competency to stand trial? Did requiring Hinckley to undergo a psychiatric examination without a lawyer present violate Hinckley's Sixth Amendment right to counsel? Such questions not only had a bearing on the insanity defense, but they also spoke to the rights of persons who were involuntarily detained not to be subjected to medical examinations against their will.

In a portion of the opinion to which the court refers in its decision but which is not included in this excerpt, the judges considered a related quandary: whether confiscation of Hinckley's diary by custodial personnel was an infringement on Hinckley's rights as a detained person. Was the diary (which provided evidence of his motivations for attempting to shoot the president) also evidence of his mental capacity? The eventual decision by the court—that the diary would be suppressed as evidence due to the circumstances of its seizure—had a perceptible impact on the government's case. The prosecution could not employ the diary to show that Hinckley was mentally competent enough to brood about the crime for months, in effect stalking not only President Ronald Reagan but also the previous president, Jimmy Carter.

Once Hinckley's criminal trial was conducted, the resulting jury verdict of not guilty by reason of insanity proved explosive. The verdict was a spur in numerous state and federal efforts to make the insanity defense less attractive and less available to defendants. Several jurisdictions reacted to Hinckley's acquittal by implementing standards for insanity that hearkened to the M'Naghten Rules of the mid–nineteenth century.

COURT OPINION BY JUSTICE PARKER. The defendant John W. Hinckley, Jr. is charged in a multi-count indictment with attempted assassination of the President of the United States. . . .

Counsel for the defendant have filed a number of pretrial motions, four of which are addressed in this Memorandum Opinion. Two motions seek to suppress statements, and any fruits thereof, made by Hinckley during the course of court-ordered examinations dealing with his competency to stand trial and the defendant's mental condition at the time of the alleged offenses and legal responsibility for the acts charged in the indictment. The orders were entered on March 31, and April 2, 1981. The remaining two are (1) a motion to suppress statements made by Hinckley to law enforcement officials on March 30, 1981, the day of his arrest; and (2) a motion to suppress certain documents seized from the defendant's cell in July, 1981 by correctional officers at the Federal Correctional Institution, Butner, North Carolina (Butner) where he was held as a pretrial detainee for mental evaluation.

. . . The Court determines that the appellate decisions of this jurisdiction provide solid support for the court-ordered evaluations and examinations. Accordingly, the defendant's challenges should be rejected.

As to the statements made by Hinckley at the time of his arrest and the seizure of certain personal papers and documents at Butner, the Court determines that the March 30 statements and the documents seized at Butner should be suppressed. The reasons for these conclusions are set out in the discussion which follows.

. . . On March 31, 1981 Magistrate Arthur Burnett ordered an examination to determine Hinckley's competency to stand trial. The examination was conducted on April 1, 1981, by Dr. James L. Evans, a psychiatrist, who reported that the defendant was competent. On

April 2, 1981 Chief Judge William B. Bryant issued an order for an examination to determine Hinckley's: (1) competency to stand trial; and (2) mental condition and legal responsibility for his actions on March 30, 1981. Under Judge Bryant's order the defendant was committed to Butner, where he underwent physical, psychiatric and a battery of psychological examinations. The examination was completed and a report submitted to the Court on July 29, 1981.

Defendant's counsel contend that the use of the examination by Dr. Evans, ordered pursuant to 18 U.S.C. § 4244, is strictly limited by the provisions of the statute to a determination of the defendant's competency to stand trial; and that use of any evidence from this examination on the issue of guilt in any trial on the substantive charges would violate the statutory limitation of section 4244.

Hinckley's counsel raise additional objections to the Butner examination: that the Court lacked authority to order a compulsory examination to ascertain the competency and legal responsibility for the alleged offenses, over the defendant's objections; that use of any statements obtained from the examination would violate Hinckley's Fifth Amendment privilege against self-incrimination; and that use of the statements—obtained in the absence of counsel—would violate his Sixth Amendment right to counsel.

The government in opposition notes that the law in this circuit is well-settled that evidence from a section 4244 examination may be utilized at trial for the limited purpose of opposing an insanity defense. The government also argues that the Butner examination was plainly permissible and consistent with the Court's inherent authority to order an examination to determine competency and responsibility; that, because evidence from the examination would only be used to oppose an insanity defense rather than to establish guilt, it would not be incriminating within the terms of the Fifth Amendment privilege; and finally, that the Sixth Amendment creates no right to the presence of counsel at a defendant's examination by government or court-ordered psychiatrists.

... The provisions of the order are consistent with the current standard in this circuit applicable to the insanity defense.

Section 4244 provides, in relevant part:

> Whenever after arrest ... the United States Attorney has reasonable cause to believe that a person charged with an offense ... may be presently insane or otherwise so mentally incompetent as

> to be unable to understand the proceedings against him or properly to assist in his own defense, he shall file a motion for a judicial determination of such mental competency of the accused. . . . (T)he court shall cause the accused . . . to be examined as to his mental condition by at least one qualified psychiatrist, who shall report to the Court. . . . No statement made by the accused in the course of any examination into his sanity or mental competency provided for by this section . . . shall be admitted in evidence against the accused on the issue of guilt in any criminal proceeding. A finding by the judge that the accused is mentally competent to stand trial shall in no way prejudice the accused in a plea of insanity as a defense to the crime charged; such finding shall not be introduced in evidence on that issue nor otherwise be brought to the notice of the jury. . . .

Defendant argues that, since the statute, by its terms, only empowers an examination to determine competency, any evidence generated at Butner is not admissible on the responsibility question. Furthermore, he argues that section 4244's prohibition on the use of any evidence obtained in an examination against a defendant on the issue of guilt prohibits its use at a later trial. In so arguing, defendant contends that his capacity at the time of the offense is a component of guilt within the meaning of the provision.

Even the defendant acknowledges, however, that it has long been the rule in this circuit that section 4244 does not limit the use of evidence obtained in psychiatric examinations to a determination of competency. Section 4244's prohibition on the use of defendant's statements to establish guilt does not prevent their use in opposing a defendant's insanity defense. Only recently, Judge Spottswood Robinson, writing just prior to becoming Chief Judge of the District of Columbia Circuit, held that use of psychiatric testimony from a compelled examination was not inconsistent with section 4244's provision.

Even without regard to the court's specific statutory authority, for more than twenty years it has been the rule in this circuit that the "federal courts have inherent power—indeed, a solemn obligation—to call for a psychiatric evaluation of criminal responsibility in a case where it is obvious that the trial will revolve around the issue of the accused's mental state at the time of the crime." Whitlock, at 1106, citing *Winn v. United States*, 106 U.S. App. D.C. 133 (D.C.Cir. 1959). . . .

Defendant's argument that this widely accepted rule is inapplicable in this case because defense counsel immediately sought a complete examination on its own is unavailing. Although some of these decisions note defendant's inability to afford psychiatric counsel, the basis for the court's power in this regard is "not only to protect the rights of the accused," but also to protect "society's great interest in hospitalizing the accused if his violent act sprang from mental disorder." Winn, 270 F.2d at 327. . . .

Here, the circumstances suggesting that defendant's mental state would be an issue at trial were more than sufficient to invoke the Court's responsibility to examine his mental capacity. Beyond the circumstances of the alleged incident itself, the Court was made aware that the defendant had been under psychiatric care immediately prior to March 30, 1981. Furthermore, at the same time that Hinckley's counsel argued against committing him to Butner for examination, they too sought immediate access to raise the insanity defense. These substantial indications that defendant's mental state would be an issue at trial led the court, in a sound exercise of discretion, to invoke its inherent authority to have Hinckley undergo a mental evaluation.

. . . [The defendant] argues that his Fifth Amendment privilege against self-incrimination and Sixth Amendment right to counsel were violated by the April 2nd commitment order to Butner. . . . [The] Supreme Court concluded that psychiatric testimony at the death penalty phase of a Texas murder trial, based upon a court-ordered psychiatric examination to determine competency to stand trial without warning the defendant that the evidence would be used affirmatively to persuade the jury to return the death sentence and without opportunity to refuse to submit to an examination for that purpose, violated the defendant's privilege against self-incrimination. Because his counsel was never notified of the examination or that evidence from the undisclosed examination would be used in the penalty phase of the proceeding, the Court also concluded that the defendant was denied the right to counsel in determining whether or not to submit to the examination.

Defendant finds support . . . for the proposition that use of statements obtained from him and conclusions reached by the Butner psychiatrists, based on those statements would be incriminatory within the meaning of the Fifth Amendment if used by the government to oppose his insanity defense. Such evidence, he argues is testimonial within the terms of the privilege.

The verbal content of any communication between the defendant and mental health experts may well be an essential basis for a meaningful psychiatric examination, see id. at 1873 n.8; *Battie v. Estelle*, 655 F.2d 692, at 699–700 (5th Cir. 1981). While this suggests that the psychiatric conclusions—in addition to defendant's own statements obtained at Butner—are composed largely of testimonial evidence, the Court cannot agree that use of this evidence to controvert defendant's insanity defense would be incriminating within the terms of the privilege. . . .

Had this testimony (obtained in a compelled examination) been admitted for its tendency to buttress appellant's guilt, the self-incrimination question would generate grave concern. But the challenged testimony was elicited solely for the purpose of supporting the experts' conclusions that appellant was criminally responsible for her actions at the time of the offense.

. . . The defendant asks too much.

. . . As long as Hinckley's counsel intends to offer evidence of insanity at trial, suppression of evidence obtained from the compelled examination at Butner is not required to protect defendant's privilege against self-incrimination.

Defendant also argues that the Butner examination was conducted in violation of his right to the effective assistance of counsel under the Sixth Amendment. In *Estelle* the Supreme Court concluded that such a violation was present because the defendant's counsel was not notified in advance that the psychiatric examination would be used in the death penalty stage of trial. Finding that this examination "proved to be a 'critical stage' of the aggregate proceedings" against the defendant, the court found a violation in denying him the advice of counsel in determining whether to submit to the interview. 101 S. Ct. at 1877.

Here the defendant does not argue that he was denied counsel in determining whether to submit to the Butner examination. Rather, he claims that the Sixth Amendment required either the presence of counsel at the examination or the imposition of procedures, such as video recording of the interview sessions with the psychiatrists, to enable defense counsel to reconstruct the examination. Defendant does not explain why he did not seek these procedures at the time of commitment to Butner, nor why there was no similar objection to the absence of such safeguards during examinations by government-retained experts.

Even absent these inconsistencies, however, defendant's position finds little support. The right to have counsel present during psychiatric interviewing has been consistently rejected by federal circuit courts. See, *United States v. Cohen*, 530 F.2d at 48; *United States v. Albright*, 388 F.2d at 726. The majority opinion in *Estelle* also raised the concern that presence of counsel at a psychiatric examination might be disruptive and carefully pointed out that the decision in no way suggested such a right. 101 S. Ct. 1877 n.14.

Nor is an audio recording of psychiatric proceedings required by the Sixth Amendment to enable counsel to reconstruct the examination. . . .

In light of the foregoing, the motion to suppress statements obtained during the competency examination ordered on March 31st warrants little discussion.

In the hearings before the Magistrate, the prosecutor and defendant's then-appointed counsel agreed that a competency evaluation was necessary. The Magistrate ordered a section 4244 examination on March 31st. A subsequent motion to vacate that order filed by Hinckley's retained counsel was denied. Dr. James Evans of the Forensic Psychiatry Division of the District of Columbia Mental Health Administration examined Hinckley and on April 1st reported that he understood the charges and indictment against him; was able to confer and consult with his counsel; and was competent to participate in these proceedings.

Focusing on section 4244's prohibition on the use of any evidence obtained in the examination against the defendant on the issue of guilt, defendant seeks to suppress any statements made to Dr. Evans and conclusions of the doctor based on those statements from use at trial. However, as already noted in connection with the Butner motion, this circuit has determined on several occasions that the statute's definition of guilt is limited to the elements of the offense, and does not include the issue of defendant's insanity. . . . Thus evidence from the examination which tends to show that the defendant did not lack criminal responsibility because of his mental state at the time of the offense is available to the government in responding to defendant's insanity defense. However, the government has the burden and the responsibility of making a clear showing to the trial court that the evidence or statements fall within that area, meet that test and are otherwise admissible. Failure to meet that burden could result in a rejection of such evidence or statements. . . .

The *Quinlan* Case and the Right to Die (1976)

The Quinlan *case had profound implications for questions concerning the end of life. It involved the legal standing of a family member (in this case a parent) to make vital decisions for an incompetent relative. The courts that decided the case, first a New Jersey Superior Court and then the New Jersey Supreme Court, were aware of the broad applicability of their decisions. Indeed, the* Quinlan *case eventually did have an impact on a number of areas of law and medicine. For example, the case led to the widespread adoption of living wills and other advanced care directives by patients, so that patients' express wishes would be well documented if the patients became incapacitated and could not express their desires about medical treatment. The New Jersey courts' decisions also showed great sensitivity to the emotional turmoil that must have been experienced by the Quinlan family, which sought to discontinue life support for their daughter. The Quinlans were devout Roman Catholics, and they availed themselves of advice from spiritual counselors before deciding to pursue the request to terminate artificial respiration. The decision of the New Jersey Supreme Court contains significant references to the policies of the Catholic Church on the problem at hand because the court considered the seriousness of the Quinlan family's moral position to be relevant. Medical advisors and authorities had a pivotal role in the* Quinlan *case. They provided testimony about Karen Ann Quinlan's physical condition and prognosis; they also testified about the current standards within the medical community in evaluating "brain death." Through their writings on the ethical issues connected with dying, physicians suggested alternate ways of managing such difficult cases in the future, such as ethics committees that were empowered to make decisions without asking courts' permission.*

COURT OPINION BY CHIEF JUSTICE HUGHES. The central figure in this tragic case is Karen Ann Quinlan, a New Jersey resident. At the age of 22, she lies in a debilitated and allegedly moribund state at Saint Clare's Hospital in Denville, New Jersey. The litigation has to do, in final analysis, with her life,—its continuance or cessation,—and the responsibilities, rights and duties, with regard to any fateful decision concerning it, of her family, her guardian, her doctors, the hospital, the State through its law enforcement authorities, and finally the courts of justice. . . .

Joseph Quinlan sought the adjudication of that incompetency. He wished to be appointed guardian of the person and property of his daughter. It was proposed by him that such letters of guardianship, if granted, should contain an express power to him as guardian to authorize the discontinuance of all extraordinary medical procedures now allegedly sustaining Karen's vital processes and hence her life, since these measures, he asserted, present no hope of her eventual recovery. A guardian *ad litem* was appointed by Judge Muir to represent the interest of the alleged incompetent.

By a supplemental complaint, in view of the extraordinary nature of the relief sought by plaintiff and the involvement therein of their several rights and responsibilities, other parties were added. These included the treating physicians and the hospital, the relief sought being that they be restrained from interfering with the carrying out of any such extraordinary authorization in the event it were to be granted by the court. Joined, as well, was the Prosecutor of Morris County (he being charged with responsibility for enforcement of the criminal law), to enjoin him from interfering with, or projecting a criminal prosecution which otherwise might ensue in the event of, cessation of life in Karen resulting from the exercise of such extraordinary authorization were it to be granted to the guardian. The Attorney General of New Jersey intervened . . . on behalf of the State of New Jersey. . . . Its basis, of course, was the interest of the State in the preservation of life, which has an undoubted constitutional foundation.

The matter is of transcendent importance, involving questions related to the definition and existence of death; the prolongation of life through artificial means developed by medical technology undreamed of in past generations of the practice of the healing arts; the impact of such durationally indeterminate and artificial life prolongation on the rights of the incompetent, her family and society in general; the bearing of constitutional right and the scope of judicial responsibility, as to the appropriate response of an equity court of justice to the extraordinary prayer for relief of the plaintiff. Involved as well is the right of the plaintiff, Joseph Quinlan, to guardianship of the person of his daughter.

. . . After certification the Attorney General filed as of right a cross-appeal challenging the action of the trial court in admitting evidence of prior statements made by Karen while competent as to her distaste for continuance of life by extraordinary medical procedures, under circumstances not unlike those of the present case. These quoted statements were made in the context of several conversations with regard to others terminally ill and being subjected to like heroic measures. The statements were advanced as evidence of what she would want done in such a contingency as now exists. She was said to have firmly evinced her wish, in like circumstances, not to have her life prolonged by the otherwise futile use of extraordinary means. Because we agree with the conception of the trial court that such statements, since they were remote and impersonal, lacked significant probative weight, it is not of consequence to our opinion that we decide whether or not they were admissible hearsay. Again, after certification, the guardian of the person of the incompetent (who had been appointed as a part of the judgment appealed from) resigned and was succeeded by another, but that too seems irrelevant to decision. . . .

Essentially then, appealing to the power of equity, and relying on claimed constitutional rights of free exercise of religion, of privacy and of protection against cruel and unusual punishment, Karen Quinlan's father sought judicial authority to withdraw the life-sustaining mechanisms temporarily preserving his daughter's life, and his appointment as guardian of her person to that end. His request was opposed by her doctors, the hospital, the Morris County Prosecutor, the State of New Jersey, and her guardian *ad litem.*

. . . On the night of April 15, 1975, for reasons still unclear, Karen Quinlan ceased breathing for at least two 15 minute periods. She received some ineffectual mouth-to-mouth resuscitation from friends. She was taken by ambulance to Newton Memorial Hospital. There she had a temperature of 100 degrees, her pupils were unreactive and she was unresponsive even to deep pain. The history at the time of her admission to that hospital was essentially incomplete and uninformative.

Three days later, Dr. Morse examined Karen at the request of the Newton admitting physician, Dr. McGee. He found her comatose with evidence of decortication, a condition relating to derangement of the cortex of the brain causing a physical posture in which the upper extremities are flexed and the lower extremities are extended. She required a respirator to assist her breathing. Dr. Morse was unable to obtain an adequate account of the circumstances and events leading up to Karen's admission to the Newton Hospital. Such initial history or etiology is crucial in neurological diagnosis. Relying as he did upon the Newton Memorial records and his own examination, he concluded that prolonged lack of oxygen in the bloodstream, anoxia, was identified with her condition as he saw it upon first observation. When she was later transferred to Saint Clare's Hospital she was still unconscious, still on a respirator and a tracheotomy had been performed. On her arrival Dr. Morse conducted extensive and detailed examinations. An electroencephalogram (EEG) measuring electrical rhythm of the brain was performed and Dr. Morse characterized the result as "abnormal but it showed some activity and was consistent with her clinical state." Other significant neurological tests, including a brain scan, an angiogram, and a lumbar puncture were normal in result. Dr. Morse testified that Karen has been in a state of coma, lack of consciousness, since he began treating her. He explained that there are basically two types of coma, sleep-like unresponsiveness and awake unresponsiveness. Karen was originally in a sleep-like unresponsive condition but soon developed "sleep-wake" cycles, apparently a normal improvement for comatose patients occurring within three to four weeks. In the awake cycle she blinks, cries out and does things of that sort but is still totally unaware of anyone or anything around her.

Dr. Morse and other expert physicians who examined her characterized Karen as being in a "chronic persistent vegetative state." Dr. Fred Plum, one of such expert witnesses, defined this as a "subject who remains with the capacity to maintain the vegetative parts of neurological function but who no longer has any cognitive function." Dr. Morse, as well as the several other medical and neurological experts who testified in this case, believed with certainty that Karen Quinlan is not "brain dead." They identified the Ad Hoc Committee of Harvard Medical School report (*infra*) as the ordinary medical standard for determining brain death, and all of them were satisfied that Karen met none of the criteria specified in that report and was therefore not "brain dead" within its contemplation. . . .

Because Karen's neurological condition affects her respiratory ability (the respiratory system being a brain stem function) she requires a respirator to assist her breathing. From the time of her admission to Saint Clare's Hospital Karen has been assisted by an MA-1 respirator, a sophisticated machine which delivers a given volume of air at a certain rate and periodically provides a "sigh" volume, a relatively large measured volume of air designed to purge the lungs of excretions. Attempts to "wean" her from the respirator were unsuccessful and have been abandoned.

The experts believe that Karen cannot now survive without the assistance of the respirator; that exactly how long she would live without it is unknown; that the strong likelihood is that death would follow soon after its removal, and that removal would also risk further brain damage and would curtail the assistance the respirator presently provides in warding off infection. It seemed to be the consensus not only of the treating physicians but also of the several qualified experts who testified in the case, that removal from the respirator would not conform to medical practices, standards and traditions.

The further medical consensus was that Karen in addition to being comatose is in a chronic and persistent "vegetative" state, having no awareness of anything or anyone around her and existing at a primitive reflex level. Although she does have some brain stem function (ineffective for respiration) and has other reactions one normally associates with being alive, such as moving, reacting to light, sound and noxious stimuli, blinking her eyes, and the like, the quality of her feeling impulses is unknown. She grimaces, makes stereotyped cries and sounds and has chewing motions. Her blood pressure is normal.

Karen remains in the intensive care unit at Saint Clare's Hospital, receiving 24-hour care by a team of four nurses characterized, as was the medical attention, as "excellent." She is nourished by feeding by way of a nasal-gastro tube and is routinely examined for infection, which under these circumstances is a serious life threat. The result is that her condition is considered remarkable under the unhappy circumstances involved.

Karen is described as emaciated, having suffered a weight loss of at least 40 pounds, and undergoing a continuing deteriorative process. Her posture is described as fetal-like and grotesque; there is extreme flexion-rigidity of the arms, legs and related muscles and her joints are severely rigid and deformed.

From all of this evidence, and including the whole testimonial record, several basic findings in the physical area are mandated. Severe brain and associated damage, albeit of uncertain etiology, has left Karen in a chronic and persistent vegetative state. No form of treatment which can cure or improve that condition is known or available. As nearly as may be determined, considering the guarded area of remote uncertainties characteristic of most medical science predictions, she can *never* be restored to cognitive or sapient life. Even with regard to the vegetative level and improvement therein (if such it may be called) the prognosis is extremely poor and the extent unknown if it should in fact occur.

She is debilitated and moribund and although fairly stable at the time of argument before us (no new information having been filed in the meanwhile in expansion of the record), no physician risked the opinion that she could live more than a year and indeed she may die much earlier. Excellent medical and nursing care so far has been able to ward off the constant threat of infection, to which she is peculiarly susceptible because of the respirator, the tracheal tube and other incidents of care in her vulnerable condition. Her life accordingly is sustained by the respirator and tubal feeding, and removal from the respirator would cause her death soon, although the time cannot be stated with more precision. The determination of the fact and time of death in past years of medical science was keyed to the action of the heart and blood circulation, in turn dependent upon pulmonary activity, and hence cessation of these functions spelled out the reality of death. . . .

But, as indicated, it was the consensus of medical testimony in the instant case that Karen, for all her disability, met none of these criteria, nor indeed any comparable criteria extant in the medical world and representing . . . prevailing and accepted medical standards. We have adverted to the "brain death" concept and Karen's disassociation with any of its criteria, to emphasize the basis of the medical decision made by Dr. Morse. When plaintiff and his family, finally reconciled to the certainty of Karen's impending death, requested the withdrawal of life support mechanisms, he demurred. His refusal was based upon his conception of medical standards, practice and ethics described in the medical testimony, such as in the evidence given by another neurologist, Dr. Sidney Diamond, a witness for the State. Dr. Diamond asserted that no physician would have failed to provide respirator support at the outset, and none would interrupt its life-saving course thereafter, except in the case of cerebral death. In the latter case, he thought the respirator would in effect be disconnected from one already dead, entitling the physician under medical standards and, he thought, legal concepts, to terminate the supportive measures. We note Dr. Diamond's distinction of major surgical or transfusion procedures in a terminal case not involving cerebral death, such as here:

> The subject has lost human qualities. It would be incredible, and I think unlikely, that any physician would respond to a sudden hemorrhage, massive hemorrhage or a loss of all her defensive blood cells, by giving her large quantities of blood. I think that

major surgical procedures would be out of the question even if they were known to be essential for continued physical existence.

This distinction is adverted to also in the testimony of Dr. Julius Korein, a neurologist called by plaintiff. Dr. Korein described a medical practice concept of "judicious neglect" under which the physician will say:

> Don't treat this patient anymore, . . . it does not serve either the patient, the family, or society in any meaningful way to continue treatment with this patient.

Dr. Korein also told of the unwritten and unspoken standard of medical practice implied in the foreboding initials DNR (do not resuscitate), as applied to the extraordinary terminal case:

> Cancer, metastatic cancer, involving the lungs, the liver, the brain, multiple involvements, the physician may or may not write: Do not resuscitate. . . . [I]t could be said to the nurse: if this man stops breathing don't resuscitate him. . . . No physician that I know personally is going to try and resuscitate a man riddled with cancer and in agony and he stops breathing. They are not going to put him on a respirator. . . . I think that would be the height of misuse of technology.

While the thread of logic in such distinctions may be elusive to the non-medical lay mind, in relation to the supposed imperative to sustain life at all costs, they nevertheless relate to medical decisions, such as the decision of Dr. Morse in the present case. We agree with the trial court that that decision was in accord with Dr. Morse's conception of medical standards and practice.

We turn to that branch of the factual case pertaining to the application for guardianship, as distinguished from the nature of the authorization sought by the applicant. The character and general suitability of Joseph Quinlan as guardian for his daughter, in ordinary circumstances, could not be doubted. The record bespeaks the high degree of familial love which pervaded the home of Joseph Quinlan and reached out fully to embrace Karen, although she was living elsewhere at the time of her collapse. The proofs showed him to be deeply religious, imbued with a morality so sensitive that months of tortured indecision preceded his belated conclusion (despite earlier moral judgments reached by the other family members, but unexpressed to him in order not to influence him) to seek the termination of life-supportive measures sustaining Karen. A communicant of the Roman Catholic Church, as were other family members, he first sought solace in private prayer looking with confidence, as he says, to the Creator, first for the recovery of Karen and then, if that were not possible, for guidance with respect to the awesome decision confronting him.

To confirm the moral rightness of the decision he was about to make he consulted with his parish priest and later with the Catholic chaplain of Saint Clare's Hospital. He would not, he testified, have sought termination if that act were to be morally wrong or in conflict with the tenets of the religion he so profoundly respects. He was disabused of doubt, however, when the position of the Roman Catholic Church was made known to him as it is reflected in the record in this case. While it is not usual for matters of religious dogma or concepts to enter a civil litigation (except as they may bear upon constitutional right, or sometimes, familial matters), they were rightly admitted in evidence here. The judge was bound to measure the character and motivations in all respects of Joseph Quinlan as prospective guardian; and insofar as these religious matters bore upon them, they were properly scrutinized and considered by the court. . . .

Medicine with its combination of advanced technology and professional ethics is both able and inclined to prolong biological life. Law with its felt obligation to protect the life and freedom of the individual seeks to assure each person's right to live out his human life until its natural and inevitable conclusion. Theology with its acknowledgment of man's dissatisfaction with biological life as the ultimate source of joy defends the sacredness of human life and defends it from all direct attacks.

These disciplines do not conflict with one another, but are necessarily conjoined in the application of their principles in a particular instance such as that of Karen Ann Quinlan. Each must in some way acknowledge the other without denying its own competence. The civil law is not expected to assert a belief in eternal life; nor, on the other hand, is it expected to ignore the right of the individual to profess it, and to form and pursue his conscience in accord with that belief. Medical science is not authorized to directly cause natural death; nor, however, is it expected to prevent it when it is inevitable and all hope of a return to an even partial exercise of human life is irreparably lost. Religion is not expected to define biological death; nor, on its part, is it expected to relinquish its responsibility to assist man in the formation and pursuit of a correct conscience as to the acceptance of natural death when science has confirmed its inevitability beyond any hope other than that of preserving biological life in a merely vegetative state. . . .

In the present public discussion of the case of Karen Ann Quinlan it has been brought out that responsible people involved in medical care, patients and families have exercised the freedom to terminate or withhold certain treatments as extraordinary means in cases judged to be terminal, i.e., cases which hold no realistic hope for some recovery, in accord with the expressed or implied intentions of the patients themselves. To whatever extent this has been happening it has been without sanction in civil law. Those involved in such actions, however, have ethical and theological literature to guide them in their judgments and actions. Furthermore, such actions have not in themselves undermined society's reverence for the lives of sick and dying people.

It is both possible and necessary for society to have laws and ethical standards which provide freedom for decisions, in accord with the expressed or implied intentions of the patient, to terminate or withhold extraordinary treatment in cases which are judged to be hopeless by competent medical authorities, without at the same time leaving an opening for euthanasia. Indeed, to accomplish this, it may simply be required that courts and legislative bodies recognize the present standards and practices of many people engaged in medical care who have been doing what the parents of Karen Ann Quinlan are requesting authorization to have done for their beloved daughter.

Before turning to the legal and constitutional issues involved, we feel it essential to reiterate that the "Catholic view" of religious neutrality in the circumstances of this case is considered by the Court only in the aspect of its impact upon the conscience, motivation and purpose of the intending guardian, Joseph Quinlan, and not as a precedent in terms of the civil law. If Joseph Quinlan, for instance, were a follower and strongly influenced by the teachings of Buddha, or if, as an agnostic or atheist, his moral judgments were formed without reference to religious feelings, but were nevertheless formed and viable, we would with equal attention and high respect consider these elements, as bearing upon his character, motivations and purposes as relevant to his qualification and suitability as guardian. . . .

At the outset we note the dual role in which plaintiff comes before the Court. He not only raises, derivatively, what he perceives to be the constitutional and legal rights of his daughter Karen, but he also claims certain rights independently as parent. Although generally a litigant may assert only his own constitutional rights, we have no doubt that plaintiff has sufficient standing to advance both positions. . . .

We think the contention as to interference with religious beliefs or rights may be considered and dealt with without extended discussion, given the acceptance of distinctions so clear and simple in their precedential definition as to be dispositive on their face. Simply stated, the right to religious beliefs is absolute but conduct in pursuance thereof is not wholly immune from governmental restraint. . . . So it is that, for the sake of life, courts sometimes (but not always) order blood transfusions for Jehovah's Witnesses (whose religious beliefs abhor such procedure), *Application of President & Directors of Georgetown College, Inc.*, 118 *U.S. App. D.C.* 80, 331 *F.* 2d 1000 [1010] (D.C. Cir.) (1964). . . . The public interest is thus considered paramount, without essential dissolution of respect for religious beliefs. . . .

Similarly inapplicable to the case before us is the Constitution's Eighth Amendment protection against cruel and unusual punishment which, as held by the trial court, is not relevant to situations other than the imposition of penal sanctions. . . .

So it is in the case of the unfortunate Karen Quinlan. Neither the State, nor the law, but the accident of fate and nature, has inflicted upon her conditions which though in essence cruel and most unusual, yet do not amount to "punishment" in any constitutional sense. Neither the judgment of the court below, nor the medical decision which confronted it, nor the law and equity perceptions which impelled its action, nor the whole factual base upon which it was predicated, inflicted "cruel and unusual punishment" in the constitutional sense.

It is the issue of the constitutional right of privacy that has given us most concern, in the exceptional circumstances of this case. Here a loving parent, *qua* parent and raising the rights of his incompetent and profoundly damaged daughter, probably irreversibly doomed to no more than a biologically vegetative remnant of life, is before the court. He seeks authorization to abandon specialized technological procedures which can only maintain for a time a body having no potential for resumption or continuance of other than a "vegetative" existence. . . .

We have no hesitancy in deciding . . . that no external compelling interest of the State could compel Karen to endure the unendurable, only to vegetate a few measurable months with no realistic possibility of returning to any semblance of cognitive or sapient life. We perceive no thread of logic distinguishing between such a choice on Karen's part and a similar choice which, under the evidence in this case, could be made by a competent patient terminally ill, riddled by cancer and suffering great pain; such a patient would not be resuscitated or put on a respirator in the example described by Dr. Korein, and *a fortiori* would not be kept *against his will* on a respirator.

Although the Constitution does not explicitly mention a right of privacy, Supreme Court decisions have recognized that a right of personal privacy exists and that certain areas of privacy are guaranteed under the Constitution. The Court has interdicted judicial intrusion into many aspects of personal decision, sometimes basing this restraint upon the conception of a limitation of judicial interest and responsibility, such as with regard to contraception and its relationship to family life and decision. *Griswold v. Connecticut,* 381 *U.S.* 479 (1965). The Court in *Griswold* found the unwritten constitutional right of privacy to exist in the penumbra of specific guarantees of the Bill of Rights "formed by emanations from those guarantees that help give them life and substance." 381 *U.S.* at 484. Presumably this right is broad enough to encompass a patient's decision to decline medical treatment under certain circumstances, in much the same way as it is broad enough to encompass a woman's decision to terminate pregnancy under certain conditions. *Roe v. Wade,* 410 *U.S.* 113, 153 (1973). Nor is such right of privacy forgotten in the New Jersey Constitution. *N.J. Const.* (1947), Art. I, par. 1.

The claimed interests of the State in this case are essentially the preservation and sanctity of human life and defense of the right of the physician to administer medical treatment according to his best judgment. In this case the doctors say that removing Karen from the respirator will conflict with their professional judgment. The plaintiff answers that Karen's present treatment serves only a maintenance function; that the respirator cannot cure or improve her condition but at best can only prolong her inevitable slow deterioration and death; and that the interests of the patient, as seen by her surrogate, the guardian, must be evaluated by the court as predominant, even in the face of an opinion *contra* by the present attending physicians. Plaintiff's distinction is significant. The nature of Karen's care and the realistic chances of her recovery are quite unlike those of the patients discussed in many of the cases where treatments were ordered. In many of those cases the medical procedure required (usually a transfusion) constituted a minimal bodily invasion and the chances of recovery and return to functioning life were very good. We think that the State's interest *contra* weakens and the individual's right to privacy grows as the degree of bodily invasion increases and the prognosis dims. Ultimately there comes a point at which the individual's rights overcome the State interest. It is for that reason that we believe Karen's choice, if she were competent to make it, would be vindicated by the law. Her prognosis is extremely poor,—she will never resume cognitive life. And the bodily invasion is very great,—she requires 24 hour intensive nursing care, antibiotics, the assistance of a respirator, a catheter and feeding tube.

Our affirmation of Karen's independent right of choice, however, would ordinarily be based upon her competency to assert it. The sad truth, however, is that she is grossly incompetent and we cannot discern her supposed choice based on the testimony of her previous conversations with friends, where such testimony is without sufficient probative weight. Nevertheless we have concluded that Karen's right of privacy may be asserted on her behalf by her guardian under the peculiar circumstances here present. If a putative decision by Karen to permit this non-cognitive, vegetative existence to terminate by natural forces is regarded as a valuable incident of her right of privacy, as we believe it to be, then it should not be discarded solely on the basis that her condition prevents her conscious exercise of the choice. The only practical way to prevent destruction of the right is to permit the guardian and family of Karen to render their best judgment, subject to the qualifications hereinafter stated, as to whether she would exercise it in these circumstances. If their conclusion is in the affirmative this decision should be accepted by a society the overwhelming majority of whose members would, we think, in similar circumstances, exercise such a choice in the same way for themselves or for those closest to them. It is for this reason that we determine that Karen's right of privacy may be asserted in her behalf, in this respect, by her guardian and family under the particular circumstances presented by this record. . . .

Having declared the substantive legal basis upon which plaintiff's rights as representative of Karen must be deemed predicated, we face and respond to the assertion on behalf of defendants that our premise unwarrantably offends prevailing medical standards. We thus turn to consideration of the medical decision supporting the determination made below, conscious of the paucity of pre-existing legislative and judicial guidance as to the rights and liabilities therein involved.

A significant problem in any discussion of sensitive medical-legal issues is the marked, perhaps unconscious, tendency of many to distort what the law is, in pursuit of an exposition of what they would like the law to be. Nowhere is this barrier to the intelligent resolution of legal controversies more obstructive than in the debate over patient rights at the end of life. Judicial refusals to order lifesaving treatment in the face of contrary claims of bodily self-determination or free religious exercise are too often cited in support of a preconceived "right to die," even though the patients, wanting to live, have claimed no such right. Conversely, the assertion of a religious or other objection to lifesaving treatment is at times condemned as attempted suicide, even though suicide means something quite different in the law.

Perhaps the confusion there adverted to stems from mention by some courts of statutory or common law condemnation of suicide as demonstrating the state's interest in the preservation of life. We would see, however, a real distinction between the self-infliction of deadly harm and a self-determination against artificial life support or radical surgery, for instance, in the face of irreversible, painful and certain imminent death. The contrasting situations mentioned are analogous to those continually faced by the medical profession. When does the institution of life-sustaining procedures, ordinarily mandatory, become the subject of medical discretion in the context of administration to persons *in extremis*? And when does the withdrawal of such procedures, from such persons already supported by them, come within the orbit of medical discretion? When does a determination as to either of the foregoing contingencies court the hazard of civil or criminal liability on the part of the physician or institution involved?

The existence and nature of the medical dilemma need hardly be discussed at length, portrayed as it is in the present case and complicated as it has recently come to be in view of the dramatic advance of medical technology. The dilemma is there, it is real, it is constantly resolved in accepted medical practice without attention in the courts, it pervades the issues in the very case we here examine. The branch of the dilemma involving the doctor's responsibility and the relationship of the court's duty was thus conceived by Judge Muir:

> Doctors to treat a patient, must deal with medical tradition and past case histories. They must be guided by what they do know.

> The extent of their training, their experience, consultation with other physicians, must guide their decision-making processes in providing care to their patient. The nature, extent and duration of care by societal standards is the responsibility of a physician. The morality and conscience of our society places this responsibility in the hands of the physician. What justification is there to remove it from the control of the medical profession and place it in the hands of the courts? (137 *N.J. Super.* at 259).

. . . [The] law, equity and justice must not themselves quail and be helpless in the face of modern technological marvels presenting questions hitherto unthought of. Where a Karen Quinlan, or a parent, or a doctor, or a hospital, or a State seeks the process and response of a court, it must answer with its most informed conception of justice in the previously unexplored circumstances presented to it. That is its obligation and we are here fulfilling it, for the actors and those having an interest in the matter should not go without remedy. . . .

But insofar as a court, having no inherent medical expertise, is called upon to overrule a professional decision made according to prevailing medical practice and standards, a different question is presented. As mentioned below, a doctor is required "to exercise in the treatment of his patient the degree of care, knowledge and skill ordinarily possessed and exercised in similar situations by the average member of the profession practicing in his field." *Schueler v. Strelinger,* 43 *N.J.* 330, 344 (1964). If he is a specialist he "must employ not merely the skill of a general practitioner, but also that special degree of skill normally possessed by the average physician who devotes special study and attention to the particular organ or disease or injury involved, having regard to the present state of scientific knowledge." *Clark v. Wichman,* 72 *N.J. Super.* 486, 493 (App. Div. 1962). This is the duty that establishes his legal obligations to his patients. (137 *N.J. Super.* at 257–58). . . .

In regard to the foregoing it is pertinent that we consider the impact on the standards both of the civil and criminal law as to medical liability and the new technological means of sustaining life irreversibly damaged. The modern proliferation of substantial malpractice litigation and the less frequent but even more unnerving possibility of criminal sanctions would seem, for it is beyond human nature to suppose otherwise, to have bearing on the practice and standards as they exist. The brooding presence of such possible liability, it was testified here, had no part in the decision of the treating physicians. . . . The agitation of the medical community in the face of modern life prolongation technology and its search for definitive policy are demonstrated in the large volume of relevant professional commentary. . . .

We glean from the record here that physicians distinguish between curing the ill and comforting and easing the dying; that they refuse to treat the curable as if they were dying or ought to die, and that they have sometimes refused to treat the hopeless and dying as if they were curable. In this sense, as we were reminded by the testimony of Drs. Korein and Diamond, many of them have refused to inflict an undesired prolongation of the process of dying on a patient in irreversible condition when it is clear that such "therapy" offers neither human nor humane benefit. We think these attitudes represent a balanced implementation of a profoundly realistic perspective on the meaning of life and death and that they respect the whole Judeo-Christian tradition of regard for human life. No less would they seem consistent with the moral matrix of medicine, "to heal," very much in the sense of the endless mission of the law, "to do justice." . . .

Nevertheless, there must be a way to free physicians, in the pursuit of their healing vocation, from possible contamination by self-interest or self-protection concerns which would inhibit their independent medical judgments for the well-being of their dying patients. We would hope that this opinion might be serviceable to some degree in ameliorating the professional problems under discussion. . . .

The evidence in this case convinces us that the focal point of decision should be the prognosis as to the reasonable possibility of return to cognitive and sapient life, as distinguished from the forced continuance of that biological vegetative existence to which Karen seems to be doomed. . . .

We . . . sense from the whole record before us that while Mr. Quinlan feels a natural grief, and understandably sorrows because of the tragedy which has befallen his daughter, his strength of purpose and character far outweighs these sentiments and qualifies him eminently for guardianship of the person as well as the property of his daughter. Hence we discern no valid reason to overrule the statutory intendment of preference to the next of kin.

. . . Some time has passed since Karen's physical and mental condition was described to the Court. At that time her continuing deterioration was plainly projected. Since the record has not been expanded we assume that she is now even more fragile and nearer to death than she was then. Since her present treating physicians may give reconsideration to her present posture in the light of this opinion, and since we are transferring to the plaintiff as guardian the choice of the attending physician and therefore other physicians may be in charge of the case who may take a different view from that of the present attending physicians, we herewith declare the following affirmative relief on behalf of the plaintiff. Upon the concurrence of the guardian and family of Karen, should the responsible attending physicians conclude that there is no reasonable possibility of Karen's ever emerging from her present comatose condition to a cognitive, sapient state and that the life-support apparatus now being administered to Karen should be discontinued, they shall consult with the hospital "Ethics Committee" or like body of the institution in which Karen is then hospitalized. If that consultative body agrees that there is no reasonable possibility of Karen's ever emerging from her present comatose condition to a cognitive, sapient state, the present life-support system may be withdrawn and said action shall be without any civil or criminal liability therefor on the part of any participant, whether guardian, physician, hospital or others. We herewith specifically so hold.

The Meaning of Informed Consent: *Canterbury v. Spence* (1972)

Since the beginning of the twentieth century, American courts recognized the principle of informed consent. Courts required that physicians tell patients of medical procedures that were to be performed and secure their permission for those specific procedures. Such had not always been the case; in the early days of anesthesia, for example, courts allowed some physicians to practice "involuntary anesthetization" (for instance, on patients who were delirious or drunken) if they did so within currently accepted standards of practice. In a series of cases in the early 1900s, however, courts required that consent be freely given and connected with each particular procedure. The decision in Schloendorff v. Society of New York Hospitals *(1914) contained a famous warning by Justice Cardozo that "every human being of adult years and sound mind has the right to determine what shall be done with his own body" (125). That statement was a basis of subsequent decisions that further specified exactly how and when consent should be obtained. In later decisions, courts mandated that for consent to be informed, physicians had to let patients know of the alternatives to the procedures that were being recommended, as well as the possible outcomes of the procedures.*

By the 1960s and 1970s, courts went so far as to warn physicians that failing to tell patients of the risks from not undergoing tests, surgeries, or other procedures could amount to the absence of informed consent. The case of Canterbury v. Spence *was a watershed decision because even in the face of some questions about how patient Canterbury sustained all of the injuries of which he complained (that is, whether he was injured more by the surgery under discussion or a fall from a hospital bed), the court held Dr. Spence to a high standard with regard to informed consent. The court determined that neither Canterbury (nineteen years old at the time) nor his mother had been warned in sufficient detail about the risks attendant to a spinal operation. It was not a good defense for a physician to contend that the operation carried only a minor risk of complications and that warning of those rare possible complications might deter the patient from seeking needed treatment. The court took pains to emphasize that physicians' "duty to disclose" the risks of treatment was especially important when patients were of socioeconomic backgrounds that might make them deferential to doctors' authority—as had been the case with patient Canterbury and his mother.*

COURT OPINION BY CIRCUIT JUDGE ROBINSON. This appeal is from a judgment entered in the District Court on verdicts directed for the two appellees at the conclusion of plaintiff-appellant Canterbury's case in chief. His action sought damages for personal injuries allegedly sustained as a result of an operation negligently performed by appellee Spence, a negligent failure by Dr. Spence to disclose a risk of serious disability inherent in the operation, and negligent post-operative care by appellee Washington Hospital Center. On close examination of the record, we find evidence which required submission of these issues to the jury. We accordingly reverse the judgment as to each appellee and remand the case to the District Court for a new trial.

The record we review tells a depressing tale. A youth troubled only by back pain submitted to an operation without being informed of a risk of paralysis incidental thereto. A day after the operation he fell from his hospital bed after having been left without assistance while voiding. A few hours after the fall, the lower half of his body was paralyzed, and he had to be operated on again. Despite extensive medical care, he has never been what he was before. Instead of the back pain, even years later, he hobbled about on crutches, a victim of paralysis of the bowels and urinary incontinence. In a very real sense this lawsuit is an understandable search for reasons.

At the time of the events which gave rise to this litigation, appellant was nineteen years of age, a clerk-typist employed by the Federal Bureau of Investigation. In December, 1958, he began to experience severe pain between his shoulder blades. He consulted two general practitioners, but the medications they prescribed failed to eliminate the pain. Thereafter, appellant secured an appointment with Dr. Spence, who is a neurosurgeon.

Dr. Spence examined appellant in his office at some length but found nothing amiss. On Dr. Spence's advice appellant was x-rayed, but the films did not identify any abormality. Dr. Spence then recommended that appellant undergo a myelogram—a procedure in which dye is injected into the spinal column and traced to find evidence of disease or other disorder—at the Washington Hospital Center.

Appellant entered the hospital on February 4, 1959. The myelogram revealed a "filling defect" in the region of the fourth thoracic vertebra. Since a myelogram often does no more than pinpoint the location of an aberration, surgery may be necessary to discover the cause. Dr. Spence told appellant that he would have to undergo a laminectomy—the excision of the posterior arch of the vertebra—to correct what he suspected was a ruptured disc. Appellant did not raise any objection to the proposed operation nor did he probe into its exact nature.

Appellant explained to Dr. Spence that his mother was a widow of slender financial means living in Cyclone, West Virginia, and that she could be reached through a neighbor's telephone. Appellant called his mother the day after the myelogram was performed and, failing to contact her, left Dr. Spence's telephone number with the neighbor. When Mrs. Canterbury returned the call, Dr. Spence told her that the surgery was occasioned by a suspected ruptured disc. Mrs. Canterbury then asked if the recommended operation was serious and Dr. Spence replied "not anymore than any other operation." He added that he knew Mrs. Canterbury was not well off and that her presence in Washington would not be necessary. The testimony is contradictory as to whether during the course of the conversation Mrs. Canterbury expressed her consent to the operation. Appellant himself apparently did not converse again with Dr. Spence prior to the operation.

Dr. Spence performed the laminectomy on February 11 at the Washington Hospital Center. Mrs. Canterbury traveled to Washington, arriving on that date but after the operation was over, and signed a consent form at the hospital. The laminectomy revealed several anomalies: a spinal cord that was swollen and unable to pulsate, an accumulation of large tortuous and dilated veins, and a complete absence of epidural fat which normally surrounds the spine. A thin hypodermic needle was inserted into the spinal cord to aspirate any cysts which might have been present, but no fluid emerged. In suturing the wound, Dr. Spence attempted to relieve the pressure on the spinal cord by enlarging the dura—the outer protective wall of the spinal cord—at the area of swelling.

For approximately the first day after the operation appellant recuperated normally, but then suffered a fall and an almost immediate setback. Since there is some conflict as to precisely when or why appellant fell, we reconstruct the events from the evidence most favorable to him. Dr. Spence left orders that appellant was to remain in bed during the process of voiding. These orders were changed to direct that voiding be done out of bed, and the jury could find that the change was made by hospital personnel. Just prior to the fall, appellant summoned a nurse and was given a receptacle for use in voiding, but was then left unattended. Appellant testified that during the course of the endeavor he slipped off the side of the bed, and that there was no one to assist him, or side rail to prevent the fall.

Several hours later, appellant began to complain that he could not move his legs and that he was having trouble breathing; paralysis seems to have been virtually total from the waist down. Dr. Spence was notified on the night of February 12, and he rushed to the hospital. Mrs. Canterbury signed another consent form and appellant was again taken into the operating room. The surgical wound was reopened and Dr. Spence created a gusset to allow the spinal cord greater room in which to pulsate.

Appellant's control over his muscles improved somewhat after the second operation but he was unable to void properly. As a result of this condition, he came under the care of a urologist while still in the hospital. In April, following a cystoscopic examination, appellant was operated on for removal of bladder stones, and in May was released from the hospital. He reentered the hospital the following August for a 10-day period, apparently because of his urologic problems. For several years after his discharge he was under the care of several specialists, and at all times was under the care of a urologist. At the time of the trial in April, 1968, appellant required crutches to walk, still suffered from urinal incontinence and paralysis of the bowels, and wore a penile clamp.

In November, 1959 on Dr. Spence's recommendation, appellant was transferred by the F.B.I. to Miami where he could get more swimming and exercise. Appellant worked three years for the F.B.I. in Miami, Los Angeles and Houston, resigning finally in June, 1962. From then until the time of the trial, he held a number of jobs, but had constant trouble finding work because he needed to remain seated and close to a bathroom. The damages appellant claims include extensive pain and suffering, medical expenses, and loss of earnings.

Appellant filed suit in the District Court on March 7, 1963, four years after the laminectomy and approximately two years after he attained his majority. The complaint stated several causes of action against each defendant. Against Dr. Spence it alleged, among other things, negligence in the performance of the laminectomy and failure to inform him beforehand of the risk involved. Against the hospital the complaint charged negligent post-operative care in permitting appellant to remain unattended after the laminectomy, in failing to provide a nurse or orderly to assist him at the time of his fall, and in failing to maintain a side rail on his bed. Appellant introduced no evidence to show medical and hospital practices, if any, customarily pursued in regard to the critical aspects of the case, and only Dr. Spence, called as an adverse witness, testified on the issue of causality. Dr. Spence described the surgical procedures he utilized in the two operations and expressed his opinion that appellant's disabilities stemmed from his pre-operative condition as symptomatized by the swollen, non-pulsating spinal cord. He stated, however, that neither he nor any of the other physicians with whom he consulted was certain as to what that condition was, and he admitted that trauma can be a cause of paralysis. Dr. Spence further testified that even without trauma paralysis can be anticipated "somewhere in the nature of one percent" of the laminectomies performed, a risk he termed "a very slight possibility." He felt that communication of that risk to the patient is not good medical practice because it might deter patients from undergoing needed surgery and might produce adverse psychological reactions which could preclude the success of the operation.

At the close of appellant's case in chief, each defendant moved for a directed verdict and the trial judge granted both motions. The basis of the ruling, he explained, was that appellant had failed to produce any medical evidence indicating negligence on Dr. Spence's part in diagnosing appellant's malady or in performing the laminectomy; that there was no proof that Dr. Spence's treatment was responsible for appellant's disabilities; and that notwithstanding some evidence to show negligent post-operative care, an absence of medical testimony to show causality precluded submission of the case against the hospital to the jury. The judge did not allude specifically to the alleged breach of duty by Dr. Spence to divulge the possible consequences of the laminectomy.

We reverse. The testimony of appellant and his mother that Dr. Spence did not reveal the risk of paralysis from the laminectomy made out a prima facie case of violation of the physician's duty to disclose which Dr. Spence's explanation did not negate as a matter of law. There was also testimony from which the jury could have found that the laminectomy was negligently performed by Dr. Spence, and that appellant's fall was the consequence of negligence on the part of the hospital. The record, moreover, contains evidence of sufficient quantity and quality to tender jury issues as to whether and to what extent any such negligence was causally related to appellant's post-laminectomy condition. These considerations entitled appellant to a new trial. . . .

Suits charging failure by a physician adequately to disclose the risks and alternatives of proposed treatment are not innovations in American law. They date back a good half-century, and in the last decade they have multiplied rapidly. There is, nonetheless, disagreement among the courts and the commentators on many major questions, and there is no precedent of our own directly in point. For the tools enabling resolution of the issues on this appeal, we are forced to begin at first principles.

. . . The root premise is the concept, fundamental in American jurisprudence, that "every human being of adult years and sound mind has a right to determine what shall be done with his own body. . . ." True consent to what happens to one's self is the informed exercise of a choice, and that entails an opportunity to evaluate knowledgeably the options available and the risks attendant upon each. The average patient has little or no understanding of the medical arts, and ordinarily has only his physician to whom he can look for enlightenment with which to reach an intelligent decision. From these almost axiomatic considerations springs the need, and in turn the requirement, of a reasonable divulgence by physician to patient to make such a decision possible.

. . . Patients ordinarily are persons unlearned in the medical sciences. Some few, of course, are schooled in branches of the medical profession or in related fields. But even within the latter group variations in degree of medical knowledge specifically referable to particular therapy may be broad, as for example, between a specialist and a general practitioner, or between a physician and a nurse. It may well be, then, that it is only in the unusual case that a court could safely assume that the patient's insights were on a parity with those of the treating physician. The doctrine that a consent effective as authority to form therapy can arise only from the patient's understanding of alternatives to and risks of the therapy is commonly denominated "informed consent." . . .

In duty-to-disclose cases, the focus of attention is more properly upon the nature and content of the physician's divulgence than the patient's understanding or consent. Adequate disclosure and informed consent are, of course, two sides of the same coin—the former a sine qua non of the latter. But the vital inquiry on duty to disclose relates to the physician's performance of an obligation, while one of the difficulties with analysis in terms of "informed consent" is its tendency to imply that what is decisive is the degree of the patient's comprehension. As we later emphasize, the physician discharges the duty when he makes a reasonable effort to convey sufficient information although the patient, without fault of the physician, may not fully grasp it. . . . Even though the fact-finder may have occasion to draw an inference on the state of the patient's enlightenment, the fact-finding process on performance of the duty ultimately reaches back to what the physician actually said or failed to say. And while the factual conclusion on adequacy of the revelation will vary as between patients—as, for example, between a lay patient and a physician-patient—the fluctuations are attributable to the kind of divulgence which may be reasonable under the circumstances.

. . . A physician is under a duty to treat his patient skillfully but proficiency in diagnosis and therapy is not the full measure of his responsibility. The cases demonstrate that the physician is under an obligation to communicate specific information to the patient when the exigencies of reasonable care call for it. Due care may require a physician perceiving symptoms of bodily abnormality to alert the patient to the condition. It may call upon the physician confronting an ailment which does not respond to his ministrations to inform the patient thereof. It may command the physician to instruct the patient as to any limitations to be presently observed for his own welfare, and as to any precautionary therapy he should seek in the future. It may oblige the physician to advise the patient of the need for or desirability of any alternative treatment promising greater benefit than that being pursued. Just as plainly, due care normally demands that the physician warn the patient of any risks to his well-being which contemplated therapy may involve.

The context in which the duty of risk-disclosure arises is invariably the occasion for decision as to whether a particular treatment procedure is to be undertaken. To the physician, whose training enables a self-satisfying evaluation, the answer may seem clear, but it is the prerogative of the patient, not the physician, to determine for himself the direction in which his interests seem to lie. To enable the patient to chart his course understandably, some familiarity with the therapeutic alternatives and their hazards becomes essential.

A reasonable revelation in these respects is not only a necessity but, as we see it, is as much a matter of the physician's duty. It is a duty to warn of the dangers lurking in the proposed treatment, and that is surely a facet of due care. It is, too, a duty to impart information which the patient has every right to expect. The patient's reliance upon the physician is a trust of the kind which traditionally has exacted obligations beyond those associated with armslength transactions. His dependence upon the physician for information affecting his well-being, in terms of contemplated treatment, is well-nigh abject. As earlier noted, long before the instant litigation arose, courts had recognized that the physician had the responsibility of satisfying the vital informational needs of the patient. More recently, we ourselves have found "in the fiducial qualities of [the physician-patient] relationship the physician's duty to reveal to the patient that which in his best interests it is important that he should know." [brackets in original] We now find, as a part of the physician's overall obligation to the patient, a similar duty of reasonable disclosure of the choices with respect to proposed therapy and the dangers inherently and potentially involved.

Some doubt has been expressed as to ability of physicians to suitably communicate their evaluations of risks and the advantages of optional treatment, and as to the lay patient's ability to understand what the physician tells him. . . . We do not share these apprehensions. The discussion need not be a disquisition, and surely the physician is not compelled to give his patient a short medical education; the disclosure rule summons the physician only to a reasonable explanation. . . . That means generally informing the patient in nontechnical terms as to what is at stake: the therapy alternatives open to him, the goals expectably to be achieved, and the risks that may ensue from particular treatment and no treatment. . . . So informing the patient hardly taxes the physician, and it must be the exceptional patient who cannot comprehend such an explanation at least in a rough way.

This disclosure requirement, on analysis, reflects much more of a change in doctrinal emphasis than a substantive addition to malpractice law. It is well established that the physician must seek and secure his patient's consent before commencing an operation or other course of treatment. It is also clear that the consent, to be efficacious, must be free from imposition upon the patient. It is the settled rule that therapy not authorized by the patient may amount to a tort—a common law battery—by the physician. And it is evident that it is normally impossible to obtain a consent worthy of the name unless the physician first elucidates the options and the perils for the patient's edification. Thus the physician has long borne a duty, on pain of liability for unauthorized treatment, to make adequate disclosure to the patient. The evolution of the obligation to communicate for the patient's benefit as well as the physician's protection has hardly involved an extraordinary restructuring of the law.

We discard the thought that the patient should ask for information before the physician is required to disclose. Caveat emptor is not the norm for the consumer of medical services. Duty to disclose is more than a call to speak merely on the patient's request, or merely to answer the patient's questions; it is a duty to volunteer, if necessary, the information the patient needs for intelligent decision. The patient may be ignorant, confused, overawed by the physician or frightened by the hospital, or even ashamed to inquire. . . . Perhaps relatively few patients could in any event identify the relevant questions in the absence of prior explanation by the physician. Physicians and hospitals have patients of widely divergent socio-economic backgrounds, and a rule which presumes a degree of sophistication which many members of society lack is likely to breed gross inequities. . . .

Duty to disclose has gained recognition in a large number of American jurisdictions, but more largely on a different rationale. The majority of courts dealing with the problem have made the duty depend on whether it was the custom of physicians practicing in the community to make the particular disclosure to the patient. If so, the physician may be held liable for an unreasonable and injurious failure to divulge, but there can be no recovery unless the omission forsakes a practice prevalent in the profession. We agree that the physician's noncompliance with a professional custom to reveal, like any other departure from prevailing medical practice, may give rise to liability to the patient. We do not agree that the patient's cause of action is dependent upon the existence and nonperformance of a relevant professional tradition.

There are, in our view, formidable obstacles to acceptance of the notion that the physician's obligation to disclose is either germinated or limited by medical practice. To begin with, the reality of any discernible custom reflecting a professional consensus on communication of option and risk information to patients is open to serious doubt. We sense the danger that what in fact is no custom at all may be taken as an affirmative custom to maintain silence, and that physician-witnesses to the so-called custom may state merely their personal opinions as to what they or others would do under given conditions. We cannot gloss over the inconsistency between reliance on a general practice respecting divulgence and, on the other hand, realization that the myriad of variables among patients makes each case so different that its omission can rationally be justified only by the effect of its individual circumstances. Nor can we ignore the fact that to bind the disclosure obligation to medical usage is to arrogate the decision on revelation to the physician alone. Respect for the patient's right of self-determination on particular therapy demands a standard set by law for physicians rather than one which physicians may or may not impose upon themselves. . . .

We have admonished, however, that "the special medical standards are but adaptions of the general standard to a group who are required to act as reasonable men possessing their medical talents presumably would." There is, by the same token, no basis for operation of the special medical standard where the physician's activity does not bring his medical knowledge and skills peculiarly into play. And where the challenge to the physician's conduct is not to be gauged by the special standard, it follows that medical custom cannot furnish the test of its propriety, whatever its relevance under the proper test may be. The decision to unveil the patient's condition and the chances as to remediation, as we shall see, is ofttimes a non-medical judgment and, if so, is a decision outside the ambit of the special standard. Where that is the situation, professional custom hardly furnishes the legal criterion for measuring the physician's responsibility to reasonably inform his patient of the options and the hazards as to treatment. . . .

Thus we distinguished, for purposes of duty to disclose, the special and general-standard aspects of the physician-patient relationship. When medical judgment enters the picture and for that reason the special standard controls, prevailing medical practice must be given its just due. In all other instances, however, the general standard exacting ordinary care applies, and that standard is set by law. In sum, the physician's duty to disclose is governed by the same legal principles applicable to others in comparable situations, with modifications only to the extent that medical judgment enters the picture. We hold that the standard measuring performance of that duty by physicians, as by others, is conduct which is reasonable under the circumstances.

. . . Once the circumstances give rise to a duty on the physician's part to inform his patient, the next inquiry is the scope of the disclosure the physician is legally obliged to make. The courts have frequently confronted this problem but no uniform standard defining the adequacy of the divulgence emerges from the decisions. Some have said "full" disclosure, a norm we are unwilling to adopt literally. It seems obviously prohibitive and unrealistic to expect physicians to discuss with their patients every risk of proposed treatment—no matter how small or remote . . . —and generally unnecessary from the patient's viewpoint as well. Indeed, the cases speaking in terms of "full" disclosure appear to envision something less than total disclosure, leaving unanswered the question of just how much.

In our view, the patient's right of self-decision shapes the boundaries of the duty to reveal. That right can be effectively exercised only if the patient possesses enough information to enable an intelligent choice. The scope of the physician's communications to the patient, then, must be measured by the patient's need, and that need is the information material to the decision. Thus the test for determining whether a particular peril must be divulged is its materiality to the patient's decision: all risks potentially affecting the decision must be unmasked. And to safeguard the patient's interest in achieving his own determination on treatment, the law must itself set the standard for adequate disclosure. . . .

. . . There is no bright line separating the significant from the insignificant; the answer in any case must abide a rule of reason. Some dangers—infection, for example—are inherent in any operation; there

> is no obligation to communicate those of which persons of average sophistication are aware. Even more clearly, the physician bears no responsibility for discussion of hazards the patient has already discovered, or those having no apparent materiality to patients' decision on therapy. The disclosure doctrine, like others marking lines between permissible and impermissible behavior in medical practice, is in essence a requirement of conduct prudent under the circumstances. Whenever nondisclosure of particular risk information is open to debate by reasonable-minded men, the issue is for the finder of the facts. . . .

The Right to Refuse Treatment: *Georgetown College v. Jones* (1964)

Some of the medicolegal controversies that have come before the courts have been actual medical emergencies, in which physicians have had to act first and determine the appropriateness of their actions later. Georgetown College v. Jones *was a particularly dramatic case in a factual sense and one that also represented a fundamental quandary: how to balance the right for a patient to determine what medical treatment her body should receive with the duty of physicians to perform lifesaving treatments. The physicians' dilemma was particularly interesting when Mrs. Jesse Jones refused on religious grounds emergency medical treatment that doctors thought would save her life. Thus Mrs. Jones claimed that to force her to receive blood products violated her First Amendment right to exercise her religion. The hospital administrators who faced Mrs. Jones's refusal for treatment approached one judge who would not order a blood transfusion; they pursued their quest for judicial authorization, however, and located another judge who would. After Mrs. Jones was discharged from the hospital, fully recovered, she sought to have the hospital's action declared unconstitutional. In allowing the decision of the judge who issued the order to remain in force, the U.S. Court of Appeals for the District of Columbia stood on the point that the matter was moot; Mrs. Jones was out of danger. The dissenters from the decision raised several contentious questions, however, including whether it was appropriate for a single judge to make the determination to authorize the transfusion when matters of such fundamental importance were at stake.*

DISSENTING OPINION BY CIRCUIT JUDGE MILLER. In giving the reasons for my unwillingness to agree to the foregoing order, I think it expedient to begin at the beginning by sketching the story of the circumstances which led to its entry; for, standing alone, it has the appearance of an innocuous routine order.

On September 17, 1963, two attorneys appeared at the chambers of District Judge Edward A. Tamm and tendered the following order, which they requested him to sign:

ORDER

United States District Court for the District of Columbia Civil Division

In re: Application of the President and Directors of Georgetown College, Inc., a Body Corporate

This cause having come on to be heard upon application of The President and Directors of Georgetown College, Inc., a body corporate, owning and operating Georgetown University Hospital, and it being represented by counsel for the applicant that a Mrs. Jesse E. Jones is presently a patient at Georgetown University Hospital and that she is in extremis and it being further represented that the physician in attendance, the chief resident at Georgetown Hospital, Edwin Westura, is of the opinion that blood transfusions are necessary immediately in order to save her life and it being further represented by the applicant that consent to the administration thereof can be obtained neither from the patient nor her husband; it is therefore

ORDERED that the applicant acting through its duly accredited and licensed physicians in attendance may administer such transfusions as are in the opinion of the physicians in attendance necessary to save her life.

Although the proposed order was styled 'Application of The President and Directors of Georgetown College, Inc., a Body Corporate,' there was no such proceeding pending in the District Court; there had been no complaint, petition or formal written application filed. The only 'application' was the oral request of the attorneys that the tendered order be signed and entered. To this day, there is nothing on file in the District Court Clerk's office with reference to this 'application.' Judge Tamm endorsed on the paper the word 'Denied,' which of course meant that he was denying the oral application for the order. It is plain, I think, that at the very least Judge Tamm's denial was based on the fact that there was nothing before him upon which he could act, that the jurisdiction of the District Court had not been properly invoked, and that there was no pending case or controversy.

About 4:00 P.M. on September 17 the same attorneys appeared, unannounced, at the chambers of a judge of this court and requested an immediate review of Judge Tamm's action denying the application for authority to administer a transfusion to a patient at the hospital, said to be in imminent danger of death from loss of blood. They did not file a written petition for review of Judge Tamm's refusal to sign the order but merely orally requested a single judge to take the action which Judge Tamm had just refused to take. The appellate judge spoke by telephone with the hospital's chief resident physician who confirmed the representations made by counsel and thereupon the judge proceeded to the hospital. There he spoke to the husband of the patient who advised that, on religious grounds, he would not approve a blood transfusion for his wife. The judge advised the husband to obtain counsel immediately but, after brief consideration, the husband declined to do so. The judge then called at the patient's room and repeated to her what the doctors had said. Her only reply audible to him was, 'Against my will.'

Then, at 5:20 P.M. on September 17, at Georgetown Hospital, the appellate judge signed the order which Judge Tamm had declined to sign and then signed the following additional order, which was filed by our Clerk the same day:

> The applicant having appeared before me for the issuance of a writ permitting the applicant to administer such transfusions as are in the opinion of the physicians in attendance necessary to save the life of Mrs. Jesse E. Jones and it appearing that on September 17, 1963, the District Court denied such application; and a hearing having been conducted before me at which all the interested parties were present and upon due consideration had thereon, I signed, pursuant to the provisions of Section 1651, Title 28, United States Code, the attached order granting such relief which counsel had presented to the District Court Judge and which had been denied by him, it is therefore
>
> ORDERED that the Clerk of this court is hereby directed to file this memorandum order and attachment.

The blood transfusion was accomplished immediately after the order was signed.

On September 19 the appellate judge filed a memorandum concerning his action, in which he said inter alia:

> . . . It was obvious that the woman was not in a mental condition to make a decision. I was reluctant to press her because of the seriousness of her condition and because I felt that to suggest repeatedly the imminence of death without blood might place a strain on her religious convictions. I asked her whether she would oppose the blood transfusion if the court allowed it. She indicated, as best I could make out, that it would not then be her responsibility. . . .

And on September 20—three days after the transfusion had been accomplished—the hospital filed affidavits by four physicians to the effect that the transfusion had been necessary.

On October 14, 1963, Jessie [spelling per court decision] E. Jones, the patient, filed a petition for a rehearing en banc and for an order vacating and quashing the order of September 17 which authorized the transfusion. The petition states the question presented as follows:

> The question is whether a free adult citizen of the United States can be forced against her will to accept medical treatment to which she objects on both religious and medical grounds. 'This case is of vital importance and rehearing should be granted due to the broad implications of the question presented. The right of free exercise of religion and the right of a free citizen to have his body inviolate are all a part of the rights guaranteed by the Constitution. The problem raised here additionally affects all doctor-patient-hospital relationships throughout the entire country. Thus, while the fact issue may be unusual, the principle is broad and vital and these important qualities make this a case which peculiarly calls for reconsideration by the full Court en banc and the right of a rehearing.

The petition contains extensive arguments in support of the following propositions:

1. Respondent has a constitutionally guaranteed right to the free exercise of her religion, which includes the right to 'abstain from blood.' The order of the Court and the action of the applicant in forcing blood upon her is a violation of her conscience and of the liberty guaranteed by the First Amendment to the Constitution of the United States.
2. Respondent as a free citizen of the United States has been deprived of her liberty by the invasion of her person without due process of law contrary to the Fifth Amendment to the Constitution of the United States.
3. The precedent created here is a threat to so many other persons that judicial substitution of medical discretion for individual discretion should be examined in principle to see where it is leading.
4. Respondent is still subject to the order of the Court dated September 17, 1963. Her liberty continues to be infringed until the order is quashed, and the Court should therefore grant a rehearing.

Such is the petition for rehearing en banc which is being denied without comment by the foregoing order. I presume the reason which actuates the majority is the theory that the order of September 17 is now moot in that the transfusion has been administered and the patient has left the hospital. The petition for rehearing presents a strong argument to the contrary which merits consideration.

I am not now concerned, however, with the substantive questions presented by the petition for rehearing; I am disturbed by the procedural aspects of the situation. In the description of the nature of the proceedings the petition for rehearing says: 'The procedure by which the matter came before this Court is not clear to counsel, but no issue is raised on the point at this time.'

It seems clear to me, however, that the matter did not properly come before this court and that, had it been duly presented on appeal, one judge of this court was not authorized to make a summary disposition of the matter on the merits. . . .

Under Article III, Section 2, of the Constitution of the United States, the judicial power extends only to cases and controversies. Although this Section defines and limits judicial power, it does not prescribe the particular method by which that power may be invoked. . . .

. . . I do not mean to impugn the motives of our colleague who signed these orders. He was impelled, I am sure, by humanitarian impulses and doubtless was himself under considerable strain because of the critical situation in which he had become involved. In the interval of about an hour and twenty minutes between the appearance of the attorneys at his chambers and the signing of the order at the hospital, the judge had no opportunity for research as to the substantive legal problems and procedural questions involved. He should not have been asked to act in these circumstances.

I suggest it is not correct to suppose that, where there is a serious emergency in life, a judge of a district or a circuit court may act to meet it, regardless of whether he is empowered by law to do so. This situation shows the truth of the adage that hard cases make bad law.

COURT OPINION BY CIRCUIT JUDGE BURGER. I believe we should dismiss the petition for rehearing en banc for want of a justiciable controversy, as Judge Danaher does, rather than merely deny it.

This episode presents on the one hand an example of a grave dilemma which confronts those who engage in the healing arts and on the other hand some very basic and fundamental issues on the nature and scope of judicial power. We can sympathize with the one but we cannot safely or appropriately temporize with the other; we have an obligation to deal with the basic question whether any judicially cognizable issue is presented when a legally competent adult refuses, on grounds of conscience, to consent to a medical treatment essential to preserve life. At the outset I would assume that we cannot make a judicial appraisal of justiciability on the basis of any consequences attributable to the order issued in the name of this court. The end, desirable as it obviously developed, cannot establish the existence of a case or controversy if such did not exist independent of the sequel to the enforced medical treatment.

. . . The threshold issue, therefore, is whether the hospital had a right which it was entitled to require the court to enforce. It is not always easy to separate the concepts of standing of a party and justiciability of an issue; the two tend to blend and merge at times. But it would seem beyond challenge that the party seeking relief has the burden of showing affirmatively a legally protected right which is invaded or is about to be invaded by an opposing party.

What, then, is the legally enforceable 'right' of the hospital in this context? We can assume first that a hospital, like a doctor, has certain responsibilities and duties toward a person who, by choice or emergency, comes under its care. No affirmative act of the patient is suggested as invading or threatening any right of the hospital. So we must decide whether an 'invasion' of legal right can be spelled out of a relationship between the patient's refusal to accept a standard medical treatment thought necessary to preserve life and the possible consequences to the hospital if, relying on her refusal of consent, it fails to give a transfusion and death or injury follows. The possible economic impact, apart from the moral implications inherent in its responsibilities, perhaps presented an arguable basis for the hospital's claim of protected economic right. It stood in an unenviable 'Good Samaritan' posture when the patient categorically refused to consent to a blood transfusion called for by a medical emergency. (The existence of an emergency is assumed although there is no record to show when the patient reached the hospital or when an emergency was thought to arise.) The choice between violating the patient's convictions of conscience and accepting her decision was hardly an easy one.

However, since it is not disputed that the patient and her husband volunteered to sign a waiver to relieve the hospital of any liability for the consequences of failure to effect the transfusion, any claim to a protected right in the economic damage sphere would appear unsupported. Can a legally protected right arise out of some other duty-right of the hospital toward a patient, such as a moral obligation to preserve life at all costs? For me it is difficult to construct an actionable or legally protected right out of this relationship. The affirmative enforcement of a right growing out of a possible moral duty of the hospital toward a patient does not seem to meet the standards of justiciability especially when the only remedy is judicial compulsion touching the sensitive area of conscience and religious belief. Because Mrs. Jones could invoke judicial power to enjoin a blood transfusion does not mean, as a corollary, that the hospital has a comparable right to compel it.

"Limitation on 'the judicial Power of the United States' is expressed by the requirement that a litigant must have 'standing to sue' or, more comprehensively, that a federal court may entertain a controversy only if it is 'justiciable.' Both characterizations mean that a court will not decide a question unless the nature of the action challenged, the kind of injury inflicted, and the relationship between the parties are such that judicial determination is consonant with what was, generally speaking, the business of the Colonial courts and the courts of

Westminster when the Constitution was framed." *Joint Anti-Fascist Refugee Committee v. McGrath,* supra, 341 U.S. at 150, 71 S.Ct. at 637 (separate opinion of Frankfurter, J.).

The Standard suggested by Mr. Justice Frankfurter is not archaic or obsolete any more than is the Constitution simply because it is nearly 200 years old. Moreover, Justice Frankfurter did not mean that this concept of justiciability would forever rigidly embalm all remedies and all actions in the mold of 18th century courts. Legal claims concerning atomic energy and the space age may well arise and the standard suggested by Justice Frankfurter is sufficiently malleable to encompass claims and remedies not dreamed of 200 years ago or even a generation ago, provided always they are within the general competence of the courts. What he was pointing to was the appropriateness for judicial treatment, the fitness for adjudication, which in turn depend upon a showing of invasion of a legally protected right.

The breadth of the Frankfurter definition also makes manifest that he was not addressing himself narrowly to the limited nature of federal judicial power as distinguished from that of state courts of general jurisdiction, for the Colonial courts and those of Westminster of the 1780's were courts of general jurisdiction. Rather he was attempting to contrast the proper scope of judicial business with the business of legislatures, executives and sovereigns, see *Pauling v. McNamara,* No. 17797, D.C.Cir., Dec. 23, 1963, and, by inference, those matters which are strictly a private concern and thus beyond reach of all governmental power. We cannot neatly divide all of life's problems and decisions into three compartments and assign one to each of the three great Branches of Government. The cases in which vaccination was compelled for smallpox and other communicable diseases are not in point for such compulsion was enforcement of public health measures under the police power.

Mr. Justice Brandeis, whose views have inspired much of the 'right to be let alone' philosophy, said in *Olmstead v. United States,* 277 U.S. 438, 478, 48 S.Ct. 564, 572 (1928) (dissenting opinion): 'The markers of our Constitution . . . sought to protect Americans in their beliefs, their thoughts, their emotions and their sensations. They conferred, as against the Government, the right to be let alone—the most comprehensive of rights and the right most valued by civilized man.'

Nothing in this utterance suggests that Justice Brandeis thought an individual possessed these rights only as to sensible beliefs, valid thoughts, reasonable emotions, or well-founded sensations. I suggest he intended to include a great many foolish, unreasonable and even absurd ideas which do not conform, such as refusing medical treatment even at great risk.

That judicial power is narrow and limited is a concept deeply embedded in our System. Thus the need for external restraints on the powers of Federal Judges was plainly an important corollary to their constitutionally secured tenure. It was quite as clear in the 1780's as it is today that men are not notorious for exercising self-restraint when they possess both permanent tenure and plenary power. Under our System no single Branch of Government has both, and no single Branch of Government could safely be entrusted with both.

Confronted by a unique episode such as this, it seems to me we must inquire where an assumption of jurisdiction over such matters could lead us. (There is another interesting facet which needs only to be mentioned briefly: the emergent nature of the factual situation confronting the hospital demonstrates that what on its face was 'interlocutory relief' was really the ultimate relief. Once granted, no more remained for any court to consider. Were we to view the claims now as moot, we would have to acknowledge their mootness as soon as the challenged order was acted upon. This was in effect not only a form of instant relief but perhaps also instant mootness. This does not appear to be a situation of preserving a status quo in order to preserve jurisdiction but rather one where the interim relief was the total relief.) Physicians, surgeons and hospitals—and others as well—are often confronted with seemingly irreconcilable demands and conflicting pressures. Philosophers and theologians have pondered these problems and different religious groups have evolved different solutions; the solutions and doctrines of one group are sometimes not acceptable to other groups or sects. Various examples readily come to mind: a crisis in childbirth may require someone to decide whether the life of the mother or the child shall be sacrificed; absent a timely and decisive choice both may die. May the physician or hospital require the courts to decide? A patient may be in a critical condition requiring, in the minds of experts, a certain medical or surgical procedure. If the patient has objections to that treatment based on religious conviction, or if he rejects the medical opinion, are the courts empowered to decide for him?

Some of our greatest jurists have emphasized the need for judicial awareness of the limits on judicial power which is simply an acknowledgement of human fallibility. Cardozo, in *The Nature of the Judicial Process,* said:

> The judge, even when he is free, is still not wholly free. He is not to innovate at pleasure. He is not a knight-errant, roaming at will in pursuit of his own ideal of beauty or of goodness. He is to draw his inspiration from consecrated principles. He is not to yield to spasmodic sentiment, to vague and unregulated benevolence. He is to exercise a discretion informed by tradition, methodized by analogy, disciplined by system, and subordinated to the primordial necessity of order in the social life. Wide enough in all conscience is the field of discretion that remains.

It is at the periphery of the boundaries of power where the guidelines are less clear that an appealing claim presents difficult choices, but this is precisely the area in which restraint is called for in light of the absolute nature of our powers and the finality which often, as here, attends our acts. But we should heed Cardozo's counsel of restraint and reconcile ourselves to the idea that there are myriads of problems and troubles which judges are powerless to solve; and this is as it should be. Some matters of essentially private concern and others of enormous public concern, are beyond the reach of judges. . . .

The Beginning of Life and Parental Rights: *Miller v. Columbia/HCA* (2000)

The case of Miller v. Columbia/HCA *(2000) was a lawsuit pitting the parents of a gravely injured child against the management of the hospital where the child was born. So-called birth-injury cases have become quite common in the United States, in part contributing to rapidly rising insurance rates among American obstetricians. But the parents of the injured child who were suing Columbia/HCA were employing a somewhat novel legal argument. They contended that their daughter, Sidney Miller, was injured just after her birth because of the hospital's policy of resuscitating their extremely premature daughter in spite of their express wish that Sidney not be kept alive. Whereas the Millers had won a very large settlement from the hospital company in 1998, the Texas Court of Appeals in 2000 ruled against*

Sidney's family, deciding that the Millers were not entitled to the damages that had been awarded earlier.

COURT OPINION BY JUDGE EDELMAN. HCA, Inc., HCA–Hospital Corporation of America, Hospital Corporation of America, and Columbia/HCA Healthcare Corporation (collectively "HCA") appeal a judgment entered in favor of Sidney Ainsley Miller ("Sidney"), by and through her next friend, Karla H. Miller, and Karla H. Miller ("Karla") and J. Mark Miller ("Mark"), individually (collectively, the "Millers"). Among other things, HCA contends that a health care provider is not liable in tort for administering urgently needed life-sustaining medical treatment to a newborn infant contrary to the pre-birth instructions of her parents not to do so. After a lengthy struggle with the difficult issues presented, we conclude that HCA is not liable under the facts of this case, reverse the judgment of the trial court, and render a take-nothing judgment.

Although the tragic circumstances of this case are far more numerous, those pertinent to this appeal can be summarized as follows. Early on August 17, 1990, Karla was admitted to Woman's Hospital of Texas (the "hospital") with symptoms of premature labor. An ultrasound revealed that her fetus, weighing approximately 629 grams, had an estimated gestational age of 23 weeks. In addition, Karla was feared to have an infection that could endanger her life. Dr. Jacobs, Karla's attending obstetrician, and Dr. Kelley, a neonatologist, informed the Millers that if the baby were born alive and survived, she would suffer severe impairments. Accordingly, the Millers orally requested that no heroic measures be performed on the baby after her birth. Dr. Kelley recorded the Millers' oral request in the medical records, and Dr. Jacobs informed the nursing staff that no neonatologist would be needed at delivery.

However, after further consultation, Dr. Jacobs concluded that if the Millers' baby was born alive and weighed over 500 grams, the medical staff would be obligated by law and hospital policy to administer life-sustaining procedures even if the Millers did not consent to it. Dr. Jacobs explained this to Mark who verbally reiterated his and Karla's desire that their baby not be resuscitated.

Sidney was born late that night. The attending neonatologist, Dr. Otero, determined that Sidney was viable and instituted resuscitative measures. Although Sidney survived, she suffers, as had been anticipated, from severe physical and mental impairments and will never be able to care for herself.

The Millers filed this lawsuit against HCA, asserting: (1) vicarious liability for the actions of the hospital in: (a) treating Sidney without consent; and (b) having a policy which mandated the resuscitation of newborn infants weighing over 500 grams even in the absence of parental consent; and (2) direct liability for failing to have policies to prevent such treatment without consent. Based on the jury's findings of liability and damages, the trial court entered judgment in favor of the Millers in the amount of $29,400,000 in past and future medical expenses, $13,500,000 in punitive damages, and $17,503,066 in prejudgment interest.

... Although the Millers contend that the resuscitation performed on Sidney itself contributed to her impairment, they do not assert that the liability imposed against HCA was predicated on negligence in the *manner* that the resuscitation was performed but only in that it was performed at all, *i.e.*, without their consent and against their instructions. This is consistent with the fact that although the jury charge based HCA's liability, in part, on an agency relationship between the hospital and Dr. Otero, no question was submitted as to any negligence by Dr. Otero (or any other doctor).

... On the one hand, Texas law expressly gives parents a right to consent to their children's medical care. ... Thus, unless a child's need for life-sustaining medical treatment is too urgent for consent to be obtained from a parent or other person with legal authority (the "emergency exception"), a doctor's treatment of the child without such consent is actionable even if the condition requiring treatment would eventually be life-threatening and the treatment is otherwise provided without negligence. ... Obviously, the logical corollary of a right of consent is a right not to consent, *i.e.*, to refuse medical treatment. *See Cruzan v. Director, Mo. Dep't of Health*, 497 U.S. 261, 270. ... In addition, in Texas, the Advance Directives Act, formerly the Natural Death Act (collectively, the "Act"), allows parents to withhold or withdraw life-sustaining medical treatment from their child where the child's condition has been certified in writing by a physician to be terminal, *i.e.*, incurable or irreversible and such that even providing life-sustaining treatment will only temporarily postpone death. ...

... The liberty interest of parents in the care, custody, and control of their children is also a fundamental right protected by the Due Process Clause of the Fourteenth Amendment to the United States Constitution. *See, e.g., Troxel v. Granville*, 530 U.S. 57 (2000). The Due

Process Clause does not permit a State to infringe on this fundamental right of parents to make childrearing decisions simply because a state judge believes a "better" decision could be made. *See Troxel,* 120 S. Ct. at 2064. *See also Cruzan v. Director, Mo. Dep't of Health,* 497 U.S. 261, 269 (1990) (noting that because every adult of sound mind has a right to determine what will be done with his body, a surgeon who performs an operation without a patient's consent is liable for assault); *Gravis v. Physicians & Surgeons Hosp.,* 427 S.W.2d 310, 311 (Tex. 1968) ("In the absence of exceptional circumstances, . . . a surgeon is subject to liability for assault and battery where he operates without the consent of the patient or the person legally authorized to give such consent").

. . . Depending on the circumstances, a parent's refusal of non-urgently needed or non-life-sustaining medical treatment for their child might legitimately be based, for example, on a desire to seek additional medical opinions on the treatment options or to select a different health care provider to administer the treatment.

. . . Although Texas does so by way of the Act, states are not required to authorize anyone besides the individual patient to exercise that patient's right to refuse life-sustaining medical treatment. *See Cruzan,* 497 U.S. at 286–87. The choice between life and death is obviously a deeply personal decision of overwhelming finality. *See id.* at 281. Sustaining life maintains the status quo (albeit sometimes at tremendous financial and emotional cost). *See id.* at 283. It keeps open the option to act on a change of heart, subsequent advancements in medical treatment, or natural improvement in a patient's medical condition. A decision to withhold life-sustaining medical treatment ends life permanently and irrevocably. The decision whether to do so in a particular case can obviously differ among those who are similarly afflicted, but the decision an infant might have made for herself about consenting to medical treatment under the circumstances cannot be known by others. . . . On the other hand, parents have a legal duty to provide needed medical care to their children. . . . Thus, the failure of a parent to provide such care is a criminal offense when it causes injury or impairment to the child.

. . . The third competing legal and policy interest is that of the state, acting as *parens patriae,* to guard the well-being of minors, even where doing so requires limiting the freedom and authority of parents over their children.

. . . But does a parent have a right to deny urgently needed life-sustaining medical treatment to their child, *i.e.*, to decide, in effect, to let their child die? In Texas, the Legislature has expressly given parents a right to withhold medical treatment, urgently needed or not, for a child whose medical condition is certifiably terminal, but it has not extended that right to the parents of children with non-terminal impairments, deformities, or disabilities, regardless of their severity. In addition, although the Act expressly states that it does not impair or supersede any legal right a person may have to withhold or withdraw life-sustaining treatment in a lawful manner, the parties have cited, and we have found, no other statutory or common law authority allowing urgently needed life-sustaining medical treatment to be withheld from a non-terminally ill child by a parent. To infer that parents have a general common law right to withhold such treatment from a non-terminally ill child would, in effect, mean that the Legislature has afforded greater protection to children who are terminally ill than to those who are not. On the contrary, if anything, the state's interest in preserving life is greatest when life *can* be preserved and then weakens as the prognosis dims. *See Cruzan*, 497 U.S. at 270–71.

. . . More importantly, to infer that parents have a common law right to withhold urgently needed life-sustaining treatment from non-terminally ill children would pose imponderable legal and policy issues. For example, if parents *had* such a right, would it apply to otherwise healthy, normal children or only to those with some degree of abnormality? If the latter, which circumstances would qualify, which would not, and how could any such distinctions be justified legally? . . . In light of the high value our law places on preserving human life, and especially on protecting the life and well-being of minors, we perceive no legal basis or other rationale for concluding that Texas law gives parents a common law right to withhold urgently needed life-sustaining medical treatment from children in circumstances in which the Act does not apply. Moreover, in Texas, a child born alive after a premature birth (or abortion) is entitled to the same rights as are granted by the State to any other child born alive after normal gestation.

Having recognized, as a general rule, that parents have no right to refuse urgently-needed life-sustaining medical treatment to their non-terminally ill children, a compelling argument can be made to carve out an exception for infants born so prematurely and in such poor condition that sustaining their life, even if medically possible, cannot be justified. To whatever extent such an approach would be preferable from a policy standpoint to having no such an exception, and to whatever extent such an approach is available to the Legislature or a higher court, we do not believe it is an alternative available to this court because: (1) a sufficient record does not exist in this case to identify where to "draw the line" for such an exception; and, more importantly, (2) it is not within the province of an intermediate appellate court to, in effect, legislate in that manner.

To the extent a parent's right to refuse urgently-needed life-sustaining medical treatment for their child exists only under the Act, *i.e.*, only where the child's condition is certifiably terminal, it logically follows that this right does not exist and cannot be exercised until a child's condition can be evaluated adequately to determine whether the condition is indeed terminal. Correspondingly, to the extent a child's condition has not been certified as terminal, a health care provider is under no duty to follow a parent's instruction to withhold urgently-needed life-sustaining medical treatment from their child.

In a situation where non-urgently needed or non-life-sustaining medical treatment is proposed for a child, a court order is needed to override a parent's refusal to consent to the treatment because a determination of such issues as the child's safety, welfare, and best interest can vary under differing circumstances and alternatives. By contrast, where life-sustaining medical treatment is urgently needed, time constraints will often not permit resort to the courts. Where the need for such treatment can be anticipated before it becomes acute, the circumstances might allow the parents to remove the child from the health provider's care; and, under existing legal principles, the treatment cannot lawfully be provided without consent before the need for it becomes acute in any event. However, where the need for life-sustaining medical treatment is or becomes urgent while a non-terminally ill child is under a health care provider's care, and where the child's parents refuse consent to that treatment, we do not believe that a court order is necessary to override that refusal because no legal or factual issue exists for a court to decide regarding the provision of such treatment. This is because: (1) a court cannot decide the issue of impairment versus no life at all; and, thus, (2) a court could not conclude that the parents were entitled to withhold the treatment if the child's condition is not terminal.

In this case, the Millers had a right to refuse urgently needed life-sustaining medical treatment for Sidney only to the extent that her condition was certifiably terminal and other requirements of the Act were satisfied. Although there was considerable doubt that Sidney would be born alive at all and that, if and when born alive, she could be kept alive, there is no evidence that her condition before or after birth was (or could have been) certified as terminal. In addition, the record is clear that at the time Sidney was born, her need for life-sustaining procedures was urgent. Following her birth, Sidney's condition proved, with the efforts of her doctors, not to be terminal. Under these circumstances, the Millers had no right to deny the urgently needed life-sustaining medical treatment to Sidney, and no court order was needed to overcome their refusal to consent to it.

Based on the foregoing, we sustain HCA's contentions that it did not owe the Millers a tort duty to: (a) refrain from resuscitating Sidney; (b) have no policy requiring resuscitation of patients like Sidney without consent; and (3) have policies prohibiting resuscitation of patients like Sidney without consent. However, before concluding this opinion, we will briefly discuss a few additional authorities which have been extensively briefed by the parties but which we do not believe bear on the disposition of the controlling issue of duty. . . .

In light of our determination that HCA did not owe the Millers the tort duties upon which liability was predicated in this case, it is not necessary for us to address HCA's remaining issues. Accordingly, the judgment of the trial court is reversed, and judgment is rendered that the Millers take nothing on their claims against HCA.

The Supreme Court Rules on Partial-Birth Abortions, *Stenberg v. Carhart* (2000)

After the decision on abortion in Roe v. Wade *(1973), the abortion controversy deepened in American society. Questions about the morality of legalizing abortions wracked state legislatures and divided the Supreme Court. In the decision of* Planned Parenthood v. Casey *(1992), by a bare majority the Court managed to agree that if states were going to regulate abortions, they could not place an "undue burden" on the woman who sought the procedure. But beyond that basic agreement,* Casey *indicated that the court was badly split on other issues connected to state regulations on abortions.*

In Stenberg v. Carhart, *the court struck down Nebraska's prohibition on one form of late-term abortion, the so-called partial-birth abortion (specifically a procedure called D&X). The list of opinions, concurring opinions, and dissenting opinions in itself conveys a sense of the Supreme Court's deep divisions in* Stenberg v. Carhart. *Justice Breyer delivered the opinion of the Court, in which Justices Stevens, O'Connor, Souter, and Ginsburg joined. Justice Stevens filed a concurring opinion, in which Justice Ginsburg joined. Justice O'Connor filed a concurring opinion. Justice Ginsburg filed a concurring opinion, in which Justice Stevens joined. Chief Justice Rehnquist and Justice Scalia filed dissenting opinions. Justice Kennedy filed a dissenting opinion, in which Chief Justice Rehnquist joined. Justice Thomas filed a dissenting opinion, in which Chief Justice Rehnquist and Justice Scalia joined.*

It was not surprising that the Court should rely on medical testimony (including an amicus curiae *brief from the American College of Obstetricians and Gynecologists, the ACOG), for the Court often had leaned on the opinions of professional medical organizations in abortion cases. The majority of the Court appeared sympathetic to the ACOG's contention that the Nebraska law did not distinguish adequately between the D&X procedure and other abortion methods that were utilized in the second trimester. In addition, medical authorities argued that physicians ought to have the option of employing the D&X because in some circumstances it was safer than other methods for the woman undergoing an abortion.*

Stenberg v. Carhart *was notable for the anger with which the justices spoke to their colleagues. Another of the striking aspects of the decision was the barely disguised distaste with which some of the dissenters characterized Dr. Carhart and, by implication, other practitioners who performed procedures such as the D&X. In addition, the decision was an unusually frank expression of several justices' belief that legislators rather than judges should address this vexing issue.*

COURT OPINION BY JUSTICE BREYER. We again consider the right to an abortion. We understand the controversial nature of the problem. Millions of Americans believe that life begins at conception and consequently that an abortion is akin to causing the death of an innocent child; they recoil at the thought of a law that would permit it. Other millions fear that a law that forbids abortion would condemn many American women to lives that lack dignity, depriving them of equal liberty and leading those with least resources to undergo illegal abortions with the attendant risks of death and suffering. Taking account of these virtually irreconcilable points of view, aware that constitutional law must govern a society whose different members sincerely hold directly opposing views, and considering the matter in light of the Constitution's guarantees of fundamental individual liberty, this Court, in the course of a generation, has determined and then redetermined that the Constitution offers basic protection to the woman's right to choose. *Roe* v. *Wade*, 410 U.S. 113 (1973); *Planned Parenthood of Southeastern Pa.* v. *Casey*, 505 U.S. 833 (1992). We shall not revisit those legal principles. Rather, we apply them to the circumstances of this case.

Three established principles determine the issue before us. We shall set them forth in the language of the joint opinion in *Casey*. First, before "viability . . . the woman has a right to choose to terminate her pregnancy." 505 U.S. at 870.

Second, "a law designed to further the State's interest in fetal life which imposes an undue burden on the woman's decision before fetal viability" is unconstitutional. 505 U.S. at 877. An "undue burden is . . . shorthand for the conclusion that a state regulation has the purpose or effect of placing a substantial obstacle in the path of a woman seeking an abortion of a nonviable fetus." *Ibid.*

Third, "'subsequent to viability, the State in promoting its interest in the potentiality of human life may, if it chooses, regulate, and even proscribe, abortion except where it is necessary, in appropriate medical judgment, for the preservation of the life or health of the mother.'" 505 U.S. at 879 (quoting *Roe* v. *Wade*, 410 U.S. at 164–165).

We apply these principles to a Nebraska law banning "partial birth abortion." The statute reads as follows:

> No partial birth abortion shall be performed in this state, unless such procedure is necessary to save the life of the mother whose life is endangered by a physical disorder, physical illness, or physical injury, including a life-endangering physical condition caused by or arising from the pregnancy itself. Neb. Rev. Stat. Ann. § 28–328(1) (Supp. 1999).

The statute defines "partial birth abortion" as: "an abortion procedure in which the person performing the abortion partially delivers vaginally a living unborn child before killing the unborn child and completing the delivery." § 28–326(9). It further defines "partially delivers vaginally a living unborn child before killing the unborn child" to mean "deliberately and intentionally delivering into the vagina a living unborn child, or a substantial portion thereof, for the purpose of performing a procedure that the person performing such procedure knows will kill the unborn child and does kill the unborn child." *Ibid.*

The law classifies violation of the statute as a "Class III felony" carrying a prison term of up to 20 years, and a fine of up to $25,000. §§ 28–328(2), 28–105. It also provides for the automatic revocation of a doctor's license to practice medicine in Nebraska. § 28–328(4).

We hold that this statute violates the Constitution.

Dr. Leroy Carhart is a Nebraska physician who performs abortions in a clinical setting. He brought this lawsuit in Federal District Court seeking a declaration that the Nebraska statute violates the Federal Constitution, and asking for an injunction forbidding its enforcement. After a trial on the merits, during which both sides presented several expert witnesses, the District Court held the statute unconstitutional. 11 F. Supp. 2d 1099 (Neb. 1998). On appeal, the Eighth Circuit affirmed. 192 F.3d 1142 (1999). . . . We granted certiorari to consider the matter.

Because Nebraska law seeks to ban one method of aborting a pregnancy, we must describe and then discuss several different abortion procedures. Considering the fact that those procedures seek to terminate a potential human life, our discussion may seem clinically cold or callous to some, perhaps horrifying to others. There is no alternative way, however, to acquaint the reader with the technical distinctions among different abortion methods and related factual matters, upon which the outcome of this case depends. For that reason, drawing upon the findings of the trial court, underlying testimony, and related medical texts, we shall describe the relevant methods of performing abortions in technical detail. . . .

The question before us is whether Nebraska's statute, making criminal the performance of a "partial birth abortion," violates the Federal Constitution, as interpreted in *Planned Parenthood of Southeastern Pa.* v. *Casey* . . . and *Roe* v. *Wade*. . . . We conclude that it does for at least two independent reasons. First, the law lacks any exception "'for the preservation of the . . . health of the mother.'" *Casey,* 505 U.S. at 879. . . . Second, it "imposes an undue burden on a woman's ability" to choose a D&E abortion, thereby unduly burdening the right to choose abortion itself. 505 U.S. at 874. We shall discuss each of these reasons in turn.

. . . The fact that Nebraska's law applies both pre- and postviability aggravates the constitutional problem presented. The State's interest in regulating abortion previability is considerably weaker than postviability. . . . Since the law requires a health exception in order to validate even a postviability abortion regulation, it at a minimum requires the same in respect to previability regulation. . . .

. . . The quoted standard also depends on the state regulations "promoting [the State's] [bracketed in original] interest in the potentiality of human life." The Nebraska law, of course, does not directly further an interest "in the potentiality of human life" by saving the fetus in question from destruction, as it regulates only a *method* of performing abortion. Nebraska describes its interests differently. It says the law "'shows concern for the life of the unborn,'" "prevents cruelty to partially born children," and "preserves the integrity of the medical profession." Brief for Petitioners 48. But we cannot see how the interest-related differences could make any difference to the question at hand, namely, the application of the "health" requirement.

Consequently, the governing standard requires an exception "where it is necessary, in appropriate medical judgment for the preservation of the life or health of the mother," *Casey, supra,* at 879, for this Court has made clear that a State may promote but not endanger a woman's health when it regulates the methods of abortion.

. . . Nebraska responds that the law does not require a health exception unless there is a need for such an exception. And here there is no such need, it says. It argues that "safe alternatives remain available" and "a ban on partial-birth abortion/D&X would create no risk to the health of women." Brief for Petitioners 29, 40. The problem for Nebraska is that the parties strongly contested this factual question in the trial court below; and the findings and evidence support Dr. Carhart. The State fails to demonstrate that banning D&X without a health exception may not create significant health risks for women, because the record shows that significant medical authority supports the proposition that in some circumstances, D&X would be the safest procedure.

We shall reiterate in summary form the relevant findings and evidence. On the basis of medical testimony the District Court concluded that "Carhart's D&X procedure is . . . safer than the D&E and other abortion procedures used during the relevant gestational period in the 10 to 20 cases a year that present to Dr. Carhart." 11 F. Supp. 2d at 1126. It found that the D&X procedure permits the fetus to pass through the cervix with a minimum of instrumentation. *Ibid.* It thereby "reduces operating time, blood loss and risk of infection; reduces complications from bony fragments; reduces instrument-inflicted damage to the uterus and cervix; prevents the most common causes of maternal mortality (DIC and amniotic fluid embolus); and eliminates the possibility of 'horrible complications' arising from retained fetal parts." *Ibid.*

The District Court also noted that a select panel of the American College of Obstetricians and Gynecologists concluded that D&X "'may be the best or most appropriate procedure in a particular circumstance to save the life or preserve the health of a woman'" [italics in original] 11 F. Supp. 2d at 1105, n. 10 (quoting ACOG Statement, App. 600–601) (but see an important qualification, *infra,* at 14)....

Nebraska, along with supporting *amici,* replies that these findings are irrelevant, wrong, or applicable only in a tiny number of instances. It says (1) that the D&X procedure is "little-used," (2) by only "a handful of doctors." Brief for Petitioners 32. It argues (3) that D&E and labor induction are at all times "safe alternative procedures." *Id.* at 36. It refers to the testimony of petitioners' medical expert, who testified (4) that the ban would not increase a woman's risk of several rare abortion complications (disseminated intravascular coagulopathy and amniotic fluid embolus), *id.* at 37; App. 642–644.

The Association of American Physicians and Surgeons et al., *amici* supporting Nebraska, argue (5) that elements of the D&X procedure may create special risks, including cervical incompetence caused by overdilitation, injury caused by conversion of the fetal presentation, and dangers arising from the "blind" use of instrumentation to pierce the fetal skull while lodged in the birth canal. See Brief for Association of American Physicians and Surgeons et al. as *Amici Curiae* 21–23....

Nebraska further emphasizes (6) that there are no medical studies "establishing the safety of the partial-birth abortion/D&X procedure," Brief for Petitioners 39, and "no medical studies comparing the safety of partial-birth abortion/D&X to other abortion procedures," *ibid.* It points to, *id.* at 35, (7) an American Medical Association policy statement that "'there does not appear to be any identified situation in which intact D&X is the only appropriate procedure to induce abortion,'" Late Term Pregnancy Termination Techniques, AMA Policy H-5.982 (1997). And it points out (8) that the American College of Obstetricians and Gynecologists qualified its statement that D&X "may be the best or most appropriate procedure," by adding that the panel "could identify no circumstances under which [the D&X] procedure . . . would be the only option to save the life or preserve the health of the woman." [bracketed in original] App. 600–601.

We find these eight arguments insufficient to demonstrate that Nebraska's law needs no health exception. For one thing, certain of the arguments are beside the point. The D&X procedure's relative rarity (argument [1]) is not highly relevant. The D&X is an infrequently used abortion procedure; but the health exception question is whether protecting women's health requires an exception for those infrequent occasions. A rarely used treatment might be necessary to treat a rarely occurring disease that could strike anyone—the State cannot prohibit a person from obtaining treatment simply by pointing out that most people do not need it. Nor can we know whether the fact that only a "handful" of doctors use the procedure (argument [2]) reflects the comparative rarity of late second term abortions, the procedure's recent development, . . . the controversy surrounding it, or, as Nebraska suggests, the procedure's lack of utility.

For another thing, the record responds to Nebraska's (and *amici*'s) medically based arguments. In respect to argument (3), for example, the District Court agreed that alternatives, such as D&E and induced labor, are "safe" but found that the D&X method was significantly *safer* in certain circumstances. . . . In respect to argument (4), the District Court simply relied on different expert testimony—testimony stating that "'another advantage of the Intact D&E is that it eliminates the risk of embolism of cerebral tissue into the woman's blood stream.'" 11 F. Supp. 2d at 1124. . . .

In response to *amici*'s argument (5), the American College of Obstetricians and Gynecologists, in its own *amici* brief, denies that D&X generally poses risks greater than the alternatives. It says that the suggested alternative procedures involve similar or greater risks of cervical and uterine injury, for "D&E procedures, involve similar amounts of dilitation" and "of course childbirth involves even greater cervical dilitation." Brief for American College of Obstetricians and Gynecologists et al. as *Amici Curiae* 23. The College points out that Dr. Carhart does not reposition the fetus thereby avoiding any risks stemming from conversion to breech presentation, and that, as compared with D&X, D&E involves the same, if not greater, "blind" use of sharp instruments in the uterine cavity. *Id.* at 23–24.

We do not quarrel with Nebraska's argument (6), for Nebraska is right. There are no general medical studies documenting comparative safety. Neither do we deny the import of the American Medical Association's statement (argument [7])—even though the State does omit the remainder of that statement: "The AMA recommends that the procedure not be used *unless alternative procedures pose materially greater risk to the woman.*" Late Term Pregnancy Termination Techniques, AMA Policy H-5.982 (emphasis added).

We cannot, however, read the American College of Obstetricians and Gynecologists panel's qualification (that it could not "identify" a circumstance where D&X was the "only" life- or health-preserving option) as if, according to Nebraska's argument (8), it denied the potential health-related need for D&X. . . .

The word "necessary" in *Casey*'s phrase "necessary, in appropriate medical judgment, for the preservation of the life or health of the mother" (505 U.S. at 879), . . . cannot refer to an absolute necessity or to absolute proof. Medical treatments and procedures are often considered appropriate (or inappropriate) in light of estimated comparative health risks (and health benefits) in particular cases. Neither can that phrase require unanimity of medical opinion. Doctors often differ in their estimation of comparative health risks and appropriate treatment. And *Casey*'s words "appropriate medical judgment" must embody the judicial need to tolerate responsible differences of medical opinion—differences of a sort that the American Medical Association and American College of Obstetricians and Gynecologists' statements together indicate are present here.

For another thing, the division of medical opinion about the matter at most means uncertainty, a factor that signals the presence of risk, not its absence. That division here involves highly qualified knowledgeable experts on both sides of the issue. Where a significant body of medical opinion believes a procedure may bring with it greater safety for some patients and explains the medical reasons supporting that view, we cannot say that the presence of a different view by itself proves the contrary. Rather, the uncertainty means a significant likelihood that those who believe that D&X is a safer abortion method in certain circumstances may turn out to be right. If so, then the absence of a health exception will place women at an unnecessary risk of tragic health consequences. If they are wrong, the exception will simply turn out to have been unnecessary.

In sum, Nebraska has not convinced us that a health exception is "never necessary to preserve the health of women." . . . Rather, a statute that altogether forbids D&X creates a significant health risk.

The statute consequently must contain a health exception. . . . By no means must a State grant physicians "unfettered discretion" in their selection of abortion methods. But where substantial medical authority supports the proposition that banning a particular abortion procedure could endanger women's health, *Casey* requires the statute to include a health exception when the procedure is "'necessary, in appropriate medical judgment, for the preservation of the life or health of the mother.'" 505 U.S. at 879. Requiring such an exception in this case is no departure from *Casey,* but simply a straightforward application of its holding.

. . . [Using] this law some present prosecutors and future Attorneys General may choose to pursue physicians who use D&E procedures, the most commonly used method for performing previability second trimester abortions. All those who perform abortion procedures using that method must fear prosecution, conviction, and imprisonment. The result is an undue burden upon a woman's right to make an abortion decision. We must consequently find the statute unconstitutional.

The judgment of the Court of Appeals is *Affirmed.*

DISSENTING OPINION BY JUSTICE SCALIA. I am optimistic enough to believe that, one day, *Stenberg* v. *Carhart* will be assigned its rightful place in the history of this Court's jurisprudence beside *Korematsu* and *Dred Scott.* The method of killing a human child—one cannot even accurately say an entirely unborn human child—proscribed by this statute is so horrible that the most clinical description of it evokes a shudder of revulsion. And the Court must know (as most state legislatures banning this procedure have concluded) that demanding a "health exception"—which requires the abortionist to assure himself that, in his expert medical judgment, this method is, in the case at hand, marginally safer than others (how can one prove the contrary beyond a reasonable doubt?)—is to give live-birth abortion free rein. The notion that the Constitution of the United States, designed, among other things, "to establish Justice, insure domestic Tranquility, . . . and secure the Blessings of Liberty to ourselves and our Posterity," prohibits the States from simply banning this visibly brutal means of eliminating our half-born posterity is quite simply absurd. . . .

. . . As long as we are debating this issue of necessity for a health-of-the-mother exception on the basis of *Casey,* it is really quite impossible for us dissenters to contend that the majority is *wrong* on the law—any more than it could be said that one is *wrong in law* to support or oppose the death penalty, or to support or oppose mandatory minimum sentences. The most that we can honestly say is that we disagree with the majority on their policy-judgment-couched-as-law. And those who believe that a 5-to-4 vote on a policy matter by unelected lawyers should not overcome the judgment of 30 state legislatures have a problem, not with the *application* of *Casey,* but with its *existence. Casey* must be overruled.

While I am in an I-told-you-so mood, I must recall my bemusement, in *Casey,* at the joint opinion's expressed belief that *Roe* v. *Wade* had "called the contending sides of a national controversy to end their national division by accepting a common mandate rooted in the Constitution," *Casey,* 505 U.S. at 867, and that the decision in *Casey* would ratify that happy truce. It seemed to me, quite to the contrary, that "*Roe* fanned into life an issue that has inflamed our national politics in general, and has obscured with its smoke the selection of Justices to this Court in particular, ever since"; and that, "by keeping us in the abortion-umpiring business, it is the perpetuation of that disruption, rather than of any *Pax Roeana,* that the Court's new majority decrees." 505 U.S. at 995–996. Today's decision, that the Constitution of the United States prevents the prohibition of a horrible mode of abortion, will be greeted by a firestorm of criticism—as well it should. I cannot understand why those who *acknowledge* that, in the opening words of Justice O'Connor's concurrence, "the issue of abortion is one of the most contentious and controversial in contemporary American society," *ante* at 1, persist in the belief that this Court, armed with neither constitutional text nor accepted tradition, can resolve that contention and controversy rather than be consumed by it. If only for the sake of its own preservation, the Court should return this matter to the people—where the Constitution, by its silence on the subject, left it—and let *them* decide, State by State, whether this practice should be allowed. *Casey* must be overruled.

DISSENTING OPINION BY JUSTICE KENNEDY, JOINED BY CHIEF JUSTICE REHNQUIST. For close to two decades after *Roe* v. *Wade,* the Court gave but slight weight to the interests of the separate States when their legislatures sought to address persisting concerns raised by the existence of a woman's right to elect an abortion in defined circumstances. When the Court reaffirmed the essential holding of *Roe,* a central premise was that the States retain a critical and legitimate role in legislating on the subject of abortion, as limited by the woman's right the Court restated and again guaranteed. . . . The political processes of the State are not to be foreclosed from enacting laws to promote the life of the unborn and to ensure respect for all human life and its potential. . . . The State's constitutional authority is a vital means for citizens to address these grave and serious issues, as they must if we are to progress in knowledge and understanding and in the attainment of some degree of consensus.

The Court's decision today, in my submission, repudiates this understanding by invalidating a statute advancing critical state interests, even though the law denies no woman the right to choose an abortion and places no undue burden upon the right. The legislation is well within the State's competence to enact. Having concluded Nebraska's law survives the scrutiny dictated by a proper understanding of *Casey,* I dissent from the judgment invalidating it.

The Court's failure to accord any weight to Nebraska's interest in prohibiting partial-birth abortion is erroneous and undermines its discussion and holding. The Court's approach in this regard is revealed by its description of the abortion methods at issue, which the Court is correct to describe as "clinically cold or callous." *Ante,* at 3–4. The majority views the procedures from the perspective of the abortionist, rather than from the perspective of a society shocked when confronted with a new method of ending human life. Words invoked by the majority, such as "transcervical procedures," "osmotic dilators," "instrumental disarticulation," and "paracervical block," may be accurate and are to some extent necessary, *ante,* at 5–6; but for citizens who seek to know why laws on this subject have been enacted across the Nation, the words are insufficient. Repeated references to sources understandable only to a trained physician may obscure matters for persons not trained in medical terminology. Thus it seems necessary at the outset to set forth what may happen during an abortion.

The person challenging Nebraska's law is Dr. Leroy Carhart, a physician who received his medical degree from Hahnemann Hospital and University in 1973. . . . Dr. Carhart performs the procedures in a clinic in Nebraska, . . . and will also travel to Ohio to perform abortions there. . . . Dr. Carhart has no specialty certifications in a field related to childbirth or abortion and lacks admitting privileges at any hospital. . . . He performs abortions throughout pregnancy, including when he is unsure whether the fetus is viable. . . . In contrast to the physicians who provided expert testimony in this case (who are board certified instructors at leading medical education institutions and members of the American Board of Obstetricians and Gynecologists), Dr. Carhart performs the partial-birth abortion procedure (D&X) that Nebraska seeks to ban. He also performs the other method of abortion at issue in the case, the D&E.

As described by Dr. Carhart, the D&E procedure requires the abortionist to use instruments to grasp a portion (such as a foot or hand) of a developed and living fetus and drag the grasped portion out of the uterus into the vagina. Dr. Carhart uses the traction created by the opening between the uterus and vagina to dismember the fetus, tearing the grasped portion away from the remainder of the body. *Ibid.* The traction between the uterus and vagina is essential to the procedure because attempting to abort a fetus without using that traction is described by Dr. Carhart as "pulling the cat's tail" or "dragging a string across the floor, you'll just keep dragging it. It's not until something grabs the other end that you are going to develop traction." *Id.* at 62. The fetus, in many cases, dies just as a human adult or child would: It bleeds to death as it is torn limb from limb. . . . The fetus can be alive at the beginning of the dismemberment process and can survive for a time while its limbs are being torn off. Dr. Carhart agreed that "when you pull out a piece of the fetus, let's say, an arm or a leg and remove that, at the time just prior to removal of the portion of the fetus, . . . the fetus [is] alive" [bracketed in original]. *Id.* at 62. Dr. Carhart has observed fetal heartbeat via ultrasound with "extensive parts of the fetus removed," *id.* at 64, and testified that mere dismemberment of a limb does not always cause death because he knows of a physician who removed the arm of a fetus only to have the fetus go on to be born "as a living child with one arm." *Id.* at 63. At the conclusion of a D&E abortion no intact fetus remains. In Dr. Carhart's words, the abortionist is left with "a tray full of pieces." *Id.* at 125.

The other procedure implicated today is called "partial-birth abortion" or the D&X. The D&X can be used, as a general matter, after 19 weeks gestation because the fetus has become so developed that it may survive intact partial delivery from the uterus into the vagina. *Id.* at 61. In the D&X, the abortionist initiates the woman's natural delivery process by causing the cervix of the woman to be dilated, sometimes over a sequence of days. *Id.* at 492. The fetus' arms and legs are delivered outside the uterus while the fetus is alive; witnesses to the procedure report seeing the body of the fetus moving outside the woman's body. Brief for Petitioners 4. At this point, the abortion procedure has the appearance of a live birth. As stated by one group of physicians, "as the physician manually performs breech extraction of the body of a live fetus, excepting the head, she continues in the apparent role of an obstetrician delivering a child." Brief for Association of American Physicians and Surgeons et al. as *Amici Curiae* 27. With only the head of the fetus remaining in utero, the abortionist tears open the skull. According to Dr. Martin Haskell, a leading proponent of the procedure, the appropriate instrument to be used at this stage of the abortion is a pair of scissors. . . . Witnesses report observing the portion of the fetus outside the woman react to the skull penetration. . . . The abortionist then inserts a suction tube and vacuums out the developing brain and other matter found within the skull. The process of making the size of the fetus' head smaller is given the clinically neutral term "reduction procedure." . . . Brain death does not occur until after the skull invasion, and, according to Dr. Carhart, the heart of the fetus may continue to beat for minutes after the contents of the skull are vacuumed out. . . . The abortionist next completes the delivery of a dead fetus, intact except for the damage to the head and the missing contents of the skull.

Casey is premised on the States having an important constitutional role in defining their interests in the abortion debate. It is only with this principle in mind that Nebraska's interests can be given proper weight. The State's brief describes its interests as including concern for the life of the unborn and "for the partially-born," in preserving the integrity of the medical profession, and in "erecting a barrier to infanticide." Brief for Petitioners 48–49. A review of *Casey* demonstrates the legitimacy of these policies. The Court should say so.

States may take sides in the abortion debate and come down on the side of life, even life in the unborn. . . .

States also have an interest in forbidding medical procedures which, in the State's reasonable determination, might cause the medical profession or society as a whole to become insensitive, even disdainful, to life, including life in the human fetus. Abortion, *Casey* held, has consequences beyond the woman and her fetus. The States' interests in regulating are of concomitant extension. *Casey* recognized that abortion is, "fraught with consequences for . . . the persons who perform and assist in the procedure [and for] society which must confront the knowledge that these procedures exist, procedures some deem nothing short of an act of violence against innocent human life" 505 U.S. at 852.

A State may take measures to ensure the medical profession and its members are viewed as healers, sustained by a compassionate and rigorous ethic and cognizant of the dignity and value of human life, even life which cannot survive without the assistance of others. *Ibid.; Washington* v. *Glucksberg,* 521 U.S. 702 (1997).

... The issue is not whether members of the judiciary can see a difference between the two procedures. It is whether Nebraska can.

... The Court fails to acknowledge substantial authority allowing the State to take sides in a medical debate, even when fundamental liberty interests are at stake and even when leading members of the profession disagree with the conclusions drawn by the legislature ... disagreements among medical professionals "do not tie the State's hands in setting the bounds of ... laws. In fact, it is precisely where such disagreement exists that legislatures have been afforded the widest latitude." 521 U.S. at 360, n. 3. Instead, courts must exercise caution (rather than require deference to the physician's treatment decision) when medical uncertainty is present. *Ibid.* ("When a legislature 'undertakes to act in areas fraught with medical and scientific uncertainties, legislative options must be especially broad and courts should be cautious not to rewrite legislation'") (quoting *Jones* v. *United States,* 463 U.S. 354 [1983]).

... Instructive is *Jacobson* v. *Massachusetts,* 197 U.S. 11 (1905), where the defendant was convicted because he refused to undergo a smallpox vaccination. The defendant claimed the mandatory vaccination violated his liberty to "care for his own body and health in such way as to him seems best." 197 U.S. at 26. He offered to prove that members of the medical profession took the position that the vaccination was of no value and, in fact, was harmful. 197 U.S. at 30. The Court rejected the claim, establishing beyond doubt the right of the legislature to resolve matters upon which physicians disagreed:

> Those offers [of proof by the defendant] in the main seem to have had no purpose except to state the general theory of those of the medical profession who attach little or no value to vaccination as a means of preventing the spread of smallpox, or who think that vaccination causes other diseases of the body. What everybody knows the court must know, and therefore the state court judicially knew, as this court knows, that an opposite theory accords with the common belief, and is maintained by high medical authority. We must assume that, when the statute in question was passed, the legislature of Massachusetts was not unaware of these opposing theories, and was compelled, of necessity, to choose be-

> tween them. It was not compelled to commit a matter involving the public health and safety to the final decision of a court or jury. It is no part of the function of a court or a jury to determine which one of two modes was likely to be the most effective for the protection of the public against disease. That was for the legislative department to determine in the light of all the information it had or could obtain. It could not properly abdicate its function to guard the public health and safety. *Ibid.* [bracketed in original]

The *Jacobson* Court quoted with approval a recent state-court decision which observed, in words having full application today:

> The fact that the belief is not universal [in the medical community] is not controlling, for there is scarcely any belief that is accepted by everyone. The possibility that the belief may be wrong, and that science may yet show it to be wrong, is not conclusive; for the legislature has the right to pass laws which, according to common belief of the people, are adapted to [address medical matters]. "In a free country, where government is by the people, through their chosen representatives, practical legislation admits of no other standard of action." *Id.* at 35 (quoting *Viemeister* v. *White*, 179 N.Y. 235, 241 [1904]). [bracketed in original]

Justice O'Connor assures the people of Nebraska they are free to redraft the law to include an exception permitting the D&X to be performed when "the procedure, in appropriate medical judgment, is necessary to preserve the health of the mother." *Ante*, at 5. The assurance is meaningless. She has joined an opinion which accepts that Dr. Carhart exercises "appropriate medical judgment" in using the D&X for every patient in every procedure, regardless of indications, after 15 weeks' gestation. *Ante*, at 18–19 (requiring any health exception to "tolerate responsible differences of medical opinion" which "are present here"). A ban which depends on the "appropriate medical judgment" of Dr. Carhart is no ban at all. He will be unaffected by any new legislation. This, of course, is the vice of a health exception resting in the physician's discretion.

. . . Ignoring substantial medical and ethical opinion, the Court substitutes its own judgment for the judgment of Nebraska and some 30 other States and sweeps the law away. The Court's holding stems from misunderstanding the record, misinterpretation of *Casey*, outright refusal to respect the law of a State, and statutory construction in conflict with settled rules. The decision nullifies a law expressing the will of the people of Nebraska that medical procedures must be governed by moral principles having their foundation in the intrinsic value of human life, including life of the unborn. Through their law the people of Nebraska were forthright in confronting an issue of immense moral consequence. The State chose to forbid a procedure many decent and civilized people find so abhorrent as to be among the most serious of crimes against human life, while the State still protected the woman's autonomous right of choice as reaffirmed in *Casey.* The Court closes its eyes to these profound concerns.

From the decision, the reasoning, and the judgment, I dissent.

The *Baby M* Case, Artificial Reproduction, and Family Law (1988)

When Mary Beth Whitehead gave birth to a baby girl in March 1986, she formed an immediate attachment to the child. For many mothers, that would have been a positive development. To Mrs. Whitehead, it presented a terrible dilemma. The child had been conceived through artificial reproductive technology. Prior to being inseminated with the sperm of a man who was not her husband, Whitehead had signed a surrogacy agreement to surrender the baby to its biological father, William Stern. In return for her conceiving, carrying, and then giving up the child, Mrs. Whitehead was paid $10,000. When Whitehead decided that she could not relinquish the baby to Stern, he and his wife Betsy were terribly disappointed. Long wishing to bear a child of their own, they had been frustrated by Betsy Stern's poor health. Until the actual birth of the baby, the surrogacy contract had seemed the answer to the Sterns' childlessness as well as Mrs. Whitehead's economic difficulties.

The Baby M *case drew a great deal of attention as it was being argued in New Jersey courts. Not only was the controversy surrounding custody of "Baby M" of interest to the families involved. It figured in the ideologies and agendas of organizations such as the American Adoption Congress, the Catholic League for Religious and Civil Rights, Concerned United Birthparents, the Eagle Forum, the National Center on Women and Family Law, a feminist group including Betty Friedan and Gloria Steinem, and RESOLVE (a support group for persons facing infertility issues), which all submitted briefs. Faced with a Solomon-like decision as to how the child should be apportioned between two sets of claimants, the court indicated that it was in the child's best interests to spend some time with both biological parents. Although the biological father, William Stern, was to have primary custody, the child's biological mother (surrogate parent Mary Beth Whitehead) was promised a hearing in a lower court, to determine Whitehead's access to the child through visitation.*

The case immediately made commercial surrogacy agreements in New Jersey illegal; soon other states followed. In future, surrogacy agreements had to have much different provisions than the contract signed by Mary Beth Whitehead and William Stern. Not only were the agreements required to be noncommercial in nature (money could not be paid for the baby, but only for expenses such as medical fees); they had to include provisions so that the biological mother could change her mind about keeping her child.

COURT OPINION BY CHIEF JUSTICE WILENTZ. In this matter the Court is asked to determine the validity of a contract that purports to provide a new way of bringing children into a family. For a fee of $10,000, a woman agrees to be artificially inseminated with the semen of another woman's husband; she is to conceive a child, carry it to term, and after its birth surrender it to the natural father and his wife. The intent of the contract is that the child's natural mother will thereafter be forever separated from her child. The wife is to adopt the child, and she and the natural father are to be regarded as its parents for all purposes. The contract providing for this is called a "surrogacy contract," the natural mother inappropriately called the "surrogate mother."

We invalidate the surrogacy contract because it conflicts with the law and public policy of this State. While we recognize the depth of the yearning of infertile couples to have their own children, we find the payment of money to a "surrogate" mother illegal, perhaps criminal, and potentially degrading to women. Although in this case we grant custody to the natural father, the evidence having clearly proved such custody to be in the best interests of the infant, we void both the termination of the surrogate mother's parental rights and the adoption of the child by the wife/stepparent. We thus restore the "surrogate" as the mother of the child. We remand the issue of the natural mother's visitation rights to the trial court, since that issue was not reached below and the record before us is not sufficient to permit us to decide it *de novo.*

We find no offense to our present laws where a woman voluntarily and without payment agrees to act as a "surrogate" mother, provided that she is not subject to a binding agreement to surrender her child. Moreover, our holding today does not preclude the Legislature from altering the current statutory scheme, within constitutional limits, so as to permit surrogacy contracts. Under current law, however, the surrogacy agreement before us is illegal and invalid.

. . . In February 1985, William Stern and Mary Beth Whitehead entered into a surrogacy contract. It recited that Stern's wife, Elizabeth, was infertile, that they wanted a child, and that Mrs. Whitehead was willing to provide that child as the mother with Mr. Stern as the father.

The contract provided that through artificial insemination using Mr. Stern's sperm, Mrs. Whitehead would become pregnant, carry the child to term, bear it, deliver it to the Sterns, and thereafter do whatever was necessary to terminate her maternal rights so that Mrs. Stern could thereafter adopt the child. Mrs. Whitehead's husband, Richard . . . was also a party to the contract; Mrs. Stern was not. Mr. Whitehead promised to do all acts necessary to rebut the presumption of paternity under the Parentage Act. *N.J.S.A.* 9:17–43a(1), –44a. Although Mrs. Stern was not a party to the surrogacy agreement, the contract gave her sole custody of the child in the event of Mr. Stern's death. Mrs. Stern's status as a nonparty to the surrogate parenting agreement presumably was to avoid the application of the baby-selling statute to this arrangement. *N.J.S.A.* 9:3–54.

Mr. Stern, on his part, agreed to attempt the artificial insemination and to pay Mrs. Whitehead $10,000 after the child's birth, on its delivery to him. In a separate contract, Mr. Stern agreed to pay $7,500 to the Infertility Center of New York ("ICNY"). The Center's advertising campaigns solicit surrogate mothers and encourage infertile couples to consider surrogacy. ICNY arranged for the surrogacy contract by bringing the parties together, explaining the process to them, furnishing the contractual form . . . and providing legal counsel.

The history of the parties' involvement in this arrangement suggests their good faith. William and Elizabeth Stern were married in July 1974, having met at the University of Michigan, where both were Ph.D. candidates. Due to financial considerations and Mrs. Stern's pursuit of a medical degree and residency, they decided to defer starting a family until 1981. Before then, however, Mrs. Stern learned that she might have multiple sclerosis and that the disease in some cases renders pregnancy a serious health risk. Her anxiety appears to have exceeded the actual risk, which current medical authorities assess as minimal. Nonetheless that anxiety was evidently quite real, Mrs. Stern fearing that pregnancy might precipitate blindness, paraplegia, or other forms of debilitation. Based on the perceived risk, the Sterns decided to forego having their own children. The decision had special significance for Mr. Stern. Most of his family had been destroyed in the Holocaust. As the family's only survivor, he very much wanted to continue his bloodline.

Initially the Sterns considered adoption, but were discouraged by the substantial delay apparently involved and by the potential problem they saw arising from their age and their differing religious backgrounds. They were most eager for some other means to start a family.

The paths of Mrs. Whitehead and the Sterns to surrogacy were similar. Both responded to advertising by ICNY. The Sterns' response, following their inquiries into adoption, was the result of their longstanding decision to have a child. Mrs. Whitehead's response apparently resulted from her sympathy with family members and others who could have no children (she stated that she wanted to give another couple the "gift of life"); she also wanted the $10,000 to help her family.

Both parties, undoubtedly because of their own self-interest, were less sensitive to the implications of the transaction than they might otherwise have been. Mrs. Whitehead, for instance, appears not to have been concerned about whether the Sterns would make good parents for her child; the Sterns, on their part, while conscious of the obvious possibility that surrendering the child might cause grief to Mrs. Whitehead, overcame their qualms because of their desire for a child. At any rate, both the Sterns and Mrs. Whitehead were committed to the arrangement; both thought it right and constructive.

Mrs. Whitehead had reached her decision concerning surrogacy before the Sterns, and had actually been involved as a potential surrogate mother with another couple. After numerous unsuccessful artificial inseminations, that effort was abandoned. Thereafter, the Sterns learned of the Infertility Center, the possibilities of surrogacy, and of Mary Beth Whitehead. The two couples met to discuss the surrogacy arrangement and decided to go forward. On February 6, 1985, Mr. Stern and Mr. and Mrs. Whitehead executed the surrogate parenting agreement. After several artificial inseminations over a period of months, Mrs. Whitehead became pregnant. The pregnancy was uneventful and on March 27, 1986, Baby M was born.

Not wishing anyone at the hospital to be aware of the surrogacy arrangement, Mr. and Mrs. Whitehead appeared to all as the proud parents of a healthy female child. Her birth certificate indicated her name to be Sara Elizabeth Whitehead and her father to be Richard Whitehead. In accordance with Mrs. Whitehead's request, the Sterns visited the hospital unobtrusively to see the newborn child.

Mrs. Whitehead realized, almost from the moment of birth, that she could not part with this child. She had felt a bond with it even during pregnancy. Some indication of the attachment was conveyed to the Sterns at the hospital when they told Mrs. Whitehead what they were going to name the baby. She apparently broke into tears and indicated that she did not know if she could give up the child. She talked about how the baby looked like her other daughter, and made it clear that she was experiencing great difficulty with the decision.

Nonetheless, Mrs. Whitehead was, for the moment, true to her word. Despite powerful inclinations to the contrary, she turned her child over to the Sterns on March 30 at the Whiteheads' home.

The Sterns were thrilled with their new child. They had planned extensively for its arrival, far beyond the practical furnishing of a room for her. It was a time of joyful celebration—not just for them but for their friends as well. The Sterns looked forward to raising their daughter, whom they named Melissa. While aware by then that Mrs. Whitehead was undergoing an emotional crisis, they were as yet not cognizant of the depth of that crisis and its implications for their newly-enlarged family.

Later in the evening of March 30, Mrs. Whitehead became deeply disturbed, disconsolate, stricken with unbearable sadness. She had to have her child. She could not eat, sleep, or concentrate on anything other than her need for her baby. The next day she went to the Sterns' home and told them how much she was suffering.

The depth of Mrs. Whitehead's despair surprised and frightened the Sterns. She told them that she could not live without her baby, that she must have her, even if only for one week, that thereafter she would surrender her child. The Sterns, concerned that Mrs. Whitehead might indeed commit suicide, not wanting under any circumstances to risk that, and in any event believing that Mrs. Whitehead would keep her word, turned the child over to her. It was not until four months later, after a series of attempts to regain possession of the child, that Melissa was returned to the Sterns, having been forcibly removed from the home where she was then living with Mr. and Mrs. Whitehead, the home in Florida owned by Mary Beth Whitehead's parents.

The struggle over Baby M began when it became apparent that Mrs. Whitehead could not return the child to Mr. Stern. Due to Mrs. Whitehead's refusal to relinquish the baby, Mr. Stern filed a complaint seeking enforcement of the surrogacy contract. He alleged, accurately, that Mrs. Whitehead had not only refused to comply with the surrogacy contract but had threatened to flee from New Jersey with the child in order to avoid even the possibility of his obtaining custody. The court papers asserted that if Mrs. Whitehead were to be given notice of the application for an order requiring her to relinquish custody, she would, prior to the hearing, leave the state with the baby. And that is precisely what she did. After the order was entered, *ex parte,* the process server, aided by the police, in the presence of the Sterns, entered Mrs. Whitehead's home to execute the order. Mr. Whitehead fled with the child, who had been handed to him through a window while those who came to enforce the order were thrown off balance by a dispute over the child's current name.

The Whiteheads immediately fled to Florida with Baby M. They stayed initially with Mrs. Whitehead's parents, where one of Mrs. Whitehead's children had been living. For the next three months, the Whiteheads and Melissa lived at roughly twenty different hotels, motels, and homes in order to avoid apprehension. From time to time Mrs. Whitehead would call Mr. Stern to discuss the matter; the conversations, recorded by Mr. Stern on advice of counsel, show an escalating dispute about rights, morality, and power, accompanied by threats of Mrs. Whitehead to kill herself, to kill the child, and falsely to accuse Mr. Stern of sexually molesting Mrs. Whitehead's other daughter.

Eventually the Sterns discovered where the Whiteheads were staying, commenced supplementary proceedings in Florida, and obtained an order requiring the Whiteheads to turn over the child. Police in Florida enforced the order, forcibly removing the child from her grandparents' home. She was soon thereafter brought to New Jersey and turned over to the Sterns. The prior order of the court, issued *ex parte,* awarding custody of the child to the Sterns *pendente lite,* was reaffirmed by the trial court after consideration of the certified representations of the parties (both represented by counsel) concerning the unusual sequence of events that had unfolded. Pending final judgment, Mrs. Whitehead was awarded limited visitation with Baby M.

The Sterns' complaint, in addition to seeking possession and ultimately custody of the child, sought enforcement of the surrogacy contract. Pursuant to the contract, it asked that the child be permanently placed in their custody, that Mrs. Whitehead's parental rights be terminated, and that Mrs. Stern be allowed to adopt the child, *i.e.,* that, for all purposes, Melissa become the Sterns' child.

The trial took thirty-two days over a period of more than two months. It included numerous interlocutory appeals and attempted interlocutory appeals. There were twenty-three witnesses to the facts recited above and fifteen expert witnesses, eleven testifying on the issue of custody and four on the subject of Mrs. Stern's multiple sclerosis; the bulk of the testimony was devoted to determining the parenting arrangement most compatible with the child's best interests. Soon after the conclusion of the trial, the trial court announced its opinion from the bench. 217 *N.J. Super.* 313 (1987). It held that the surrogacy contract was valid; ordered that Mrs. Whitehead's parental rights be terminated and that sole custody of the child be granted to Mr. Stern; and, after hearing brief testimony from Mrs. Stern, immediately entered an order allowing the adoption of Melissa by Mrs. Stern, all in accordance with the surrogacy contract. Pending the outcome of the appeal, we granted a continuation of visitation to Mrs. Whitehead, although slightly more limited than the visitation allowed during the trial.

Although clearly expressing its view that the surrogacy contract was valid, the trial court devoted the major portion of its opinion to the question of the baby's best interests. The inconsistency is apparent. The surrogacy contract calls for the surrender of the child to the Sterns, permanent and sole custody in the Sterns, and termination of Mrs. Whitehead's parental rights, all without qualification, all regardless of any evaluation of the best interests of the child. As a matter of fact the contract recites (even before the child was conceived) that it is in the best interests of the child to be placed with Mr. Stern. In effect, the trial court awarded custody to Mr. Stern, the natural father, based on the same kind of evidence and analysis as might be expected had no surrogacy contract existed. Its rationalization, however, was that while the surrogacy contract was valid, specific performance would not be granted unless that remedy was in the best interests of the child. The factual issues confronted and decided by the trial court were the same as if Mr. Stern and Mrs. Whitehead had had the child out of wedlock, intended or unintended, and then disagreed about custody. The trial court's awareness of the irrelevance of the contract in the court's determination of custody is suggested by its remark that beyond the question of the child's best interests, "[a]ll other concerns raised by counsel constitute commentary." 217 *N.J. Super.* at 323.

On the question of best interests—and we agree, but for different reasons, that custody was the critical issue—the court's analysis of the testimony was perceptive, demonstrating both its understanding of the case and its considerable experience in these matters. We agree substantially with both its analysis and conclusions on the matter of custody.

. . . Mrs. Whitehead appealed. This Court granted direct certification. 107 *N.J.* 140 (1987). The briefs of the parties on appeal were joined by numerous briefs filed by *amici* expressing various interests and views on surrogacy and on this case. We have found many of them helpful in resolving the issues before us.

Mrs. Whitehead contends that the surrogacy contract, for a variety of reasons, is invalid. She contends that it conflicts with public policy since it guarantees that the child will not have the nurturing of both natural parents—presumably New Jersey's goal for families. She further argues that it deprives the mother of her constitutional right to the companionship of her child, and that it conflicts with statutes concerning termination of parental rights and adoption. With the contract thus void, Mrs. Whitehead claims primary custody (with visitation rights in Mr. Stern) both on a best interests basis (stressing the "tender years" doctrine) as well as on the policy basis of discouraging surrogacy contracts. She maintains that even if custody would ordinarily go to Mr. Stern, here it should be awarded to Mrs. Whitehead to deter future surrogacy arrangements.

In a brief filed after oral argument, counsel for Mrs. Whitehead suggests that the standard for determining best interests where the infant resulted from a surrogacy contract is that the child should be placed with the mother absent a showing of unfitness. All parties agree that no expert testified that Mary Beth Whitehead was unfit as a mother; the trial court expressly found that she was *not* "unfit," that, on the contrary, "she is a good mother for and to her older children," 217 *N.J. Super.* at 397; and no one now claims anything to the contrary.

One of the repeated themes put forth by Mrs. Whitehead is that the court's initial *ex parte* order granting custody to the Sterns during the trial was a substantial factor in the ultimate "best interests" determination. That initial order, claimed to be erroneous by Mrs. Whitehead, not only established Melissa as part of the Stern family, but brought enormous pressure on Mrs. Whitehead. The order brought the weight of the state behind the Sterns' attempt, ultimately successful, to gain possession of the child. The resulting pressure, Mrs. Whitehead contends, caused her to act in ways that were atypical of her ordinary behavior when not under stress, and to act in ways that were thought to be inimical to the child's best interests in that they demonstrated a failure of character, maturity, and consistency. She claims that any mother who truly loved her child might so respond and that it is doubly unfair to judge her on the basis of her reaction to an extreme situation rarely faced by any mother, where that situation was itself caused by an erroneous order of the court. Therefore, according to Mrs. Whitehead, the erroneous *ex parte* order precipitated a series of events that proved instrumental in the final result.

The Sterns claim that the surrogacy contract is valid and should be enforced, largely for the reasons given by the trial court. They claim a constitutional right of privacy, which includes the right of procreation, and the right of consenting adults to deal with matters of reproduction as they see fit. As for the child's best interests, their position is factual: given all of the circumstances, the child is better off in their custody with no residual parental rights reserved for Mrs. Whitehead.

Of considerable interest in this clash of views is the position of the child's guardian *ad litem,* wisely appointed by the court at the outset of the litigation. As the child's representative, her role in the litigation, as she viewed it, was solely to protect the child's best interests. She therefore took no position on the validity of the surrogacy contract, and instead devoted her energies to obtaining expert testimony uninfluenced by any interest other than the child's. We agree with the guardian's perception of her role in this litigation. She appropriately refrained from taking any position that might have appeared to compromise her role as the child's advocate. She first took the position, based on her experts' testimony, that the Sterns should have primary custody, and that while Mrs. Whitehead's parental rights should not be terminated, no visitation should be allowed for five years. As a result of subsequent developments, mentioned *infra,* her view has changed. She now recommends that no visitation be allowed at least until Baby M reaches maturity.

Although some of the experts' opinions touched on visitation, the major issue they addressed was whether custody should be reposed in the Sterns or in the Whiteheads. The trial court, consistent in this respect with its view that the surrogacy contract was valid, did not deal at all with the question of visitation. Having concluded that the best interests of the child called for custody in the Sterns, the trial court enforced the operative provisions of the surrogacy contract, terminated Mrs. Whitehead's parental rights, and granted an adoption to Mrs. Stern. Explicit in the ruling was the conclusion that the best interests determination removed whatever impediment might have existed in enforcing the surrogacy contract. This Court, therefore, is without guidance from the trial court on the visitation issue, an issue of considerable importance in any event, and especially important in view of our determination that the surrogacy contract is invalid.

. . . We have concluded that this surrogacy contract is invalid. Our conclusion has two bases: direct conflict with existing statutes and conflict with the public policies of this State, as expressed in its statutory and decisional law.

One of the surrogacy contract's basic purposes, to achieve the adoption of a child through private placement, though permitted in New Jersey "is very much disfavored." *Sees v. Baber*, 74 *N.J.* 201, 217 (1977). Its use of money for this purpose—and we have no doubt whatsoever that the money is being paid to obtain an adoption and not, as the Sterns argue, for the personal services of Mary Beth Whitehead—is illegal and perhaps criminal. *N.J.S.A.* 9:3–54. In addition to the inducement of money, there is the coercion of contract: the natural mother's irrevocable agreement, prior to birth, even prior to conception, to surrender the child to the adoptive couple. Such an agreement is totally unenforceable in private placement adoption. *Sees,* 74 *N.J.* at 212–14. Even where the adoption is through an approved agency, the formal agreement to surrender occurs only *after* birth (as we read *N.J.S.A.* 9:2–16 and 17, and similar statutes), and then, by regulation, only after the birth mother has been offered counseling. *N.J.A.C.* 10:121A–5.4(c). Integral to these invalid provisions of the surrogacy contract is the related agreement, equally invalid, on the part of the natural mother to cooperate with, and not to contest, proceedings to terminate her parental rights, as well as her contractual concession, in aid of the adoption, that the child's best interests would be served by awarding custody to the natural father and his wife—all of this before she has even conceived, and, in some cases, before she has the slightest idea of what the natural father and adoptive mother are like.

The foregoing provisions not only directly conflict with New Jersey statutes, but also offend long-established State policies. These critical terms, which are at the heart of the contract, are invalid and unenforceable; the conclusion therefore follows, without more, that the entire contract is unenforceable.

. . . The surrogacy contract conflicts with: (1) laws prohibiting the use of money in connection with adoptions; (2) laws requiring proof of parental unfitness or abandonment before termination of parental rights is ordered or an adoption is granted; and (3) laws that make surrender of custody and consent to adoption revocable in private placement adoptions.

(1) Our law prohibits paying or accepting money in connection with any placement of a child for adoption. *N.J.S.A.* 9:3–54a. Violation is a high misdemeanor. *N.J.S.A.* 9:3–54c. Excepted are fees of an approved agency (which must be a non-profit entity, *N.J.S.A.* 9:3–38a) and certain expenses in connection with childbirth. *N.J.S.A.* 9:3–54b. . . .

Mr. Stern knew he was paying for the adoption of a child; Mrs. Whitehead knew she was accepting money so that a child might be adopted; the Infertility Center knew that it was being paid for assisting in the adoption of a child. The actions of all three worked to frustrate the goals of the statute. It strains credulity to claim that these arrangements, touted by those in the surrogacy business as an attractive alternative to the usual route leading to an adoption, really amount to something other than a private placement adoption for money.

The prohibition of our statute is strong. Violation constitutes a high misdemeanor, *N.J.S.A.* 9:3–54c, a third-degree crime, *N.J.S.A.* 2C:43–1b, carrying a penalty of three to five years imprisonment. *N.J.S.A.* 2C:43–6a(3). The evils inherent in baby-bartering are loathsome for a myriad of reasons. . . .

. . . Mrs. Whitehead, shortly after the child's birth, had attempted to revoke her consent and surrender by refusing, after the Sterns had allowed her to have the child "just for one week," to return Baby M to them. The trial court's award of specific performance therefore reflects its view that the consent to surrender the child was irrevocable. We accept the trial court's construction of the contract; indeed it appears quite clear that this was the parties' intent. Such a provision, however, making irrevocable the natural mother's consent to surrender custody of her child in a private placement adoption, clearly conflicts with New Jersey law. . . .

. . . The surrogacy contract violates the policy of this State that the rights of natural parents are equal concerning their child, the father's right no greater than the mother's. . . . The whole purpose and effect of the surrogacy contract was to give the father the exclusive right to the child by destroying the rights of the mother.

The policies expressed in our comprehensive laws governing consent to the surrender of a child . . . stand in stark contrast to the surrogacy contract and what it implies. Here there is no counseling, independent or otherwise, of the natural mother, no evaluation, no warning.

. . . Mrs. Whitehead was examined and psychologically evaluated, but if it was for her benefit, the record does not disclose that fact. The Sterns regarded the evaluation as important, particularly in connection with the question of whether she would change her mind. Yet they never asked to see it, and were content with the assumption that the Infertility Center had made an evaluation and had concluded that there was no danger that the surrogate mother would change her mind. From Mrs. Whitehead's point of view, all that she learned from the evaluation was that "she had passed." It is apparent that the profit motive got the better of the Infertility Center. Although the evaluation was made, it was not put to any use, and understandably so, for the psychologist warned that Mrs. Whitehead demonstrated certain traits that might make surrender of the child difficult and that there should be further inquiry into this issue in connection with her surrogacy. To inquire further, however, might have jeopardized the Infertility Center's fee. The record indicates that neither Mrs. Whitehead nor the Sterns were ever told of this fact, a fact that might have ended their surrogacy arrangement.

Under the contract, the natural mother is irrevocably committed before she knows the strength of her bond with her child. She never makes a totally voluntary, informed decision, for quite clearly any decision prior to the baby's birth is, in the most important sense, uninformed, and any decision after that, compelled by a pre-existing contractual commitment, the threat of a lawsuit, and the inducement of a $10,000 payment, is less than totally voluntary. Her interests are of little concern to those who controlled this transaction.

Although the interest of the natural father and adoptive mother is certainly the predominant interest, realistically the *only* interest served, even they are left with less than what public policy requires. They know little about the natural mother, her genetic makeup, and her psychological and medical history. Moreover, not even a superficial attempt is made to determine their awareness of their responsibilities as parents.

Worst of all, however, is the contract's total disregard of the best interests of the child. There is not the slightest suggestion that any inquiry will be made at any time to determine the fitness of the Sterns as custodial parents, of Mrs. Stern as an adoptive parent, their superiority to Mrs. Whitehead, or the effect on the child of not living with her natural mother.

This is the sale of a child, or, at the very least, the sale of a mother's right to her child, the only mitigating factor being that one of the purchasers is the father. Almost every evil that prompted the prohibition on the payment of money in connection with adoptions exists here. The differences between an adoption and a surrogacy contract should be noted, since it is asserted that the use of money in connection with surrogacy does not pose the risks found where money buys an adoption. . . .

First, and perhaps most important, all parties concede that it is unlikely that surrogacy will survive without money. Despite the alleged selfless motivation of surrogate mothers, if there is no payment, there will be no surrogates, or very few. That conclusion contrasts with adoption; for obvious reasons, there remains a steady supply, albeit insufficient, despite the prohibitions against payment. The adoption itself, relieving the natural mother of the financial burden of supporting an infant, is in some sense the equivalent of payment.

Second, the use of money in adoptions does not *produce* the problem—conception occurs, and usually the birth itself, before illicit funds are offered. With surrogacy, the "problem," if one views it as such, consisting of the purchase of a woman's procreative capacity, at the risk of her life, is caused by and originates with the offer of money.

Third, with the law prohibiting the use of money in connection with adoptions, the built-in financial pressure of the unwanted pregnancy and the consequent support obligation do not lead the mother to the highest paying, ill-suited, adoptive parents. She is just as well-off surrendering the child to an approved agency. In surrogacy, the highest bidders will presumably become the adoptive parents regardless of suitability, so long as payment of money is permitted.

Fourth, the mother's consent to surrender her child in adoptions is revocable, even after surrender of the child, unless it be to an approved agency, where by regulation there are protections against an ill-advised surrender. In surrogacy, consent occurs so early that no amount of advice would satisfy the potential mother's need, yet the consent is irrevocable.

The main difference, that the unwanted pregnancy is unintended while the situation of the surrogate mother is voluntary and intended, is really not significant. Initially, it produces stronger reactions of sympathy for the mother whose pregnancy was unwanted than for the surrogate mother, who "went into this with her eyes wide open." On reflection, however, it appears that the essential evil is the same, taking advantage of a woman's circumstances (the unwanted pregnancy or the need for money) in order to take away her child, the difference being one of degree.

In the scheme contemplated by the surrogacy contract in this case, a middle man, propelled by profit, promotes the sale. Whatever idealism may have motivated any of the participants, the profit motive predominates, permeates, and ultimately governs the transaction. The demand for children is great and the supply small. The availability of contraception, abortion, and the greater willingness of single mothers to bring up their children has led to a shortage of babies offered for adoption. . . . The situation is ripe for the entry of the middleman who will bring some equilibrium into the market by increasing the supply through the use of money.

Intimated, but disputed, is the assertion that surrogacy will be used for the benefit of the rich at the expense of the poor. . . . In response it is noted that the Sterns are not rich and the Whiteheads not poor. Nevertheless, it is clear to us that it is unlikely that surrogate mothers will be as proportionately numerous among those women in the top twenty percent income bracket as among those in the bottom twenty percent. *Ibid.* Put differently, we doubt that infertile couples in the low-income bracket will find upper income surrogates.

In any event, even in this case one should not pretend that disparate wealth does not play a part simply because the contrast is not the dramatic "rich versus poor." At the time of trial, the Whiteheads' net assets were probably negative—Mrs. Whitehead's own sister was foreclosing on a second mortgage. Their income derived from Mr. Whitehead's labors. Mrs. Whitehead is a homemaker, having previously held part-time jobs. The Sterns are both professionals, she a medical doctor, he a biochemist. Their combined income when both were working was about $89,500 a year and their assets sufficient to pay for the surrogacy contract arrangements.

The point is made that Mrs. Whitehead *agreed* to the surrogacy arrangement, supposedly fully understanding the consequences. Putting aside the issue of how compelling her need for money may have been, and how significant her understanding of the consequences, we suggest that her consent is irrelevant. There are, in a civilized society, some things that money cannot buy.

Key People, Laws, and Concepts

Adverse Drug Experiences (ADEs)

The Food and Drug Administration (FDA) gathers reports of reactions to drugs and other substances (such as dietary supplements, vitamins, and diet aids) from consumers and medical professionals. Those instances of problems with substances are the basis of some FDA decisions to issue warnings or recalls of products. Some recent products, such as the diet aid Metabolife, have been the subject of so many complaints to the FDA that it has set up special hot lines dedicated to those substances.

Baby M Case

An important case from 1988 concerning the rights of surrogate mothers and biological parents. The biological mother of a child born through a surrogacy arrangement, Mary Beth Whitehead, tried to retain custody of the baby, who had been fathered by William Stern. The final court decision was that a continuing relationship with both of her biological parents was in the best interests of the child. The court also invalidated the commercial surrogacy agreement, leading several other states to follow its example.

Coroner

A public official responsible for determining the cause of deaths in a locality. The coronership as an office dates to England in the twelfth century, and still is widely used in parts of the world that are English speaking. Traditionally, the coroner inquires into deaths that are sudden, mysterious, unnatural, or violent, as well as deaths that occur in certain public institutions, such as prisons, and those that take place during the performance of medical procedures. The coroner may be elected or appointed. In large urban jurisdictions in the modern United States, the coroner usually is a well-trained physician with expertise in forensic pathology. Also see *Medical Examiner (ME)* in this chapter.

Daubert Standard

A rule, enunciated by the U.S. Supreme Court in the case of *Daubert v. Merrell Dow Pharmaceuticals* (1993), giving judges the authority to act as gatekeepers for scientific (or medical) expert evidence. The rule was applicable in both civil and criminal cases, although the judiciary most often applies it in civil suits involving alleged harm from drugs. When the *Daubert* case first was decided, it initially seemed simply a barrier to "junk science" being used as the basis for expert testimony. Some judges have applied *Daubert* very broadly, however, to bar evidence that does not meet a very high scientific standard. They require, for instance, that expert testimony have passed peer review or be measurable in quantitative terms. Also see Frye *Rule or General Acceptance Test* in this chapter.

Dietary Supplement Health and Education Act (1994)

Faced with complaints from the makers of nonprescription products such as herbal supplements, vitamins, and diet aids, Congress in 1994 passed an act limiting the FDA's oversight of such products. After 1994, the FDA had less power to recall dietary supplements than to recall prescription medications; in order to pull such products off the shelves, the FDA must meet high medical and legal standards showing the products' immediate potential for harm. Passed with the strong support of the industry to be regulated, the bill enjoyed powerful advocates such as Senator Orrin Hatch (R-UT), who had close ties to the dietary supplement industry.

DNA Evidence

The use in court cases of samples from the human body that contain nucleated cells. Those cells, which may be tiny—even microscopic—in size, can be examined to determine their deoxyribonucleic acid (DNA) content. DNA samples may be obtained from many types of physical remnants connected to a case, such as hair, blood, and semen. DNA evidence can place suspects at the scenes of crimes, and it can exonerate persons who have been convicted of crimes.

DNR Order

Literally, "Do Not Resuscitate" order. Especially prior to the *Karen Ann Quinlan* case of 1976, DNR orders were an open secret in the medical community. Physicians wrote coded messages (such as "DNR," in pencil) or told hospital staffs not to apply heroic measures (including resuscitation) to patients who were suffering from terminal illnesses, such as metastatic cancer, in the event that those patients stopped breathing momentarily.

The Emergency Medical Treatment and Active Labor Act (EMTALA)

The Emergency Medical Treatment and Active Labor Act (EMTALA) was a piece of congressional legislation passed in 1986 in response to the problem of hospitals sending ill or injured patients who were without health insurance on to other medical facilities. The act requires that hospitals treat and stabilize emergency patients and attend to women in active labor, and it prohibits hospitals from transferring patients who are critically ill or in labor until they are medically stable. In spite of the seemingly broad applicability of the statute to ensure access to emergency care, courts generally have decided cases brought under the statute along narrow grounds—in effect finding ways to determine that hospitals have not violated the act.

Euthanasia

Literally, "mercy killing," euthanasia may involve the administration of a lethal dose of medicine, the use of a weapon, or the withdrawal of necessary technology that has been supplying life-sustaining functions for an ill person. Some authorities and countries distinguish between voluntary euthanasia, where a patient requests the act of killing by a physician or other person in order to be relieved of extreme pain or suffering, and involuntary euthanasia, in which a person effectively decides to commit the act of killing without the patient's permission or immediate knowledge. In most legal systems, euthanasia is considered a crime. In a few countries and in well-defined circumstances (such as in the Netherlands, under certain administrative guidelines) physicians may commit euthanasia without being prosecuted. Also see *Physician-Assisted Suicide (PAS)* in this chapter.

Forensic Odontology

The use of dental records often is critical in solving cases such as murders that occurred many years previously and in identifying human remains when the rest of the body has been destroyed. Forensic odontology is a specialty within the field of forensic pathology.

Frye Rule or General Acceptance Test

A rule for the admissibility of scientific evidence in court, requiring that scientific evidence be based on theory and methodologies commonly recognized as valid within the scientific community. This standard first was enunciated in the case of *Frye v. U.S.* (1923). The Frye rule both promoted and managed the use of scientific and medical expert testimony in court. The rule was criticized, however, as encouraging plaintiffs and defendants to counter one another with "competing experts," who sometimes could be confusing to jurors. After applying *Frye* for nearly seventy years, judges took a firmer line in admitting scientific testimony to court after the enunciation of the *Daubert* standard in 1993. *Daubert* partially superseded *Frye*. Also see Daubert *Standard* in this chapter.

Helpern, Milton

Influential advocate for medical examiner (ME) systems and world-renowned authority on forensic pathology, Dr. Helpern was the third person to serve as the chief ME with the New York City

Medical Examiner's Office. He helped found the National Association of Medical Examiners (NAME) and was its first president, serving several terms between 1966 and 1970. Helpern spearheaded the building of a modern ME's office for New York City and assisted in the development of a teaching institute for forensic pathology (later named in his honor) associated with New York University.

Informed Consent

The legal requirement that a patient be fully apprised of treatment options that are available, as well as medical and other risks attendant both to the treatment and to not receiving the treatment. Informed consent laws were expanded greatly in the later twentieth century, as medical technologies (such as options for surgery) grew increasingly varied and complex.

Irresistible Impulse Doctrine

A corollary to the rules on insanity that were applied by most U.S. courts between the *M'Naghten* case (1843) and the 1960s, the irresistible impulse doctrine provided a way for defendants to argue that they were in the grip of an uncontrollable urge when they committed a criminal act. Some jurisdictions allowed the argument that an irresistible impulse had deprived a defendant of the ability to conform his or her conduct to the law to mitigate the charges against the accused.

Kevorkian, Jack

An American physician (by training a pathologist, although currently unlicensed) and right-to-die writer and activist who by his own admission has participated in dozens of assisted suicides. In several well-publicized trials, Dr. Kevorkian won the sympathy of the jury in recounting his justifications for assisting terminally ill persons and others (such as Alzheimer's patients) to commit suicide, leading states (including Michigan) to tighten their regulations prohibiting such actions by physicians. In 1998, however, he was convicted of murder and handling a controlled substance without a license; he was sentenced to ten to twenty-five years in prison.

Kevorkian Laws

Laws and proposed laws patterned after the recommendations of Dr. Jack Kevorkian and other advocates of physician-assisted suicide (PAS). In the late 1980s and 1990s, a few states considered laws specifying certain conditions under which PAS would be legal; only Oregon actually passed such a law. A number of states, however, passed laws criminalizing PAS.

Living Will

A document prepared by a patient, specifying whether and which extraordinary measures should be undertaken in the event that the subject of the document is unable to speak for herself or himself. Since the time of the *Quinlan* case (1976), living wills have been recognized by most states. Many states have laws requiring institutions such as hospitals and nursing homes to inform patients of their right to prepare and have on file a living will.

Magrath, Thomas

Medical examiner (ME) for over twenty years in the early twentieth century in the northern district of Suffolk County (which encompasses Boston), Dr. Magrath was an outspoken and influential advocate of medical examinerships. He participated in a number of criminal trials in New England. He was best known, nationally, for giving expert testimony that reflected negatively on the defendants Sacco and Vanzetti.

Medical Examiner (ME)

The medical examiner (ME) determines the cause of death in cases of unexplained or violent fatalities. The ME has formal medical credentials; he or she is a physician who almost always is highly trained in forensic pathology. MEs frequently testify in legal proceedings, and they aid the police and prosecutors in their investigations. Most MEs are associated with the offices of MEs or coroners in local jurisdictions in the United States. A coroner often is qualified as an ME (as is the case in several large urban areas such as Los Angeles) or has MEs on staff. See *Pathologist* in this chapter.

M'Naghten Rules

A statement of the law on insanity in criminal cases, as it was understood by a set of famous judges in England after the Daniel M'Naghten trial of 1843. The rules were an effort to make the law on insanity less accessible to defendants who wished to be found not guilty by reason of insanity. The M'Naghten standards were widely applied in U.S. state courts throughout the nineteenth and much of the twentieth century.

National Childhood Vaccine Injury Act (1994)

Congressional legislation in 1994 set up a fund to compensate the children or families of persons who were injured or killed by mandatory childhood vaccinations. Proving that the injuries alleged were caused by the vaccines rather than some other factors, however, has been difficult for many litigants. Cases claiming that vaccines caused Sudden Infant Death Syndrome (SIDS) and autism have been among the types of suits that the authorities hearing these cases have rebuffed.

Noguchi, Thomas

Forensic pathologist Dr. Thomas Noguchi held the high-profile position of coroner for the County of Los Angeles from 1967 until 1982. He directed the medical investigations of a number of celebrity deaths. Despite his recognition as a leader within the professional ranks of medical examiners (MEs), his championing of the modernization of the Los Angeles coroner's facilities, and his strong work ethic, Dr. Noguchi was involved in political controversy that eventually cost him his position.

Partial-Birth Abortion

Popular term for several medical procedures related to abortion, including the procedures known as D&X (dilation and extraction) and D&E (dilation and evacuation). Those procedures involve the dismemberment and extraction of the body of a fetus during the late second trimester or in the third trimester of pregnancy—when many opponents of abortion believe that the fetus should be considered a "person" in a practical, moral, religious, and legal sense. Partial-birth abortions became a volatile political issue in the 1990s, when antiabortion activists lobbied for restrictions on late-term abortions. The publicity surrounding cases such as *Stenberg v. Carhart* (2000) helped fuel the debate about the legality and morality of partial-birth abortions.

Pathologist

A specially trained physician who specializes in the examination of dead persons. Medical examiner (ME) systems and most coroner systems in the modern United States require the participation of pathologists in medical examinations. Forensic pathologists focus on relating their findings to legal authorities such as the police or the courts. Most pathologists who work in MEs' or coroners' offices of necessity are specialists in forensic matters; they regularly testify in court and assist the police in investigations of crimes. See *Medical Examiner (ME)* in this chapter.

Physician-Assisted Suicide (PAS)

When a patient participates in his or her own demise but is aided by a medical care provider, that suicide is said to be physician assisted. Some patients who request help from their physicians in ending their own lives are physically unable to commit suicide on their own, for example because of partial paralysis. In most jurisdictions, in both the United States and around the world, physician-assisted suicide (PAS) is considered less serious as a crime than euthanasia. In some areas, such as several U.S. states, there are efforts to legalize PAS through statutes. Also see *Euthanasia* in this chapter.

Postma Case

A 1971 case in the Netherlands, after which physician-assisted suicide (PAS) began to be openly accepted by that nation's judiciary and Dutch society at large. A physician, Dr. Geertruida Postma, administered a fatal dose of morphine to her bedridden (but not terminally ill) mother; though found guilty, Dr. Postma received a very light sentence.

Quinlan Case

Those persons who were legally responsible for the medical care of Karen Ann Quinlan (in particular her parents) faced an agonizing decision when she fell into a coma in 1975: Should she be disconnected from the respirator, which seemed to be the only thing keeping her alive? In a judicial decision with profound repercussions, the Supreme Court of New Jersey in 1976 ruled that Quinlan's right to privacy entitled her (through her parents) to "choose" to refuse mechanical respiration.

Reasonable Care and Diligence

Courts in the early twentieth century began to require that in treating a patient, physicians should exercise the amount of diligence that would be commonly expected of others in their profession (and medical specialization). Failure to live up to that standard might result in a finding of negligence against the physician.

Remmerlink Commission

In 1991, an appointed committee in the Netherlands published the results of several months of study on the question of the law and practice of physician-assisted suicide (PAS) in the Netherlands. The Remmerlink Commission found that most instances of PAS had proceeded according to well-known guidelines; a few physicians, however, had engaged in the euthanasia of patients who had not given their recent and fully informed consent.

Right-Wrong Test

A leading element in the M'Naghten Rules concerning insanity. The M'Naghten standards required that in order for a defendant to succeed in a plea of not guilty by reason of insanity, he or she not only should have a disease of the mind, but also should be incapable of distinguishing right from wrong.

Rodriguez Case

A Canadian case involving a terminally ill woman, Sue Rodriguez, who requested that she be allowed to have physicians' assistance in committing suicide. The Canadian Supreme Court considered her case and narrowly rejected her arguments, igniting a public debate about suicide and euthanasia for terminally ill persons. With assistance from an unnamed physician, Ms. Rodriguez died on February 7, 1994.

Sound Methodology Test

In the case of *Daubert v. Merrell Dow Pharmaceuticals* (1993), the Supreme Court appeared to claim for federal judges the right to determine the validity of scientific evidence to be presented in court. In *Daubert*, the court de-emphasized the expert witness somewhat, noting that judges could look directly at the scientific evidence that was to be presented to ascertain whether it employed methodologies that were sound.

Spilsbury, Sir Bernard

Between the start of his career in 1910 and his death in 1947, Dr. Bernard Spilsbury was a world-renowned authority on forensic pathology. He held the position of chief pathologist for England's Home Office, which had authority to investigate crimes all over the nation. Spilsbury's assured, elegant, and competent manner at the bar made him a compelling expert witness, particularly in complex or graphically violent murder investigations.

Surrogacy

In cases where a couple is unable to conceive children, they may hire a surrogate mother to bear their child. Usually the biological father (often the male of the infertile couple) provides sperm, which is implanted in the surrogate mother through either artificial insemination or in vitro fertilization techniques. In the *Baby M* case of 1988 (see Baby M *Case* in this chapter), commercial surrogacy agreements were made illegal in New Jersey. Many other states either followed suit or placed stern restrictions on commercial surrogacy contracts.

Total Investigation

In the later twentieth century, many large medical examiners' (MEs') offices clustered medical and other investigators of deaths under the roof of one modern facility. The Coroner's Office in the County of Los Angeles, opened in 1972 under the direction of Dr. Thomas Noguchi, was considered to be one of the most modern and extensive examples of a total investigative approach and was a model for other jurisdictions.

Wild Beast Test

The requirement in English courts, prior to about 1800, that persons who claimed that their mental state absolved them from responsibility for criminal acts should have no more capacity for reason than an animal. The wild beast test seemed to carry with it a presumption that persons who were legally insane would behave in a "furious" (that is uncontrolled or maniacal) fashion.

Chronology

1194 English judges associated with the court of King Richard I (the Lion-Hearted) mandate that each county have three knights and one clerk to be "keepers of the pleas of the crown." These "crowners" (later called coroners) eventually become local officials who specialize not so much in revenue collection, but in the investigation of sudden or suspicious deaths.

1487 Parliament authorizes payment of coroners for their examinations of the bodies of murder victims.

1530 Holy Roman Emperor Charles V publishes a law code, the *Constitutio Criminalis Carolina,* including the provision that medical testimony be included in trials involving infanticide, homicide, abortion, or poisoning.

1637 A colonial governor of Maryland, Leonard Calvert, appoints a local citizen, Thomas Baldridge, to be both sheriff and coroner in Saint Mary's County, using the model of the English coronership as a guide to his duties.

1751 Parliament allows the coroner to collect fees for traveling expenses, though it restricts the payment of other fees except when the coroner can show that he has strong suspicion of a felony having been committed. This effectively limits coroners' scope for investigation.

1807 The University of Edinburgh establishes the first chair of legal medicine among English-speaking nations.

1836 Britain's parliament passes the Medical Witnesses Remuneration Act, allowing the payment of witnesses who testify on medical matters at trials and coroners' inquests. This legislation encourages the bringing into court of medical expert witnesses, especially in cases of suspected murder or other instances where medical expertise could prove useful—such as in cases of alleged insanity.

1843 The *M'Naghten* case creates controversy when defendant M'Naghten is found not guilty by reason of insanity. The M'Naghten Rules are written by eminent English judges, making a defense of insanity more difficult.

1860 The State of Maryland passes a law permitting coroners to compel that physicians testify to inquests or courts in cases of violent death.

1861 Britain's Offenses against the Person Act makes it a criminal offense to "unlawfully procure" a miscarriage.

1870 New Hampshire courts enunciate rules by which persons pleading insanity had certain legal advantages, as opposed to other jurisdictions where the M'Naghten Rules applied.

1877 The coroner system is abolished by state law in Massachusetts and is replaced by a medical examiner's (ME's) office. Only the bodies of those persons who are suspected of having died violent deaths, however, have to be examined by a forensic medical expert.

1881 The assassination of President James Garfield by Charles J. Guiteau brings the insanity defense before an American audience. Guiteau is convicted and executed in spite of his effort to employ the insanity defense.

1888 The election of coroners is abolished in England. The leaders of local governments are to appoint coroners. There are no qualifications that coroners have to be either medically or legally trained.

1889 In *Dent v. West Virginia,* the U.S. Supreme Court affirms the authority of states to issue licenses for medical practitioners.

1905 In the decision of *Jacobson v. Massachusetts,* the U.S. Supreme Court allows states to make vaccination compulsory.

1908 Attorney (and later Supreme Court Justice) Louis Brandeis writes a brief for a case that he is trying before the

U.S. Supreme Court—*Muller v. Oregon.* Novel in form and use of evidence, the Brandeis brief establishes a trend for courts to consider large numbers of sociological and scientific facts in deciding cases.

1910 The *Crippen* murder case places forensic pathologists Joseph Pepper and his pupil Bernard Spilsbury into the public eye as expert witnesses. After the *Crippen* case, forensic pathologists are much more sympathetic figures in the eyes of the public.

Edmond Locard opens a crime laboratory in Lyon, France, that serves as a model for modern forensic investigation. Widely emulated in England and the United States, the Lyon laboratory brings together experts not only in forensic pathology, but also microscopy, chemistry, physics, and biology.

1914 In the case of *Schloendorff v. The Society of the New York Hospital,* Justice Benjamin Cardozo makes an eloquent statement affirming the need for physicians to secure informed consent from their patients.

1915 An (ME's) office with wide authority is created in New York City as a replacement for the older coroner system there. The ME in New York has the authority to order autopsies in cases that seem suspicious.

1918 New York laws regulating the dispensing of birth control information are upheld in the case of *People v. Sanger,* involving birth control advocate and nurse Margaret Sanger. After the decision, however, doctors may dispense birth control information to women in order to prevent disease or protect women's health.

1923 The case of *Frye v. U.S.* establishes the requirement that in order for courts to accept expert medical and scientific evidence, that evidence must be recognized as legitimate within the general medical and scientific communities.

1926 England's coroners are required, by act of Parliament, to be qualified as either medical or legal professionals with at least five years of professional experience prior to appointment.

1927 The U.S. Supreme Court decision in *Buck v. Bell* allows states to sterilize persons whom the legislature deems unfit because of their mental disability.

1932 The United States Federal Bureau of Investigation (FBI) establishes a laboratory that is available to forensic scientists nationally. In the FBI lab as well as others built on its model, medical experts, ballistics specialists, immunologists, handwriting experts, and other nonmedical personnel work in concert to solve crimes.

1937 Harvard University's Medical School establishes a chair of legal medicine, with the purpose of encouraging students to pursue specialized training in forensic pathology.

1938 The British case of *Rex. v. Bourne* allows physicians to perform abortions as long as they justify the procedures in terms of maternal health and if the abortions are carried out in a hospital.

Congress passes a federal food and drug regulatory act, creating many of the modern functions of the Food and Drug Administration (FDA).

1939 Maryland adopts the first statewide ME system, based on the model of the New York City Medical Examiner's Office. Rather than being appointed by the state's chief executive, the state's chief ME is appointed by a board composed of various state officeholders, such as the superintendent of the state police and health department officials.

1942 An Oklahoma law mandating sterilization for felons is ruled unconstitutional (though on narrow grounds) in the case of *Skinner v. Oklahoma.*

1962 The American Law Institute (ALI) establishes standards for courts to employ in insanity cases; those principles are adopted in courts throughout the United States.

Congress passes the Kefauver-Harris Amendment in the wake of the thalidomide scare, giving broader authority to the FDA to regulate the testing of prescription drugs before they come onto the market.

1963 The investigation into the assassination of President John F. Kennedy is criticized in part because the autopsy was conducted not by the Dallas ME but by armed forces pathologists in Maryland.

1964 In the case of *Georgetown College v. Jones,* physicians and a hospital are given authority to order a lifesaving blood transfusion for a woman who had objected on religious grounds to receiving blood products.

1965 Medicare and Medicaid are set up through congressional legislation.

In the case of *Griswold v. Connecticut,* the U.S. Supreme Court identifies a right to privacy in the Constitution, striking down state laws that limit the dissemination of birth control information.

1967 Britain's Abortion Act legalizes abortions that are performed by physicians in hospitals, with certain qualifications.

1971 The FDA bans the use of the drug diethylstilbestrol (DES) among pregnant women.

1973 The *Postma* case in the Netherlands helps establish that physicians can exercise their discretion in helping patients to die. Some physicians' actions amounting to euthanasia also are countenanced by the Dutch courts.

Citing a previously identified right to privacy, the U.S. Supreme Court rules that state laws banning abortion except to save the life of the mother are unconstitutional. The decisions in the twin cases of *Roe v. Wade* and *Doe v. Bolton* that establish a "right to abortion" under the federal constitution prove immediately controversial, spawning the formation of "right to life" advocacy groups.

1976 The *Quinlan* decision inspires discussions about the "right to die."

1984 A New Jersey court awards damages to the Cipollone family in the smoking-related death of Rose Cipollone; it is one of the first jury awards concerning tobacco use.

1986 The trial and decision in the *Baby M* case bring legal controversies concerning assisted reproduction (AR) to the attention of the American public.

DNA evidence is first used in a criminal case in the United States.

The Emergency Medical Treatment and Active Labor Act (EMTALA) is passed by Congress, requiring hospitals to stabilize and treat emergency cases before transferring them to other facilities.

1990 The decision by the U.S. Supreme Court in *Cruzan v. Director, Missouri Department of Public Health* allows states to lean on the side of the preservation of life when patients' own wishes concerning the discontinuation of life support are not clear.

In the Patient Self Determination Act of 1990, Congress requires healthcare facilities such as hospitals and nursing homes to inform their patients of their right to file advanced directives and living wills.

Dr. Jack Kevorkian is acquitted of a first-degree murder charge arising from his assisting an Alzheimer's patient in committing suicide. In a subsequent case he also is acquitted, although eventually he is found guilty and sentenced to several years in prison.

1991 The FDA responds to questions about the safety of silicone breast implants by asking for studies from product manufacturers.

The Remmerlink Commission issues a report on the operation of legal euthanasia and PAS in the Netherlands.

1992 In *Planned Parenthood v. Casey,* the U.S. Supreme Court strikes down a spousal-notification provision in a Pennsylvania law limiting abortions. The Court fails to reach agreement, however, on other crucial aspects of the abortion controversy.

1993 The case of *Rodriguez v. Attorney General of British Columbia* galvanizes those groups and persons interested in establishing a right to die in Canada involving PAS.

The Supreme Court ruling in *Daubert v. Merrell Dow Pharmaceuticals* allows judges considerable discretion in admitting scientific and medical testimony in both criminal and civil cases, thus undermining the *Frye* rule.

1994 Oregon passes the nation's only state legislation allowing PAS—the Death with Dignity Statute. Aided by a voter referendum approving of the measure, the law goes into effect in 1997.

Congress passes the Dietary Supplement Health and Education Act, allowing dietary supplements and vitamins to be less stringently regulated (especially by the FDA) than prescription drugs.

1997 The U.S. Supreme Court decides the related cases of *Washington v. Glucksberg* and *Vacco v. Quill*, concerning the authority of states to regulate the "right to die."

1998 The case of *Kass v. Kass* highlights family-law issues related to the storage of embryos created through artificial reproductive technology.

Dr. Jack Kevorkian is sentenced to ten to twenty-five years for murder in the first PAS case in which he is convicted.

2000 The U.S. Supreme Court decides a case involving partial-birth abortions, rebuffing Nebraska's effort to ban those procedures but also indicating deep divisions within the Court about the subject of abortion.

2002 The U.S. government reaches a settlement with Dow Corning, a leading breast-implant maker, to compensate federal authorities who had paid millions of dollars for breast implants through programs such as Medicare and Medicaid.

2003 The U.S. government files suit against tobacco manufacturers such as Philip Morris, claiming that tobacco companies conspired to sell their products to minors and hid the dangers of tobacco from smokers.

Table of Cases

Attorney General v. Times Newspapers Ltd., Q.B. 752 (1975)
Barber v. Superior Court, 195 Cal. 484 (1983)
Barbour et al. v. Dow Corning et al., LEXIS 1316 (Conn. Super. 2002)
Bennan v. Parsonnet, 83 N.J.L. 20 (1912)
Blum v. Yaretsky, 457 U.S. 991 (1982)
Brophy v. New England Sinai Hospital, 497 N.E. 2d 626 (Sup. Jud. Ct. Mass. 1986)
Brown v. Board of Education of Topeka, Kansas, 347 U.S. 483 (1954)
Buck v. Bell, 274 U.S. 200 (1927)
Canterbury v. Spence, 464 F.2d 772 (1972)
Children's Healthcare is a Legal Duty, Inc., v. Vladeck, 938 F. Supp. 1466 (1996)
Cipollone v. Liggett Group, Inc., 505 U.S. 504 (1992)
Cloer v. Gynecology Clinic, Inc., 528 U.S. 1099 (2000)
Collins v. Texas, 223 U.S. 288 (1912)
Compagnie Francaise v. State Board of Health, 186 U.S. 380 (1902)
Coppolino v. Florida, FL 234 So. 2d 120 (1969)
Coulatti v. Franklin, 439 U.S. 379 (1979)
County v. Earls, 122 S. Ct. 2559 (2002)
Crane v. Johnson, 242 U.S. 339 (1917)
Cremonese v. City of New York, 267 N.Y. Supp. 897 (1966)
Cruzan v. Director, Missouri Department of Public Health, 497 U.S. 261 (1990)
Daubert v. Merrell Dow Pharmaceuticals, 509 U.S. 579 (1993)
Dent v. West Virginia, 129 U.S. 114 (1889)
Doe v. Bolton, 410 U.S. 179 (1973)
Durham v. United States, 214 F.2d 864 (1954)

Eisenstadt v. Baird, 405 U.S. 438 (1972)
Ellis v. C. R. Bard and Baxter Healthcare Corporation, 311 F.3d 1272 (2002)
Feguer v. United States, 302 F.2d 214 (1962)
Fein v. Permanente Medical Group, 38 Cal. 3d 137 (1985)
Feingold v. Commonwealth State Board of Chiropractic, 568 A.2d 1365 (1980)
Ferguson v. City of Charleston, 532 U.S. 67 (2001)
Frye v. United States, 293 F. 103 (D.C. Cir. 1923)
Georgetown College v. Jones, 118 U.S. App. D.C. 90, 331 F.2d 1010 (1964)
Gerstein v. Pugh, 420 U.S. 103 (1975)
Gonzalez v. United States, 284 F.3d 281 (2002)
Gramm v. Boener, 56 Ind. 497 (1877)
Gravis v. Physicians and Surgeons Hospital, 427 S.W. 2d 310 (Tex., 1968)
Griswold v. Connecticut, 381 U.S. 479 (1965)
Hales v. Petit, 1 Plowden 253 (1562) (England)
Harris v. McRae, 488 U.S. 297 (1980)
Hawker v. New York, 170 U.S. 189 (1898)
Helling v. Carey, 83 Wash. 2d 514 (1974)
Helms v. Secretary of Health and Human Services, 10 Fed. Appx. 934 (2001)
Hermanson v. Florida, 570 So. 2d 322 (1990)
Hymowitz v. Eli Lilly, 73 N.Y. 2d 487 (1989)
In re Baby M, 109 N.J. 396 (1988)
In re Guess, 976 F.2d 998 (1992)
In re Jane Doe, 262 Ga. 389, 418 S.E. 2d 3 (1992)
In re Quinlan, 137 N.J. Super. 227 (1975)
In re Quinlan, 70 N.J. 10 (1976)
In re Thaw, 138 A.D. 91; 122 N.Y.S. 970 (1910)
In the matter of Charlotte F. Tavel, 661 A.2d 1061 (1995)
Jackson v. Rupp, 228 So. 2d 916 (1969)
Jacobson v. Commonwealth of Massachusetts, 197 U.S. 11 (1905)
Josiah Sutton v. The State of Texas, Tex. App. LEXIS 337 (2001)
Kass v. Kass, 91 N.Y. 2d 554 (1998)
Kawaauhau v. Geiger, 523 U.S. 57 (1998)
Kerr v. Inamed, 51 Fed. Appx. 718 (2002)
Krauel v. Iowa Methodist Medical Center, 95 F.3d 674 (1996)

Lochner v. New York, 198 U.S. 45 (1905)
McGuire v. Rix, 118 Neb. 434 (1929)
Michals v. Baxter Healthcare Corp., 289 F.3d 402 (2002)
Miller v. Columbia/HCA, 36 S.W. 3d 187 (2000)
Mitchell v. Davis, 205 S.W. 2d 812 (Tex. Civ. App. Dallas 1947)
Mohr v. Williams, 95 Minn. 261 (1905)
Mulcahy v. Lilly, 386 N.W. 2d 67 (1986)
Muller v. Oregon, 208 U.S. 412 (1908)
Nabours v. Commissioner of Social Security, 50 Fed. Appx. 272 (2002)
Parham v. J. R., 442 U.S. 584 (1979)
Pegram v. Herdrich, 530 U.S. 211 (2000)
People v. Sanger, 222 N.Y. 192 (1918)
Phillips v. Hillcrest Medical Center, 244 F.3d 790 (2001)
Pike v. Honsinger, 155 N.Y. 201 (1898)
Planned Parenthood of Central Missouri v. Danforth, 428 U.S. 52 (1976)
Planned Parenthood of Southeastern Pennsylvania v. Casey, 505 U.S. 833 (1992)
Quill v. Vacco, 80 F.3d 716 (1996)
Rasmussen v. Fleming, 741 P.2d 674 (1987)
Regina re Regina v. Truscott, 62 D.L.R. (2d) 545 (1967) (Canada)
Regina v. McNaghten, 4 State Trials (N.S.) 847 (1843) (England)
Regina v. Truscott, 125 C.C.C. 100 (1959) (Canada)
Rex v. Bourne, 1 K. B. 687 (1938) (England)
Rex v. Crippen, 1 K. B. 687 (1938) (England)
Rex v. Hadfield, 27 State Trials (N.S.) 1281 (1800) (England)
Reynolds v. McNichols, 488 F.2d 1378 (1973)
Rish et al. v. Sally Johnson et al. and the U.S. Government, 131 F.3d 1092 (1997)
Rodriguez v. Attorney General of British Columbia, 3 W.W.R. 553 (1993) (Canada)
Roe v. Wade, 110 U.S. 113 (1973)
Sacco v. Massachusetts, 275 U.S. 574 (1927)
Schloendorff v. The Society of New York Hospital, 211 N.Y. 125 (1914)
Skinner v. Oklahoma, 316 U.S. 535 (1942)
Small v. Howard, 128 Mass. 131 (1880)
Smith v. United States, 36 F.2d 548 (1929)

Snell v. United States, 16 App. D.C. 501 (1900)
State ex rel. Kellogg v. Currens and the Wisconsin Board of Medical Examiners, 111 Wisc. 431 (1901)
State of Ohio v. Freida Miller, Ohio 948 (2003)
State v. Hinze, 441 N.W. 2d 593 (1989)
State v. Pike, 49 N.H. 399 (1870)
Stenberg v. Carhart, 530 U.S. 914 (2000)
Stiver v. Parker, 975 F.2d 261 (1992)
Strnad v. Strnad, 78 N.Y.S. 2d 390 (1948)
Taylor v. United States, 7 App. D.C. 27 (1895)
Toledo v. Medical Engineering Corp., 50 Pa. D&C. 4th 129 (2001)
Truman v. Thomas, 27 Cal. 3d 285 (1980)
United States v. Currens, 290 F.2d 751 (1961)
United States v. Guiteau, 1 Mackey 498 (1882)
United States v. Hinckley, 525 F. Supp. 1342 (1981)
United States v. LeBeau, LEXIS 1501 (U.S. App. 1993)
Vacco v. Quill, 521 U.S. 793 (1997)
Voinovich et al. v. Women's Medical Professional Corporation, 523 U.S. 1036 (1998)
Washington, et al., Petitioners v. Walter Harper, 494 U.S. 210 (1990)
Washington v. Glucksberg, 521 U.S. 702 (1997)
Wilkinson v. Duff, LEXIS 236 (W. Va. 2002)
Wood v. Thompson, 265 U.S. 1026 (2001)

Annotated Bibliography

Books and Articles

Atkinson, Jim. "**Wrongful Life?**" *Texas Monthly* 30 (December 2002): 88–94.

Examination of *Miller v. Columbia/HCA,* a Texas case in which parents of a child who was born with severe disabilities sued the hospital where the child was born. The parents contended that the hospital ignored their directions with regard to the care offered to their baby, and as a result the child survived with severe impairments, rather than succumbing close to the time of birth. The case tested the strength of hospitals to make and follow their own protocols on caring for persons with severe disabilities against parental rights to determine whether their children should be kept alive by heroic means.

Battin, Margaret P., Rosamund Rhodes, and Anita Silvers, eds. ***Physician Assisted Suicide: Expanding the Debate.*** New York: Routledge, 1998.

A collection of articles concerning specific aspects of the debate over physician-assisted suicide (PAS) and euthanasia. Focuses on the United States, but also includes examples from other nations. Includes the texts of several important primary sources, such as "the *amicus curiae* 'philosophers' brief" that was submitted by several imminent ethicists on behalf of the right-to-die position in *Washington v. Glucksberg.* Several of the essays stress the deleterious effects of proposed legislation on minorities and persons with disabilities.

Blanche, Tony, and Brad Schreiber. ***Death in Paradise.*** Los Angeles: General Publishing Group, 1998.

An illustrated history of the coroner's office in the County of Los Angeles. The authors provide a history geared to lay readers. They chronicle the evolution of the office of coroner in nineteenth- and early twentieth-century southern California. Their focus is on the lure of the area for those interested in quick riches and therefore the vicinity's propensity for violent—and often newsworthy—crime.

Childs, Richard. "**The Passing of Lay Coroners.**" *Journal of Forensic Sciences* 19 (January 1974): 8–11.

A brief review of the activities of municipal reformers, particularly the National Municipal League (NML), in making state and local medical examiner (ME) systems more uniform and eliminating the office of coroner from many jurisdictions in the United States. Focuses on the period between 1920 and about 1970, with particular emphasis on the 1950s and 1960s.

Cohen, Michael. ***Complementary and Alternative Medicine: Legal Boundaries and Regulatory Perspectives.*** Baltimore: Johns Hopkins University Press, 1998.

A well-informed discussion of current law on alternative and complementary medicine. Includes descriptions of historical developments including state regulations on licensing for alternative practitioners such as massage therapists, homeopaths, and chiropractors. The author provides a clear explanation of the process by which new drugs are approved by the FDA.

Dworkin, Roger. ***Limits.*** Bloomington: Indiana University Press, 1996.

A discussion of the cases and dilemmas related to biomedical ethics, with an emphasis on the ways in which law has proved unable to resolve controversies or has created further difficulties in trying to reach resolutions. The Supreme Court decisions related to abortion and end-of-life issues come in for particularly sharp criticism.

Ficarra, Bernard J. "**History of Legal Medicine.**" *Legal Medicine Annual* (1976): 1–27.

An overview of the intersection between medical expertise and justice throughout history. The discussion includes European, English, and American historical developments since the early modern era and has a section dealing with punishments for medical malpractice in the ancient world.

Gawande, Atul. ***Complications: A Surgeon's Notes on an Imperfect Science.*** New York: Picador, 2002.

Readable series of essays on the current practice of surgery. Gawande offers a surgeon's perspective on malpractice suits, among other topics. He argues that the most effective brakes upon negligent physicians come from within the medical profession itself (e.g., the weekly "morbidity and mortality" discussions held at most teaching hospitals) rather than through legal actions that pit doctors against patients. He also discusses some of the technological innovations that recently have led to a dramatic decrease in mortality from anesthesia.

Hanzlick, Randy. "**History of the National Association of Medical Examiners and Its Meetings, 1966–93.**" *American Journal of Forensic Medicine and Pathology* 16 (1994): 278–313.

An account of the founding of the National Association of Medical Examiners (NAME), including lists of NAME presidents, meeting locations, and topics of papers presented at the annual conferences. The article is a serious organizational history, but it does make apparent the ironic sense of humor that often characterizes the offices of medical examiners (MEs). The titles of conference presentations demonstrate the range of subjects in which forensic pathologists have expertise. There have been numerous papers, for example, on child abuse, AIDS, aircraft disasters, Sudden Infant Death Syndrome (SIDS), cult-related deaths, gunshot wounds, serial murder, odontology, deaths under anesthesia, suicides, and drownings. The association also has heard research on the serious subject of deaths caused by animals; many of those papers feature titles that are a tribute to members' sense of humor, such as "Bear with Us" and "The Revenge of Mr. Ed."

Hanzlick, Randy, and Debra Combs. "**Medical Examiner and Coroner Systems: History and Trends.**" *Journal of the American Medical Association* 279 (1998): 870–874.

An argument that medical examiners (MEs) usually provide more professional and effective investigations into unnatural deaths than coroners. Hanzlick and Combs's survey of local and state systems for death investigation reveals that just less than half of the nation's population is served by coroners and the rest by MEs. The authors describe a certain amount of momentum in the adoption of ME systems in the beginning and middle years of the twentieth century. On the other hand, they note and lament a slowing of the adoption of ME systems in the later part of the century.

Helpern, Milton. "**The Role of the Forensic Pathologist in the Administration of Justice.**" *American Journal of Clinical Pathology* 59 (1973): 605–612.

An address given by the eminent forensic pathologist Dr. Milton Helpern at the inauguration of a lecture series on forensic pathology by the American Society of Clinical Pathologists. In the speech, Dr. Helpern reflects on decades of research, practice, and organizational effort as one of the leading forensic pathologists in the United States. Helpern includes accounts of efforts by pathologists during the 1930s and 1940s to organize themselves into professional groups; it was an era when autopsies still were known by the ominous term "necropsies." He reviews the advantages of the performance of autopsies by specially trained pathologists.

Jennett, Bryan. ***The Vegetative State: Medical Facts, Ethical and Legal Dilemmas.*** Cambridge: Cambridge University Press, 2002.

A review of medical, legal, and ethical issues connected to the condition known as "persistent vegetative state" (a term that the author helped coin). Focuses on law and ethics in the United Kingdom, but includes several key cases from the United States and Canada, as well. The author gained his medical experience at first by working with polio patients; he then focused on traumatic brain-injury victims. Provides a detailed and readable discussion of leading cases in the United Kingdom and the United States.

Kass, Leon R. ***Life, Liberty, and the Defense of Dignity.*** San Francisco: Encounter Books, 2002.

An opinionated and thoughtful exploration of the ethical and moral questions related to the right-to-die debate. Kass argues that the *Glucksberg* and *Quill* decisions left room for the Supreme Court to broaden the scope of a right to die. He notes the efforts of groups involved in the controversy to market themselves more effectively by dropping the term "euthanasia" from their names. Kass, a physician, served as the chair of a Council on Bioethics, appointed by President George W. Bush.

Knightley, Phillip, et al. ***Suffer the Children: The Story of Thalidomide.*** New York: Viking Press, 1979.

Dramatic and well-written account of the development of thalidomide by the drug company Chemie Grunenthal, the drug's medical testing, and the massive international recriminations of the thalidomide controversy. Prepared by the staff of the *Sunday Times.*

Noguchi, Thomas, and Joseph DiMona. ***Coroner.*** Boston: G. K. Hall, 1984.

A description of the duties of coroners in late twentieth-century America, from the standpoint of a controversial holder of the Los Angeles County coronership, Dr. Thomas Noguchi. Noguchi, an eminent forensic pathologist, was in several instances a lightning rod for controversy. Noguchi provides details of how coroners and other medicolegal officials work at crime scenes, and he discusses working relationships with law-enforcement officials. He centers his account on controversial cases on which he worked as a forensic pathologist.

O'Neill, Onora. ***Autonomy and Trust in Bioethics.*** Cambridge: Cambridge University Press, 2002.

Polished and compelling arguments by a leading British bioethicist. Although focused on British developments, many of the contentions by the author are applicable to the United States, where bioethics originated as a term and where many of the field's fiercest battles have been fought. O'Neill is particularly incisive in discussing the concept of informed consent, which courts rather than medical communities imposed on the doctor-patient relationship.

Presswalla, Faruk B. "**Historical Evolution of Medico-Legal Investigative Systems.**" *Medico-Legal Bulletin* 25 (1976): 1–8.

A review of the origins of the coroner's office in England from medieval times, with a brief discussion of the development of medical examiner (ME) systems in the United States and the modern English coronership. Includes list of typical duties and qualifications of MEs in New York City, which the author argues features a modern and well-respected office. Describes the systems of medicolegal investigation—still based on the coronership—in modern England.

Rich, Ben A. ***Strange Bedfellows: How Medical Jurisprudence Has Influenced Medical Ethics and Medical Practice.*** New York: Kluwer Academic Publishers, 2001.

A well-crafted argument that law has exercised a positive influence on bioethics in recent years. Rich focuses on the change from a paternalistic model of physician-patient interaction to one based on a more equitable relationship influenced, for example, by the court-ordered precepts of informed consent.

Rothman, David J. ***Strangers at the Bedside: A History of How Law and Bioethics Transformed Medical Decision Making.*** New York: Basic Books, 1991.

A historical perspective on the development of bioethics in the United States, focusing on the 1960s and 1970s. Rothman's pioneering and critically acclaimed book examines the impact that a variety of interests have had upon the physician-patient relationship. He argues, in fact, that that relationship (which used to be mostly personal and private) has been profoundly affected by the presence of insurers, hospital corporations, lawyers, legislative policymakers, administrative regulators, and, of course, the courts.

Scherer, Jennifer M., and Rita J. Simon. ***Euthanasia and the Right to Die: A Comparative View.*** Lanham, MD: Rowman and Littlefield, 1999.

Comparison of right-to-die legislation and court cases in a number of nations, beginning with the United States but also including European and non-Western countries. Includes a discussion of key arguments by several sides in the debate over euthanasia and physician-assisted suicide (PAS). Describes leading organizations and authors in the controversies, such as Derek Humphry. Particularly convincing with respect to the social and economic factors influencing policy in each country.

Shapiro, E. Donald, and Anthony Davis. "**Law and Pathology through the Ages: The Coroner and His Descendants—Legitimate and Illegitimate.**" *New York State Journal of Medicine* 72 (April 1972): 805–809.

Brief but thorough discussion of coroners within court systems, focusing on English policies, laws, and practices connected with the coroner. Also includes a description of the origins and modern features of American medical examiner (ME) systems.

Starr, Paul. ***The Social Transformation of American Medicine.*** New York: Basic Books, 1982.

An influential history of medicine in the United States. Starr is especially convincing with respect to the connections between physicians and their professional organizations, and medical practitioners and the hospital. He is well informed about the parallels between American medicine and that of other nations. For example, he describes the elite social status of British and American physicians in the eighteenth century as opposed to the lesser stature of surgeons in that era. In his detailed citations of examples, however, he does not spend much time on court cases.

Steadman, Henry, et al. ***Before and After Hinckley: Evaluating Insanity Defense Reform.*** New York: Guilford Press, 1993.

A study of the effect of the *Hinckley* decision on several states' laws. The authors identify several states as representative of certain typical legal reactions to the Hinckley verdict—e.g., they focus on California's reiteration of the M'Naghten Rules and Montana's aboliton of the insanity defense altogether. They track the number of pleas of not guilty by reason of insanity or other alternatives that were allowed by state law, before and after the *Hinckley* verdict, and describe the motivations of legislators who sought to change their states' laws regarding insanity.

Thomasma, David C., Thomasina Kimbrough-Kushner, et al., eds. ***Asking to Die: Inside the Dutch Debate about Euthanasia.*** Dordrecht, The Netherlands: Kluwer Academic Publishers, 1998.

Thorough review of twentieth-century legal developments in the Netherlands concerning right-to-die issues. The Netherlands is considered one of the nations most receptive to physician-assisted suicide (PAS) and euthanasia. The volume provides detailed discussion of several policies—judicial, medical, and administrative—along with source materials such as interviews with patients and physicians who were involved in leading cases. The authors note the complex interaction between judicial decisions, public opinion, partisan politics, particular pressure groups (such as the Royal Dutch Medical Association), and administrative and private authorities (such as the administrators of assisted-care facilities). The book displays sympathy for individual physicians faced with difficult decisions, especially when the gravely ill persons who requested help in suicide were members of the physicians' own families. Includes some discussion of related cases from other nations, such as Canada and the United States.

Van der Maas, P. J., G. Van der Wal, et al. "**Euthanasia, Physician-Assisted Suicide, and Other Medical Practices Involving the End of Life in the Netherlands.**" *New England Journal of Medicine* 335 (1996): 1699–1705.

A well-informed review of the key laws, judicial decisions, administrative procedures, and political controversies connected with end-of-life issues. The authors focus primarily on the Netherlands, but also include comparisons and contrasts with other countries. There are several references to key cases in the United States and Britain.

Websites

http://bioethics.gov/
Website for the President's Council on Bioethics. Includes citations to and texts of several articles and reports concerning bioethical issues such as the debate about human cloning and the stem cell controversy. Contains a "bookshelf," with well-chosen literary selections illustrating varying views on bioethical controversies—such as Nathaniel Hawthorne's memorable short story "The Birthmark," about a physician who tries to remove the only blemish from his beautiful wife's face and in so doing causes a tragedy.

http://www.collphyphil.org/
Website for the College of Physicians of Philadelphia. Their collection focuses on the role of physicians in history and contemporary society.

http://echo.gmu.edu/center/
Website for the Virtual Center for Science and Technology, a reviewing and cataloging site on the history of science, technology, and medicine.

http://histmed.org/
Website for the American Association for the History of Medicine (AAHM). AAHM sponsors scholarly conferences on all aspects of medical history and publishes the *Bulletin of the History of Medicine.*

http://www.nlm.nih.gov/
Website for the U.S. National Library of Medicine in Bethesda, Maryland. Provides access to the comprehensive collections in the U.S. National Library of Medicine, which has extensive resources on U.S. medical history.

Index

About the Author

Elisabeth Cawthon received her Ph.D. in legal history from the University of Virginia. She has been a visiting faculty member at the University of New Hampshire and Brown University. Since 1988, she has taught at the University of Texas at Arlington, where she recently has served as associate professor and university distinguished teaching professor. She is the author of *English Law and the American Experience* (1994).